Stress and Your Health

Stress and Your Health

Stress and Your Health

From Vulnerability to Resilience

Hymie Anisman

WILEY Blackwell

This edition first published 2015
© 2015 John Wiley & Sons, Ltd.

Registered Office
John Wiley & Sons, Ltd, The Atrium, Southern Gate, Chichester, West Sussex, PO19 8SQ, UK

Editorial Offices
350 Main Street, Malden, MA 02148-5020, USA
9600 Garsington Road, Oxford, OX4 2DQ, UK
The Atrium, Southern Gate, Chichester, West Sussex, PO19 8SQ, UK

For details of our global editorial offices, for customer services, and for information about how
to apply for permission to reuse the copyright material in this book please see our website at
www.wiley.com/wiley-blackwell.

The right of Hymie Anisman to be identified as the author of this work has been asserted in
accordance with the UK Copyright, Designs and Patents Act 1988.

Library of Congress Cataloging-in-Publication data

Anisman, Hymie.
  Stress and your health : from vulnerability to resilience / Hymie Anisman.
    pages cm
  Includes bibliographical references and index.
  ISBN 978-1-118-85028-2 (hardback) – ISBN 978-1-118-85024-4 (paper)
1. Stress (Psychology) 2. Health. 3. Psychophysiology. I. Title.
  BF575.S75A55 2015
  613–dc23
                                                        2014048339

A catalogue record for this book is available from the British Library.

Cover image: © Cristiana Ceppas Photography

Set in 9/10.5pt Sabon by SPi Publisher Services, Pondicherry, India

1 2015

For Ralph and Ann

Contents

Preface

Being the good son, I would frequently visit my mom, who lived in Montreal, about a two-hour drive from Ottawa. She and her sister, Esther, were very close, figuratively as well as literally, as they lived next door to one another. Having retired from their self-owned businesses, they would spend hours sitting on the porch talking. The conversations were particularly animated, using a combination of English and Yiddish, and some Polish words were occasionally thrown in when they began gossiping about any neighbor who walked by. They were at times very analytical, as they not only gossiped but also speculated about the individual motivations associated with recent events. They delved into politics (what was Kennedy thinking running around with all those women? What in the world did John Profumo, Secretary of State in the British government, see in a 19-year-old model, Christine Keeler?), history (they never got over the split between Elizabeth Taylor and Eddie Fisher), and business (the news report that so-and-so, a corrupt businessman, maintained a coterie of young woman that he used to attract potential customers).

One Sunday morning in the mid-1970s I showed up only to see the two of them sitting glumly, arms crossed, looking straight ahead, hardly acknowledging me. I soon learned from my mom that their neighbor Mrs K. had died.

"I guess that was pretty well inevitable," I said, "as cancer had spread to multiple places throughout her body. The fact that she lasted as long as she did was actually fairly surprising and sad as it is, she was, I heard, in a lot of pain."

"No," my mom said, and after a thoughtful pause she added, "inevitable it wasn't. She got sick only because her husband was a useless good-for-nothing, who wasn't nice to her ... the stress he brought on her caused her to get cancer."

"Mom, please. She developed cancer. God knows why she was the unlucky one. It's a disease of aging, and whether he was nice to her or not had nothing to do with it."

She, of course, objected to my perspective and we debated for some time. My aunt remained silent, occasionally catching my mother's eye and then she would slowly close her eyes and nod, which roughly translated as "forgive me for saying so, dear sister, but your son's a dope. Well meaning, but a dope all the same."

At some point my uncle showed up, and he was immediately confronted by my mother saying, "We need an opinion from you. Your wife, Esther, my wonderful younger sister, and I both say that stress causes cancer. He [with a thrust of her head in my general direction] says it doesn't. What do you say?"

He looked at each of us, and in a Solomonic way said, "It's hard to know. Maybe it does, and maybe it doesn't' (his equivalent of cutting the baby in two).

However, his prevarication wasn't going to work, and my mother said, "Maybe this ... maybe that ... Stop being a nebbish. Yes or no."

Knowing what was good for him, he quickly moved to the "Yes" side.

Gloatingly, my mom turned to me saying, "Three to one for us; obviously, stress causes cancer and that's why Mrs K got sick."

With increasing exasperation, I said, "Just because the three of you vote in the same way doesn't make it so. Whoever heard of taking a vote on a scientific debate! You think we're electing someone to parliament. Cancer is a disease of aging, not of stress, and as it happens I work in the area of stress, and I know what there is to know about that topic."

"First of all," my mom replied, "it wasn't just three to one. Your uncle and aunt were two of the three, and by saying what you did, you disrespected them. So, you should apologize. I, as your mother, who worked long and hard to make sure that there was nothing you didn't have, know my place, and don't ask for an apology. Second, I didn't say that cancer isn't an illness that comes from being old. But, did you ever think that maybe stress makes you old before your years. Stress makes your hair gray and so does getting old."

I apologized to my aunt and uncle, although I couldn't see why that was necessary, but couldn't help adding petulantly, "In case you've forgotten, I do have a PhD, and here you are lecturing me about stress. Did I ever tell you how to run your business?" Not a smart move on my part.

She was quiet (always a bad sign), and then said, while nodding her head, "Yup, yup, yup ... If you're such a smarty pants, then how come you're a PhD working in research, and you're not a real doctor."

A mean shot if there ever was one, but on my drive home, while brooding, I wondered whether there wasn't something to her notion about stress and cancer. Even if stress didn't cause cancer to come about, was it possible that stressful experiences might promote the growth of a tumor that was already present? On returning to Ottawa I told my graduate student Lawrence Sklar about my visit, and he in his customary way was skeptical for a minute, and then said, "Who knows. Maybe she's right." He ended up going to a university in Kingston and talking to a cancer researcher there who provided him with several tumor cell lines that could be transplanted into a mouse, where the tumor would then grow. To make a very long story short, one of these cell lines was responsive to stressors, possibly because of hormonal changes that occurred in a stressed mouse, so that the transplanted tumor grew more quickly. We conducted a fairly large set of experiments, and over the ensuing few years published some of this work. The very first of these papers appeared in a prestigious journal (Sklar and Anisman, 1979), which made me very full of myself, and on my next trip to Montreal, I showed this two-page paper (the journal always insisted on brevity) to my mom.

She held the apparently flimsy two-page paper, which was actually one piece of paper with printing on both sides, making it appear that much less impressive, and said, "That's nice. You say that that you wrote that stress causes cancer?"

She was obviously returning to the debate of several years earlier, so I interrupted with "No, we showed that stress causes an already present cancer to grow faster."

"OK, that's very nice also. So, tell me, to do experiments like this it took years, and costs how much?"

"About $20,000," I replied (this was the 1970s and things were so much cheaper then). To which she said, "Go figure. I told you the same thing for free."

Typically, scientific discoveries are made through long diligent experimentation, based on the work of numerous earlier studies in the field. At other times discoveries come about because of sheer luck, happenstance, or having a mom being adamant in her opinions. On occasion, it might even be advantageous not to be an expert within a field so that you can see the general picture without getting caught up in the details, although it's likely that this is an exception to the rule.

The fact that I was willing to engage in my mom's notion about stress and disease, even if it wasn't evidence based, was reinforced by the fact that I had long been enchanted by folk wisdom, and there's something especially endearing about folk medicine. To be sure, many of us consider folk wisdom as quaint, but often dismiss it as old wives' or grandma tales. Yet, there are instances where it becomes part of our collective wisdom, as in the case of parents still telling their kids not to go out in the winter with wet hair. There are oodles of folk medicines that have evolved based on hearsay, rather than scientific evidence, including beliefs that involved stressors. Among other things, stressors made you old before your years; stressors weaken your protective systems so that you're more likely to catch a cold; stressors cause apoplexy (primarily stroke). As we'll see in this book, many of these beliefs were subsequently validated through strict experimental analyses, although many others weren't. Some folk wisdom, while quaint, really is a bunch of baloney, but there's a fair bit that might not be delicatessen grade but is still tasty. In this book, we'll take a broad perspective concerning stress and illness, covering information from valid scientific studies on a range of conditions, and occasionally we'll also debunk a few myths.

H.A., Ottawa

Acknowledgments

There are so many people to whom I owe much gratitude and appreciation. I am especially indebted to my closest collaborators and friends, Kim Matheson and Zul Merali, as well as Shawn Hayley, Alfonso Abizaid, Mike Poulter, Steve Ferguson, Alex Kusnecov, Cath Haslam, Alex Haslam, and Nyla Branscombe, who in one fashion or another influenced my notions regarding stress and distress. My graduate students also shaped my thoughts, just as I might have shaped theirs, and as there have been many dozens, I won't name them all. However, several graduate and undergraduate students were particularly helpful in diminishing the technical jargon, although some of it necessarily had to be included as there weren't obvious alternative terms that could be used. So, I'm very indebted to Opal McInnis, Robyn McQuaid, Rob Gabrys, Katie Trenouth, Tetyana Maniuk, Kasia Szyszkowicz, Thomas Ritchie, and Tamir Streiner. Of course, I'm especially grateful for having Andy Peart and Karen Shield as editors at Wiley-Blackwell, who know how to get things done in the most practical ways, making the venture a pleasant one, as well as Ann Bone, who copy edited this book so that it reads so much better than it would have otherwise.

I'm indebted to the agencies that sponsored my research over the years; the Natural Science and Research Council of Canada, The Canadian Institutes of Health Research, The Ontario Mental Health Foundation, The Canada Foundation for Innovation, as well as the Canada Research Chairs program.

As always, I'm thankful for the influences of Helen and Simon, and for the constant unconditional support from Simon, Rebecca, Jessica, and Max, and of course, Maida.

1

Stressors, Stress, and Distress

Getting past the surface

There are a few lucky people who seem to float through life, largely unaffected by the aggravations and hardships that others so often endure. They've got terrific jobs, a nice home and fancy car, a summer cottage, and a stash of cash based on investments made on their behalf starting the day they were born. They attend top universities, run in the best social circles, and have loads of good friends and alliances. We envy these luckiest people in the world, and might even delight when, on the odd occasion, they actually do suffer a setback, and we don't feel the least bit guilty about this *schadenfreude*. Yet, if you were to look beyond the surface, you might find that their lives aren't dust-free and they're not immune from life stressors. They might have multiple problems, including family and health issues, financial problems that are being covered up, children with a huge sense of entitlement, and they suffer the same diseases that other people do. I don't mean to make anyone feel sorry for the members of the country-club set who happened to have hit a few road bumps, nor do I want to compare their problems to yours. Instead, the point is that although life is hard for lots of people, but pretty sweet for others, at least on the surface, virtually everyone will encounter challenges that scar them. In dealing with our own problems, it's not profitable to look around to see how much better anyone else seems to have it.

What this book is about

When you encounter stressors, particularly those that are fairly disturbing, do you fret, get overly emotional, or get stuck in neutral just hoping everything will get better, eventually? Or, do you look at the situation logically and make efforts to solve the problem? The two aren't mutually exclusive, although for most individuals emotional reactions tend to occur more readily in response to stressful situations. In general, there isn't a right way or a wrong way to deal with stressors, since the best method often depends

Stress and Your Health: From Vulnerability to Resilience, First Edition. Hymie Anisman.
© 2015 John Wiley & Sons, Ltd. Published 2015 by John Wiley & Sons, Ltd.

on the specific situation in which we find ourselves. However, using ineffective or counterproductive methods of dealing with stressors will usually result in our load getting progressively heavier and it might eventually increase vulnerability to any of several psychological and physical disturbances.

Whether it's heart disease, cancer, diabetes, or any of a number of psychological disturbances, there's a premise that holds true: the longer it goes untreated, the further the illness will progress, and the more difficult it will be to treat. Like physical wounds, those of a psychological nature will fester, and early detection and treatment is essential. Better still would be to preemptively intervene in the processes that lead to disease. My intention with this book is to provide information regarding the multiple processes that

Good thing you were here or I might have been far off track

When it comes to politics, fixing the economy, and the state of international relations, many people believe that they have some special insights, and that everyone ought to be sharing their opinion, and if you don't then you're obviously ignorant. This also seems to be true of stress processes and the relationship between stressful events and the development of illnesses. When they learn that I work on stress processes, some people feel compelled to offer me advice about what sort of research I should be doing, how it should be done, and why the approach I've been taking is way off base and even irrelevant. It's even come from a (non-blood) relative who suggested that "we need to separate ourselves from our brain, and think on a higher plain." I have no idea what that meant, but this was the same guy who was near apoplectic when I disagreed with his contention that we use only 10 percent of our brain. This notion has been around for a long time, and somewhere there must have been a teacher who started this widely disseminated and readily accepted myth. With the analogy to an iceberg in which only 10 percent is above the surface, that teacher likely influenced views of brain functioning to a greater extent than have 99 percent of neuroscientists.

Of course, all these stress experts are also competing with the advice concerning stress and coping offered by magazines in the waiting room of your doctor's office or at the checkout stand at the supermarket – 10 fast and easy steps to rid yourself of stress; 12 ways of coping with a cruddy relative; 34 ways to find balance; the 17 best ways of getting rid of bad karma, and contacting your inner self. I haven't seen it yet, but I'm anticipating "Want to feel better? – 81 ways to get even with the people you don't like." I'm really not all that down on self-help advice obtained from magazines, but it strikes me as odd that anyone would use this sort of advice to deal with stressful events. Given the health burden that can be created by stressful events, it's too important a matter to rely on advice offered in a magazine article written by someone who spoke to someone who sat on a bus beside a self-proclaimed expert in the field, possibly my non-blood relative. If you had a suspicious lump in your breast or fairly severe chest pain that radiated down your left arm every time you exerted yourself, would you rely on one of these magazine articles for treatment options? They might have some great cooking recipes, but don't rely on them for ways of coping to minimize distress.

influence the impact of stressors on well-being, after which we'll consider factors that can minimize the negative effects of stressor experiences. In this regard, we'll examine the right steps that ought to be taken at the first whiff of danger, thereby minimizing the negative impact that would otherwise occur. Moreover, we'll consider what can be done to limit the psychological and physiological disturbances that could emerge in response to various chronic challenges. The information provided is based on well-controlled research concerning the actions of stressors. As there's also a fair bit of incorrect information that gets passed around, as we go we'll also dispel some of these myths.

What do we mean when we talk about stressors?

Although it's often thought that stressors will have negative effects, this isn't always the case. In some instances, stressors may, in fact, cause us to be alert and ready to deal with events that could potentially cause harm, they can promote biological changes that facilitate coping, and they can facilitate learning about how to engage subsequent stressful events. In essence, our cognitive and biological systems help us deal with immediate challenges, and these experiences may leave us better equipped to deal with further insults. One issue that needs to be dealt with is how to know under what conditions stressors can have positive effects, and under what conditions do they cause damage? Answering this can be difficult, and there isn't a single rule that can guide us in relation to all situations or for all individuals. Among other things, the effects of stressors depend on when in the course of a person's development they occurred, and their effects can be modified further by a broad constellation of psychosocial and experiential factors. In some instances, stressor experiences can have transient effects that are soon forgotten. But they can also have far-reaching consequences, potentially marking us for decades, and as we'll see, some stressor experiences can even have intergenerational consequences, affecting our children and their children.

What we know concerning the impact of stressors has come from research conducted in both humans and animals (mostly rats and mice). Of course, the effects of various stressors and other manipulations in animals aren't always generalizable to humans, so interpreting the findings from animal studies and applying them to humans isn't simple or straightforward. Later, we'll consider when it might or might not be appropriate to make these generalizations, but for the moment the information will be presented with only occasional warnings about their relevance or meaningfulness.

Stressors, as most of us have discovered, can come in several forms. They can be purely psychological (sometimes referred to as psychogenic) or physical (neurogenic), and they might vary across several dimensions, such as their severity, controllability, predictability, ambiguity, uncertainty, complexity, volatility, chronicity, and intermittence. The response to stressors can also vary with several features inherent to the organism, including the species, strain, race/culture, sex, age, and personality factors, as well as previous stressor experiences, including those encountered prenatally or in early life. Some events or stimuli are appraised as stressors on the basis of our experiences, others are innately driven, such as predator odors. Innate and learned stressors can activate diverse neurobiological circuits and might thus have repercussions that are distinct from one another. Thus, pathological conditions brought on by one or another type of stressor might call for different remedies.

We typically don't think of viral or bacterial challenges as being stressors, and their actions are in many ways very different from those elicited by psychological or physical challenges. We don't appraise these "systemic" insults in the same way as we might

What's a stressor?

So that we're all working from the same playbook, let's define a few terms and concepts. A "stressor" is a stimulus or event that is appraised, judged, or perceived as being aversive and which causes a "stress response," which is often referred to as "stress." There isn't actually "a" stress response, but instead there are many stress responses that comprise cognitive, behavioral, and biological changes. These stress responses have multiple adaptive functions, helping us deal with and diminish the negative effects of the stressor. For instance, biological stress responses that occur in the brain may guide our appraisals of stressors and facilitate the adoption of appropriate coping responses, and they also act to direct energy resources toward places they are needed (e.g., muscles, so we can run from danger) and away from processes that are not essential at the moment (e.g., reproduction, eating, digestion). The term "distress" in this book refers to the biological and psychological states or responses that evolve as a result of a failure to adapt to stressor events.

There have been occasional discussions as to what constitutes a stressor. Is jumping out of a plane a stressor for an experienced skydiver given that some of the biological responses elicited are reminiscent of the stress response seen in other stressful situations? Frankly, I don't have the patience or interest in these largely academic discussions that are often boring and have no resolution. Instead, I often fall back on US Supreme Court Justice Potter Stewart's comment in dealing with the definition of pornography, "I can't define it, but I know it when I see it" (*Jacobellis v. Ohio*, 1964). Even this isn't entirely accurate in relation to stressors, but it shuts down debates that I don't want to get into. The essential issue is that what constitutes a stressor is highly subjective; what I see as being stressful might not be something you see in the same way.

There's also the issue of whether or not something can be stressful if we aren't consciously aware of its presence. There are, as we'll see, a variety of environmental challenges, including bacterial or viral infection, that can instigate biological stress responses, just like those elicited by psychological challenges, without our being aware of their presence. Likewise, stressors that we experienced as infants, even if we have no recollection of them, can have lasting repercussions and can affect responses to stressors encountered many years later. This challenges the often used definition that a stressor is something that is "appraised, judged or perceived to be aversive." So, unlike the pornography that Justice Stewart recognized when he saw it, there are occasions where stressors can elicit their effects even when they're unseen or unrecognized.

appraise psychological or physical stressors, and often we are unaware that our body has been infiltrated by these invaders. Yet, through their effects on brain neuronal activity, systemic challenges that involve activation of our immune system can affect cognitive processes and mood. Just as the pain elicited by a neurogenic stressor, such as a sprained ankle, makes us cautious and protective of the injured area so that the tissue can heal properly, we're blessed with a very clever adaptive network wherein the brain knows about the presence of a systemic challenge, such as the presence of a virus, well before we actually become sick, so that we can behave in ways, such as slowing down, to preserve energy that will help us deal with symptoms that might be just around the corner.

Stress responses can arise as a consequence of an event that has already occurred, such as the termination of a romantic relationship, loss of a loved one, business failure, natural disaster, or being ostracized by your previous best friends. Stressors of this sort often diminish us, even if they do so in different ways, and in some instances may give rise to intense depressive mood. Other stressors, in contrast, don't reflect events that have already happened, but instead concern anticipated events, such as impending surgery, having to speak in a public forum, or even the fear of encountering the bully in the school yard or in the workplace. These anticipatory stressors are usually accompanied by anxiety, and if they go on long enough or are sufficiently severe, depressive mood might also arise.

The characteristics of stressors: comparing apples, oranges, and lemons

What makes some stressors appear relatively modest, whereas others are so severe that they are incapacitating? Although this seems like the type of question that can readily be answered, it's actually fairly complex given the broad constellation of factors that ultimately determine how a stressor affects us. The perceived severity of a stressor is, of course, closely related to the development of pathological conditions, but focusing on this alone is simplistic, and a direct linear relationship might not exist between the severity or intensity of a stressor and the negative consequences that follow. Besides, stressors come in many forms and vary across multiple dimensions, making it exceptionally difficult to define which stressors are more severe than others. How does one compare the negative attributes of illness, loss of a loved one, severe shame and ostracism, or the fear of harm coming to one's children? These stressors are different across so many domains that they can hardly be compared to one another, and there likely isn't much value in doing so.

As we're on the topic of stressor severity, let's also consider that it isn't just relatively severe stressors that have negative consequences. Day-to-day hassles frequently create considerable strain for some individuals and their impact shouldn't be underestimated. When there are enough of them, especially when they're superimposed on a backdrop of major stressors, they can be especially damaging. Many of us know the feeling of trying to deal with some fairly intense stressor only to be subjected to some trivial event that needs to be dealt with so that our resources have to be redirected to where they need to be. Unless we're able to compartmentalize emotions and issues, we might find our abilities to deal with important issues to be disturbed.

One of the most cogent factors concerning the impact of stressors concerns their perceived controllability. In studies conducted on animals during the 1960s and 1970s, Maier and Seligman (1976) revealed that stressor events that the animals could bring to an end by making particular responses did not have particularly negative effects on later behavior. However, animals exposed to a stressor that was identical, except that its termination was not under their control, subsequently demonstrated profound performance impairments when they were tested in a situation where they could escape from a physical stressor. These animals seemed to accept the stressor passively, exhibiting few efforts to escape. They were thought to have formed the cognition that "nothing I do matters," which essentially amounted to learning that they were helpless in controlling their own destiny, and hence they gave up efforts of trying to escape. These uncontrollable stressor experiences had several behavioral consequences beyond simply affecting the animal's motivation or ability to escape from other stressors. Among other things, these animals displayed disturbed social interactions, with a diminished capacity to obtain positive feelings from stimuli or events that would otherwise have been interpreted as rewarding or pleasurable. It may be particularly significant that if animals were first trained in a situation in which they could determine outcomes, essentially learning that "I have control over this situation," then later uncontrollable stressor experiences did not lead to behavioral impairments. From a clinical perspective, these findings suggest that if individuals had the cognitive mindset established that control over events was possible, this would immunize them against the adverse actions that might otherwise be imparted by later uncontrollable events.

It's unfortunate that we might find ourselves in situations where we have limited control over our destinies, which could potentially result in feelings of helplessness. At the extreme, no doubt, are the experiences of those caught up in wars where they could do little but suffer as they and those around them were victimized. We've recently seen this happening in Syria, Sudan, and the Congo, and we've been witness to the establishment of concentration camps that were used for acts of genocide. Although these are instances outside of the norm of usual human experiences, many of us encounter relatively common stressors that could leave us feeling helpless. Consider, for instance, the dehumanizing experiences associated with intrusive medical procedures and severe illnesses, the distress created by natural disasters that range across floods, hurricanes, tornadoes, and earthquakes, or the distress caused by repeated bullying or experiencing repeated discrimination. Equally disturbing, but creating different types of emotions, is the distress that comes from watching the demise of a parent through dementia, or being unable to prevent the death of a child through cancer.

Beyond the severity and controllability of a stressor, the impact of a stressor on well-being is also influenced by its predictability. The occurrence of some stressors is perfectly predictable. University students know that when exam time rolls around they'll be feeling stressed, accountants know that March is going to be a hectic time, and when you've got an appointment at a colonoscopy clinic you know it's not going to be a picnic (maybe that isn't the best choice of words), but in each instance you have the opportunity to prepare yourself. There are, in contrast, occasions when the occurrence of stressors is entirely unpredictable, and our responses in these situations are likely to be quite

Going to the happy place

Oddly, I'm reminded of my youngest kid's experience of uncontrollability, saying "I hate school! I don't wanna go anymore. I just sit there ... bored ... It's my life, you know, and I don't have any control, or choice, or anything." His older brother then interjected with "You're going! You don't have a say in the matter. You just go! – Don't you get it? You're not in charge when you go to school. They're in charge and you just do what you're told. In fact, you're not supposed to like school. That's why they call it 'school'. If they wanted you to like it, then they'd call it 'the happy place.'" Somehow, that seemed to make a lot of sense.

different. Some of these stressors are somewhat unpredictable, such as being in a traffic accident and suffering a couple of bruises. I say that they're *somewhat* unpredictable as accidents happen all of the time, but there aren't warning signs that tell us that "today's the day." Other trauma events are far more devastating and are entirely unpredictable. Who could have predicted 9/11, or earthquakes, tsunamis, or the floods secondary to hurricanes in New Orleans or New York? As the well-known expression goes, "It's difficult to make predictions, especially about the future."

Let's look at yet another instance concerning unpredictability in relation to stressors. In Canada, where there is socialized medicine, an individual might need to have surgery to deal with a problem, such as a herniated C6 disc that creates considerable pain. However, the wait-list for most non-emergency conditions is invariably long, sometimes exceeding a year. So the surgery, which is distressing to say the least, will happen; however, it's unpredictable when this will happen, and aside from fretting, all that can be done is gobble Percocet (a combination of oxycodon and acetaminophen) for pain control, despite the high risk for addiction. Few among us care for this sort of suspense, and if given the option most people would choose to deal with predictable rather than unpredictable stressors. However, it is also the case that knowing precisely when an event will occur allows for anxiety to build up as the due date approaches, and so there are individuals who might choose unpredictability.

Predictability and unpredictability refer to events that will almost certainly occur, but we might not know when the event will occur. So, for instance, we know that we will die some day (it's an inherited characteristic!), but most often we don't know precisely when this will happen. It's unpredictable. Uncertainty is related to unpredictability, but it is usually considered in the context of events that might or might not occur (e.g., it's uncertain whether a particular flu virus will be transmittable between humans, and whether it has the potential to kill large masses of people). Once again, certainty promotes or allows for preparatory responses, whereas uncertainty might leave us in limbo, not sure if we should be engaging in particular behaviors to ward off the threat or whether this would simply comprise pointless action. As there isn't a certainty that the event will happen, we can fall back on the hope that it won't occur, providing us with a ray of hope in situations that are otherwise bleak, as in the case of individuals who are experiencing an illness that is usually fatal, but there is a chance of recovery, however small.

The brain abhors a vacuum

What happens to brain functioning when situations are either uncertain, ambiguous or unknowable? When brain activity was assessed under conditions that involve various levels of "knowability," neuronal activity in portions of the frontal cortex associated with executive functioning, such as planning and decision-making, markedly increased as the ambiguity and uncertainty of the situation increased. Essentially, the brain doesn't like ambiguity, and works hard to make sense of uncertain situations. One wonders, however, whether in filling in the blanks when insufficient information is available, the brain is actually making correct guesses or confabulating with any information that happens to serve the purpose.

Individuals differ appreciably in their intolerance of uncertainty, a characteristic (trait) that individuals bring into situations. Those who are relatively intolerant of uncertainty tend to display elevated levels of anxiety and distress in response to uncertain daily stressors, and express the desire to reduce uncertainty through persistent information-seeking in an effort to obtain factual certainties. Other individuals seem better able to cope with uncertainty, expressing the attitude of "whatever happens, happens." We sometimes see these characteristics in the context of a particular gene or gene mutation (variant) that increases the probability of developing an illness but doesn't guarantee that the disease will actually emerge. Women of certain ethnic groups (e.g., Eastern European Jewish women of Ashkenazi descent) are at increased risk of developing breast cancer owing to the increased inheritance of BRCA1 and BRCA2 gene mutations. Thus, if they had a close relative with this disease, increasing the odds that they too carry this gene, the person might not want to live in suspense, waiting for the shoe to drop, and might thus go for genetic testing to determine if they carry one of these mutations. If the tests are positive some women opt for a double mastectomy and ovariectomy to preclude the possibility of developing breast or ovarian cancer. Others, in contrast, even with a family history of the disease, might choose not to be tested. They prefer not to know and are seemingly able to vanquish these thoughts so that their daily routine is not affected.

Ambiguity, like its cousins, unpredictability and uncertainty, is a further characteristic of stressors that determines how powerful they can be. A situation is said to be ambiguous when there's insufficient information available concerning the probability of an event occurring, or when multiple but inconsistent bits of information are available regarding a potential threat. For example, discomfort can arise as a result of a set of suspicious symptoms that don't form a pattern that is sufficiently coherent to allow for a firm illness diagnosis. Likewise, most of us have heard that government agencies are on the alert for a terrorist attack when they encounter increased internet chatter, or when certain individuals or groups have suddenly dropped off the grid. However, these cues are vague and don't give sufficient information about what might be happening, and hence they are especially potent in creating anxiety.

Reluctant symptoms

Cars sometimes make odd noises that seem to come and go. Computers often misbehave in a similar manner, first showing and then not showing puzzling characteristics. Often the symptoms disappear when you visit the auto mechanic or get the IT technician to look at your computer. Sometimes the same type of thing happens regarding chest, head or stomach pains. Frustratingly, the medical tests come back with a series of inconsistent results, or results that suggest that there's nothing wrong with you and you're viewed suspiciously as if you're either very neurotic or a candidate for a diagnosis of Munchausen's Syndrome. This isn't uncommon and people are frequently sent home after visiting a hospital emergency room having been told that there's nothing wrong with them, when in actuality they're in a perilous condition. Of course, within an hour or so after leaving the hospital, the symptoms re-emerge, and you might wonder whether dropping dead will be the necessary clue to convince the doctors that there is, in fact, something amiss.

Both ambiguity and uncertainty occur frequently and many of us will have experienced the anxiety elicited by such events. For example, if you're over 60 then you may already have had medically related experiences where you're simply unsure what you should be doing. "This feeling in my chest seems like indigestion, but it might also be a heart attack. What do I do now? Do I rush off to the hospital and potentially make a fool of myself if it turns out to be a false alarm, or should I just sit here and hope it passes?" Often these experiences are "just" false alarms, and when the symptoms disappear we likely forget about them. If they reappear, we might then have tests done, and there are occasions where these tests yield distressing outcomes (oddly, the statement that "the test turned out to be 'positive'" is actually bad news). This is accompanied by considerable distress, including uncertainties pertaining to the illness prognosis, and the availability of a competent and experienced medical practitioner (Does this doctor have the experience and skill that will be needed or is he or she a new graduate who had to repeat the module on the kidney after figuring it wouldn't be on the exam?).

Some events that we encounter call for particular measures to be taken fairly quickly. If you feel pain in your chest or a suspicious lump upon a breast examination, then it's obviously advisable to seek medical attention. Other events, however, comprise much greater complexity, and as the situation plays out, uncertainty and unpredictability might increase rather than diminish. We simply can't get a grip on the situation; the chess pieces seem to be moving every which way, and finding a path through the phalanx becomes baffling. When we encounter complex situations of this sort, some individuals simply abandon active efforts to change things, letting fate decide outcomes. For some, this strategy is the worst of all worlds, even as we're being pushed by an inner voice saying "do something, anything, just do something." As we'll find in discussing decision-making processes, we have specific strategies that we use in these situations, although sometimes they're not particularly effective.

Related to some of these stressor characteristics is the volatility of a stressful situation, essentially meaning the extent to which the situation is unstable. Some stressors we meet tend to mosey along, getting somewhat better or somewhat worse, but generally following along a given trajectory. Other stressor conditions are more volatile, exploding suddenly in unexpected ways, or changing rapidly over time, making it difficult to adjust to or cope with the situation. Obviously, these situations require individuals to be nimble and able to change coping strategies readily.

Many of us seem to have a need to feel as if we're in control of our destiny. In fact, we might even go so far as to delude ourselves into thinking that we have control under conditions in which we most certainly don't. Most of us also behave as if life is predictable, and so we plan for the future, as we should, and act as if we can reasonably anticipate what's in store for us. Typically, we can make some fairly informed decisions about the future, often ignoring the possibility that our beliefs about the predictability and controllability of life events are actually illusory. It's not for nothing that we have expressions such as "mann tracht und Gott lacht," literally meaning "man thinks (plans) and god laughs" or Woody Allen's rephrased version, "If you want to make God laugh, tell him about your plans." We have a need for control, for order and for predictability so that we can operate to make sure our futures are secure and that our expectations and hopes are met. Because of our illusions of control over life circumstances, we might be unprepared to deal with unpredictable, ambiguous stressful situations when they do arise. These might comprise unforeseen challenges that affect us individually, such as being afflicted by rare illnesses or those that aren't rare, but weren't expected. There are also highly unlikely events that can affect people, such as becoming collateral damage when a part of a building suddenly collapses, or being hit by

Optimism bias or plain stupid

Individuals often have a sense of invulnerability (especially younger people), believing that bad things might happen to others, but not to them. In recent studies conducted with Sheena Taha, we observed an optimism bias in relation to severe illness (breast and prostate cancer) as well as in relation to being infected by a potential virus, such as H5N1, at some point in the future. In both instances, participants reported that it was much more likely that members of the general public would contract H5N1 or cancer (54% and 71%, respectively) than they would themselves (32% and 45%, respectively). They also believed that the chances of illness being contracted by their close friends were lower than those of the general population (34% and 50% for H5N1 and cancer, respectively), perhaps reflecting "immunity by proxy." Interestingly, the individual's optimism bias was entirely altered if they thought that an acquaintance or family member had contracted the illness. One sees these same optimism biases and the sense of invulnerability in relation to other illnesses, including the development of skin cancer among those spending time in the sun, and lung disease among those who smoke.

lightning, or having a helicopter crash out of the sky. There are also many unexpected events that affect whole communities and countries, including terrorist attacks, wars, nuclear plant meltdowns, hurricanes, famines, and floods. There are even "unknown unknowns" that can affect us. Given the sheer number of potential bullets that might be aimed at us, what are the odds of dodging all of them? Bad things do happen, and as we've heard in Robert Kushner's book published many years ago, they even happen to good people.

Chronic stressors and allostatic overload

Many of the stressors we encounter are blessedly transient and not overly severe, and their effects on our well-being are limited and some of the experiences are quickly forgotten. However, some stressors, as brief as they might be, can have lasting ramifications, especially as the rumination that comes with some stressors can serve as a persistent reminder of negative experiences. By example, being publicly shamed and humiliated can have lasting effects, and it isn't unusual for individuals to ruminate for lengthy periods, sometimes years, over events that led to these feelings.

The stressors we encounter are frequently chronic, and as aversive as they might be, when they occur on a predictable basis we might be able to find ways to adapt and contend with them, and many of our stress-sensitive biological systems likewise become less reactive. However, when stressors are chronic and unpredictable, occur intermittently, or are ambiguous and uncontrollable, adaptation is less likely, and it is difficult to establish adequate coping methods, or to take preparatory steps that enable effective coping. Persistent stressors, such as acting as a caregiver for a parent with Alzheimer's or a child with exceptional needs, dealing with chronic illness, or financial problems, may comprise challenges that can change from day to day, thus straining our ability to cope effectively, and our biological coping resources may become overly taxed, eventually culminating in pathological outcomes.

We ordinarily encounter varied conditions that call for behavioral or physiological adaptations so that our internal environment remains stable, a process referred to as homeostasis. For example, body temperature is regulated, in part, by sweating or shivering in response to heat or cold, respectively, and regulatory processes are likewise present to make sure that our biological systems don't fluctuate wildly. To a significant extent, homeostatic changes are fairly slow-moving as the consequences aren't all that great if you sweat a few moments earlier or a few moments later. Many of the biological changes that occur in response to stressors operate on similar principles, but adaptive responses are more urgent and thus occur quickly. This process, referred to as allostasis, involves multiple biological mechanisms within the brain, as well as endocrine, immune, and peripheral nervous systems. As impressive as our adaptability might be, in response to stressors that are chronic, variable and unpredictable, the strain on biological systems may become excessive, resulting in *allostatic overload*, which may increase vulnerability to illness (McEwen, 2007). Another form of allostatic overload, termed "Type 2" allostatic overload, may also develop through more subtle and insidious challenges that comprise sustained social disturbances or social conflict. These social or community stressors can similarly undermine our well-being, unless measures are taken to modify the social structures that support them (McEwen and Wingfield, 2003).

Before you go...

Any number of disasters can befall us, but we really don't expect them to happen, at least not yet, and probably not to us. Yet, the probability of dying of heart disease is about 34% and that of cancer is about 16–17% (although survival has been increasing for several cancers), Type 2 diabetes occurs in about 3.5% of individuals and is climbing, autoimmune disorders occur at 3.1%, then there's kidney, pancreatic or liver disease, as well as serious automobile accidents that lead to severe disability or death. The list goes on and on, and although we don't know specifically how we'll fare in the future, we can pretty much count on not getting away untouched.

Each stressor we experience is different from every other stressor, and how each individual interprets or responds to a stressor is likely very different from how others see or respond to these stressors. Still, there are some features of stressors themselves that can influence their perceived aversiveness. These features, together with personality characteristics and biological sensitivity and reactivity, can influence the potential for pathological outcomes emerging.

2

Individual Differences in Relation to Stressors and Stress Responses

Comparing cows

Based on our experiences, expectancies and desires, we often make judgments about potential stressors. We likewise make judgments concerning how stressors affect others, and then either commiserate with them or minimize what they're experiencing. A parent dealing with a teenage offspring who has suddenly developed a zit and is having a hissy, might first be empathetic and supportive, but as the hysteria continues, the parent's patience runs short and they might say something unsupportive, such as "Oh, gimme a break. It's just a zit, not a tumor. Pull yourself together." Explicit here is the comparison between the distress that should be felt in response to a zit versus a tumor, but for the kid with the zit, these comparisons are meaningless. At night, all cows look black.

One of the most predictable things about stressors concerns the wide differences that are evident among individuals when confronted by challenges. Some individuals are able to deal well with stressors and don't fall apart even under the most stressful conditions, whereas others, when given the slightest opportunity, do the Henny-Penny thing, shouting to anyone that will listen that the sky is falling. Stressors obviously aren't perceived in the same way by all people and they can understandably have very different effects across individuals. What's viewed as very stressful by one person might be seen as a minor inconvenience by a second. Furthermore, even if individuals perceived the stressor similarly, they might be inclined to use different methods of dealing (coping) with stressors that aren't equally effective. And, even if they use comparable coping methods, the neurobiological impact of the stressor might differ between these individuals. Given the diversity of psychological, emotional, cognitive and biological responses that exist among us, some individuals will succumb to the adverse effects of stressors, whereas the same experiences will have only a modest impact on others.

Stress and Your Health: From Vulnerability to Resilience, First Edition. Hymie Anisman.
© 2015 John Wiley & Sons, Ltd. Published 2015 by John Wiley & Sons, Ltd.

Vulnerability and resilience

Vulnerability and resilience are sometimes incorrectly seen as being at opposite ends of a continuum. In the context of illness or in dealing with stressors, vulnerability typically refers to the susceptibility of a person, group, or even a whole society to disturbances that develop in response to particular environmental or social challenges. Resilience, in contrast, refers to the ability or disposition to recover readily from illness, but in the context we're dealing with, it can also be taken to mean that an individual has the capacity to limit or preclude the detrimental effects of a stressor.

Vulnerability is in a sense easy to understand, and there are a great many factors that can favor the development of illness. Genetic or poor early life experiences, the wrong hormonal or other chemical mix, lousy parenting, or just repeated encounters with nasty events might cumulatively influence our vulnerability to illness. In contrast, it's more difficult to define what factors make us resilient in the face of multiple challenges that can harm us. In a way, it's reminiscent of the contrast concerning the difficulty of creating an elegant and exciting piece of art, and how simple it is to damage it by anybody with the intent to do so.

Most of us have heard of the person who seems perfectly healthy, but who then dies unexpectedly. It required only a single malfunction, an aneurysm or a pulmonary embolism, to undo all that was "healthy" about that individual. Ordinarily, stressors affect numerous biological systems concurrently or sequentially, essentially placing a load on these systems. As strong as our defensive systems might be, if the load is heavy enough then the weakest link supporting these systems might give way, culminating in a pathological condition. For one person it may be the heart, for another it may be aspects of the brain or particular hormonal systems. For an individual to be resilient it might be necessary for weak links to be absent, but let's face it, with enough of a load, any weaknesses that are present will emerge. To limit these outcomes it might be necessary to find ways of diminishing the load or, failing this, to have back-up systems in place that compensate when particular links fail.

Multiple factors likely contribute to resilience, many of which sound like motherhood statements, but this doesn't make them any less important. Resilience factors have included psychosocial and cognitive factors, such as an individual's tenacity, trust in one's instincts, feelings of control, the ability to problem solve, having a positive outlook on life, the ability to gain from both rewarding and negative experiences, spirituality, readiness to respond appropriately to cues that signal danger, as well as the ability to adapt and be flexible to change. Moreover, even in the face of factors that make an individual vulnerable to pathology, whether it involves adverse early experiences or genetic influences, having a strong social identity, being connected to others, and having a good social support network can do wonders in offsetting some of the potential adverse effects of stressors. Of course, some of these resilience factors might be especially useful in some situations and hardly relevant in others. For instance, having a strong social identity might be particularly effective in protecting us from discriminatory events, whereas optimism might be more useful in dealing with illnesses. In this, and several ensuing chapters, we'll consider various factors that influence vulnerability to the negative outcomes of stressors as well as those that favor resilience.

Genetic influences

The field of genetics has changed considerably since the time Gregor Mendel was messing around with pea plants in the 1850s, and marked changes have even evolved since the time I was an undergraduate student. At that time, our introduction to genetics comprised a description of Mendelian inheritance where we were led to believe that we inherited certain genotypes (specific genes received from our parents), much like pea plants did, which then somehow affected our phenotype (what we looked like or how we behaved). We also learned that we inherited one component or allele of a gene from our father and one from our mother, and these inherited gene components could be dominant or recessive. If you inherited a dominant gene it determined your phenotype, and the alternative phenotype could only emerge if you inherited a recessive gene from each of your parents. Thus, if your father had a combination of a dominant and a recessive gene that made him tall, and your mother was similarly heterozygous for this gene (having one dominant tall gene and one recessive short gene), the offspring could potentially inherit the recessive gene from each parent, so that he or she would be short, unlike either parent (this greatly relieved this kid, Murray, who didn't resemble either of his parents in any way, being a foot taller than either of them, but in later years we nonetheless nicknamed him "Mrs Robinson's kid"). At some point, it was acknowledged that inheritance could be incomplete and hence we might not be exactly like either of our parents with respect to any given feature. As an afterthought, as if it were barely important, we were also told that most traits in humans weren't determined by single genes, but reflected polygenic actions (the actions of many genes). So, unlike pea plants, people aren't simply tall or short, green or yellow, or round or wrinkled. There are all sorts of levels of in-between. It all seemed pretty simple and we accepted what we were told, although there was the nagging feeling that to some extent we were being scammed. Although it was reasonable to assume that we inherited particular genes that molded us in some form, we were never told how this happened. You simply inherited something, and somehow this translated into hair or eye color, height, particular behavioral traits, or whether we would succumb to some illness.

It's all magic

Years before my confusion about how a genotype translated into a phenotype, actually in Grade 3, we were told that the earth was created in six days and on the seventh day God rested. That seemed pretty reasonable, as creating the earth was a pretty big job, even for God. But, when I asked our teacher what existed before the world was created, he replied that there had been nothing. I responded, saying, "well, there had to be something." A bit annoyed he responded by saying "nothing. There was nothing. How hard is it to understand that there was nothing? ... An empty space, nothing." As I persisted saying that "even nothing is something," he became very perplexed saying "Mr Anisman ... There was nothing. And, if God wanted you to understand more about what nothing means, then he would have given you a bigger brain rather than the pee-wee you have." Some years later I had an almost identical discussion with my biology teacher when I wondered how genes were translated into the products that we were made of. It just seemed odd that having a particular gene somehow made us appear in one form or another. He didn't have any answers at that time, and he became irritated as I kept pushing, but being a Darwinist, he didn't resort to the assertion that God gave me a tiny brain.

Another premise that was emphasized was that the genes you inherited were those that you were stuck with for better or worse. If you had the "wrong" genes it wasn't anybody's fault, that's just the way it was. Yet another bit that was thrown in was that somehow genes and the environment could interact with one another, but nobody seemed to have a clue concerning how this occurred, and this topic was, in fact, shunted off to the side after being mentioned as a small part of a hypothetical mathematical formula related to factors that govern the inheritance of particular phenotypes. The impression we were left with was that genes had some effect and so did the environment, and together these largely determined our phenotype. The possibility of the environment actually influencing our genes wasn't something that we needed to concern ourselves with.

The last two decades have seen a revolution within molecular biology and all related fields of medicine and neuroscience. Not only has the genome been unraveled, but genetic correlates of some diseases have been identified, and in many instances we know the precise steps by which genes influence biological processes that end up creating a given phenotype. There have also been remarkable advances in defining how environmental conditions, such as stressors, might influence the expression of genetic factors. Skeptics will say that defining the genome hasn't led to any major cures; stem cells haven't panned out as a panacea for everything as was at first so enthusiastically predicted. But it's still early and science progresses in steps, sometimes giant steps and sometimes just baby steps.

Many of the myths that dominated the field just a few years ago have been abandoned in the face of hard data. Contrary to earlier precepts, the influence of genes is not immutable, but can be affected by environmental factors that moderate how these gene effects are expressed. Indeed, stressful events as well as several environmental toxins may affect the expression of genes, but without actually altering the sequence of amino acids that make up these genes. Essentially, the gene responsible for a given outcome can be silenced even though the actual gene sequence has remained intact. These so called "epigenetic" changes may influence neurobiological processes and may influence vulnerability to a variety of disease conditions, including some forms of cancer and autoimmune disorders, such as rheumatoid arthritis, and may contribute to stress responses over the course of an organism's life. It's especially interesting that epigenetic changes that occurred within germline cells (i.e., the sperm or ovum) could be transmitted from parent to child so that the children inherit the gene in its silenced form and could, in theory, transmit the silenced gene to their own offspring. In effect, environmental toxins and stressors can have consequences that travel across successive generations, showing up in the children and grandchildren of those who had initially experienced the stressor or environmental toxin.

In addition to epigenetic processes, gene mutations frequently appear on a DNA strand that can influence phenotypic expression. Numerous mutations appear within the genome and multiple mutations can even appear within a single gene. Mutations may comprise deletions, insertions, or changes of several nucleotides, whereas others may involve only a single nucleotide. Many mutations are fairly common and those that are present in more than 1 percent of the population are referred to as polymorphisms. If the polymorphism entails only a single nucleotide alteration, it is referred to as a single nucleotide polymorphism or SNP (pronounced as "snip"). In an effort to understand the processes leading to pathological conditions, one approach has involved the identification of particular gene polymorphisms and tying these to specific pathological states. This has entailed finding a sample (cohort) of individuals who have or do not have a particular phenotype or a family history for that phenotype, or alternatively

Et voilà, a behavioral phenotype appears

People typically believe that by inheriting certain genes, particular phenotypes appear, but they give little thought to how this comes about. There's really no reason for them to be concerned with what genes do and how they do it, any more than they need to know how a microwave oven works in order to reheat yesterday's leftovers. Still, misconceptions about genes lead people to think incorrectly about genetically related diseases, and they obviously won't see the significance of stressors or other life experiences interacting with genes in affecting a variety of our abilities.

Chromosomes inherited from our parents comprise lengthy DNA strands, made up of a series of four nucleotides, guanine (G), adenine (A), cytosine (C) and thymine (T). Much like letters strung together to make words, these nucleotides in sets of three make up particular amino acids, and a sequence of amino acids makes up a gene, just as a set of letters form a word, and a sequence of words make up a sentence. This gene, alone or in combination with other genes, serves as the blueprint for the creation of RNA and the expression of particular phenotypes. Using the DNA as a template, RNA is formed through a process called transcription, and for all intents, the RNA that is manufactured looks exactly like the DNA (except for the nucleotide thymine being replaced with uracil). The specific sequence (or ingredients) of the messenger RNA (mRNA) produced through this process is then decoded so that specific chains of amino acids are created that will end up forming a protein. The process of mRNA being converted to proteins is ongoing and new proteins are formed as others are used. These proteins make up every characteristic of which you're made up (hair, skin, kidney cells, liver cells), including hormones and immune factors, and contribute to the formation of neurotransmitters. These neurobiological changes contribute to all aspects of our daily functioning, including our behaviors, the way we deal with stressors, and whether pathology will be induced when stressors are not dealt with appropriately.

We have about 20,000 genes comprised of about 3 billion bases. As impressive as that is, consider that even though as many as 10 trillion cells are made over a lifetime, every cell, with some odd exceptions, comprises exactly the same sequence of bases. Understandably, the more cell replication occurs, the more likely it is for errors to occur on a DNA strand. Some of these errors can be fairly complex involving large changes in parts of a chromosome, whereas others seem pretty small, amounting to a change of a single nucleotide. It doesn't sound as if those small changes can have much of an effect, but they might. Just as changing one letter or word can change the entire meaning of a sentence, if the characteristics of the DNA are altered, even when this is no more than a single nucleotide, the protein that ought to be formed might be altered.

A gene contains the information for the formation of a phenotype, and nearby sequences of amino acids, referred to as promoter regions, tell the primary gene when to turn on or off, or even when to interact with other genes. Importantly, environmental events, including stressors, can affect biochemical processes which influence these promoters, and hence can alter the genes' impact on hormonal and neurotransmitter production, and all the other biological factors that come to affect behavior.

finding a sufficiently large group of random individuals, and then assessing whether there is a match between the presence of certain genes or mutations and the appearance of pathology.

This ought to be simple enough, but there's no reason to believe that complex behaviors involve a single gene; instead they likely involve a compilation of several genes as well as environmental contributions or the presence of stressors. The difficulties are compounded by the fact that many psychological disturbances have overlapping symptoms and it is possible that they also have gene influences in common. Furthermore, even if individuals have similar symptoms it doesn't necessarily mean that these stem from the same underlying biological causes. Two individuals can exhibit a particular biological modification, but this could have come about through different routes, much in the same way that your bank account can be low either because you're spending too much, or not earning enough, or because of a bank error, or unknown to you someone has been removing money. As well, given the vast number of mutations that exist, sometimes varying dramatically across cultures, it can be difficult to link a particular mutation to a specific pathology. Conducting analyses of such phenomena requires a huge number of participants and even then, finding the genetic source for particular pathological conditions is akin to finding a specific needle in a pile of needles.

Paralleling the human studies, there has been considerable research in animals that has attempted to link genetic factors and the development of pathological conditions. Using inbred mice in which all members of the strain are genetically identical to one another, or animals that are selectively bred for particular phenotypes, certain genes have been tied to disturbances reminiscent of psychopathological conditions in humans. In addition, sophisticated methods have been developed, including those in which genes can be engineered, which permit analyses of what happens to behavioral and biochemical outcomes when certain genes are deleted from or inserted into the genome. Likewise, procedures have been developed to assess what happens when a gene's function is either increased or decreased at different times of life and in specific brain regions. When genetic approaches in animals are coupled with the analysis of early life experiences, social processes, stressor effects and other experiences, it may be possible to identify the array of factors that influence vulnerability to stress-related disturbances.

Age

The extent to which a person is affected by stressors has a lot to do with their age. Most everyone knows that vulnerability to certain illnesses, such as those that are virally related, are elevated in the very young and in the very old, and stressors at these times also have particularly dramatic effects. But these aren't the only phases of life in which stressors can have powerful effects. Stressors encountered prenatally as a result of a pregnant woman being stressed can affect later pathological outcomes. As well, stressors experienced during life transition periods, such as adolescence, can engender adverse consequences that may carry through to later periods in life so that vulnerability to pathology may persist even years later. These persistent effects of stressors may be due to altered psychosocial processes or neurobiological mechanisms that are affected by stressors. Knowing what influences these processes might be instrumental in developing approaches to blunt the negative consequences of stressors. In Chapter 8, as well as in other chapters dealing with specific pathological conditions, we'll talk more about stressor effects across the life span, so for the moment we'll move on.

Sex

Women usually have it tougher than do men. They're the partner who gives birth, typically carries the bulk of the childrearing load and takes care of the home, generally is more likely to care for sick family members and act as a caregiver for elderly parents, all the while juggling employment and multiple other demands. With so much to do, it's a good thing men are around to provide able direction. To add to their already sizable burden, relative to men, women are more likely to develop illnesses, such as autoimmune disorders (those in which the immune system turns on the individual, as in the case of multiple sclerosis, lupus erythematosus, rheumatoid arthritis), posttraumatic stress disorder (PTSD) and major depression. This health disparity might be attributable to the stress burden carried, coupled with socialization processes in women that promote certain behavioral styles, or the use of less adaptive coping strategies to deal with stressors, or it might be that stressors are simply appraised and dealt with differently by males and females. For example, in some situations males tend to examine issues from a broad perspective, whereas females are more detail oriented, which could potentially influence how stressors are dealt with. It is also possible that the effects observed are specific to certain stressors, in that interpersonal challenges might have greater effects in females, whereas work-related performance pressures have greater effects in males. As well, variations of sex hormones might directly, or indirectly through actions on brain functioning, contribute to some of the effects of stressors on female behavioral and cognitive responses. Indeed, stress-provoked neuronal activity within numerous cortical and limbic brain regions varies over the estrous cycle, and the effects on the stress hormone, cortisol, are more pronounced during the latter part of the menstrual cycle (luteal phase), during which the hormone progesterone is high. As we'll see in Chapter 4 and 5, however, the notion that women are frailer than men and less able to deal with hardships might simply be a myth.

Personality differences in relation to stress responses

Personality factors seem to be fundamental in determining how individuals respond to stressors. Personality traits are usually seen as stable characteristics of an individual, although they're not entirely fixed in stone, and can be modified to some degree by experiences. These characteristics are likely formed by several factors, including genetic contributions, parenting received, and the socialization that occurred in early life or adolescence, as well as the general environment in which kids were raised.

It is perhaps predictable that individuals who are generally *optimistic* and approach situations with a positive outlook tend to be more resilient than individuals who approach these situations with a pessimistic perspective. Among other things, optimists have been found to be better able to regulate hormonal and immunological stress responses, less likely to suffer burnout or depression, and more adept at handling severe stressors, such as breast cancer and radical prostatectomy. Interestingly, studies that evaluated brain changes that occurred in those who were positive versus negative thinkers indicated different neuronal activation patterns that could potentially reflect hard-wired characteristics.

Having a resilient personality was similarly linked to an individual's self-efficacy, which comprises the belief that tasks can be accomplished and difficulties resolved through one's own efforts. Paralleling these findings, high levels of mastery and hardiness were accompanied by a better ability to deal with stressors and a diminished likelihood of succumbing to stress-related pathology. Likewise, people who have an internal locus of control, meaning that they tend to have the view that events in life arise primarily because of their own behaviors and actions, tend to deal with stressors better than do those with an external locus of control, who generally believe that fate, chance, or powerful others determine the events they encounter and the consequences of these experiences. There is also ample reason to believe that elements of what are known as the Big Five personality dimensions contribute to the way in which stressors affect the individual. This conceptual framework of personality comprises openness (imagination and insight), conscientiousness (thoughtfulness, being goal directed, organized, detail oriented), extraversion (excitability, sociability, assertiveness, emotional expressiveness), agreeableness (prosocial behaviors, such as trust, altruism, kindness, affection), and neuroticism (emotional instability, sadness, anxiety, moodiness, irritability), with the last of these being most closely aligned with how individuals respond to stressors. As we'll see later, these personality dimensions influence how we appraise and cope with stressors, and they also have a say in how our biological systems respond to such events, and thus may have profound consequences for our general well-being and in the development of stress-related psychological and physical illnesses.

Previous stressor experiences

Our behavioral and biological responses to stressors are greatly influenced by our previous experiences with different challenges. Whereas mild or moderate stressors, especially if experienced early in life, might enhance hardiness and the ability to deal with challenges, strong stressors might "sensitize" biological systems so that when stressors are again encountered, the systems are too reactive or their activation is too persistent, and as a result negative repercussions may evolve. Whether they occur in childhood or during adulthood, these experiences might influence later sensitivity to stressors, appraisals of events, and coping processes, and can also affect lifestyles and general worldview, and may even affect the propensity for further stress encounters.

As we'll see repeatedly, an important characteristic of brain neurons is that they are plastic or malleable, so that as a result of experiences, including stressors, the strength of connections between neurons can change, thereby influencing memory of events as well as later responses to stressors. The altered responses to later stressors can develop as a result of prenatal stressors or those experienced when we were very young, and thus we may be unlikely to remember them. Thus, the adverse effects that occur aren't simply based on our memory of earlier experiences, but might reflect a change of the developmental trajectory related to biological processes, or it might be that neuronal processes can become "sensitized" so that greater responses are elicited when stressors are encountered years later. With each stressor experience the sensitized responses might become more pronounced and behavioral disturbances will be more readily provoked. Eventually, very little stimulation will be necessary to promote the exaggerated neuronal changes so that behavioral and emotional disturbances can even be instigated by minor stressors that would otherwise be insignificant.

Stress generation

Sometimes we're chance victims of negative events, sometimes others create stressors for us, and sometimes people run into problems simply because of the situation in which they find themselves. The concept of "stress generation," as this is known, isn't an attempt to blame the victim, but rather it means that sometimes, for any number of reasons, people might be disposed to doing the wrong thing at the wrong time, and they might even do this repeatedly. Unfortunately, often enough they might not be aware that they're doing this and so it's difficult for them to engage in useful corrective actions. Readers of Tolstoy's *Anna Karenina* will recall that she was pushed to a depressive state and became both possessive and paranoid about her partner's supposed trysts, which caused him to distance himself. Rampant insecurities caused her to persist in her ways instead of changing her behavior, leading to dissolution of the relationship and the loss of an important resource that could have served as a stress buffer.

Stress generation is not an infrequent occurrence, often being apparent among individuals with depressive features, especially if the individual has a tendency to blame others for negative events or is inclined to shy away from social interactions, thus alienating others and thereby further undermining social support. Stress generation is also common among individuals who are emotionally sensitive and thus more likely to find themselves in interpersonal conflicts, as well as among those with a perfectionist streak who might also alienate others because of their excessive demands or because of their own failures to meet commitments. Likewise, sociotropy, a personality trait comprising high levels of dependence and excessive need to please others, tends to be associated with stress generation, and it seems that among individuals whose self-esteem is based largely on their relationship with others, interpersonal conflicts can be created through their own behaviors, leading to unhappiness or depression, and further stress generation. As well, there are times when individuals find themselves unable to take control of their situation, and through a sequence of unfortunate events find themselves encountering a cycle of stressors. For example, intimate partner violence may lead to depression, which may hinder appropriate actions being taken, leaving victims still more prone to being a prime target for further abuse. So, as much as most of us would like to diminish distress that can upset our lives, often stress breeds stress, and active steps or external help is necessary to limit this cycle of hurt.

Before you go...

We frequently make the incorrect assumption that if we find a particular experience to be stressful, then others would see this situation similarly. To the contrary, however, inter-individual differences exist regarding stress responses and variables that influence our vulnerability to stress-related pathology and stress resilience. Multiple factors encourage these differences, including genetic influences, personality types, age, sex, previous stressful experiences, and the inclination for generating stressors. As well, interactions between genes and the environment, including the silencing of gene actions, have much to do with these individual differences. Thus, it's probably not a good idea to assume that any given stressor will affect you in the same way that they affect others, and likewise, methods that were effective in diminishing distress in others might not be similarly useful for you. In offering advice to others, we frequently assume that our actions if we were in their situation are essentially what they ought to be doing, and we then throw up our hands when they don't follow our advice. Consider that your advice, presented from a distance, may be missing nuances of the situation, or alternatively, your advice might be straining the coping abilities and psychological resources of the other person.

3

Appraising Stressful Events

Appraisal and misappraisals

This guy was accused of borrowing a book and then thoughtlessly returning it in a tattered condition. In his defense, he argued that (a) I never borrowed the book, (b) it was already tattered when I got it, and (c) it was in perfectly good condition when I returned it. Obviously this isn't a great defense strategy. In much larger real-life cases another strategy that has been used, largely unsuccessfully, has been termed the "idiot defense" or the "ostrich defense." In this instance, the defendant, the president or CEO of a company, maintained that in running a multibillion dollar corporation they couldn't reasonably be expected to be aware of every little thing that was going on, and instead relied on subordinates to handle day-to-day events. Their job was to develop global strategies and not to get bogged down with nitty-gritty issues. However, it wasn't the nitty-gritty that was the problem, but instead it involved events that were happening right in the head office, and it was thought that if they didn't know what had been happening, then they should have.

Lots of us actually do the very same thing frequently, and continue to do so even as we acknowledge that it's not a great idea. How often do individuals have physical symptoms that are threatening, but choose to ignore them with the hope that they'll just go away? Likewise, it's not unusual for a parent to see their kid's behavior as "just being a phase" instead of a kid "out of control." Further, how often do individuals evaluate a situation and then optimistically believe that the outcome will be consistent with the most hopeful projections as opposed to those that are more realistic. Appraising events with blinders on and then engaging in avoidance and denial might be useful under certain circumstances, but more often it amounts to the idiot defense.

Stress and Your Health: From Vulnerability to Resilience, First Edition. Hymie Anisman.
© 2015 John Wiley & Sons, Ltd. Published 2015 by John Wiley & Sons, Ltd.

Appraising stressors

Guidance through primary and secondary appraisals

How we perceive and appraise stressors is fundamental in determining the coping strategies that we use to deal with challenges, and conversely our coping abilities or the specific coping methods used may influence how we appraise stressors. Ordinarily, when confronted by a potential stressor our brain is involved in focusing attention on those aspects of the situation that are likely to be particularly relevant, and it also seems that there are brain regions that are actively involved in suppressing the influence of irrelevant stimuli that might distract us. How we appraise events, understandably, contributes to the development of stress-related psychological disturbances and physical illnesses, and can influence our ability to recover from these conditions. One of the most detailed analyses linking stressors, appraisals and coping was suggested about 30 years ago by Lazarus and Folkman (1984) and still holds considerable sway. According to their perspective, when we are confronted with a potential stressor, we typically make an evaluation or "primary appraisal" regarding the threat or challenge it represents. This appraisal is likely influenced by the attributes of the potential threat, as well as personality characteristics, previous stressor experiences, and the person's specific abilities and beliefs. If a situation is perceived as being threatening, then the primary appraisal is followed by "secondary appraisals" in which an assessment is made concerning whether we have the resources necessary to contend with the threat. The secondary appraisals may comprise an assessment as to our potential behavioral and cognitive control over the situation, whether the situation is one that allows for a degree of choice over the coping strategies available, and to what extent we can predict and prepare for stressful events. These various attributes of secondary appraisal are fundamental in determining the strategies that are used to cope with the challenge.

In some instances, a threat is very clear and certain, but in other instances it is blurred by ambiguity and uncertainty, and our appraisals may rely largely on our previous experiences, things we've heard from others, or gut responses. On some occasions when a threat is imminent and particularly dangerous, appraisals need to occur very quickly, and coping responses are initiated almost reflexively. In other instances, appraisals are complex, and multiple reappraisals guide the individual's thoughts and behaviors. For example, when individuals unexpectedly find themselves jobless, their first reaction might be shock or a need to understand why this occurred. They probably consider the psychological toll that might accompany being "let go," including the shame of letting family members, coworkers and friends know. Soon afterward, secondary appraisals would follow in which the individual would consider how severe this threat is with respect to their immediate financial needs given their obligations and needs, including the availability of employment insurance or previous savings, and what the likelihood is of getting another job soon. Clearly, the primary and secondary appraisals vary based on whether the threat only affects them or whether it also affects dependents, such as children or elderly parents, whether they're near retirement and would have left the job soon, as well as the extent to which their identity was tied to the job. Ultimately, these considerations contribute to the actions the individual takes to cope with what has occurred and how they will deal with other events that will soon unfold.

Thinking fast and slow

When we ask "Do I have the resources to contend with this stressor?" or "What route should I take in dealing with the stressor?" we are essentially tapping into our ability to make sound decisions. The processes involved in decision-making are complex, involve many variables and call upon the effective function of several brain regions. Some of the most influential work in the field of decision-making came from Kahneman and Tversky (1974) who defined numerous processes related to decision-making and why we sometimes make decisions that appear somewhat irrational. Their work, which garnered a Nobel Prize for Kahneman (Amos Tversky, sadly, died before the prize was awarded), has a lot to say about how we appraise and respond to stressors, although their theorizing was not specifically focused on stressor appraisals. They indicated that to a significant extent decisions or attributions are based on "heuristics," which simply means strategies or shortcuts that are made on the basis of information that is readily at hand, often related to experiences or rules that had previously been established. This is especially important during stressful situations when individuals often are not in a position to go through lengthy processes to make decisions, and it may be more pragmatic to resort to past practices, educated guesses, or rules of thumb. In this regard, a "representative heuristic" might be endorsed in which individuals consider whether their current perspective regarding a given situation is consistent with everyday experiences. For instance, even the seemingly simple task of making judgments about other people might require considerable information, and so we might use bits of information that are readily at hand to make our initial judgments.

The heuristic view was subsequently extended in several ways, including the incorporation of *fast* and *slow* thinking, which recently appeared in the popular literature. Like others, Kahneman (2011) suggested that decision-making involves dual systems comprising System 1 or Fast Thinking that is rapid, automatic, driven by emotions and the subconscious, involves the incorporation of new ideas into an existing schema, and can be primed to react in a particular way in response to environmental events. A more cognitively based system, termed System 2 or Slow Thinking, is based on logic and conscious efforts, typically kicking in when relatively complex decisions need to be made. This system is ruled by memories that could potentially affect our logical thinking and can modify the automatic responses that would otherwise prevail.

Consider for a moment that upon encountering a sudden stressful occurrence similar to one we had previously experienced, we might react exactly as we previously did. If we had encountered the event on many occasions, then our responses might have become second-nature and the resulting actions seem well rehearsed and effective. For this very reason it is often suggested that when going into some novel situation, a practice run, even cognitively, might be valuable. There are occasions, however, in which stressors are encountered that are entirely out of the range of our experiences and more apt to be met with confused or disorganized appraisals, and it may take a few moments to understand what it is that's actually happening. It is then that slow thinking or secondary appraisals might be needed for appropriate decisions to be made, but in these confused situations it might still be our fast thinking responses that prevail.

How we behave in many situations is largely determined by whether and how we've been primed to respond. Indeed, it's impressive how sensitive our appraisals are even to fairly subtle cues that serve to prime us to think or behave in certain ways. If my friend thinks someone is two-faced, and he lets me know this, even innocuously, then when I meet this person I likely will be cautious or even negative in relation to him or her. Likewise, a person in a "uniform" or a relatively tall person is viewed as more authoritative than others, even if there isn't any reason to believe that this person is particularly competent. In the same way, as much as we might not want to accept it, stereotypes about certain groups or cultures can influence our appraisals, even if we are not consciously aware that this is occurring. Our appraisals, and our misappraisals, intrude on many day-to-day appraisals and action, and it's likely that we haven't a clue that our behaviors are being directed by priming stimuli.

Trusting your gut

The activity of millions of neurons within several brain regions are involved in keeping short-term memories intact. Disruption of systematic neuronal firing that keeps memories active may result in disturbed short-term memory, as we typically see when we try to keep a phone number in mind only to have someone ask us a question. Short-term memory is similarly disrupted by stressful events, and in making decisions under these circumstances one would be better off relying on well-entrenched heuristics. People working in high-pressure situations (first responders, surgeons, air-traffic controllers) are well rehearsed and trained so that when stressors occur, heuristics are available that allow for rapid and automatic decision-making.

In situations that are ambiguous, making decisions is understandably difficult, and we are especially likely to rely on our intuitions that comprise trusting our gut instincts. In fact, those with expertise or knowledge of a topic fare better in making gut-based responses compared to those without the same level of expertise. Interestingly, when individuals were explicitly told to ignore their gut instincts and respond solely on a logical, analytical basis, the performance of experts and non-experts was comparable. It seems that even though we say that a particular decision was instinctive, it is likely formed through experience-based heuristics.

Just about anyone who has written a multiple choice exam might commiserate with the thought: "should I change my answer or stick with my first response?" Although common wisdom has been "stick with your first response," several studies that assessed this indicated that it wasn't necessarily a good strategy. However, there is a compromise position. If you are well prepared and know your stuff, then go with your first instinct, as the heuristics involved will take you to the right place, unless of course on rereading the question you become certain of an alternative answer. If, in contrast, you don't know your stuff, then analytical processes won't get you anywhere and so you might as well go with your gut, which also amounts to sticking with your first response.

That doesn't sound like much of a compromise. It reminds me of a recent item on a social media site where this fellow wrote to say "My girlfriend wanted to get a kitten. I didn't. So we both compromised and got a kitten."

Our automatic responses, including those comprising our stressor appraisals, are related to several processes relevant to heuristic processes. In this regard, appraisals might be influenced by "associative coherence," meaning the degree to which an event is consistent with our preconceived or primed "intuitions." We might also engage in "attribute substitution," which means that when a situation is fairly complex, decisions might be based on a simpler question without us necessarily being aware that this is being done. So, if we are primed to believe that Rebecca is a charitable person, we might make other attributions about her, including that she is kind, warm and friendly, even though we actually know very little about her. The judgments we make can also be influenced by the perceived ease or difficulty involved in coming to a decision, referred to as "processing fluency." Certainly, easy appraisals or solutions are preferred over those that are complex, but we might mistakenly assume that the simpler solutions are more likely to be correct.

Priming against bad news

Do I want the bad news or the good news first? Is there a more stupid question on this earth? Right, I'd like the good news first because I want to live in anticipation of horror as long as I possibly can. Of course the person delivering the news wants to get to the good things first in the hope that it will buffer against the effects of the bad news. So what's the best approach when you've got to cause someone distress? Some people have argued in favor of first delivering some good news in the hope of tempering the bad news that follows, and then provide the rest of the good. Probably the best advice is not to start the conversation with "Do you want the good news or the bad news first." This said, it might be possible to couch the negative information in a relatively positive framework. So, a doctor delivering bad news to a patient might say "I hope you'll live a very nice, comfortable life, but we have some issues to take care of first." The key in delivering this news is basically putting oneself in the other person's shoes and then determining the preferred strategy.

Guideposts and anchors

It isn't unusual to find ourselves having to make some fairly important decisions even though we have limited knowledge about a given topic. In such instances we might look for guideposts or anchors that point us in particular directions. Kahneman indicated that in some instances, such as buying a house or a car, most of us will actually know little about how much they might actually be worth. The anchors might be the asking price for the house, what other houses in the area have sold for recently, advice from friends who probably know little more than we do, or we foolishly might ask the real-estate agent who is desperate to sell a property in a sluggish market and might say anything to do so. The anchor, in a sense, has limited bearing on the true worth of the house, but instead is a reflection of what someone is willing to pay. The vendor, by posting an asking price sets the anchor, and regardless of whether it had been set 10 or 20 percent higher or lower, we would have gone through the same trepidations and discomfort simply because we have no idea what the actual value of the house might be. In some instances the starting point might be so far off the mark that we wouldn't consider the purchase, but if it is "in the ball park" then we might proceed with negotiations. In this instance, potential buyers might rely on Slow thinking, but sometimes their desires might outweigh their common sense, and there are more than just a few people who, following the exhilaration of getting a new house, experience buyer's regret.

We might, unfortunately, encounter a somewhat similar dilemma when it comes to our health. Having been diagnosed with a severe illness, such as breast or prostate cancer, the oncologist might recommend several possible therapeutic routes. Often, this also entails an anchor being set in the form of statistics regarding survival rates and other related issues. The patient wants to survive, of course, but also wants to avoid pain and disfigurement, and maintain their quality of life. So they're in a position of choosing their poison, and this might entail trying to "get a better deal." In addition to talking to their oncologist or the surgeon about the short- and long-term side effects of the treatments, as well as the survival rates associated with them, they might gather information, through the web for example, concerning survival rates among those with an illness very similar to their own, rather than relying on global statistics. As much as we think we're making decisions based on logical thinking, the fact is that we might not be in a position to make good judgments. For that matter, our decisions in relation to treatment options might be influenced by what we've heard, or to subtle influences. Even how information is framed might lead to different decisions. Being told that a surgical procedure is associated with a 90 percent survival rate has a very different effect than being told that this procedure has a 10 percent mortality rate, even though the outcome is the same in both instances.

There are occasions, which include making decisions regarding medical options, in which the correctness of our decisions might be only slightly better than how we'd fare if we were responding based on guesses. When things work out well we're tempted to take credit for the decision, but when things turn sour, we might hear a lot of either "if only" or "who could have known that ...?" In situations where decisions are difficult to reach, and we certainly don't want to carry the blame for bad decisions, we might opt to alter the responsibility for decisions or leave it to fate.

How we behave in decision-making situations can also be influenced by our natural tendency to loss aversion being stronger than our desire for gains. There are occasions when our decisions consist of not taking a certain course of action, such as not making a particular investment or accepting a particular strategy in the treatment of an illness, and as a result we miss an opportunity. Essentially, an individual might bemoan a loss of $50,000 in selling a house much more than they would regret not buying a house that would have yielded a $50,000 profit, even though both options would leave them shy of the same amount of money. Thus, even if they could afford a financial loss, individuals will frequently "play it safe" when they shouldn't. Of course, if a person wants something badly enough, there is a tendency to underestimate costs and overestimate benefits, leading to unwise, risky decisions. As well, sunk-costs in losing financial situations (i.e., how much has already been invested for naught) have a way of stopping us from thinking through our decisions properly. Given the choice, we're apt to chase our losses, so that having lost a sum of money, say for instance in buying a stock that's a dud, we're likely to stick with the stock in the hope that it will bounce back, even though cashing out and betting on another stock is a much wiser decision.

The way we perceive losses or missed opportunities is influenced by contextual or background conditions. Basically, when you're riding a high, most everything looks good, and even situations that are transparently threatening might look manageable. However, when you're in a slump, you might feel that the world and fate are conspiring against you, and your appraisals regarding just about everything turn very negative. When our mood is poor, we might not see things the way they really are, but might instead see it from a narrow, dark, gloomy place that simply doesn't favor good decision-making. At these times, it's likely best to step outside of the situation before making appraisals, or it might be advisable to try to gain insight from others outside of the situation as they might be able to see things from another perspective.

Beyond the contribution of anchors and situational factors, various personality characteristics have been linked to decision-making. To be sure, intense stressors will likely be perceived similarly among most people, but less intense stressors or those that are ambiguous will be associated with diverse appraisals. Individuals who see the world positively will likely interpret potential threats differently from those who see things from a negative perspective, and those with good self-esteem and feelings of mastery will have a different take on challenges relative to those with less positive self-perceptions. Optimistic individuals dealing with a cancer diagnosis, for instance, fare better than those who are more pessimistic, at least with respect to their mood and how they deal

Little devil and little angel

I had always assumed that the little devil and the little angel that guided some of my bad and good behaviors sat on my left and right shoulders, respectively. It's more realistic to believe that these two are actually situated in my head within the lateral frontal pole of each of the two hemispheres of the brain. Activity in these sites lets us know when we've blundered in our behavior or decision-making, such as when we open our mouths and out comes something really dopey that we instantly regret, or when we know we should have done something charitable, but instead just walked on by. This region seems to be unique to humans and in a sense it might serve as our conscience. However, given that so many blunders are apt to occur, and irrational and bad behaviors are as common as they are, it seems that either the lateral frontal pole is sometimes absent, asleep at the switch, or just can't tell the difference between alternatives.

with this dreadful experience. However, I wonder whether those with an optimistic personality style were also less likely to have the suspicious lump checked simply because they optimistically thought that there was nothing to worry about. Similarly, what can we say about people who are optimistic not because of a personality trait, but because their religion suggests that their prayers will reach God's ear, and hence radical procedures aren't necessary, or that children needn't be vaccinated because God will protect them?

Appraisals based on what others think

Our appraisals and decisions aren't only guided by our own previous experiences, but might also be based on what others think. We not only follow what other people do or say, but we make suppositions about the perspectives of others, and then behave accordingly. This occurs across many stressful situations, but is particularly evident in relation to those that are ambiguous and uncertain. Some people have a great deal of self-confidence and a wish to be masters of their own destiny, and thus choose to rely on their own judgments. Others, perhaps because they're more social, or possibly owing to self-doubts and insecurities, prefer to respond on the basis of what others think. In fact, consultation and obtaining information from appropriate sources, whether they have a unique expertise or represent larger groups (e.g., focus groups), can be exceptionally useful. But there are occasions when the appraisals and actions made by groups might not be a proper course of action. This is especially the case when the members of the group are too homogeneous and alternative perspectives are not well represented. As well, appraisals and decisions made by a group are often riskier than those made by any single individual. This phenomenon, known as the "risky shift," might come about owing to a diffusion of responsibility (we're all in this together, and we'll share the blame if things don't work out well), or it might be that individuals are apt to follow the behavior of those who are seen as more inclined to take on a risky position. Regardless of why it occurs, in some contexts it's important to consider that the decision made by a group might not be preferable if you end up suffering the loss on your own.

Most of us likely see ourselves as being fairly rational, probably even more rational than the next person. Still, irrational behaviors and some very bad decisions seem to

Rational decisions for which there are no great solutions

Anyone who has read *Sophie's Choice* will know that there are occasions where decision-making is nearly impossible. Every solution is bad and the option considered at any given moment is the one that seems least desirable. The greater the stakes the more difficult it might be for decisions to be made, especially when a decision, once made, can't be reversed.

Sometimes the possible decisions individuals are required to make are at a very different level, such as making moral decisions, where it could be argued there isn't a right or a wrong choice. In an experimental setting this is assessed under conditions where individuals are presented with a situation that entails two unappealing choices (e.g., the participant is offered the hypothetical possibility of sacrificing one person in order to save the lives of several others). You'd think that such decisions would be based on logic, moral views, or empathy, but the decisions that are made in these situations are markedly influenced by recent stressors that individuals have encountered.

emerge in many different situations, and we have interesting ways of rationalizing them. As we saw earlier, one unfortunate consequences of being stressed is that it may promote behaviors that contribute to the generation of still more stress. As well, stressors might make individuals more inflexible so that they tend to hang on to long-held, outdated opinions or beliefs, or they might not be able to accept that they've made an error and thus are unlikely to change their ways. Individuals who are emotionally driven might make decisions primarily on this basis, and there are those who are so afraid of making wrong decisions, or who simply can't abide feelings of regret associated with wrong decisions, they end up not making any decisions at all. Likewise, the availability of too many choices can be daunting, and this too can result in decisions not being made. For other individuals, procrastination might be a way of dealing with the anxiety associated with making decisions (putting off seeing a doctor regarding certain suspicious symptoms), and they continue with these clearly maladaptive behaviors with the full knowledge that their procrastination might have negative consequences. Doing nothing is, after all, much easier than doing something.

Appraisals in relation to learning, memory, automaticity, expectation, and habit

We are to some extent hard-wired to respond to environmental stimuli in a standard manner. In some species, responses to warning signals are emitted to which other animals respond, without either of them having had relevant previous experiences. These automatic responses are essential as these critters might not get a second chance to heed warnings. We are also equipped with processes related to attention, learning, and memory that develop in an experience-dependent manner. Years ago, the Canadian scientist Donald Hebb (1955) formulated a view that explained how learning new information occurs, how memories and expectations are formed, and how these expectations lead us to perceive things as they should be rather than how they actually are. Hebb suggested that as we learn new information, connections between neurons are strengthened, and the assembly of cells involved in recognizing objects and responding to them are broadened. Complex learning and memory involve still greater and more complex cell assemblies or networks, and once the connections are sufficiently well ingrained, stimulating one aspect of the network will result in the entire cell assembly being triggered as if on autopilot.

For some individuals, appraisals may be warped by previous experience, and might be too automatic, rigid, and negatively biased so that all situations are seen through the same dark lens. Stressful experiences could augment these negative biases, and like habits, these negative mindsets are hard to break. This negativity is particularly pronounced among individuals who are depressed or have a propensity toward depression, as well as in the presence of certain gene polymorphisms. Having well-entrenched response styles can serve us well in solving straightforward problems, especially when challenges are consistent with those we've previously encountered. However, life often isn't all that predictable and we're apt to run into new problems for which sticking to old strategies might not be fruitful, and novel approaches to deal with these stressors might be needed.

Delusions of courage

Most of us have at some time made some fairly poor appraisals and decisions concerning far-off events that "didn't seem like a bad idea at the time." Considerable regret is expressed by the person with a fear of public speaking who agreed some time earlier to talk to a large group, or the individual who cherishes their privacy but nonetheless agreed to host a charitable event at their home. When the dreaded event is far off, individuals appraise the situation from a perspective that comprises an "illusion of courage" or perhaps, more appropriately, a "delusion of courage" so that the potential stressor feels less negative, even though they know, based on their experiences, that they won't deal well with the event when it comes to pass. Obviously, when the invitation first comes we need to make a proper appraisal concerning how we'll actually behave when the time comes to act, rather than fooling ourselves into thinking that things will be different this time. One way to do this is to imagine how you'd feel if the event were to be held tomorrow instead of many months off.

While we're on the topic of illusions and delusions, if we believe that we can influence a situation, then appraisals of that situation obviously ought to differ from those evident when we believe a situation is beyond our control. However, depending on experiences and several personality characteristics, we frequently overestimate the degree to which we actually are able to exert control over otherwise chance events. Such misappraisals might produce difficulties that hadn't been anticipated, but this illusion of control might also have some positive attributes. When we perceive events as controllable, we are generally better able to deal with stressors, and in a sense, the illusory sense of control may actually reflect an adaptive process for dealing with challenges. For instance, cancer patients who had the perception that they had some control over their illness exhibited lower levels of distress than did individuals who did not have these control perceptions. Illusory control in this instance might not affect disease progression, but it allows for lower daily distress.

Positive and negative emotions

How we appraise events can obviously influence our emotional state, and conversely, our emotional state affects our appraisals of situations. Emotions are determined by multiple processes, and because several emotions can occur concurrently, they can be exceedingly complex, and it can be difficult to identify the biological underpinnings of some emotions. Generally, it seems that although a variety of emotions can emerge under diverse conditions, they all serve several common or interrelated functions. They let others know how we're feeling so that they can take measures that are corrective (apologize), supportive (sympathize), or defensive (show aggression, indignation). They also tell us about the situation we're in, providing us with feedback regarding our actions, so that we can moderate our responses. For instance, anger is an activating emotion that might prompt an aggressive stance towards the perpetrator of a threat, such as one that involves a racial slur or one that undermines our self-esteem. Concurrently, such a stressor may also cause feelings of shame or embarrassment, especially if the slur occurs in front of others, which promote withdrawal or suppression, thus making it less likely that the individual will act on their anger. This might save them from the ill-feelings of bystanders who might view aggression as socially unacceptable, although doing nothing in response to discrimination might subsequently lead to pervasive rumination about the event and what should or could have been done differently.

It may be particularly relevant that positive emotions and cognitions can alter the way we appraise and respond to stressful events, and could preclude the despair and depression that might otherwise be elicited by negative situations. A particularly interesting perspective regarding positive emotions was advanced by Fredrickson (2004), who offered the "Broaden-and-Build" Theory of Positive Emotions. According to this perspective, beyond their obvious actions, positive emotions enhance our ability to expand our repertoire of behavioral and cognitive tendencies, and leave behind the negative and narrow set of behaviors that are otherwise encouraged. While in a positive state we might develop social contacts and other tools and abilities that facilitate the behavioral flexibility that will be needed to deal with negative events that might come up at some future time. There has indeed been the view that having a positive disposition and mood can be powerful enough to prevent or undo the adverse effects of negative events, including cardiovascular disturbances that might otherwise be provoked by chronic stressor experiences. It's entirely possible that positivity and the increased flexibility it encourages can limit the development of pathological conditions, but it's a bit of a stretch to accept that these emotions can "undo" physical damage that has already been created. Can positive emotions and increased cognitive flexibility serve to reduce plaque formation associated with coronary artery disease? Probably not, but this doesn't mean that a positive framework won't be effective in limiting further stressor-related aggravation of a pathological condition.

Emotions can influence how we appraise or interpret events and hence our decision-making ability, particularly if the decisions are complex and involve a stressful component. In his book *Getting Past No*, which deals with how to negotiate, Ury (1993) suggested that when stress is high, and emotions are peaking, it's best to "go to the balcony." Essentially, remove yourself from the situation and become an observer, a fly on the wall, rather than being enmeshed in the turmoil. Thus, it might become possible to see the scene for what it is, unhampered by emotional responses or baggage. This same phenomenon, in psychological terms, is referred to as "self-distancing." When someone has wronged you, whether it involved a snub at a social gathering, being cut off in traffic, or something that is more profound, we can seethe

Understanding our emotions

Our behaviors and attitudes are influenced by both negative and positive emotions, but it may be more difficult to understand and deal with emotions that are a combination of negative and positive feelings that yield "mixed emotions" or those that are "bittersweet." Memories of the way things used to be can fill us with both passion and regret, or watching adult kids leave home can promote both pride and emptiness, and having a loved one pass after a lengthy illness can similarly result in both sadness and relief. It's hard to be happy and sad at the same time and our feelings thus might change from moment to moment.

Although we usually know what we feel, there are times when it's actually difficult for us to define or understand our own emotions, and a number of emotions we feel might differ from one another in subtle ways. As with many other things we've discussed, individuals vary in their emotional intelligence just as they do with respect to social intelligence. Emotional intelligence is a complex ability that involves emotional perception and expression, emotional understanding, and emotional regulation. Some people are exceptionally adept at appreciating their own emotions and understanding those of others, whereas there are individuals who are much less competent in this regard. In fact, about 4–8 percent of individuals express a trait referred to as alexithymia which is characterized by an inability of individuals to identify or describe their own feelings or to understand the feelings and emotions of others. In some instances, these individuals need to watch others in emotionally charged situations so that they know how they should react. This sort of disturbance might hamper the ability to appraise socially stressful situations and to gain the social support needed to cope effectively, and might thus be associated with stress-related pathologies, such as depressive disorders and PTSD.

and ruminate over it, or we can distance ourselves and work things out so that we can eventually simply let it go. It might be satisfying to get even with someone who has wronged us, but it's a lot healthier to move on, and as we'll see later there are easy ways of doing this.

Gauging stressors

Our perceptions of stressors are highly subjective, and it's difficult to get a sense of what someone else means when they say that they feel slightly stressed, moderately stressed, very stressed, or crawling-out-of-their-skin stressed. Researchers and clinicians sometimes distinguish between different types of stressors, such as major stressors versus day-to-day hassles, and ask how frequently these events were experienced and to what extent they were perceived as distressing. Typically, this information is obtained through questionnaires, or through structured (or semistructured) interviews that involve some preset questions. Being able to attach stress level to a number is sometimes preferred as it allows for comparisons across individuals or groups, or changes that occur over time within an individual. Several questionnaires were developed in an effort to get at the distress that individuals are experiencing. Most of these "major life events scales" have been used to predict the relations between stressors and the occurrence of illness or disturbed quality of life. Some scales are based on the notion that a stressor ought to be considered in terms of the social adjustment that it provokes over a set period of time, say six months or a year (Social Readjustment Scale), whereas others focus on major life stressors or traumatic experiences that might have occurred over a protracted time span (e.g., the Traumatic Life Events Questionnaire). Still others are used to assess distress associated with specific types of events, such as psychological abuse or breast cancer.

It's not my intent to be critical of these scales, but it is sometimes difficult to evaluate stressors that individuals have experienced, or to validate the severity of these stressors, using questionnaires that are based on self-reports of past experiences. First, evaluation of the distress experienced by an individual over some set period of time is based on "scaled scores." What this means is that a large group of people were previously given the questionnaire and asked to rate how stressful each event was perceived to be. Yet one of the most fundamental characteristics about stressors is that what's stressful to you might be more or less stressful to others. Thus, basing the distress of an individual on what a group of others expressed on average, possibly under very different circumstances, might not be all that useful. It's also more than a little troublesome to suppose that one can assign a number to a compilation of stressors experienced and expect that this number is somehow meaningful. For instance, does it make any sense to suggest that the "death of a child," which rates 100 (the maximum score), is in some fashion equivalent to a combination of several seemingly moderate stressors, such as "moving home," "trouble with in-laws," "minor illness," and "changes in work hours." As well, the scales don't consider the context in which a stressor had occurred. Typically, "death of a loved one" is a severe stressor, but this depends on how the death occurred. Was it suicide, accidental death, or did it occur following a long and painful illness?

A further problem with stress measurement in many experimental settings is that they involve individuals reporting on events they previously experienced. The way individuals perceive, recall or interpret the past may be subject to what is referred to as "retrospective bias." When an individual is in a dejected state, they will recollect the past from this dark, gloomy state, and we can pretty well count on past experiences being perceived negatively. Likewise, having come to this depressed state, they often want to know why this occurred. Is it something they did, is someone else to blame, or is it simply a matter of bad luck? People who are depressed, for instance, might be looking for reasons to which they could attribute their depression, and they sometimes lay blame inappropriately. The fact is that there are times when we simply can't be trusted to recollect or appraise our past experiences accurately, and among individuals with current problems this difficulty is still greater.

The best way to evaluate the relations between stressful events and later outcomes is by prospectively assessing stressor experiences. This entails tracking people for extended times and relating their stressful experiences to adverse outcomes that might develop. This is an onerous task that takes a long time to complete, and for many reasons, including boredom with the study, being busy, moving, illness or death, individuals frequently drop out of extended experimental studies. Indeed, the participants who complete these studies may well be those who are most dedicated to the project, or those with lots of time on their hands, and the data obtained might not be representative of individuals at large. So, no matter how it's sliced, measuring stress is difficult, and even under the best of circumstances it may provide a distorted perspective. In this regard, even when a prospective analysis is conducted and then related to the appearance of a pathological condition, it can't be concluded that the stressful events caused the

The medical default mode

You might visit the doctor with a set of symptoms that are a bit vague. It doesn't appear as if you're in any imminent danger, but things aren't quite right. The doctor has no way of making a firm diagnosis, and so asks (perhaps in desperation) whether you've been experiencing more stress than usual. When asked this question you pause, thinking, but your hesitation might be enough for the doctor to suggest that you start relaxing a bit more, take it easy, and change your lifestyle. This is all good advice, but may or may not be relevant to your symptoms. It was an "out" for the doctor, and you're content to be told that you're not, in fact, suffering some horrid disease. However, how did the doctor come to the conclusion that you were experiencing lots of stress and whether this had anything to do with your symptoms? There are tests doctors can use to check your blood pressure, heart rate and body temperature, and they can send you off to check your blood sugar, electrolytes, this and that hormone, immune competence and a bunch of other stuff that could potentially serve as indices of stress perception (and coping). However, your doctor didn't use any of these and instead came to the conclusion through default, given that nothing else could be detected within the brief visit.

pathological outcome. When two events occur closely in time it doesn't necessarily mean that one provoked the other. It could be a chance occurrence or that the two are caused by some other common factor. During a storm, the falling rain doesn't cause the lightning, the thunder, or the movement of the clouds.

Before you go…

Most of us are required to deal with multiple demands concurrently, but individuals are very different in their ability to do so. For some of us the opportunity to juggle multiple challenges is exciting, whereas others seem largely incapable of shifting from one issue to another, often finding this exceptionally frustrating and distressing. For them the accumulation of day-to-day hassles over an extended period may be associated with a range of illnesses, including depression, irritable bowel syndrome, and diabetes. The situation becomes that much worse when hassles are superimposed on major life stressors and even those of us who are adept at juggling effectively might become too enmeshed in the situation to make proper appraisals and to deal with a single issue at a time. For that matter, for some people appraisals of a new problem can't even be considered until earlier issues have been resolved.

Typically, we ought to be able to assess stressors fairly accurately, and then initiate behaviors to diminish or eliminate the challenges that confront us. However, our accuracy can be biased, and among some individuals even the mildest challenges can engender negative responses that make things seem worse than they actually are. So, in dealing with stressors the essential first step is to appraise stressors appropriately, which will then guide individuals as to how these stressors ought to be dealt with. It's unfortunate that we so often misappraise stressful events, including those that ought to be handled simply. It's also too bad that we are plagued by many biases that affect our appraisals and hence the decisions that we make. Among many others, we suffer hindsight bias (I knew it all along), belief bias (evaluation of the logical strength of an argument is determined by our beliefs), bias bias (belief that others are more biased than you are), reactance bias (reacting in a manner opposite to the one which others are pushing you toward), confirmation bias (looking for information that confirms our views, while ignoring any contradicting them), self-serving bias (claiming responsibility for success and passing off the blame for failures), illusory superiority (overestimating our positive qualities and underestimating negative qualities), and my favorite, the "Lake Wobegon" bias (derived from the Garrison Keillor's book in which all the children of the town are above average). There are near a hundred biases that have been evaluated in the scientific literature, and they share the feature that they affect our appraisals, decision-making and memory of events, and for better or worse they might have effects on our well-being in response to stressors.

4

Coping with Stressors

Learning from our plant friends

Humans and animals often find themselves in competition with other organisms and thus operate with a focus on survival. A neurogeneticist colleague pointed out that "survival of the fittest" can also mean "demise of the least fit" and so competition can be especially vigorous, particularly as resources become scarce. Competition is not limited to organisms with a brain, also being seen across plant species. Moreover, plants, like humans and other animals, can also behave cooperatively and benefit from one another. For instance, the shade provided by one species allows a second to remain moist and hence more likely to survive under blistering sun. The use of nutrients is sometimes also shared between different species. As a situation becomes increasingly threatening for the survival of plants, their behavior might change, but it might not entail an "every plant for himself" strategy. In fact, actions that might have hindered a neighbor's growth actually diminish, especially in highly competitive species (grasses) so that more vulnerable species (trees) are more likely to survive. Remarkably, when a bug starts to graze on a seemingly helpless plant, the plant actually responds by producing and releasing chemicals that might cause the bug to leave. But, more than this, once these chemicals are released into the air, nearby plants respond to these signals by manufacturing chemicals that similarly repel predatory insects. Unfortunately for the plants, some well-adapted insects have developed so that these protective plant signals are used as markers that help them locate potential plant prey. The latter unfortunate outcome aside, it seems that plants can teach humans a fair bit in relation to social behavior. If they aren't mowed down by natural and unnatural challenges, they might have still more to tell us. For the moment, however, the essential message is that having friends who can be counted on is a great way of coping with challenges.

Stress and Your Health: From Vulnerability to Resilience, First Edition. Hymie Anisman.
© 2015 John Wiley & Sons, Ltd. Published 2015 by John Wiley & Sons, Ltd.

First responses to stressors

When confronted with a stressor the behavioral responses of animals narrow to a subset of behaviors that comprise those that are highest in their defense repertoire, whereas those that are less important for their immediate survival, such as foraging, feeding, sexual behavior, and exploration, are suppressed. If a particular defensive response does not eliminate the challenge, then that behavior might temporarily be dropped and replaced by one that is more effective. Persisting with the same unsuccessful response would obviously be counterproductive, but in the face of uncontrollable and unpredictable events, animals might do precisely that. The very same thing might occur in humans faced with strong stressors. Often we turn to strategies that are highest in our repertoire, essentially resorting to the tried and true, even if it isn't the most logical or effective approach under particular circumstances. Indeed, people often make very bad decisions in stressful circumstances, and it's not unusual for them to do so again and again.

Having made an appraisal that a stressor is imminent or present, we engage one or more coping methods to deal with the challenge. To a certain extent, the way we cope with stressors might reflect a behavioral *style* that is somewhat fixed. Some people are disposed to tackle stressors by thinking about them and then responding on the basis of logical and thoughtful deductions, whereas others might be more disposed to avoid dealing with issues confronting them or they might use emotional ways of dealing with stressful events. Even though we might have an inclination to cope in preestablished ways, the specific coping strategies that we use may also vary with the different stressors encountered and the context in which they appear, and they may vary over time as the stressor plays out and its multiple ramifications unfold. In essence, although coping might reflect a disposition that we bring to a situation, the coping methods that we endorse also depend on other factors.

Coping methods

There are dozens of coping methods that can be used, which largely fall into about 15 or so general methods that comprise three broad classes that are described as problem-focused, emotion-focused, and avoidant coping strategies. Some of the most common methods of coping with stressors are provided in the accompanying box. As you read through these you might recognize what it is that you do when you encounter stressors of varied sorts.

In view of the importance of coping methods in diminishing distress associated with negative events, the question often asked concerns which coping strategies are the most effective or adaptive and which are ineffective or maladaptive? The view is often taken that problem-focused strategies are good, emotion-focused coping is not, and avoidant coping is very bad. At first blush this sounds fairly reasonable, but it's hardly this simple. Particular strategies aren't inherently either good or bad, but instead their value depends on the specific stressor and the situation in which it occurs. Avoidance/denial might be an optimum strategy if nothing the individual does can actually change the course of events. In the case of an individual learning that they have a terminal illness, there may be little to be gained by problem-solving efforts, although they can provide hope that mitigates other bad emotional outcomes. Avoidance coping, in contrast, might allow the individual to function on a day-to-day basis without being preoccupied by their illness, and in some situations it might also provide temporary relief until more effective strategies are found. Emotion-focused coping is also seen negatively, but the emotional release obtained by venting or crying shouldn't be discounted. More importantly, in emotionally charged situations, certain emotion-focused coping strategies, described as emotional approach coping, might help people acknowledge and understand their own feelings in

Coping methods

Problem-focused strategies
Problem solving: Finding a solution to limit or eliminate a stressor.
Cognitive restructuring (also termed *positive reframing*): Diminishing distress by reassessing the situation or placing a new spin on it, or simply by finding a silver lining to a black cloud. In response to severe stressors, individuals might cope by finding meaning (benefit finding) from stressful experiences.

Avoidant or disengagement strategies
Active distraction: The use of active behaviors (e.g., going to movies, working out) as a distraction from ongoing problems.
Cognitive distraction: The use of cognitive methods (e.g., thinking about issues unrelated to the stressor, such as immersing ourselves in work) as a distraction from ongoing problems.
Denial/emotional containment: Not thinking about the problem, or convincing ourselves that a particular situation is not particularly serious.
Humor: Using humor to diminish the stress in certain situations, or simply to put on a brave face.
Drug use: Using drugs to escape from stressors or to feel good even in the face of stressors.

Emotion-focused strategies
Emotional expression: Coping with an event by expressing emotions (e.g., crying, anger, and even aggressive behaviors).
Other-blame: Blaming others for adverse events. It can be used as a way of making sense of some situations or in an effort to avoid being the one blamed.
Self-blame: Blaming ourselves for events that occurred. Sometimes, the blame is accurately placed, but there are also instances where individuals do this inappropriately.
Rumination: Continued thoughts about an issue or event; often these take on a negative tone that includes self-pity, thoughts of revenge, or replaying the events and the strategies that could have been used to deal with events.
Wishful thinking: Thinking what it would be like if the stressor were gone, or what it was like in happier times when the stressor had not surfaced.
Passive resignation: Acceptance of a situation as it is when an individual believes that they have no control over the stressor or their own destiny, or it may simply be a case of accepting the future without regret or malice ("it is what it is").

Social support
Social support seeking: Seeking individuals, usually others within our group, to help us cope with stressful experiences. This form of support can serve multiple functions, and is often combined with other coping methods.

Religion
Religiosity (internal): Using a belief in God to deal with stressful events. This may entail the simple belief in a better hereafter, a belief that a merciful god will help attenuate negative events, or, when things don't work out, falling back onto "God works in mysterious ways."
Religiosity (external): Using a social component associated with religion where similar-minded people come together (congregate) and serve as supports for one another.

relation to a stressor, thus facilitating their ability to come to terms with their feelings and allowing them to move on. Of course, it also lets others know about your distress, and provided that this coping method doesn't become habitual, others may offer support.

When faced with a stressor some individuals might make inappropriate appraisals of the situation and as a result may choose poor coping methods. Others might make appropriate appraisals but nevertheless choose entirely inappropriate or inadequate methods of coping. To address the issue of how individuals dealt with different stressors, and how effective they believed these methods to be, Kim Matheson and I developed a coping instrument, the Survey of Coping Profile Endorsement (SCOPE), which asked individuals how they would cope with stressors in general (coping styles) or in response to specific events (strategies) (Matheson and Anisman, 2003). We also asked them to appraise how effective they thought these strategies might be in dealing with challenges. There were many individuals, particularly those with an inclination toward depression, where the appraisals made were perfectly fine, but the coping methods they selected would likely be ineffective and even counterproductive. What was especially interesting was that they often recognized that their coping efforts, such as rumination and self-blame, would be ineffective, but used them all the same. One could almost hear them saying "I just didn't know what else to do."

Assuming that appropriate appraisals have been made, what makes some individuals seemingly better able to cope effectively than others? In a stressful situation in which a particular strategy proves ineffective in attenuating distress, alternative strategies ought to be adopted, but because cognitive functioning might be impaired in these situations, finding and using alternative coping responses might be hindered. In other situations, particularly those that involve a high degree of ambiguity, individuals may find themselves uncertain about what to do, and end up taking few coping initiatives on their own.

In considering the effectiveness of coping strategies, it is important to consider that we generally don't use any particular strategy in isolation from others, but instead use several strategies concurrently. Individuals might ruminate and concurrently self-blame, which is notoriously ineffective. Among individuals who are prone to depression, rumination typically occurs together with emotion-focused coping or with a failure to make efforts to disengage from these negative strategies (e.g., "I'm just such a loser; I should do something, but nothing I try ever works out. I just want to put the covers over my head, hide, and never see the world again"). In healthy, well-adjusted individuals, rumination occurs less frequently than it does among depression-prone individuals, and when it does occur, it might be accompanied by a broad constellation of problem- and emotion-focused strategies that are more apt to produce effective outcomes. (e.g., "This situation makes me feel miserable to the extent that I just want to cry, but if I hash it out with my friends they might have some suggestions that can help").

Personal growth and finding meaning

In response to mild or moderate stressors, coping through cognitive restructuring might take the form of finding something positive in the situation – the proverbial silver lining to a dark cloud. A form of cognitive restructuring, termed posttraumatic growth, sometimes referred to as finding meaning, or benefit finding, may also occur in response to severe, traumatic events, such as loss of a child, severe illness, or any of several other misfortunes that can befall us. Living through traumatic circumstances may result in the individual trying to make sense of the event and finding some benefit from the experience. Survivors of seriously distressing circumstances might use these experiences as an opportunity to improve their physical and mental health, or they may engage in a cause so that others won't have similar experiences (e.g., banning assault weapons, initiating a campaign to eliminate drunk driving, or helping those with spinal injuries or Parkinson's disease). Alternatively, individuals can learn from their experiences even if their actions are more self-focused. For instance, cancer survivors might indicate that they had benefited from living through a cancer experience in the sense that they developed greater appreciation of the positive things in their lives, and obtained greater life satisfaction and spiritual well-being.

As much as individuals might want to find meaning in horrible events, this doesn't guarantee that meaning or benefits will actually be derived from these efforts. Certain types of events lend themselves to finding meaning or personal growth. For instance, this could occur among individuals going through a struggle to survive an illness or those engaged in taking on large corporations that are viewed as being responsible for deaths due to negligence, or individuals campaigning to save others from grief. Likewise, meaning obtained through caregiving to those afflicted by Parkinson's disease or spinal cord injury can be psychologically healing. However, it's something else entirely to find meaning in relation to a person who has experienced a severe head injury falling down their stairs at home after consuming a bit too much scotch, or a death that occurred while a person was engaged in a risky behavior, such as transforming themselves into a human glider. Friends and relatives might console themselves by saying "Well, at least he died doing what he loved," even if the person who died might not have seen it that way.

Coping through religion

For some people religion is viewed as something that is profoundly bad, having contributed to enormous strife for numerous groups over many centuries. Others view it as cultish and based on illogical thinking, or it's viewed as neither bad nor good, but is instead seen as benign, even if it is nonsensical. But, for a great number of people, religion is a core component of their identity, and it can serve as an effective coping strategy, providing comfort, especially when all else has failed. Religion fosters a system of beliefs that allows individuals to find meaning in an experience, and may serve to limit feelings of hopelessness because events might be "under God's control." Beyond these attributes, religion might provide a social support network from like-minded people to promote solace and peace of mind and may also facilitate problem-focused coping. Spirituality has indeed been linked to lower depression and correspondingly greater density of brain regions, such as the prefrontal cortex and hippocampus, which are diminished among depressed individuals.

Karl Marx obviously wasn't a fan of religion and disparagingly stated that "Religion is the sigh of the oppressed creature, the heart of a heartless world, and the soul of soulless conditions. It is the opium of the people." Okay, some of us might see religion as an absurd way of coping, but if it works for some people, then we ought to wish them our best. I'm not judgmental when it comes to using particular coping strategies, and as Lennon (as opposed to Lenin) indicated, "whatever gets you through the night." This said, simply praying that things get better ought to be accompanied by more practical methods of coping, including help-seeking. But, even if religion is the opium of the masses, there are some occasions where it might be just what's needed, serving as an alternative to Prozac or Valium.

Social support

Having support from family and friends, or from our social group, is among our most important ways of diminishing the effects of stressors, and seeking support is an understandably common way of coping. The positive actions of support are apparent through an individual's subjectively appraised stress reduction, as well as through altered biological stress responses. Among other things, social support may limit excessive and prolonged hormonal, neurochemical, and immunological changes that ordinarily occur in response to chronic stressors, and thus could limit the adverse effects on well-being that might otherwise occur, and having social support may influence the development of or recovery from some illnesses.

It's not just any support that is useful, and ultimately the stress-buffering effects of social support are related to the quality of the support, rather than the amount of support available. As well, its effectiveness also depends on whom the support comes from and how the recipient perceives and interprets the motives and goals of the supportive individual or group. If a support provider and the support recipient share an identity (i.e., they are part of the same ingroup), then the positive effects of support may be more beneficial than when support is obtained from someone who doesn't share the same identity. Thus, social support groups that comprise others with similar problems can be particularly effective in buffering stressor effects. Whether it is a support group for families of children with cancer, or family members dealing with drug-addicted individuals, support from someone "who understands my pain" is better than that which comes from others, no matter how well intentioned they might be.

As the characteristics of a stressor may change over time, it can reasonably be expected that the coping methods adopted will vary accordingly, and so will the nature of the social support obtained. For example, upon learning that they have a potentially fatal illness, individuals might seek support from those with whom they're close in the hope of bolstering their spirits and obtaining encouragement. Soon afterward there may be a need for support in obtaining information, such as which treatments are available and which have proved best. Subsequently, the support might be of an instrumental nature that comprises being taken to treatment sessions or having day-to-day needs met. Still later, in a worst-case scenario, social support may be used to provide comfort, distraction, and finding peace.

There's no question about the importance of social support for well-being, but the sword cuts both ways and there are occasions when negative aspects of support can emerge. It might not often be the case, but social support can make an individual feel that others see them as less competent in contending with difficulties, or it may cause individuals to feel indebted, which can be uncomfortable enough to fracture a relationship. Most of us appreciate help but cherish our independence, and so offering support sometimes needs to be done diplomatically.

Loneliness

Loneliness can be a pervasive, all-encompassing feeling characterized by distress, a sense of isolation and a lack of intimacy, feeling disconnected from potential sources of social support, and not being accepted or belonging to a salient social group. Feelings of loneliness might occasionally be experienced by most us, and the consequences are typically mild. However, when it is chronic, it can act as a severe stressor that has profound psychological and physiological repercussions, including depression, increased risk for suicide, heightened anxiety, and drug addiction, and it may contribute to cardiovascular, immune and neuroendocrine malfunctioning as well as dementia in later life.

The bad side of identity

From what's been said regarding social identity, you'd think that it's uniformly a good thing. But it isn't always so. Indeed, in some circumstances it can be a force that fosters and supports evil. Following the trial of Adolf Eichmann, who had been engaged in the logistics associated with the extermination of the "unwanted" during World War II, various perspectives evolved to explain how he became what he was. At one extreme was Hannah Arendt's view that all of us have the potential for bad actions, just as Eichmann did. She describes "the banality of evil" as the tendency of ordinary people to conform to mass opinion and to obey orders from superiors, coupled with the tendency to do so without critically evaluating the consequences of their actions or inactions. Her views might well have been tarnished by her affection for the German philosopher Martin Heidegger, who also was a Nazi and Jew hater. However, studies by both Stanley Milgram and Philip Zimbardo demonstrated that ordinary people would indeed just follow orders and do what they were told to do or adopt the persona that they believed they should adopt. But do these studies adequately describe what humans do in horrible situations, such as those associated with the Shoah or with so many group-based atrocities. One only has to look at old film clips of the adoration given to Hitler (may his name be erased from history) to come to the belief that the behaviors of his minions comprised more than individuals simply following orders.

So, how do individuals, apparently civilized and intelligent, come to be extreme haters? Alex Haslam and Stephen Reicher have provided a remarkable analysis of the "psychology of tyranny" (2005), and Reicher, Haslam, and Rath (2008) outlined five steps involved in this process. The first step, Identification, involves the formation of an ingroup to which they can devote themselves. The second step comprises Exclusion, in which outgroups are envisaged, followed by the development of Threat, wherein these outgroup members are viewed as a challenge to the newly formed ingroup. In a related context, it is often said that if Jews hadn't existed, Hitler would have needed to invent them. The fourth step is Virtue, in which the championing of the ingroup is advanced as being a positive characteristic. Understandably, as individuals identify with the ingroup, they become more vulnerable to propaganda that supports the thoughts and actions of the group. This then makes it simpler for the fifth step to evolve, which comprises the proposed eradication of the outgroup as a means to maintain the virtue of the ingroup. In defending the actions against gays, Himmler, who was responsible for the development of extermination camps, stated that these were for the common good: "That wasn't a punishment, but simply the extinguishing of abnormal life. It had to be got rid of, just as we pull out weeds, throw them on a heap, and burn them."

Haslam and Reicher have noted that in certain experimental situations in which the participant identifies with particular roles, they're not simply following orders, but behave in line with "the endeavor of committed subject." If one can promote bad behavior within a simulated context, then we can expect that "the influence on an individual will be still greater when a whole society appears to be marching in the same footfalls." Indeed, individuals behave with zeal, energy and gusto in protecting their group from the virulence stemming from members of other groups (termed outgroup). Essentially, when someone highly identifies with a group in which racism has become the norm, then they might well develop cognitions, attitudes and emotions that might not otherwise have been evident. In this regard, racism seems to be rearing its deformed head more and more. We see it throughout the Middle East, and many countries in Europe ... yes Europe, the home of culture, democracy and liberty. Evidently, there seems to be the perspective that when everyone else in their group is a racist, it's okay for them to engage in despicable, repugnant, and immoral acts, and it may only be a matter of time when they begin to compete with one another in their endeavor to be the committed participant. This, to use a phrase borrowed from Gil Troy in one of his thoughtful editorials, is "the evil of banality."

Loneliness is common following loss or romantic break-ups, and it can be especially distressing among the aged who have lost social support resources. Indeed, loneliness can be debilitating among older individuals, and might contribute to the marked elevation of antidepressant and anti-anxiety drug intake that has been seen in this population. It is also common during "transitional" periods, including early adulthood, when individuals entering university or the job market might be separated from family and find themselves among unsympathetic people and in unfamiliar surroundings. Most individuals pass through this phase without suffering significant distress, but for some the experience can be draining. Too often, loneliness is considered as just "one of those things" that young people need to work through, and old people must endure. In neither instance is this correct, and it ought to be taken much more seriously than it usually is. Simply having a network of friends might not be the most cogent element to reduce loneliness, as reflected in the fact that one can feel lonely in a room full of people. Instead, it's the quality of the friendships that a person has that will diminish their loneliness and enhance their well-being. A few good friends with shared identities can be much more meaningful than having a broad network of surface friendships. There has been a trend in research to examine "connectedness" in relation to adverse outcomes. As indicated by Haslam et al. (2005), the essential element to bolster our well-being comes from the shared values and identities we have with other group members. If we have multiple group memberships, then all the better, provided that we share an identity of some sort with each of these. Parenthetically, given that people are now meeting in new ways, such as through the internet, and face-to-face meetings are declining, it will be interesting to see how this affects the quality of social support and loneliness, and what the effects are on well-being.

Unsupportive interactions

There are occasions when we might be unable to handle things on our own, and thus approach close friends or family members for their support with the reasonable expectation that it will be obtained. However, it might not work out as we had expected, and support might be offered conditionally, or might not be forthcoming either because of a frank refusal from a person who "doesn't want to be involved" or because someone feels incapable of being supportive. Individuals might also provide responses that aren't in the least helpful and are interpreted as being unsupportive. These can take the form of a problem being minimized (e.g., "don't you think you're overreacting?" or simply

Frenemies sitting on the fence

We might expect that when we run into rough times our friends will be there to support and help us, even if we don't explicitly ask for it. As in the case of interpersonal relationships, groups harshly treated by their own government, as well as survivors of orchestrated discrimination and even genocide, might not receive the expected support from other groups or countries. This might occur because of geopolitical considerations, or alternatively there's just no will to give support. How do the people of Darfur or Syria see the behavior of countries that haven't come to their assistance? You can count on these victims perceiving the responses as exceptionally unsupportive and they won't readily forget. Martin Luther King said, "In the end we will remember not the words of our enemies, but the silence of our friends," while Elie Wiesel, who, like King, won the Nobel Peace Prize, has repeatedly advised world leaders that "to remain silent and indifferent is the greatest sin of all." Given what we've seen repeatedly, is it any wonder that in the context of Iranian bluster and threats of annihilation toward Israel, Elie Wiesel pronounced, "History has taught us to trust the threats of our enemies more than the promises of our friends."

"I'm sure everything will work out fine"), casting blame (e.g., "I told you so"), bumbling (e.g., not knowing what to say or afraid of saying or doing the *wrong* thing; putting on an air of forced optimism), or distancing or disconnecting (e.g., when "my friend didn't want to hear about it" or "my friend pretended not to see me"). These "unsupportive" interactions can have exceptionally damaging repercussions, promoting or exacerbating a poor psychological state and could aggravate an existing physical disorder. If you've experienced these rebuffs (has anyone ever said to you, "Well, you know, there are two sides to every story"?), you might have ruminated for some time and it was unlikely that the relationship was healed easily or quickly.

For some individuals, experiencing unsupportive interactions becomes part of daily life. Those with a mental disorder or those with HIV/AIDS have frequent unsupportive encounters, sometimes intentional and sometimes not, but always hurtful. Acquaintances of individuals with mental illnesses may be uncertain about how to act and what to say, largely owing to a lack of experience, and end up avoiding those with problems. To be sure, many people are not all that competent in dealing with bad events that have happened to others, such as the death of a family member, and their clumsy behaviors might occasionally be interpreted as unsupportive. Worse still are cases where instead of immediately going to see and commiserate with the affected person, individuals shy away, and the longer they do so, the more difficult it is to meet that person later. Clearly, when your friend is hurting, it's your responsibility to offer help. The alternative is that they'll be hurt by your apparent insensitivity, and you'll have missed the opportunity to do the right thing.

In response to perceived distancing and uninterested responses of others, individuals may engage in greater use of disengagement and denial, and the use of ineffective coping methods in these situations might breed mood disturbances. Unsupportive relationships might also result in wariness of being burnt yet again, and so individuals might be reluctant to seek social support as a method of coping. There are also occasions when unsupportive relations foster further unsupportive behaviors. Take the case of a young

Just world

The more you know about people, the more you might feel you just don't understand them. Unsupportive interactions, as we've seen, come in many guises and can emerge for a variety of reasons. One of these, which is referred to as the Just World phenomenon, suggests that individuals often believe that people generally "get what they deserve and deserve what they get." Fundamentally, the world is thought to be a fair place, and hence if something bad happens to someone, then it's not because of a bad world, but instead it is attributed to that person's own behaviors. So, women who are molested brought it on themselves because of their behaviors or the places they visited, accident victims probably weren't paying attention, and people with some illness or other likely weren't taking care of themselves. From the perspective of the person who encountered the tragedy, these assumptions point to the insensitivity and callousness of others.

woman who ends up in an abusive dating relationship. If she tells others about her situation, the common response might be, and usually is, "get rid of the bum." For a variety of reasons this is not easily done even when there are no financial constraints or children that need to be considered. Thus, when the situation persists, family and friends may become frustrated and react negatively because their advice to terminate the relationship isn't accepted, and they may even distance themselves from the person being abused. This results in the abused woman feeling that she can't rely on her social network and she may stop confiding in them, thereby further isolating herself. Ironically, having run out of people to whom she can turn, the abusive partner may become her primary source of support. Alternatively, she might reorient her help seeking-behaviors, perhaps turning to anonymous sources of support (e.g., internet chat groups) where her sense of self-worth is not tied to the judgments of unsupportive others. Although this can be a good strategy in some instances, in other cases it might be ineffective or even counterproductive should an internet viper appear in the guise of someone "who wants to be there for you."

Social rejection

As social organisms, being rejected by another individual or group can create exceptionally powerful negative emotional and biological stress responses, and if feelings of rejection persist, psychological disturbances can develop. Rejection might come about for a variety of reasons, including discrimination related to gender, race, religion, sexual orientation, physical appearance, the presence of mental illness, or other illnesses, such as AIDS. Social rejection also occurs when members of the ingroup perceive an individual as somewhat different from them and particularly when that person is viewed as an embarrassment. This "black sheep effect" is reinforced because group members frequently feel that they are a unified social entity (entitativity) and those who negatively represent the group might be denigrated in an effort to preserve the group's good standing. Thus, derogation of the black sheep serves as a protective strategy to limit the threat that ingroup members will be associatively miscast ("he's not really one of us, and we're not at all like him").

Individuals who have had the experience of their best friends turning on them likely recall this with sadness. The fact that they remember this at all speaks to how distressing it was. Rejection might be relatively subtle, such as simply being ignored, being left out of social events, and generally being diminished. Targeted rejection, understandably, can be especially damaging and has been linked to the provocation or exacerbation of depressive feelings. As social media have become less private, the internet has been used in some fairly hurtful ways. Think of how you would feel if your daughter of high school age was "defriended" on her friend's Facebook page, especially when everybody on the continent was included. Defriending is already being used as a public slap to the face without even having to be in the same room with that person. So, while rejection at one time might have been kept within a small circle, it's now out there for everyone to see, and for shame and humiliation to become that much more intense.

It's a bit difficult to evaluate social rejection within a laboratory context, but several paradigms have been developed to assess the consequences of rejection on behavior and hormonal and brain functioning. A computer game, referred to as Cyberball, in which a virtual ball is tossed between three characters (icons), has been used to assess the response to rejection. One of the icons is controlled by the participant, whereas the other icons are controlled by the experimenter, although the participant believes that there are two other real people involved. Initially, the ball is tossed between the three players on an apparently random and equal basis. Shortly afterward, however, the actual participant is excluded and the ball is passed only between the other two virtual participants. As innocuous as it might seem, this manipulation elicits negative ruminative thoughts, poor mood, hostility, as well as negative self-referential cognitions ("people just don't like me") and emotions related to these feelings, especially shame and humiliation. It is likely that brain regions associated with appraisals are involved in these responses, and indeed it seems that the social pain provoked by being excluded in the Cyberball situation can be diminished by particular aspects of the prefrontal cortex.

Beyond the effects on mood, social rejection increased the level of the stress hormone cortisol, and markedly influenced neuronal activity within the anterior cingulate cortex, a brain region associated with appraisals and decision-making, as well as with depressed mood. Not unexpectedly, the effects on brain processes were particularly marked if individuals exhibited high levels of rejection sensitivity and would thus have been particularly vigilant regarding peer acceptance. A similar profile of brain changes was also evident among adolescents, but in this instance, rejection was also accompanied by decreased neuronal activity in the ventral striatum, a brain area involved in the perception of rewarding experiences. Essentially, rejection might disturb an individual's ability to sense or gain from otherwise rewarding social experiences, and the changes of brain neuronal

Does Macy's miss Gimbels?

I asked an acquaintance whether she was feeling lonely and rejected now that her kids had all left home. Philosophically, she said, "Nature has a way of making things right. Kids get progressively more obnoxious as they go through their teens, until you start to count the minutes for them to leave." Unbeknownst to me, 10 minutes earlier she had had a blow-out fight with her daughter, who threatened to exclude her from her life – the ultimate form of rejection. Remember King Lear saying, "How sharper than a serpent's tooth it is to have a thankless child!" I was taken by her apparent thoughtfulness as she slowly nodded her head, but it was at that point that she seemed to lose it, saying "they're ego thieves, kidnappers of emotions, robbers of self-esteem. Am I lonely without them? Does Macy's miss Gimbels?"

activity might be predictive of later vulnerability to depression. It is interesting as well that the emotional pain associated with ostracism shares features with physical pain, and somewhat surprisingly, acetaminophen, the pain-relieving component of drugs such as Tylenol, reduced the pain of being ostracized.

Forgiveness and trust

For positive interpersonal and intergroup relations to form and be maintained, trust is absolutely essential. As this often entails leaving oneself unprotected in the belief that no harm will occur, a breach of trust will severely impair these relationships. These occurrences might instigate negative rumination accompanied by thoughts of retribution (that's the saintly way of saying revenge), leading to a cycle of negative rumination, and further bad behaviors. To be sure, various mitigating factors might make reconciliation or peace difficult to achieve, and no one is inclined to be pushed around or be taken for a sap. Poor behavior from one individual or group toward another, irrespective of the reason, might have negative repercussions, but most often these are transient. However, when this behavior entails a breach of trust, the ramifications may be pronounced and may become exaggerated with the passage of time, and can even span generations as the recriminations become progressively greater.

There are occasions when a victimized individual or group is asked to forgive or might voluntarily choose to forgive the behaviors of a transgressor. Typically, the transgressor is sorrowful for past behaviors, and offers an apology in the hope that forgiveness can be obtained. If the recipient of the apology views it as being sincere, they might forgive the other person. The alternative is to maintain the anger and resentment, often expressed through rumination, which can adversely affect psychological and physical well-being. So, who benefits from forgiveness? Although both parties probably do, it may be particularly beneficial for the forgiver as it allows them the freedom to let go of negative thoughts, feelings, and behaviors. Of course, this by no means supports the adage of "forgive and forget"; even if forgiveness is offered, it's unlikely that strong transgressions will be forgotten (although forgiveness may facilitate forgetting of minor transgressions), and even hints of the reoccurrence of egregious behavior will cause the relation to fracture. A friend who is a linguist, Aviva Freedman, suggested that rather than using the term forgiveness, it may be more appropriate to use forbearance, defined as being patient and able to deal with a difficult person or situation without becoming angry or vengeful.

Half-truths are also half-lies

Apologies sometimes come with confessions, but these confessions might only be half-truths or partial confessions. This strategy might be adopted because they're more believable than outright lies or failures to confess. Do the words "I never had sex with that woman" ring any bells? How about "it only happened once"? Although partial confessions might seem like a good strategy, in some cases it might leave the person who confessed dissatisfied with their own behaviors and can be a source of distress. Besides, it is possible that the full truth will eventually surface, and the pain will start all over again.

There are numerous barriers to forgiveness – too many to detail here, so we'll consider just a few that are fairly common. To some extent the ability to forgive may be a dispositional characteristic, so that although some individuals have a tendency to be ready to forgive, for others forgiveness simply isn't part of their make-up. The very same thing can be said about offering apologies, as some people just don't have it in them to apologize, ever, for anything, to anybody. Furthermore, the perpetrator might not see their offense as being nearly as great as the victim does, and may even be oblivious of the degree to which their behavior was hurtful, and in these instances the victim will be less likely than the perpetrator to put things behind them. The perpetrator and victim may also have differing perceptions concerning the impact of an apology and receiving forgiveness. The perpetrator may see this as putting an end to the conflict, whereas the victim might simply see this as a possibility for a new beginning, depending how things evolve. The victim may also face additional elements that create problems; they may not be ready to forgive, and thus when the apology is offered, they might feel they "have to" accept it, but the reality is that their heart isn't in it. As well, being the victim of the obvious bad behavior of their oppressor allowed them to maintain the moral high ground, while the perpetrator was required to feel guilt and remorse. Accepting the apology means abdicating the victim role and they are now *required* to move on. Furthermore, having accepted the apology they might feel muzzled as it also means dropping the issue so that they can no longer vent feelings that have been festering for a very long time. Thus, individuals may offer surface forgiveness ("hollow forgiveness") in which they forgive but remain wary. It may be for some of these reasons that individuals are more apt to forgive if the transgressor had been punished in some way.

The greatest barrier to forgiveness involves instances where the transgression might be perceived as being just too great, the hurt too strong, and the lasting effects of the transgression too persistent, thus making forgiveness virtually impossible. In these instances the negative feelings between groups or between individuals can carry on across generations, and forgiveness likewise might not be possible until several generations have passed. In some instances, however, yesterday's enemies may turn out to be today's allies, especially when it is advantageous for groups to cooperate, or when the enemy of my enemy is my friend.

There are instances when forgiveness between groups involves an intricate dance that can turn out positively or negatively, depending on the perceptions of the players. Apologies don't erase the past, but they do send the message that past egregious behaviors are condemned, and that better relations are desired. As a result it is difficult for the recipient to do much other than to accept an apology, but this comes with a caveat with the implicit message: "It's impossible to forget the past, but we would nevertheless like to move forward. We appreciate this apology, but talk is cheap, and your apology will mean much more if it comes with actions that undo the hardships that your past behaviors have caused." Thus, if the situation between the groups doesn't improve, the attitude of the perpetrator group may be seen as yet another betrayal. In contrast, members of the perpetrator group, when confronted by protestations by the victimized group, might take the attitude of "oh brother, we apologized to them, so now what do they want?" The net result of this, predictably, is further poor relations between the groups, potentially making it still more difficult for the divide to be bridged.

Let's take another instance where an apology and the subsequent forgiveness might create problems. Abuse in a romantic relationship may be followed by apologies, and possibly forgiveness. However, accepting the apology might perpetuate the delusion (of the woman, or the man) concerning the positive attributes of the relationship. In fact, in an effort to forgive, individuals may take on blame for the events that transpired

Forgiving family conflicts

Too often, sadly, family members might not provide social supports that are needed by others, frequently behaving capriciously or in predictably unsupportive ways. There are many reasons that might have led to this. As Tolstoy's Anna Karenina said, "All happy families are alike; each unhappy family is unhappy in its own way." Possibly the worst scenarios leading to these fractures are those that have emanated from a loss of trust or earlier instances of unsupportive relations. Apologies for these events are, most unfortunately, not frequently offered and forgiveness likewise not obtained. The result is that both sides suffer. In some instances, conflicts can't be remedied as the trespasses were too great, but in other instances they can. For this to occur, both sides need to step back and view the situation as an external observer might, and then move forward in mutually agreed baby steps.

(e.g., "Oh, maybe I'm being a bit too sensitive"). Equally problematic is the fact that for some individuals and groups, receiving apologies or offers of forgiveness signals weakness on the part of the other person (or group), and thus is seen as an opportunity to reap gain at the other's expense. So, when apologies are made and forgiveness is offered, the individuals need to enter this interaction without wearing a blindfold.

Empathy

There are a lot of things that make us different from other species, but neither having an opposable thumb nor using tools are the most notable. Having complex brains and being able to express an enormous range of emotions likely set us apart from other animals. Our brain might be hard-wired for empathy, that is being able to put ourselves in another person's shoes, and this in particular makes us unique, although we've all heard about the apparent empathy sometimes reported among elephants and dolphins. In humans, empathy is seen in response to the hurt experienced by others, no matter who they are, but empathetic reactions might be more strongly elicited in relation to close others or those with whom we identify strongly. When we experience a threat within a laboratory context, certain parts of our brain may be activated. This will also occur if the threat is directed toward our friend, but less so if it is directed toward a stranger. So, when we say to a friend who is hurting that "I feel your pain," our brain might actually mean it.

Before you go...

The influence of stressors on well-being depends on an individual's ability to cope with stressors, which might comprise learned methods of dealing with challenges, inherent biological resilience, and a constellation of personality factors that act to affect our coping methods. Fundamental for our coping method and hence our well-being in the face of stressors concerns how we appraise events that are encountered. Some individuals tend to put a negative spin on events, so that the world is always a bleak place, and thus they tend to be most vulnerable to stress-induced illness. Others, despite making appropriate

Location, location, location

Some individuals seem to be inclined to use the same coping strategies over and over, despite their ineffectiveness. In contrast, other individuals are adept at using a relatively broad range of coping strategies, prepared to be flexible in their use and able to shift from one strategy to another as the situation demands or on the basis of the opportunities and resources available. If location, location, location is the maxim for the success of small businesses, then flexibility, flexibility, flexibility, should be the mantra for successful coping.

Stressors seem to occur on an unpredictable basis, and the stressors themselves seem to mutate. Thus, ways of coping need to evolve continuously in order to beat back the potential stressors that confront us. As the Red Queen said to Alice, "It takes all the running you can do, to keep in the same place."

appraisals of events, tend to use ineffective and inflexible coping methods even when the situation obviously calls for a different approach. When used often enough, these ineffective appraisal and coping methods become fairly fixed, and altering them, like breaking well-entrenched habits, is exceedingly difficult. Generally, being flexible in using particular coping strategies across situations and over time is likely the optimal strategy to deal with stressors, but simply saying this is about as useful as advising you to become taller, faster and stronger if you want to make it onto a professional sports team. In later chapters that consider treatment and intervention strategies, more specific suggestions will be described to facilitate efficient and effective ways of dealing with stressors.

5

Hormones and What They Do

Hormonal release to deal with stressors

Humans and animals have exquisitely well-integrated adaptive neurobiological systems that allow us to deal with stressors. We even have compensatory processes that kick in when a primary system stops operating effectively. Yet, each of us has weaknesses owing to genetic factors, prenatal or early postnatal experiences, or responses that developed over time when the stress load became excessive. The weak link in one individual might not be the same as that in a second, and thus identical stressors may elicit different outcomes. For one individual this might comprise processes leading to psychological disturbances, and for another it might promote the development of immunological, cardiovascular, muscular, or gastrointestinal illnesses. In some unfortunate individuals stressors might increase vulnerability to several pathological conditions.

Hormones comprise biochemical substances that are secreted from glands or cells in the body and in the brain in response to internal signals, such as altered sugar levels in the blood, as well as environmental stimuli, such as stressors. They operate to help the body meet its needs, including the activation of metabolic processes, initiation and cessation of eating, regulation of immune activity, preparing the body for transitional phases of life (puberty, parenting, bonding, menopause), and the functioning of reproductive processes, and they contribute to cell growth and the normal course of cell death. They also affect our ability to contend with stressful events by influencing our readiness to make appropriate behavioral or emotional responses, modifying cognitive processes and promoting physiological changes, including energy regulation, as well as immune and heart functioning. That's a pretty impressive load for these tiny chemical molecules, but weak links may be present so that hormonal dysfunctions might occur in the context of stressful situations, thereby increasing vulnerability to illnesses of one form or another.

Stress and Your Health: From Vulnerability to Resilience, First Edition. Hymie Anisman.
© 2015 John Wiley & Sons, Ltd. Published 2015 by John Wiley & Sons, Ltd.

What's a hormone?

Most people know something about hormones, and know that they have functions beyond the "raging hormones" that might guide teenage behaviors. Most hormones actually have multiple functions, and many contribute to our ability to contend with stressful events. Those that are particularly important for the present purposes are secreted from a part of the brain referred to as the hypothalamus which is near the base of the brain, the pituitary gland that rests on the bottom of the brain, and the adrenal glands located just above the kidney, as well as the testes and ovaries (you know where they are!). There are other glands that release essential hormones, such as the pancreas, as well as the thyroid and pineal glands, and some of these will be considered, however briefly.

Once a hormone is released into the bloodstream it will reach a target site where it will bind with a hormone receptor, which consists of a particular molecule present on a cell. Once this occurs the cell may be activated, causing further chemical changes and ultimately any of a variety of behavioral or physiological changes may occur, depending on the hormone and receptors involved. As in the case of most biological systems, stress hormones are subject to the Goldilocks effect, wherein too little or too much may cause problems. In an effort to maintain an appropriate balance of hormones and receptors, numerous checks exist within and between hormonal systems, but there are limits to the effectiveness of these back-up processes.

Linking hormones and behaviors

Considerable efforts have been made to understand how hormones are linked with particular behaviors and pathologies that come about when hormonal processes are disturbed. The aim, of course, has been to develop treatments to regulate these hormonal processes and thus alleviate hormone-related pathological conditions. To this end, one analytical method has focused on physical and behavioral disturbances present among individuals with unfortunate diseases that involve hormonal dysregulation. For instance, pituitary and adrenal adenomas (an adenoma refers to a benign tumor of glandular origin) are accompanied by high levels of the hormone cortisol, which can lead to several disturbances, including depressive symptoms. Alternatively, analyses can be conducted in patients with conditions such as Addison's disease, in which insufficient cortisol is produced, leading to still other biological changes that might culminate in psychiatric symptoms. These approaches have been helpful, but less than ideal, as many factors, including distress secondary to illness, might be responsible for the pathological conditions.

An alternative approach has involved analyses in animals in which hormone levels can be manipulated and behavioral changes assessed, or where the levels of hormones can be determined in response to stressors or other triggers and these linked to pathological outcomes. If a particular hormone is responsible for promoting symptoms of an illness, then increasing or reducing the levels of this hormone through experimental treatments ought to engender particular symptoms, which ought to diminish through treatments that bring about normalization of hormone activity.

As described earlier, one especially useful approach to assess the link between particular genes, hormones and behavioral outcomes has taken advantage of the natural genetic differences or mutations that occur at relatively high frequencies (single nucleotide polymorphisms, SNPs), and related them to particular behavioral characteristics (behavioral phenotypes). For instance, if a gene polymorphism was present so that a particular

Bridging the gap between mice and men

Researchers who work with animals typically believe that their findings are relevant to what happens in humans, and there is usually considerable congruity across species regarding the effects of stressors and pharmacological treatments. It is sometimes assumed that since approximately 99 percent of the human genome is conserved in mice, they make useful tools in identifying the contribution of certain genes to pathophysiological conditions. Animal models have been used extensively in an effort to identify the mechanisms and treatments of many psychological and physical disorders. There is no question that major health benefits have come about based on this research. This said, a European Commission workshop concluded that although animal-based research has a lot to offer, more synergy is needed between basic science researchers and clinicians working with human patients.

Ideally, there are several conditions that should be met for an animal model of a human disorder to be considered valid: (a) the animal behaviors ought to be reminiscent of the symptom profile presented in the human syndrome; (b) treatments that attenuate the illness symptoms in humans must also do so in the animal model; (c) treatments that are ineffective in attenuating the human illness should similarly be ineffective in an animal model; (d) events or stimuli that provoke or exacerbate the pathology in humans should also do so in the animal model; and finally, (e) the human and animal models ought to involve similar biological processes. In some instances these criteria can't be fully met. For instance, we might not know what the biochemical mechanisms are that are responsible for a disorder, or we might not know what remedies are effective in attenuating the disorder, as this is what we're trying to uncover. Thus, if the remaining criteria are met, it can take us forward in identifying the processes related to pathological conditions and thus develop effective treatment methods. It can be argued that simulating a psychological disorder, such as depression, can't readily be done in animals. However, this doesn't preclude the possibility of evaluating biological processes related to particular symptoms or characteristics of the disorder.

As laudable as scientific efforts might be, simply because certain criteria have been met to ensure a model's validity doesn't necessarily mean that the model is going to be useful. It's only valid within the framework that we've established to assume that something is actually valid. In a sense, it's not unlike a jury trial where even if the defendant is found not guilty, it doesn't necessarily mean that the defendant is actually innocent. It's not perfect, but it beats the alternatives.

hormone functioned less than optimally, then one would expect corresponding behavioral changes. In this way, in theory, many genes and hormones could be linked to particular pathologies. If SNPs were uncommon, then making these links might not be all that challenging, but they're estimated to occur as often as 1 in every 300 nucleotides, making it difficult to tie a given SNP of the millions that can be present to any given behavioral or pathological condition. Nonetheless, certain SNPs were identified that seemed to be related to hormonal processes and behaviors, and in some instances several SNPs on different genes were additively or synergistically related to normal and abnormal behaviors.

The data from such studies simply inform us that in some people (or animals) a behavioral phenotype occurs when a particular mutation is present, but simply because two characteristics occur concurrently doesn't necessarily mean that one caused the other. Thus, to get at causal connections, attempts are frequently made to create genetic alterations and then evaluate the physical or behavioral changes that emerge. To this end, mice and rats have been developed with their DNA engineered so that specific genes have been removed or inserted, thus allowing for the analysis of that particular gene's action in relation to an array of behavioral and physical outcomes, including the cure for diseases. In fact, genetic engineering techniques are sufficiently sophisticated so that genetic changes can be made to occur at particular sites within the brain, thus allowing researchers to study the influence of specific brain changes on pathology. As well, genes can be knocked out at specific times in the animal's life, and using a newly developed technique, referred to as optogenetics, it is possible to turn particular genes on and then off again by shining a light onto specific cells that are tagged with a light sensitive attachment. Thus, it can be determined still more precisely whether a particular gene is responsible for a given behavioral phenotype. These varied approaches have allowed scientists to get some fairly good perspectives concerning the influence of hormonal processes on behaviors and the many factors that influence how environment and experiences can modify these outcomes.

Accommodating to hostile environments

It is usually assumed that natural selection is fundamental in promoting the evolution of all organisms. If a particular trait is beneficial, then it's more likely that those organisms with that trait (phenotype) and the underlying genes (genotype) will have the opportunity to transmit that characteristic to the next generation. That sounds very nice and scientific, but it doesn't actually explain all that much more than saying that evolution moves forward because God decided that certain traits ought to be advantageous. A question that really needs to be addressed is how particular traits actually came about in the first place? Professor Masatoshi Nei (2013) suggested that evolution is driven by the occurrence of mutations which can come about by fluke or are provoked by environmental factors. If a given mutation creates a certain phenotype that is advantageous and enhances the probability of that gene being passed on, then the trait will be maintained in the organism's gene pool.

The information we get regarding adaptation to stressors often comes from mice and other little critters, but it also comes from much smaller organisms. When the bacteria Escherichia coli (E. coli) were grown in stressful environments (e.g., where they're subject to starvation or the presence of antibiotics), there was an appreciable increase in the rate of mutations. When confronted with hostile conditions, even bacteria make efforts to adapt, which takes the form of more mutations developing, thereby making it more likely that some of them will survive the onslaught, thus giving rise to generations of more resilient pathogens. As a result, we've been seeing increasingly more antibiotic-resistant bacteria, such as gonorrhea, and even lice have developed resistance to the treatments that a decade ago could readily remove them from the hair and scalps of school kids.

It also seems that "persistent bacteria" exist which have the ability to respond to antibiotic threats by going into a dormant state, during which they are resistant to the antibacterial agents, and then they emerge when the threat is gone. So, in a manner of speaking, bacteria, like humans, get on through adaptation and change, or by accommodating to the environment.

The hormonal stress response

In cooperation with brain neuronal processes, hormones contribute to various adaptive changes in response to stressors. They can blunt the physical or emotional pain that might occur, and they may influence processes relevant to appraisal, arousal, vigilance, and cognitive functioning necessary for effective coping. Moreover, hormones also regulate other biological processes, such as immune functioning, which serve to maintain our well-being, and are involved in the functioning of the autonomic nervous system that regulates peripheral organs (e.g., heart, spleen, intestine) over which we have no cognitive control.

Hormones of the autonomic nervous system

The autonomic system has two components, the sympathetic and parasympathetic systems, which are responsible for getting things going or turning things down, respectively. For example, when the sympathetic system is activated by a stressor, the resulting release of the hormones epinephrine (adrenalin) and norepinephrine (noradrenalin) stimulates receptors on the spleen so that immune molecules are sent into circulation to deal with potential systemic threats. Likewise, the heart is stimulated so that heart rate and blood pressure are increased, essentially increasing the blood oxygenation that our brain and body need. Activation of the parasympathetic system, which involves the release of another hormone-like substance, acetylcholine (ACh), keeps sympathetic activation in check, thereby maintaining the balanced functioning of organs.

The one percent doctrine

Apparently, in a meeting of several members of the Bush administration concerns were expressed about the possibility of terrorist groups seeking to obtain nuclear weapons, and Dick Cheney, then Vice President, indicated that even if this amounted to just a 1 percent possibility it had to be treated as a certainty with respect to the response that ought to be adopted. The United States could not take the risk of allowing any margin of error to creep into national defense. This very same "one percent doctrine" is exceptionally reasonable for any country to take for the sake of the well-being and safety of their citizens, although oddly, many people and politicians of some countries don't see those of other countries having the very same rights. Having terrorists in my backyard is definitely off the table, but having them in someone else's backyard is something to negotiate.

Our own naturally occurring defensive mechanisms work on the basis of the one percent doctrine. We make appraisals of potential threats, usually erring on the safe side, and then take behavioral steps to ameliorate the threat. Our biological systems are concurrently activated; they aren't sitting back hoping it's a false alarm. These systems go into action and then back off if the events are appraised as not being threatening. Often, problems arise not because systems don't react, but because they react too often or too strongly.

The hypothalamic-pituitary-adrenal (HPA) axis and glucocorticoids

In addition to activation of the autonomic nervous system, stressors give rise to a combination of other brain changes that are essential for the organism's survival. When a potential challenge is initially encountered, frontal cortical brain regions that govern appraisals and decision-making are activated, as is the amygdala, which is associated with emotions such as fear and anxiety, and the hippocampus which is involved in memory processes being established or recalled. These regions, acting in concert with one another, are responsible for figuring out what the threat is about, determining whether it's been encountered previously, and deciding on the coping strategies that should be used. Once a stimulus or event is deemed to be potentially threatening, this information is transmitted to particular neurons within the hypothalamus that release corticotropin-releasing hormone (CRH), which stimulates aspects of the pituitary gland, causing the release of another hormone, adrenocorticotropic hormone (ACTH), into the bloodstream. The ACTH makes its way to the adrenal glands where it causes the secretion of cortisol (the rodent equivalent is corticosterone), which then engenders a variety of adaptive changes. The cortisol released into the bloodstream will eventually reach the brain, where it stimulates receptors, termed glucocorticoid receptors (GR), on neurons in the hypothalamus and the hippocampus, which cause the curtailment of further CRH release from the hypothalamus. This shutdown process, or negative feedback loop, is essential because it would be counterproductive for this system to be indefinitely activated. Indeed, persistent cortisol release and excessive receptor stimulation may have damaging effects on neurons of the hippocampus. With age it is normal for hippocampal neurons to be lost and cortisol levels to be elevated, but the extent of the loss can be aggravated under conditions where high cortisol levels are sustained, as in the case of chronic stressors.

What cortisol (corticosterone) does for us

As described by Robert Sapolsky and his associates (2000), corticoids act in several beneficial ways. They are *permissive* in the sense that they allow or help other stressor-provoked hormonal changes to occur or to be amplified. For example, in the presence of cortisol, epinephrine promotes the release of free fatty acids and thus increases energy availability. This hormone can also serve in a *stimulatory* capacity in directly stimulating receptors of cells of various organs, such as the heart, or by influencing the actions of other hormones. Conversely, it can produce *suppressive* actions that inhibit the functioning of processes that might be detrimental to the organism's well-being. In this regard, cortisol may prevent excessive immune activation that could potentially have adverse effects, such as the development of illnesses where the immune system attacks aspects of the self (i.e., autoimmune disorders). As well, cortisol can delay or limit those processes which aren't essential during a crisis, such as feeding, digestion, growth, and reproduction. Finally, cortisol may serve in a *preparative* capacity in the sense that it can either increase or diminish responses to stressors experienced at some later time.

The cortisol/corticosterone response to an acute stressor

When a novel stressor is first encountered it's uncertain whether or not it is controllable or whether it will be brief or prolonged. Because cortisol release is essential for survival, a relatively fast response is needed and the organism might not have the luxury of

Glucocorticoids and mineralocorticoids

Cortisol has the ability to bind to particular receptors, dubbed glucocorticoid receptors (GR) that are found on cells throughout the body. This hormone has many positive actions and has been used clinically to treat conditions where the immune system is overly active, such as autoimmune disorders, asthma, sepsis, allergies, a variety of skin conditions, and even some types of cancer. In fact, it has so many positive actions and so many clinical uses you'd think it would be heralded as the miracle hormone, just as aspirin is touted as a miracle drug. Instead, cortisol has received the rap as being the "stress hormone" and is sometimes mistakenly thought to reflect distress, instead of being viewed as an essential adaptive hormone needed to deal with stressful events.

A second hormone class, mineralocorticoids, is also involved in the stress response. Receptors for mineralocorticoids present within the hippocampus are the first to be activated in response to stressors, and it is only with greater stressor intensities that glucocorticoid receptors are activated. Activation of hippocampal mineralocorticoid receptors may be essential for the engagement of memory systems that help us deal with threats. Several different mineralocorticoids essential for our basic functioning are present within the body. For example, aldosterone released by the adrenal gland is associated with retention of sodium and water in the body, and aldosterone disturbances may contribute to elevated blood pressure, cardiac problems, and the development of illnesses related to diabetes. Despite the many important aspects of mineralocorticoids, the focus of stress research has typically been on glucocorticoids. So, if glucocorticoids have been misunderstood, mineralocorticoids have suffered the ignominy of often being ignored.

examining all aspects of the stressor before reacting. It's clearly advantageous for relatively strong defensive responses to be mounted quickly, and then, as information is acquired regarding the characteristics of the stressor, the hormonal response can be adjusted accordingly. It also appears that adaptation may develop in response to a moderate, chronic stressor, so that the cortisol rise may be less pronounced than it was initially. The HPA system seems to be very adaptable, and it seems that once an adaptation has occurred, the introduction of a new stressor may elicit a marked HPA response. In a sense, the apparent adaptation might spare us from damage that might accrue if cortisol release went on unabated, but this essential system remains ready to react if necessary. Despite these safeguards, there are occasions when excessive functioning of this system can occur. Specifically, the adaptation is less likely to develop when the nature of the stressor itself varies, and it occurs on an intermittent, unpredictable basis, and the excessive HPA activation can have damaging effects on our well-being.

Cortisol variations in humans

The reputation of cortisol as an important hormone in dealing with stressors has been around for decades, largely based on studies in animals in which even mild stressors produced a two- to threefold increase of corticosterone, and a stronger stressor, such as physical restraint, elicited a six- to eightfold increase of the hormone, and corticosterone release was

Don't mess with momma bear

Despite the HPA system's sensitivity to stressors, stressor-elicited corticoid responses in rodents and in humans are blunted during the last trimester of pregnancy as well as during lactation. In speaking with Dominique Walker of the Douglas Hospital Research Center and McGill University, an expert on this topic, she indicated that the blunted corticosterone response in the rodent mom occurred for the sake of the pups.

> Lactation and corticosteroid secretion are linked to one another. An increase of glucocorticoids, such as that elicited during a normal stress response in the mother would increase exposure of the offspring since glucocorticoids are transferred through the milk. As the offspring brain is sensitive to glucocorticoids and exposure to excess glucocorticoids may impair brain development, we could anticipate that blunting stress responses in the mother would protect the offspring's brain from the deleterious effects of glucocorticoids. Furthermore, large stress responses might impair sequences of maternal behavior and damage the mother–infant physiological and behavioral reciprocity, so again diminished corticosterone responses are desirable.

In response to the question of whether the outcomes in rodents were also seen in humans, she indicated that they were, provided that the moms were breast-feeding and that the stressor to which they were exposed was a meaningful one.

Unlike the blunted HPA effects evident when a stressor was directed at a rodent mom, a marked corticosterone surge occurred in the mom when the threat was aimed at her pups. Evidently, rodent moms distinguish between or "filter" relevant from irrelevant stimuli, as well as different types of relevant stressors. When the threat is directed at herself she forgoes her own well-being, so that her pups are not subjected to corticoid surges. However, when the threat is directed at her offspring, the gloves come off and the HPA response in the mom is instigated so that she has the resources needed to protect her young (Walker, 2010). We often hear about the sacrifices that mothers will make for their kids, but it extends into domains that most of us haven't considered.

even elicited by cues that had previously been associated with the stressor. A pronounced disconnect exists, however, between rodent and human corticoid changes in response to stressors. Unlike the marked response evident in rodents, the effects of stressors in humans are far less pronounced. Anticipation of heart surgery, which most of us will agree is fairly threatening, causes a cortisol increase of only 30–50 percent, and academic exams are typically not associated with cortisol elevation, or lead to very limited changes. Yet, a threat to our social identity, such as sexism or racial discrimination, as well as stressors that cause shame or anger, will readily elicit cortisol elevations. Likewise, in a laboratory context, only modest cortisol increases are elicited by reminders of previous stressor experiences, whereas cortisol changes, ranging from 50 to 300 percent, are provoked when individuals are engaged in a public-speaking task followed by a verbal arithmetic test in front of a small panel of judges, a procedure known as the Trier Social Stress Test (TSST).

Why would a relatively contrived public-speaking stressor, conducted in a laboratory setting, promote greater cortisol elevations than anticipation of real-life stressors such as the distress that occurs among students prior to an exam, or just before open heart surgery? As terrifying as public speaking can be, surely it's not as distressing as open heart surgery? Clearly, there's more to the cortisol response than just the potential threat. It might be that anticipation of a stressor, irrespective of whether it involves imminent surgery or an academic exam, simply isn't as challenging to biological systems as actually undergoing a stressor. Alternatively, cortisol changes might be induced most readily in response to challenges that entail a social threat in which we are being evaluated, as in the context of public speaking, particularly if it elicits emotional responses, such as shame or self-directed anger.

Neuroendocrine changes, like some of our behaviors, vary over a 24–25 hour cycle, typically being controlled by "biological clocks" that are linked to light–dark cycles. These circadian processes permit the replenishment of hormones used up with daily activities, and disturbances of these cycles can promote health problems, and can influence the effectiveness of various drug treatments in modifying illness. Among individuals who experience frequent changes of their circadian cycles, such as shift workers, airplane pilots and stewards on international flights, the risk for illness related to hormonal disturbances, such as hypertension and diabetes, is increased.

In line with other biological systems, cortisol levels vary over the course of the day. Cortisol levels start off high in the morning, increase by about 40 percent over the first 30 minutes following awakening, and then decline over the course of the day, reaching the low point at about midnight. The early morning rise of cortisol over the initial 30 minutes following awakening is especially pronounced among highly stressed or depressed individuals. Curiously, however, the morning cortisol rise was diminished, and afternoon cortisol level increased among individuals who had experienced a strong chronic stressor, or in those with PTSD. It is uncertain whether this flattening of the diurnal cortisol curve represents an adaptive change to prevent excessive HPA functioning or whether it contributes to negative psychological and physical repercussions of stressors. Nor is it known whether the altered hormonal levels appear prior to changes of behavioral functioning, but it might turn out that these cortisol variations are useful in predicting the development of later pathological outcomes.

Risky behaviors

In stressful situations we tend to become more vigilant and less likely to expose ourselves to harm. Among stockbrokers, volatile market activity can be very stressful and be accompanied by elevated cortisol levels as well as avoidance of high risk behavior. Interestingly, during a quiet period, giving stock agents a treatment that increased their cortisol levels to an extent equivalent to that seen during hectic periods, their behaviors changed in a predictable way. They became more averse to risk and generally played it safe in their trading. Presumably, the elevated cortisol affected the brain just as a volatile market might have done, thus modifying their behavior.

Yesterday's stressors influence today's responses

Stressors that we encounter have seemingly transient hormonal effects that persist for a matter of minutes or hours, but they can nevertheless have repercussions that might be felt years later. It will be recalled that when we encounter a stressor, neuronal activation in brain regions responsible for appraisals and emotions provokes CRH release from the hypothalamus, triggering ACTH release from the pituitary and hence cortisol secretion from the adrenal gland. Likewise, if individuals are injected with CRH, thereby simulating the action of a stressor, the ACTH and cortisol elevations will follow. However, when this test was conducted among depressed women who had been abused when they were young, the ACTH response elicited by CRH treatment was diminished, indicating that HPA system functioning was down-regulated. However, if instead of CRH being administered, women were assessed following a social stressor, their HPA response wasn't diminished at all, and was, in fact, markedly exaggerated.

Biomarkers

There are instances where changes of biological factors precede or accompany pathology. They may play a provocative role in the development of illness, or they might be caused by the early processes that are associated with the disease. Regardless of whether they are causally related to the illness, these biological factors may nevertheless be important to researchers and clinicians as they could be used as predictors or (bio)markers as to whether an individual will develop a particular disturbance, or they might be indicative of which of several treatment options would be optimal. Numerous biomarkers have been identified that are associated with increased risk for specific pathological conditions. Interestingly, a set of four markers in blood, namely albumin, alpha-1-acid glycoprotein, low-density-lipoprotein particle size, and citrate, seem to be global markers of illness in that they may predict death over the ensuing five-year period.

Ideally, simply measuring resting or basal levels of a hormone in blood or saliva would be sufficient to predict vulnerability to negative outcomes. However, there are instances where basal levels of a substance might not provide the information needed for accurate prognoses. Instead, we might want to examine the hormone level when a challenge or load has been placed on the system to determine how well this is handled. To have your heart checked, simply determining its rate and blood pressure will provide important information, especially if you're walking around with fairly high blood pressure. Better information can be obtained when blood pressure and heart rate are accompanied with an electrocardiogram (EKG), and still more informative data are obtained through a stress test that consists of having you exercise on a treadmill and taking heart measures while your system is strained. In this instance, a measure is obtained regarding how quickly heart rate and blood pressure increase, how high they go, as well as how long it takes for them to normalize after you've stopped exercising. In this way we might gain data regarding how the organ (or a specific biochemical process) is performing and find out a bit about how it will function in the near future. Whether it's hearts, cars, or bridges, more information is obtained when a load is placed on it, and this should similarly be considered in relation to biomarkers for stress-related illnesses.

Clearly, negative early experiences had lasting consequences, but why were later HPA responses diminished in response to a pharmacological challenge that mimicked a stressor, but exaggerated in response to an actual stressor? It is possible that following trauma, excessively reactive HPA responses to stressful cues could result in this system becoming overly taxed and pathology would thus be more likely to occur, and thus "down-regulation" of this system occurs as an adaptive response. Yet, given this system's importance, it might be counterproductive for it to be persistently inhibited. To deal with this, the brain might behave selectively so that the response to ordinary challenges might be blunted, but override systems might exist so that in the context of particular stressors, such as those that are personally meaningful, HPA activation can be elicited.

A cacophony of hormones associated with stress, eating and energy regulation: leptin, ghrelin, CRH, and neuropeptide Y

Like other hormones, those that govern eating and energy regulation have their own daily cycles, so that some are elevated just prior to usual mealtimes, and diminished afterward. It's not just hormones that stimulate eating, as environmental stimuli also influence our motivation to eat. The smell of fresh baked bread or a smoked meat sandwich tends to encourage our appetite, and good-looking carbohydrate-rich desserts are tempting even after we've completed a meal. In effect, the biological signals that tell us we don't need any more food can be overridden by brain processes that might tell us to go for it anyway. Evidently, when it comes to food, drug addictions, and perhaps sex, aspects of the brain that control decisions concerning whether something is good for us can be hijacked by those that are responsible for what we like or crave.

My friend Zul Merali has long maintained that eating and stress systems are intertwined so that the presence of danger will often have pronounced effects on our inclination or disinclination to eat (Merali et al., 1998). Across species, aspects of the brain are hard-wired so that the search for food diminishes in the presence of a threat. When a predator is out there stalking, it's simply not a good idea for an animal to let down its guard in order to have a snack or to admire a potential mate. This is perfectly understandable from an adaptive perspective, and yet there are also instances when moderate stressful events promote eating.

Efforts to identify the processes that allow us to recognize when we're hungry, and those that tell us when we're full, have been undertaken for more than 60 years, but it's only been in the last couple of decades that a better understanding has developed regarding the hormonal processes that are involved in eating and energy regulation. In this regard, when hormones such as ghrelin or neuropeptide Y (NPY) are elevated they signal us to eat, whereas the rise of leptin, which is primarily manufactured by fat cells (adipocytes), signals us to stop eating. Ghrelin also influences the rewarding feelings derived from food by activating dopamine neurons in particular brain regions, and thus could be especially pertinent to stress-induced eating processes (Abizaid, 2009). In line with this view, eating was increased among rodents in response to ghrelin administered directly into brain regions that govern feelings of reward, but was diminished by drugs that blocked ghrelin receptors. Moreover, ghrelin administered to humans increased thoughts about food and stimulated brain processes responsible for rewarding feelings or pleasure, and cues that promote food cravings might do so through actions on ghrelin functioning.

Eating as self-medication

Deep depression and severe stressor experiences are often accompanied by reduced eating and marked weight loss. However, in the presence of moderate depression or in response to modest stressors, some individuals will reduce their eating, whereas other will increase their food consumption. The food consumed in these cases typically comprises junk food, rich in carbohydrates that offer a "quick fix." This might occur to obtain a rapid energy increase to help individuals cope, or eating might serve as a coping response that alleviates negative emotions that otherwise would have emerged. In this sense, eating might represent an effort to "self-medicate" through increased glucose availability, and if someone is eating to diminish the effects of stressors we can pretty well expect they'll select carbohydrate-rich treats rather than extraordinarily tempting celery sticks.

The increased eating that has been reported with chronic stressor experiences might also be related to variations of cortisol activity. Specifically, the cortisol release in response to a stressor stimulates calorie intake, and in the presence of insulin may contribute to the preference for high calorie foods. It also appears that the CRH release triggered by moderate stressors causes the release of dopamine, a brain neurochemical that elicits positive, rewarding feelings or makes rewarding events seem particularly salient. The increased cortisol and dopamine may also result in comfort foods generating greater pleasure than they would otherwise. Essentially, modest stressors might come to encourage eating, because tantalizing foods might seem that much yummier. As cortisol also contributes to the redistribution of fat, it will appear as abdominal fat depots, which as we'll see later might release chemicals that favor the development of coronary heart disease. Given the link between stress, cortisol, eating, and metabolic processes, Mary Dallman (2010) at the University of California (San Francisco) suggested that the current obesity epidemic might be encouraged by life stressors.

My friend Sonya Lupien (2012), a stress researcher who has worked extensively with cortisol, is fond of saying that millennia ago, our forbearers spent a large portion of their time hunting, which entailed considerable risk as the prey could easily become the predator. Thus, hunting would have promoted the release of the stress hormone cortisol that would facilitate the engagement of defensive actions. The cortisol rise would also have stimulated food intake to maximize preparedness for the next hunt, during which calories would readily be burned. Today, the hunt consists of a walk through aisles crammed with every delight, and the stressor comprises the risk of being run down by a runaway cart or being stuck in a long cash line because only three of eight cash stations are open. In essence, the cortisol release that leads to eating might not be as essential as it was for our ancestors. The carbohydrate craving and the eating of comfort foods in response to stressors might be a vestige of the cortisol release associated with the hunt, but its current value is not only limited, but may have negative health repercussions by promoting obesity.

The link between stress and eating responses is remarkably strong, and just about any drug that reduces anxiety has a propensity for increasing eating, and drugs that reduce eating generally increase anxiety. It also appears that when ghrelin is activated, as it can be in response to a moderate stressor, it has the effect of limiting excessive anxiety, and might permit feelings of reward associated with food to be elicited or even enhanced. Thus, proper food-seeking behaviors and energy stores will be maintained. Among some individuals, however, ghrelin levels not only increase in response to stressors, but might also remain elevated even after they've eaten. In essence, the shut-down mechanism for eating cessation might be inoperative, resulting in stress-elicited eating persisting, making these individuals prone to obesity.

In response to my question as to whether food can help us deal with stress, Alfonso Abizaid indicated that

> stress is, above all, a challenge that depletes our body of energy, and it's not surprising that metabolic hormones play an important role in modulating the stress response – not only in generating the energy needed to escape or face a stressor, but also to fill our energy reserves. Problems develop, however, when the stress response is constantly turned on, as this can lead to chronic energetic depletion, metabolic alterations that trigger compensatory eating, which might lead to obesity and cardiovascular disorders. Understanding these processes will be critical in preventing or treating these disorders.

Oxytocin and positive responses

Journalists found a gold mine in oxytocin, a hormone that has been associated with a range of prosocial behaviors. You name the positive social behavior and oxytocin has been implicated as a player in relation to it: attachment, bonding, maternal care, love, generosity, trust, altruism, empathy, sacrifice, social perception, the motivation to be with others, as well as the ability to infer the emotions of others based on their facial cues. It could be argued that without oxytocin or its receptors, our humanity would be diminished. For example, disturbed oxytocin functioning may be accompanied by individuals being mistrusting, seeing the world as more threatening, and less generous. As a result, the development and maintenance of relationships between individuals and groups might be undermined, and conflict resolution would be difficult.

In certain species, such as prairie voles, strong pair bonds develop that seem to be linked to oxytocin, and as might happen in humans, when prairie voles were isolated from others, they exhibited depressive-like behaviors, which could be attenuated by treating them with oxytocin. Thus, oxytocin might not only be involved in bonding, attachment, trust, and love, but might also contribute to mood states and mood disorders. In this regard one can think of the oxytocin-stress-depression constellation from a fairly simple perspective. Ordinarily, social support is one of our most effective ways of dealing with stressors, and could potentially limit the occurrence of stressor-provoked depression. However, among individuals with low oxytocin, the development of social support resources may be hampered and consequently the adverse effects of stressors will occur more readily.

A polymorphism has been identified for the gene coding for the oxytocin receptor (OXTR), so that individuals with the mutated receptor might not respond to this hormone as they would otherwise and might thus be less inclined toward prosocial behaviors. In this regard, even the social behavior of our pet dog that so often shows unconditional affection may be dependent upon whether the oxytocin receptor is operating properly. Not unexpectedly, the common response of seeking social support as a coping response in the presence of stressors is less likely to occur among individuals carrying the mutated oxytocin receptor gene. Likewise, the cortisol rise associated with a stressor can be diminished by having a friend present who could serve as a source of support, but this outcome will be precluded among individuals with the oxytocin receptor polymorphism. Evidently, the presence of this polymorphism not only limits prosocial behaviors, but diminishes the gains that can be generated by social support.

There have been indications that oxytocin could potentially be used in a clinical or quasi-clinical capacity, particularly in the context of stressful conditions. Since intra-nasal administration of oxytocin increased trust and the benefits gained from social

Love chemical? Maybe it's the "adapt well to your social surroundings chemical"

There seems to be more to oxytocin than simply the instigation of prosocial behaviors. Altruism, which refers to the tendency to help fellow group members even at a cost to oneself, seems to be strengthened by oxytocin. As Taylor et al. (2000) put it, oxytocin promotes a "tend and befriend" attitude, so that individuals with high levels of oxytocin exhibited cooperation and trust toward members of their own group even when placing themselves at risk. However, oxytocin also elicits parochial altruism wherein group members are not only true to their ingroup, but also display a "tend and defend" (defensive aggression) attitude toward competing members of other groups.

In view of the apparent social benefits that might come from heightened oxytocin levels, there might be the inclination for therapists to recommend the use of oxytocin in treating mild social anxiety. However, Mark Ellenbogen at Concordia University in Montreal showed that treatment with oxytocin might make some individuals overly sensitive to social cues (Cardoso et al., 2014). Somebody smiling at you for no reason or two people who suddenly stop talking and look slightly uncomfortable when you appear might ordinarily be off-putting, but when oxytocin levels are elevated, enhanced social reasoning and social sensitivity may lead to some very incorrect conclusions and a degree of paranoia.

Other views have emerged concerning the actions of oxytocin. One that seems to have gained increasing support is that this hormone increases social salience. Thus, when cues around us are deemed to be "safe," oxytocin might encourage prosocial behaviors, but when the environment is not deemed to be safe, oxytocin will promote defensive, antisocial behavior. It seems that oxytocin might also contribute to "social memory" so that negative social experiences, such as being bullied, will cause particular brain regions to be engaged and as a result later stressors of a similar sort will more readily create anxiety and fear. So, while some people have referred to oxytocin as the "love chemical" or the "nice chemical," it might simply represent the "being sensitive to your social surroundings chemical," although this tagline is less likely to make it on to newspaper pages.

interactions, it has been used to diminish conflict in heterosexual couples. Furthermore, oxytocin may be effective in limiting the impact of interpersonal stressors, such as social rejection, and it has been suggested that oxytocin, together with other hormones, might be useful in diminishing specific forms of anxiety that involve a social component. Thus, it could potentially be useful in the treatment of generalized social anxiety disorder, as well as facilitating the development of a social connection between patient and therapist. It also appears that oxytocin could potentially have positive effects in relation to improved brain and social functioning among children with autism who typically are averse to social interactions.

Estrogen and testosterone

Although women generally outlive men, they are more likely to develop certain illnesses, such as depression, anxiety disorders, and autoimmune disorders (i.e., disorders where the immune system attacks the self). It is sometimes assumed that such outcomes occur because women are more emotional and reactive than men, possibly owing to the involvement of estrogen, and it is the case that hormonal changes occurring over the course of the estrus cycle can influence brain processes associated with mood alterations. However, the perspective that females are less well able to handle stressors relative to men seems to be an outdated notion. In fact, there's good reason to believe that females may actually be more resilient than men. Indeed, although chronic stressors may cause disturbances of neurochemical processes necessary for attention, decision-making, and other executive processes, this was found to be less likely to occur in females, and as a result they were more able to use cognitive coping methods. If estrogen levels were reduced in females, their stressor-provoked neurochemical responses became more like those of males, whereas increasing estrogen in males provided them with increased resilience in the face of stressors. Clearly, it's about time for the term "the weaker sex" to be abandoned.

Testosterone, the primary sex hormone in males, is formed in the testes and to a limited extent by the adrenal glands. It is pivotal in the production of male reproductive tissues, the development of secondary male features, such as the growth of body hair, as well as muscle growth and bone density. As in the case of most hormones, when testosterone levels are either too high or too low, adverse outcomes may occur, including diminished life span, and in the case of particularly low testosterone levels, coronary heart disease is more common.

Several behavioral correlates have been identified in relation to testosterone. This hormone is particularly elevated in animals that were high in a dominance hierarchy or that had been superior in a dominance competition. Just as estrogen is influenced by stressors and influences stress responses, testosterone may act in a similar capacity, and the effects of stressors on brain development in males during and following adolescence is likely affected by this hormone. It also seems that the sex hormones may influence the plasticity (malleability) of brain neuronal processes, thereby affecting behavioral functioning and the propensity to develop stressor-related mental disorders.

Many similarities exist between the sexes, and there are similarly many differences, most of which we haven't touched on. One of these is that when a stressor situation is sufficiently intense, individuals may lose pleasure in otherwise rewarding activities, and both males and females are usually less inclined to engage in behaviors that lead to sex. As well, in males, stressors disturb gonadal hormone production, and erectile functioning may be impaired, possibly owing to autonomic nervous system changes that

Varied faces of hormones

Estrogen and testosterone are fundamental hormones in determining the development of male and female physical characteristics, and may be involved in sex-related behavioral differences. Some of the contributions of these hormones have been known for years, but the interpretations of their effects have changed with the times. The medical writer Randi Hutter Epstein indicated in an online blog that a bit over 60 years ago at a meeting of the American Association of Obstetricians, Gynecologists, and Abdominal Surgeons, the president of the association described women as "fickle creatures" under the control of their hormones. Perhaps feeling the stirrings of women's movements, he added that the development of hormone remedies for women might actually motivate them to dominate men. Imagine the buzz that would have created; but he went on to reassure his audience, "so long as she is controlled by her reproductive glands, she will remain basically the same loveable, gracious homemaker."

Anyone who has a female cat that hasn't been neutered will tell you that that cute little thing, at certain times, is entirely controlled by her hormones. Although that may be true for cats, surely humans have a brain that allows them to escape from this hormonal control? In the main this is probably correct. Yet, it was reported that at times near ovulation women walked relatively slowly and their gait was rated as sexier than at other times. It was suggested that as ovulation approaches, women's biologically driven unconscious behaviors include enhancing their attractiveness in order to attract more men and to increase their choice of a partner. It was also reported that ovulating women actually perceived charismatic and physically attractive men as probably being more committed partners and more devoted future fathers, even though these traits likely have little to do with physical appearance. A recent analysis of about 50 studies suggested that ovulating women might have evolved to prefer mates who have masculine facial features and body type, dominant behavior, manly scents, and the "bad-boy" behavioral style. Then, following this fertile period, their preference may shift to other traits that are more desirable in long-term mates.

While we're on this topic, at times of ovulation there may be another characteristic change of women's behavior. Specifically, it was reported in one study that they became more competitive and meaner toward other women. Games in which participants could either share amounts of money, or act greedily and want more for themselves indicated that during ovulation women cared less about the absolute amount of money they received, so long as they bettered other women. In contrast, when they played the game against men, they were more likely to share the money, or even gave the male more. One could interpret these findings in different ways. Particular hormones make women strive harder to be the best, or it might be that certain hormones might be associated with women's alpha female tendencies coming out, perhaps so that they can catch the alpha male. Perhaps so, perhaps not. I might not be the sharpest knife in the drawer, but I know enough to stay out of certain debates. I also know that potentially controversial findings need to be replicated in independent laboratories before they're fully accepted.

Having two XX chromosomes versus having one X chromosomes replaced by a puny Y

We've heard it often enough. Women are the weaker sex, and they also have to contend with much more than do men. Maybe so, I suppose, but then you have to wonder why women generally outlive men by several years, although the gap in this respect has been closing. It might simply be the case that men are more apt to undermine their longevity through their bad habits, which include smoking, eating foods that elevate cholesterol levels, coping by internalizing their emotions, and engaging in risky behaviors. It's equally possible that women have some secret biological mechanism that keeps them ticking well after the males' clocks have wound down. In this regard, multiple biological differences exist between men and women that could account for women's better health. For instance, oxytocin might encourage social support among women to a greater extent than it does among men, which could enhance survival. Likewise, estrogen enhances women's health in the sense that it acts against heart disease in premenopausal women, although they catch up after menopause. There's also reason to believe that testosterone somehow acts to reduce longevity. It's hard to know whether or not it's fiction, but it has been said that during the fourteenth to nineteenth centuries the life span of eunuchs in Korea was extended by about 15 years. Even if it's true, it's uncertain whether the extended life span was a direct result of castration or due to other factors associated with being a eunuch. Whatever the case, I'd guess that today this wouldn't catch on as a popular strategy for extending life.

influence blood flow. In females, reproduction itself, including ovulation and uterine changes necessary for successful pregnancy, might be disturbed by stressors because biological resources are redirected away from those that are important for reproduction to those necessary for dealing with environmental challenges.

There's been a lot in the news in recent years concerning the use of performance-enhancing drugs by athletes. Some of these agents elevate oxygen-carrying capacity by increasing red blood cells, whereas others facilitate the development of muscle mass. Long-distance cyclists prefer the former and weight-lifters or sprinters prefer the latter, which comprise anabolic androgenic steroids, more commonly referred to as anabolic steroids. Although they influence muscle growth that enhances strength and athletic performance, this is a deal with the devil given the multiple negative consequences elicited by these steroids. They adversely affect the heart and liver, promote elevated cholesterol and immune system disturbances, and the user's complexion takes a hit as well. Like other hormones, these anabolic steroids also affect brain functioning so that particular emotions, such as anxiety, are elevated, and cognitive functioning can potentially be disturbed.

Many of us are likely unaware that we might be affected by hormones that come from external sources. Our water supplies contain estrogen that comes from farm animals and farm fertilizers, and newspaper reports notwithstanding, only a small fraction comes from the urine of women taking the pill. Some people also willingly use steroids for other purposes, such as to minimize hair loss. Agents used in this capacity, such as Propecia and Proscar, contain finasteride, which could potentially lead to impotence,

Oh, give testosterone a break

There's no question about it at all. High levels of testosterone are viewed negatively, especially following reports that it is associated with aggression and even sexual deviancy. There have also been research reports indicating that testosterone causes males to be egocentric and disruptive when it comes to collaborative behaviors, in that males with relatively high levels of testosterone tended to give greater weight to their own judgments than to those of others in joint decision-making tasks. Yet, there seemed to be selectivity concerning occasions when testosterone levels changed. Although testosterone levels rose when males won competitions against outsiders, this didn't occur when they competed with their friend. Indeed, in the absence of a threat, testosterone was associated with reciprocity and prosocial behaviors.

There might be times, such as in crisis situations, when collaborative behaviors need to be balanced against those that are self-oriented. In a sense, the egocentrism associated with high testosterone may have high survival value, not only for the individual but for the group as a whole, especially when a threatening situation is ambiguous and an effective leader isn't present. Indeed, among animals who live in groups, such as chimpanzees, a dominant male may bully other males and females, but their presence is needed for the ultimate success of the group over other competing groups. In essence, yesterday's mean bully may be tomorrow's go-to guy. Thus, for the individuals and the group's welfare, there may be selection in favor of the bullying tendencies. I also came across a tidbit of research which suggested that testosterone levels are associated with elevated levels of honesty. I couldn't help myself and gloatingly passed this on to one my female colleagues, who indicated that she wasn't the least bit surprised. "When testosterone levels are high," she said, "it gets to the brain and makes males too dumb to lie effectively."

One more thing. Men have been ridiculed for some time in relation to their complaints about getting the proverbial "man cold." Well, people (i.e., women) making fun of men seem to ignore the fact that men often have inferior immune responses relative to women, in part owing to high testosterone levels. So, if men complain more, it might actually be because they really are sicker – but, even as I write this, I can imagine that someone will say that I'm protesting a bit too much.

erectile dysfunction, abnormal ejaculation, gynecomastia (developing enlarged breasts), testicular pain, and perhaps high-grade prostate cancer. Furthermore, finasteride might also come to cause changes of brain neurotransmitters that favor the development of anxiety and depression. So, despite the potentially high cost of a great head of hair, the words of *Saturday Night Live*'s Fernando resound that "It's better to look good than to feel good."

Before you go...

Hormonal variations elicited by stressors typically reflect adaptive responses to help the organisms deal with potential or actual challenges, although their excessive activation may have adverse consequences. Hormonal systems are well regulated so that activation remains within certain bounds, but early life negative experiences as well as genetic factors might make these biological systems more (or less) sensitive or reactive to stressors, thereby increasing the risk for the emergence of pathology. There are clearly multiple functions that are attributable to hormonal processes. Some of these are concerned with basic functions such as eating and energy regulation, and it seems that stress and eating-related hormones are reciprocally related. Thus, stressors influence eating processes, and engaging in eating can alter stress responses. Other hormones are more aligned with prosocial behaviors, and can thus indirectly influence responses to stressful experiences. In view of the complex interactions that occur between hormones and other biological mechanisms, a fuller appreciation of the factors underlying pathological conditions might require much more detailed analyses of the effects of stressors on multiple hormones, their synergistic and antagonistic actions, and individual difference factors that determine how specific individuals will be affected by hormonal changes.

6

Neurotransmitter Processes and Growth Factors

More than just a bunch of connections

Our ability to think, remember, see, and hear, the emotions we feel and express, and just about everything else about us comes about because we have a remarkable brain that evolved over millions of years through some sort of trial-and-error selection process. There's just nothing like it. Sure, Deep Blue, that nerdy computer IBM built, beat Garry Kasparov in a chess tournament, and some humans seem to be generally enamored by the idea that they can build robots to replace themselves. But there are limits to the functionality of Deep Blue or other devices that are not sentient organisms. Did Deep Blue feel good about winning, or would it have become depressed if it had lost? Did it even think how Garry felt after the whole thing was over? For that matter, did Deep Blue think that Deep Thought, its predecessor (essentially its parent) was proud of it?

There are somewhere between 85 and 100 billion cells (neurons) in the brain, each with projections that reach out to connect with many other neurons. In fact, trillions of connections can be made between neurons, and at these connections, neurochemicals can be released by the stimulating neuron to excite receptors present on an adjacent neuron. A neuron typically releases only a single type of neurochemical, but the receptors that are present on the adjacent receiving neuron come in a variety of different forms, and so can receive a range of different types of chemical messages. In a sense, each neuron can understand many languages, and then speaks in just one. It's reminiscent of the United Nations where people might speak in only one language, but through interpreters are able to understand many different languages. OK, that's a very bad example; the UN is a pretty messed-up place where nobody seems to understand anyone else, or if they do, they pretend not to.

One of the most remarkable aspects of the brain is that its many components are able to operate in a well-coordinated way. To unravel how the brain functions, we need to examine the interconnections between neurons, and the complex circuitry and the networks that are integral to our senses, emotions, and cognitions. We're not perfect, and sometimes disturbances in this circuitry occur,

Stress and Your Health: From Vulnerability to Resilience, First Edition. Hymie Anisman.
© 2015 John Wiley & Sons, Ltd. Published 2015 by John Wiley & Sons, Ltd.

leading to a variety of different pathological outcomes. Thus, adjustments of one sort or another are occasionally needed. Often we're successful in achieving this, but at other times our collective efforts have had less success. Still, we have increasingly been realizing the roots of some problems, and ways of repairing damage are being developed.

Neuronal and glial processes in relation to challenges

Brain neurons all have the function of transmitting signals to one another. When a neuron is activated, there is considerable processing that goes on within the cell body, culminating in an electrical signal being generated within a lengthy fiber, termed an axon, emanating from the cell body. The electrical signal travels down the axon to cause a neuronal chemical, termed a neurotransmitter, to be released from storage vesicles located at the end of the axon. Although 60 or so different molecules have been identified that serve in this capacity, most neurons only release a single type of neurotransmitter, but there are instances where more than one can be stored in vesicles and thus released at the same time.

The axon meets up with the many-branched receiving wires (dendrites) of close-by neurons. The point at which a connection is made between the sending and receiving neurons is referred to as a synapse. The neurotransmitter released from the end of the axon travels across a small space at the synapse, termed the synaptic cleft, to stimulate specific types of receptors that are situated on the next neuron. This, in turn, causes a further series of changes to occur within the receiving neuron, leading to it sending on the message. The multibranched dendritic tree of the receiving neuron has connections to a very large number of other neurons that can signal it, and so the behavior of this neuron is subject to multiple influences.

The neurotransmitter released into the synaptic space is degraded by enzymes that are present, or the transmitter is taken back (transported) into the cell that initially released it, through a process called reuptake. The longer the neurotransmitter stays in the synaptic cleft, the greater the opportunity to activate receptors and hence stimulate the adjacent neuron. Thus, the efficiency of the neurotransmitter can be increased by extending its time in the synaptic cleft, which can be accomplished by drugs that inhibit the enzymes that would otherwise degrade it or by inhibiting its reuptake into the neuron that released it. Alternative strategies to increase neurotransmitters have included drug treatments that reach the brain and are converted there into neurotransmitters, or administering a drug that can go directly to the receptor and either stimulate (agonists) or block it (antagonists).

At one time, the relationship between a neurotransmitter and a receptor was described as a lock-and-key arrangement, wherein little key-like chemicals floated across the synaptic cleft and fit into little locks (receptors) that more-or-less permanently resided on the dendrites or cell bodies of neurons. To some extent this analogy is still a good one, but receptors don't permanently sit on the cell surface, but instead are continuously being manufactured, and they can be also be "internalized," essentially being pulled into the cell, and consequently the number of receptors available for stimulation can vary at any given time. Moreover, as in the case of hormones, subtypes of a given transmitter receptor might be present that produce different outcomes. For instance, it had been thought that depression was due to insufficient serotonin being present, whereas schizophrenia occurred as

Going green in the neuronal world

Neuronal activity persists whether we are awake or asleep, engaged in physically or mentally strenuous tasks, or sitting around doing nothing, even when we're in a mindless state that sometimes happens when were engaged in repetitive actions. For neuronal functioning to continue under all these conditions, a lot of neurotransmitter must be produced and used efficiently. As it happens, after neurotransmitters have done their job, they don't just get tossed away as waste. In some cases, they are broken down, and their components are reformed to make the neurotransmitter. In other instances, the neurotransmitter present in the synaptic cleft is taken back up into the neuron through the process of "reuptake" so that it can be used again.

When the neurotransmitter is released, it not only stimulates receptors that are present on dendrites of an adjacent neuron, but may affect receptors present on the synaptic end of the axon that released the transmitter. When these so-called autoreceptors are triggered, which occurs more readily as the amount of neurotransmitter in the synaptic cleft increases, they tell the neuron to stop producing more transmitter. The process regarding neurotransmitter production, release and reuptake is reminiscent of industrial processes. Years ago, the Japanese auto industry created a strategy that kept costs down and allowed it to outperform companies in North America. Rather than loading up on all sorts of parts manufactured willy-nilly, the Japanese auto industry used a procedure referred to as "just in time" or "just in sequence" so that parts arrived at the plant just as they were needed. So, instead of having too many parts sitting in expensive warehouses, they were created just in time. Once cars are made, they're obviously sent to dealers who attempt to sell them. However, if the lot fills with unsold cars, for whatever reason, the dealers contact the plant asking for production and delivery to slow down. Thus, the balance between production and sales will remain stable, resources won't be used up needlessly, and the market won't be flooded with unsold cars. In a sense, neurons work on the just-in-time principle, with neurotransmitters being created on the basis of feedback obtained through autoreceptors. By the way, the car lot example has nothing to do with the word "auto" receptor, which in this context refers to "self."

a result of too much dopamine. It was subsequently demonstrated that it was more reasonable to suppose that certain serotonin receptors might be especially important in the promotion of depressive illness, and that excessive stimulation of particular dopamine receptors might contribute to schizophrenia. Thus, in accounting for stress-related illness and in developing methods to treat psychological disorders, it is not only important to know about the availability of a neurotransmitter, or the amount released, but also to consider the impact of the treatment on specific types of receptors.

A second type of cell present in the brain comprises glial cells that were at one time simply considered as support cells for neurons, but these glial cells that number a few trillion turned out to have essential functions rather than simply serving as "the help." Several types of glial cells exist, but of particular interest to us at the moment are the astrocytes and microglia, which provide nutrients to neurons, engage in the repair of cells within the brain and spinal cord, and release chemicals that contribute to the growth of cells. Like their cousins within the immune system that protect us from invaders and are involved in repair processes, the microglia within the brain are constantly on alert for damage, the presence of plaque and infectious agents, and they can respond quickly to destroy factors deemed to pose a risk to neurons. As we'll see, however, there are times when activated microglia can promote strong inflammatory responses, which could potentially cause destruction of neurons and thus contribute to the development of neurodegenerative disorders, such as Alzheimer's and Parkinson's disease, as well as psychiatric disorders.

Stressors influence neurotransmitter functioning

Peering into the brain using imaging techniques, such as fMRI and positron emission tomography (PET), have helped clarify the consequences of stressors on human brain functioning. But most of these studies are typically conducted if pathology, such as PTSD or depression, is present, and so they offer limited information about brain functioning that precedes the development of pathology, which could potentially provide information concerning vulnerability to later trauma-elicited pathology. Likewise, hardly any information is available regarding the period soon after trauma experiences, as well as over time following these experiences. A great deal of what we know concerning stressor effects on neurotransmitter functioning has come from studies in rodents, but for ethical reasons these studies don't involve severe stressors and so offer only limited information relevant to the impact of more profound and chronic challenges that humans sometimes endure.

Acetylcholine (ACh)

Acetylcholine (ACh) was the first neurotransmitter identified way back in 1914, and in 1936 Dale and Loewi shared the Nobel Prize for their discoveries. As we've seen, ACh appears in the peripheral nervous system, where it is involved in the functioning of the parasympathetic portion of the autonomic nervous system. In addition, ACh serves as a neurotransmitter within several brain regions, triggering one of two types of ACh receptors, termed muscarinic and nicotinic, and it has been implicated as playing a role in reward perceptions, attention, learning, and memory. Thus the actions of stressors on this transmitter have broad implications for cognitive processes as well as related pathologies.

Nicotine, as bad as it is when delivered through tobacco, may actually have several positive effects, presumably through its actions on nicotinic receptors in the brain. Smokers are much less likely to develop Parkinson's disease than non-smokers, and it's not a result of smokers dying of other causes before there's the opportunity of Parkinson's developing. Instead, it seems that activation of the nicotinic ACh receptors will stimulate brain dopamine neurons, which attenuate Parkinson's symptoms. In fact, trials are underway to determine whether nicotine administered through a transdermal patch or in chewing gum acts positively on symptoms of Parkinson's disease. Nicotine could also have positive effects on other processes by virtue of its ability to act as a powerful anti-oxidant, thereby protecting the brain from an excessive number of molecules containing oxygen, termed reactive oxygen species, which can be damaging to brain cells. Among individuals with early signs of Alzheimer's disease, nicotine enhanced memory and attention. It also seems that the attention-inducing actions of nicotine could serve to augment the effects of other treatments in ameliorating symptoms of attention deficit hyperactivity disorder (ADHD). It is also possible that through its attention-promoting

Reading between the lines

Emotional responses can often be read through our facial expressions and body gestures, and as poker players can attest, individuals often have "tells" that let others know about their emotions even when they're trying to cover them up. Different emotions might also be tied to diverse peripheral physiological changes. For instance, distinct patterns of cardiac and respiratory activity accompany fear, anger, sadness, and happiness. These emotional responses are largely under the control of neuronal events within several limbic brain regions. For example, activation of various components of the amygdala has been associated with fear or anxiety, whereas other midbrain regions, such as the ventral tegmentum and nucleus accumbens, are involved in reward, motivation, and positive feelings. To be sure, this is an oversimplification, as multiple brain regions cooperate with one another to produce organized outputs. Connections exist between brain regions involved in appraisal and decision-making processes and those associated with anxiety, and the expression of these emotions can be modified by ongoing events. It is also the case that some brain regions may serve multiple functions and are activated under a variety of circumstances.

In addition to brain areas responsible for detecting positive events, neurons in a particular brain region, the lateral habenula, are activated in response to negative events, such as punishment or the failure to receive reward. This might occur because of influences of the lateral habenula on brain regions that are responsible for feelings of reward. It now seems that the lateral habenula does more than this as it may be fundamental for making choices related to subjective costs in making some types of decisions. Essentially, we not only make decisions based on what we would like to gain, but also on the basis of what particular decisions will cost us. If this brain region isn't operating well, we might well be relatively indifferent in relation to the cost-benefit relationship.

Studies are often conducted in animals in an effort to determine which brain neurotransmitters in particular brain regions are linked to particular emotions. A dog or cat, and even a mouse, lets you know how they feel with very distinctive gestures, especially in relation to anger or when they're in attack mode. Other emotions, such as shame, are difficult to read in a mouse or rat. In fact, I don't know what would shame a mouse, nor do I have a clue what they look like when they do feel shame. Pet owners often believe that they communicate with their little buddies, and that they can read their pets' expressions with little difficulty, particularly the shame a dog is said to feel if it had a little accident in the living room. But perhaps the dog's behavior isn't a reflection of shame for what they did, but instead is a response to the behavior of their owner upon smelling, seeing, or stepping into the accident.

actions, nicotine might be useful in diminishing signs of schizophrenia which might be linked to "stimulus overload." Incidentally, as addictive as nicotine might be, this outcome occurs primarily when it is consumed through tobacco, which also contains several other ingredients, which as a group are responsible for the addiction potential. Thus, e-cigarettes rapidly became very popular, although there is increasing evidence attesting to its bad effects, including the promotion of cigarette smoking.

Despite the long experimental history of ACh, analyses of the effects of stressors on this neurotransmitter within the brain have been relatively sparse. Nevertheless, it is known that in rodents, psychological stressors increase ACh release within the prefrontal cortex and hippocampus, and like many other stressor effects, the ACh changes can be influenced by early life experiences. For instance, negative early events can exacerbate the ACh changes otherwise elicited by later stressors, and conversely, stressor effects were attenuated in rodents that were raised in enriched environments. The finding that

Anticholinergic agents in clinical situations

Drugs such as scopolamine and atropine, which block the effects of ACh on muscarinic receptors, have found their way into varied clinical arsenals. They are used for postoperative nausea and vomiting, and when applied as a patch they can attenuate motion/sea-sickness. They might also diminish depressive symptoms, and there have been reports that they reduce drug cravings. Scopolamine, which can be obtained from the plant Atropa belladonna, also referred to as belladonna or deadly nightshade, was used at one time in herbal medicines despite the very high toxicity of the berries of this plant. Among other things, it was also used to relieve pain, diminish menstrual difficulties, and as a muscle relaxant.

Anticholinergic agents have occasionally been used as a hallucinogenic agent, but the physical and mental side-effects can be pretty grim and so it's rarely used more than once. As well, because these agents reduce behavioral inhibition, it was at one time used as a "truth serum." Its usefulness in this capacity was limited owing to its side effects, although some countries have used it in this way during wars. Scopolamine, sometimes called burundanga in resorts within Venezuela and Thailand, has been used to drug and then rob tourists, and there have been reports that pamphlets and business cards soaked in a solution of scopolamine have been used to deliver the drug to a person's skin, although more commonly it is simply put in a person's drink. It has also been used as a date rape agent, which promotes amnesia for the period during which the drug is present in the system and shortly afterward.

Agents that increase the levels of acetylcholine often appear in insecticides. Poisoning through the use of insecticides isn't uncommon in suicide attempts, but more often poisoning results from accidental inhalation or excessive skin contact, leading to tens of thousands of deaths each year. The lethal aspects of ACh-acting agents is better known because of their tainted history as war gases used in World War I. These gases blocked the enzyme that normally degrades ACh, resulting in excessive levels of this transmitter, culminating in death. Today there are more than 70 different agents that fit this bill. Sarin, Soman, and Tabun were made in secrecy in Germany both before and during World War II for use as chemical weapons. Zyklon B, which was developed by the Nazi regime, was not used on battlefields, but instead was used to execute noncombatants in concentration camps or mobile trucks to get the job done expeditiously. Other war gases include mustard gas, chlorine, hydrogen cyanide, and those with ominous labels, such as agent 15, VX, and VR. The United Nations has condemned the use of war gases, but this didn't seem to have much effect in deterring their use in the Iran–Iraq war, the North Yemen civil war, Iraq's war on Kurds, as well as its alleged use in Chechnya, and its certain use in Syria.

ACh changes are greater in females than in males, particularly during the first half of the estrus cycle, raises the possibility that estrogen might contribute to the promotion of stressor-elicited ACh changes, and could be a factor in the development of pathology.

Serotonin, norepinephrine and dopamine

Of the many neurotransmitters that have been identified, norepinephrine, dopamine, and serotonin, which are part of a family of monoamine transmitters, have received particular attention. Neuronal activity within the hypothalamus involving these transmitters contributes to hormonal release associated with stress responses, energy regulation, feeding, and sexual behaviors. As well, their activity within various components of the prefrontal cortex and limbic brain regions contributes to appraisals, decision-making, and emotional responses. Dopamine, in particular, is thought to be involved in reward processes and motivation, and thus might be instrumental in the promotion of illnesses such as depression and drug addictions. It is usually thought that when we experience something pleasurable, it is accompanied by increased dopamine release, but it seems that dopamine activity may be elevated prior to that, and might actually be involved in the instigation of behaviors. In essence, it may encourage us to take steps to realize positive outcomes or, alternatively, withhold responses or take other actions to avoid undesirable consequences.

In the absence of a stressor, brain neuronal activity ordinarily goes on in a fairly stable manner with the production (referred to as synthesis) and use (referred to as release) of neurotransmitters matching one another, and hence the level of the transmitter remains stable. The burden of dealing with stressors is shared by behavioral and neurochemical processes, and when we're confronted by a potential threat that is appraised as being relatively mild, and can be coped with effectively, the load on neurochemical processes is limited. In this instance, a modest increase in the release of the neurotransmitter is elicited, which is met by an equivalent rate of its production, and so the level of the neurotransmitter doesn't vary appreciably. The release of the transmitter in this instance will activate neurons at critical brain sites, leading to an increase of vigilance, attention, problem-solving efforts, or any number of other behavioral, emotional and cognitive changes that facilitate coping or set in motion processes that maintain well-being. However, if the stressor encountered is severe and can't readily be dealt with through behavioral or cognitive methods, a particularly marked increase of monoamine functioning might be instigated. The resulting increase of neurotransmitter may be sufficiently great as to exceed its production, and as a result the absolute levels of the transmitter will decline, and for a time the organism is rendered less able to deal with further stressors.

As we've seen, there are often times when stressors we experience are not only strong, but also go on and on. Chronic psychological stressors may come in the form of having to deal with a serious illness, financial strains, caring for an ailing parent, family disputes, bullies repeatedly encountered at work or in the schoolyard, experiences of discrimination, or many others of a very long list. These stressors may be compounded by worry, rumination, and loss of sleep, which invariably add to the burden. Do we adapt to adverse experiences, or are the effects of stressors more and more damaging the longer we endure them? As we saw earlier in relation to hormones, both perspectives are correct. If a given stressor is encountered repeatedly, the reduction of the neurotransmitter that ordinarily occurs following an acute stressor might not occur. Compensatory changes occur, including an increase in the rate at which a neurotransmitter is produced, so that adequate supplies are maintained. However, this seeming adaptation develops

Compensatory changes to promote resilience

As we've seen, neuronal systems have remarkable ways of adapting to challenges. It is especially intriguing that these systems are blessed with compensatory abilities to take up the slack when other systems might be challenged excessively. In animals that are stressed, dopamine activity increases appreciably in brain regions associated with reward processes, and in animals that are most resilient in the face of stressors, the increased dopamine activity is still more pronounced. In mice showing increased dopamine activity, coupled with signs of depression, positive mood changes can be induced by causing the dopamine neurons to become hyperresponsive. It is as if this system compensates for dopamine changes by creating still greater neuronal responses. It remains to be understood why some animals ordinarily show this response and thus are resilient to the impact of stressors, whereas others are less able to self-regulate in this way. There is the possibility that compensatory dopamine processes can be harnessed in the treatment of human depression.

less readily if the stressor is unpredictable and varies over days, which unfortunately is characteristic of chronic stressors we frequently encounter, and such events are precisely those that favor the development of pathological outcomes.

Even if an adaptation in the form of increased synthesis of the transmitter develops in response to a chronic stressor, and the organism seems to be operating well, we shouldn't be misled into thinking that things are fine. It needs to be kept in mind that during the chronic stressor experience the rate of neurotransmitter utilization has been running on high for an extended time, and the load placed on critical brain systems might have been excessive. At some point further regulatory changes may occur in an effort to ensure that particular receptors don't become overly stimulated, and thus their number or sensitivity may diminish. Eventually, however, the allostatic load may become excessive, leading to cell loss and the development of any of several pathological outcomes. Even if adverse outcomes don't appear immediately, neuronal systems have been affected so that over time and further stressor experiences, the cumulative load might undermine adaptive biological systems, creating damage to brain processes as well as our cardiovascular and immune systems, thereby increasing the risk for later pathological outcomes.

Corticotropin releasing hormone (CRH): beyond the HPA system

Beyond its role in hypothalamic-pituitary-adrenal (HPA) functioning, CRH also operates in other brain regions that are involved in stressor appraisals and in the induction of emotional responses, such as anxiety and depressive features. Although fear and anxiety are terms that are sometimes used interchangeably, they are distinguishable from one another. Fear is an emotion elicited by a specific stimulus (object, place, or person) based on learning that the stimulus is a threat, and we have little voluntary control over its appearance or disappearance. Anxiety may also appear in anticipation of a threat, but can be engendered by diffuse stimuli, and can consist of a free-floating emotion. There have been suggestions that even though CRH plays a pivotal role in the production of both emotions, they are likely mediated by different aspects of the amygdala and

Better lucky than smart

The neurotransmitter changes that accompany stressors are reminiscent of our behaviors and reaction in a different context. On a week-to-week basis, our bank account ought to remain fairly stable, with funds leaving to pay expenses (use) being met by our salary being deposited (synthesis). Sometimes, expenses may arise that are unexpected, and we have to deal with these in some fashion. We might be able come up with a few dollars here and there, and we might cut back on some luxury items, sell off some stuff that's not essential, and thus we maintain our bank balance. If, suddenly, we hit further problems and our burden becomes relatively heavy, we might have to take on some additional part-time work to keep our balance stable, and so for the moment things still seem OK – the household expenses are handled and the kids get lunch money. Yet, simply because our bank balance has been reinstated doesn't mean everything is back to normal. The pressures on us have increased, our work–life balance is disturbed, vacation times are gone, and we have much less room to maneuver given that so much of our time and resources are taken up by the additional workload. Moreover, if yet another emergency arises, we're really in trouble. Just when we're already over-leveraged, financially, physically and mentally, we might encounter mortgage rates going up, and then both the roof shingles and the water heater need replacement. Trying to deal with unpredictable stressors that hit us one after another, especially when they're superimposed on an already heavy load that isn't being dealt with effectively, is exceedingly difficult.

Even though bankruptcy is imminent and our physical and mental health has deteriorated, further aggravating our precarious financial situation, things might miraculously turn around. We receive a promotion and a nice pay increase, the penny stock we bought years ago suddenly booms, our lucky lottery number actually paid off, or that long-lost cousin in Nicaragua really did die and leave you his fortune. In the future we'll look back and think that we dodged a bullet, and had the foresight and resilience to stay the course long enough. We might even congratulate ourselves on our wisdom in taking the actions that we did. The fact is, however, that sometimes it's better to be lucky than smart.

its extended regions. Furthermore, while anxiety responses can be activated by different stressors, including psychological threats that are learned and those that seem to be innately driven, such as responses elicited by predator cues, they might involve activation of different neural circuits. Thus, as we'll see, the treatments most effective in ameliorating excessive fear or anxiety may depend on the nature of the events that caused them to come about, such as discomfort associated with social situations versus the fear that is linked by prior physical stressors.

Two primary CRH receptor subtypes have been identified, dubbed CRH_1 and CRH_2, which seem to mediate different aspects of the behavioral stress response. One view is that activation of CRH_1 receptors in certain brain regions might contribute to emotional responses, whereas the activation of CRH_2 receptors might be principally involved in regulating coping responses. Another view has it that CRH_1 may be involved in regulating attention, executive functions, the conscious experience of emotions, and learning about these emotions, whereas CRH_2 receptors might contribute to basic processes that

Good guys or bad guys

Despite the benefits of hormonal and neurotransmitter changes that occur in response to stressful events, there are instances where these biological changes have negative consequences. After so many years of selection, one might wonder why our hormonal systems ever run amok, culminating in the development of illness. An obvious conclusion is that we aren't actually all that well adapted. Then again, there is the possibility that the seemingly negative outcomes associated with stressor-induced hormonal changes might also have positive value. Mild feelings of anxiety and depression related to hormonal changes might alert us to be vigilant and tell us to take steps to eliminate the factors that are causing us to have these feelings. In essence, these emotions have been maintained through natural selection processes because they are adaptively significant. It's unfortunate that among some individuals these emotional responses may become excessive and incapacitating.

are necessary for survival, such as feeding, reproduction, and defense. These distinctions are no small matter as they might have important implications for the treatment of disorders. For instance, patients presenting with anxiety and depression might be most efficaciously treated with drugs that antagonize CRH_1 receptors, whereas patients with eating disorders might, hypothetically, be best served by drugs targeted at CRH_2. Once the involvement of receptor subtypes in mediating specific emotions and behaviors is fully deciphered, it may be possible to develop improved treatment strategies for different anxiety-related disorders.

Glutamate

Glutamate, the most abundant excitatory neurotransmitter in the brain, has been studied for about five decades, but has been receiving increasing attention because of its involvement in memory processes, as well as in several psychopathological conditions. There are two types of glutamate receptors, ionotropic glutamate receptors and metabotropic glutamate receptors, that operate very differently from one another, and as we'll see later, they are involved in different pathologies. In response to acute stressful events glutamate release increases within brain regions, as does expression of receptors sensitive to glutamate, thereby enhancing synaptic transmission that may contribute to appraisal processes, anxiety, and memory. Although the data are limited, it appears that with repeated stressor experiences a moderate adaptation occurs with respect to glutamate release in the prefrontal cortex, but this is less notable in other brain regions. The changes specific to brain regions that are associated with chronic stressors may be significant given that glutamate disturbances or those related to glutamate receptors have been implicated in schizophrenia and depression. As well, variations of glutamate might contribute to the positive effects of antidepressant drugs, and those used in the treatment of PTSD.

Glutamate is also a major player in relation to pathology that evolves secondary to stroke and traumatic brain injury. Ordinarily, once glutamate has been released by a neuron and has done its job, it is removed by glutamate transporters, but unfortunately, under some conditions, a "glutamatergic storm" may occur, which causes cell damage or death. The negative effects of glutamate excess have been implicated in neurodegenerative disorders, including Alzheimer's disease, Parkinson's disease, amyotrophic lateral sclerosis (ALS, often referred to as Lou Gehrig's disease), multiple sclerosis, Huntington's disease, and brain damage resulting from alcoholism, as well as alcohol and benzodiazepine withdrawal. To what extent stressful events, acting on glutamate functioning, might aggravate these conditions is still an open question.

Gamma-aminobutyric acid (GABA)

Some neurotransmitters operate to excite adjacent neurons, whereas others, such as GABA, have the effect of inhibiting other neurons. In an email conversation with Michael Poulter, who has been attempting to link GABA to pathology, he indicated that "virtually all neurons in the brain are controlled by GABA activity. Its primary role is to control brain activity, facilitating the creation of brain rhythms that lead to normal brain function, and it does this by inhibiting aspects of brain excitation. Dysfunctional GABA activity has been implicated in several mental illnesses, such as depression and schizophrenia." He went on to describe the importance of inhibitory neurons, saying "it's fine to have a car with an engine that gets you moving from 0 to 60 in a just a few seconds, but as the road ends, brakes come in pretty handy." His work has revealed that stressful events affect GABA functioning within stress-sensitive brain regions, and it has also been reported that GABA levels and receptors vary in relation to general anxiety. Together with serotonin and CRH within the prefrontal cortex and hippocampus, GABA might also contribute to stress-related psychological disorders, such as depressive illness. As well, $GABA_A$ functioning may be affected by ovarian hormones, and it is possible that these interactions contribute to the sex differences that exist with respect to depression and anxiety.

Consistent with a role for GABA in stress-related disturbances, the actions of stressors on GABA functioning and on behavioral disturbances could be attenuated in animals that have received repeated antidepressant drugs over several weeks. The data concerning GABA changes in humans are admittedly sparse, but studies using imaging techniques have indicated that in response to a threat, GABA activity decreased relative to that evident during a safe period. It also appeared that among individuals who had been depressed and died by suicide, the characteristics of $GABA_A$ receptors were disturbed. Although these findings don't necessarily reflect a causal link between GABA functioning and depression or suicide, they are consistent with this supposition, and understandably have spurred research in this domain.

Cannabinoids

Endocannabinoids are naturally occurring brain chemicals that activate CB_1 receptors, which are the receptors through which delta-9-tetrahydrocannabinol (THC), the active component of marijuana, has its effects. Cannabis, of course, is known for its psychoactive effects, its ability to increase appetite, diminish nausea, reduce anxiety, and bring relief to chronic pain sufferers. Conversely, blocking these receptors increases anxiety and corticoid activity, and these actions are still more prominent following stressor challenges. It seems that communication occurs between endocannabinoid processes and HPA functioning, and as cortisol within the amygdala contributes to the consolidation or strengthening of emotionally arousing memories, activation of CB_1 receptors could indirectly contribute to emotional responses and emotional memories associated with stressors.

An interesting perspective was proposed regarding the role of cannabinoids in modulating stress responses. We won't go into the nitty-gritty of the complex, dynamic biological changes that occur, but suffice it to say that two endocannabinoids that are part of our neurobiological system, anandanine (AEA) and 2-arachodonoylglycerol (2-AG), are fundamental in stress responses. It is thought that AEA is responsible for maintaining calmness during nonstress periods and contributes to the heightened HPA response and anxiety that develop in response to a stressor. Once the initial reaction to a stressor has passed, 2-AG is activated, which serves to turn off the stress response. In effect, the stress response is not something that simply fades with the passage of time, but instead it reflects an active process involving 2-AG. Thus, the occurrence of persistent anxiety in response to stressors might be a consequence of continuous AEA activation or the failure of a 2-AG response to kick in properly.

Matt Hill, from the Hotchkiss Brain Institute, a leading researcher in the field, told me that "in general, cannabis tends to reduce stress and anxiety and promote relaxation, an effect which is believed to be mediated by the ability of cannabinoids to dampen neuronal activity in the amygdala, a brain region central to the generation of a stress response and anxious state." He went on to say:

> there are also a significant number of individuals who experience the converse, which comprises an increase in anxiety and paranoia following cannabis consumption. The mechanisms responsible for this are not entirely understood, but the research would suggest that these adverse responses are more common in women than in men, occur more readily in older individuals and can be influenced by the ambient level of environmental stress.

So once again, we see that the effects of a drug treatment can also interact with and be modified by factors related to the individual, as well as by the environmental background against which the drug is consumed. Furthermore, as most people know, cannabis also has effects on appraisal of events, and some of the stress-altering effects of cannabis might come from neurochemical changes stemming from the way individuals appraise (or misappraise) events that they encounter.

Neurotrophic factors

The focus of research related to the biological determinants of psychopathology had long been concerned with neurotransmitters, but a paradigm shift occurred with the discovery of neurotrophins, which comprise growth factors that are important for the survival of cells, cellular growth, multiplication (also referred to as proliferation), and differentiation into specialized cells. In addition to these important functions, growth factors are essential in strengthening synaptic connections that are necessary for recall of events, and dysfunctions of these growth factors have been implicated in the development of psychopathology. Two particular neurotrophins, brain-derived neurotrophic factor (BDNF) and basic fibroblast growth factor (FGF-2), have been most studied in relation to psychological disturbances. Other growth factors, such as growth hormone-releasing hormone (GHRH), nerve growth factor (NGF), neurotrophin (NT), and insulin-like growth factor 1 (IGF-1), might also contribute to psychopathological conditions, such as age-related neurodegenerative disorders like Alzheimer's disease.

There was a belief at one time that whatever neurons you were born with were more or less the maximum that you would ever have, and with age this number would dwindle. Most neurons are certainly formed prenatally but, in some parts of the adult brain, new neurons can be formed from neural stem cells, a process termed neurogenesis. Granted, these new cells are small in number, but if a few cells can manage to appear, then there may be ways of allowing for many cells to do so, and remedies for neurodegenerative disorders and other conditions might follow.

Growth factors have been receiving particular attention in relation to the impact of stressors on psychological disorders. The work of Ron Duman and his associates (e.g., Duman and Monteggia, 2006), as well as others, revealed that in rodents, acute stressors reduce BDNF and FGF-2 in brain regions, such as the hippocampus, which might contribute to depressive mood states. As in the case of several neurotransmitters, the decline of BDNF produced by acute stressors was less evident when it involved a chronic regimen in which the same stressor was administered on successive days. However, if a series of different stressors was applied over several weeks, then the BDNF and FGF-2 reductions in the hippocampus were pronounced and persistent, as were depressive-like behavioral disturbances.

Neuroplasticity

We are born with many neurons, each of which makes many connections to other neurons. The axons which transmit information make connections to dendrites through a startlingly high number of synapses. At birth, each cortical neuron is thought to have about 2,500 synapses, but with sensory experiences and learning about the world, more synapses are formed so that within a couple of years the number of synapses is increased sixfold. Some of these connections are used frequently as we perceive specific stimuli and as we gather information that builds on previous learning. Other synapses might be used infrequently, suggesting that they're not useful. So, following the "use it or lose it" principle, our remarkable brain prunes those synapses that are least used, whereas those synapses that are used a fair bit are preserved.

Our ability to acquire new information and the formation of memories is thought to occur because the synaptic connections between neurons are increased in number and the strength of the connections themselves is increased. As described earlier, a set of neurons might fire when we first see a dog, and another set of cells might fire when mom says the word "dog." Eventually, synapses will form between these sets of neurons so that the word "dog" comes to symbolize the object (the sight of the dog) and they will strengthen with repetitions of the word and sight of the dog. This neuroplasticity is necessary for specific memories concerning the dog to be maintained, but for this to occur, growth factors must be present.

Changes of neural organization can also occur in response to brain injury, presumably as an adaptive response in an effort to repair damage or to make sure that the functions of the damaged areas are dealt with by other neurons. Indeed, when a particular brain region is damaged, growth factors released from neurons or glial cells encourage neuroplastic changes in nearby neurons so that they might be able to take on the functions of the disturbed neurons.

Although BDNF is present across the brain, stressors are particularly apt to reduce this growth factor within the hippocampus, but in other brain regions that have been aligned with depressive disorders it isn't unusual to find that stressors increase BDNF expression. Interestingly, within the anterior cingulate cortex, which is important in decision-making and for the processing of emotionally salient events, the rise of BDNF expression was greater after a controllable than after an uncontrollable stressor. These findings suggest that as the organism learns about the stressor and how to deal with it, or perhaps simply as a response to being able to escape from a stressor, there is a greater call for growth factors to manage the increased neuronal connections that are being made.

It isn't certain why BDNF is reduced in some brain regions in response to stressors or in association with depressive-like behaviors, but increased in other regions. Nevertheless, it has been considered that BDNF in these brain regions operates in different capacities in relation to the symptoms that make up depressive disorders. The reduced BDNF in the hippocampus, for instance, may be linked with poor mood or the memory of events that stimulated this mood, whereas BDNF within aspects of the prefrontal cortex might influence neuronal processes responsible for cognitive and behavioral responses that support the negative thinking and biased appraisals that are seen in depressive illness. Rumination and confabulation are active processes that likely involve the establishment and engagement of multiple neural circuits which call for increased formation of synaptic connections.

Illnesses like depression and anxiety aren't readily attributable to any single process and it would be naive to suppose that a one-to-one correspondence exists between any single growth factor and depression or anxiety, and as repeatedly indicated, the processes that culminate in depression may differ across individuals. Hypothetically, BDNF may be a key factor leading to depression in one individual, whereas for another, FGF-2 or glial cell line-derived neurotrophic factor (GDNF) may be more germane. Indeed, as in the case of BDNF, stressors may influence FGF-2 and this was found to be disturbed in brain tissue of depressed individuals who had died by suicide. Likewise, GDNF levels were diminished following chronic stressors, and reduced circulating GDNF levels were associated with depressive features in animal models. Conversely, GDNF levels increased among patients who showed a positive response to electroconvulsive therapy or pharmacotherapy. There's little doubt that various growth factors contribute to stress responses and stress-related psychopathology, but it's uncertain whether they play different roles. It's hardly likely that nature or God created multiple growth factors that are entirely redundant, and we might find differences between their actions or the conditions that call upon them.

The past influences the future

Our biological systems are preprogrammed so that they are moldable by experiences, and sensitized neuronal responses ought to help us deal quickly and efficiently with a stressor encountered at some later time. Stressful events may promote or strengthen synaptic connections between neurons or sets of neurons, likely facilitated by growth factors, so that when we reexperience these events, particular behavioral and emotional responses are readily elicited. This is clearly a highly adaptive response, provided that these changes aren't excessive. Because sensitized neuronal processes are long-lasting, occur in diverse brain regions, and involve several biological substrates, excessive neuronal activation might contribute to the development of numerous disorders, including anxiety and depression, PTSD, and drug addiction, as well as neurodegenerative disorders, and may also limit the therapeutic efficacy of some treatments.

The exaggerated neurochemical changes evident upon reexposure to a stressor are not only apparent when the second hit consists of the very same stressor, but may also be evident when it involves an entirely different type of challenge. This cross-sensitization might even be apparent when the second experience comprises the intake of amphetamine or cocaine, which ordinarily engage many of the same biological processes stimulated by stressors. In effect, the response to particular drugs might be much more powerful among those who have experienced strong stressful experiences, and conversely, the use of these drugs might increase later stressor reactivity. In both instances, risks to health are elevated.

Many pathological conditions can diminish with particular treatments, or they might simply disappear with the passage of time. However, because an illness has gone, it doesn't mean it's gone for good. As neurobiological processes are subject to being sensitized and readily disturbed upon further stressor encounters, individuals will persist in being at elevated risk of a recurrence of illness even long after a stressor experience, or following the abatement of a stress-related disorder. So, unlike baseball games, it actually ain't over even when it's over.

Before you go...

The purpose of this chapter wasn't to provide a catalogue of neurotransmitters affected by stressors, and indeed those mentioned are only a few of very many that vary across brain regions. Instead, the purpose was to offer a broad perspective of how neurotransmitters could be affected by stressors, and under what conditions, as well as how these outcomes could potentially be related to pathology. Only a few neurotransmitters were covered and these were described in a rudimentary way. Increasingly more chemicals are being discovered that can act as neurotransmitters (e.g., endorphin, dynorphin, enkephalin), and gaseous substances, such as nitric oxide, can also act in this capacity, and many of these can be affected by stressors.

Neurochemical changes elicited by stressors are meant to facilitate our ability to contend with challenges and thus diminish vulnerability to pathological outcomes. However, there are limits to the effectiveness of these systems, and when stressor-provoked biological changes are sustained, as occurs in response to relatively strong, uncontrollable, chronic stressors, behavioral and physical disturbances might ensue. Furthermore, beyond the immediate effects of stressors, by promoting the sensitization of neuronal processes they may have consequences long after the initial stressor has terminated, being seemingly long forgotten. As we've learned more about the effects of stressors on hormonal processes, neurotransmitters, and growth factors, their importance in the development of pathology has become certain. Still, there are many issues that are unresolved concerning the links between stressor-related neurobiological changes and threats to mental or physical health. For that matter, it is often difficult to identify which of these serve in a protective capacity, which contribute to the damaging effects of stressors, and which are simply bystanders without any relevant function.

7

Immunological Effects of Stressors

Putting things into perspective

History has a way of making us appear so much more knowledgeable and astute than those of earlier generations. Why would anyone have thought that a blood-letting routine or drilling holes in people's skulls would have any positive effects, and isn't that business with leeches to draw out poisons really gross? However, before our hubris goes way over the top, we need to think that at some time in the future they'll be saying in wonderment that people in the early part of the twenty-first century actually resorted to chemotherapy and radiation to treat cancer, used powerful immunosuppressive agents to attenuate the symptoms of autoimmune disorders, and didn't even know how to deal with a simple flu epidemic.

It takes a fair degree of arrogance to be critical of researchers and practitioners who came before us, given the exponential growth of knowledge that has occurred over just the past two or three decades. Indeed, it wasn't long ago that basic medical texts declared that the brain and the immune system were independent of one another, and indeed this was the perspective prevailing until the last couple of decades of the twentieth century. Generations of medical students were trained to believe that immunological processes were disconnected from neurological and psychiatric illnesses, except perhaps in making some treatments a bit more difficult. If patients were being treated for an immunologically related problem or disease, this had little to do with behavioral and cognitive disturbances, or previous stressor experiences. Interactive processes involving immune processes and biological mechanisms related to psychological processes were acknowledged, but not really used in a diagnostic, prognostic, or treatment capacity.

These narrow perspectives have largely been abandoned and replaced with the view that multidirectional communication occurs between the immune, endocrine, autonomic, and central nervous systems. Recognition that hormones could affect immune functioning came fairly early, but there was more resistance to the notion that the immune system could affect the brain, and there has been increasing acknowledgment that inflammatory immune factors can cause or worsen psychiatric and neurologically based illnesses.

Stress and Your Health: From Vulnerability to Resilience, First Edition. Hymie Anisman.
© 2015 John Wiley & Sons, Ltd. Published 2015 by John Wiley & Sons, Ltd.

A brief look at how the immune system works

The job of the immune system is to fend off challenges that we encounter every day in the form of bacteria, viruses, and a plague of other invaders that seem to be hell-bent on causing us harm. As wonderfully effective as it is in protecting us from all manner of creepy, microscopic bad guys, our immune system isn't perfect and we occasionally do get sick with colds, influenza, and other infectious or bacterially related illnesses. As well, sometimes the immune system behaves as if it's confused and turns against the self, creating a different type of havoc in the form of an autoimmune disorder.

The notion that stressful events result in our immune system being compromised and hence lead to disease is intuitively appealing, and one that people seem to be inclined to accept, even if they are entirely unaware of hard data supporting this conclusion. In fact, when individuals develop an illness, they might be motivated to find a cause for their suffering, and thus might attribute their misfortune to stressors that they had previously encountered. Those who are more skeptical or rational might view this as happenstance and give limited credence to the assumption that since stressors and illness occurred contemporaneously, the stressful experience *caused* the illness. As it happens, however, controlled studies supported the claim that stressful events, owing to effects on hormonal and immune processes, might provoke some physical illnesses and exacerbate the course of illnesses that were already present.

It's become a cliché, but in explaining immunity an analogy is often drawn between its functioning and that of an army operating to defeat enemy forces. Our immune army, like any other, has lots of needs in order to operate most effectively. It must be able to recognize the enemy forces made up of viruses, bacteria and other microbes that are generally referred to as antigens, and it should be able to do this reliably. It's obviously not in our best interest for the immune system to behave irrationally or impulsively, leading to mistakes that cause the death of our own cells through "friendly fire" or cause "collateral damage." Being able to identify the enemy can occur either because it was met previously, or it can simply be deduced on the basis of the immune system's ability to recognize that a particle encountered is not one of us, and therefore might be a threat.

To deal with wily enemies like viruses and bacteria, there needs to be considerable coordination between the forces available, which requires effective communication between cells. Although the immune system is not as sophisticated as the brain in this regard, immune cells have the capacity to communicate with one another so that proper functions are conducted at the right time. Troops are needed to conduct a variety of different functions; some engage the enemy at the front line, slowing their momentum so that strong forces can be mustered to deal with the invader, whereas others make up the heavy artillery units that use several ways to attack and destroy enemy forces in different places. As well, special ops units are needed to go out on search-and-destroy missions, and there are those that wait in hiding to ambush the enemy. Once the enemy is defeated, a mechanism is needed to get the troops to stand down, especially if the immune cells develop too rapacious an appetite for killing and direct their actions toward parts of the self. But it wouldn't be wise to assume that the enemy is gone forever, as they might amass at some later time and present an even greater threat. Thus, immune cells need to have a memory of the enemy, so that if the bad guys reappear, immune cells are capable of mounting a rapid and a strong response before any damage is done. Napoleon could have learned a lot from the immune system.

Cells of the immune system

Immune cells monitor the organism's internal environment to sense the presence of bacteria and viruses, or look for damaged tissue that needs to be cleared. Recognition of threats occurs, in part, through the ability of immune cells to recognize what the "self" comprises, so that anything "other" than self can be treated as foreign. The information regarding what the self consists of largely occurs in the developing fetus, during which time immune cells are "learning" what's me and what's not. These recognition abilities are part of what is referred to as "innate immunity." An organism will also learn about certain viruses and bacteria through postnatal experiences, and this "adaptive" or "acquired" immunity plays an important role in defending us from agents that our bodies have seen on an earlier occasion.

Having been exposed to a foreign particle, several types of immune cells go into action to deal with the potential threat. These immune cells generally fall into two categories of white blood cells, monocytes and lymphocytes. The monocytes are attracted to sites of injury, where they transform into macrophages that break down foreign matter, such as bacteria and dead tissue, through a process referred to as "phagocytosis." They literally devour the foreign particle, after which a portion of the foreign matter is presented to lymphocytes, which then take steps to identify it, destroying the particle if it is deemed to be foreign, and establishing a memory of it in case it's encountered subsequently.

The lymphocytes comprise T and B cells that are produced by the thymus and bone marrow, respectively. One type of T cell, called helper T cells (Th1 cells), will make a decision, based on their experiences, as to whether a potential invader resembles anything the cells have encountered previously, and if there is a genuine threat, they will inform other T cells as well as B cells of this. Both the T and B cells will multiply so that an adequate force is available, and then they will proceed to destroy the foreign matter, but they do so through different processes. The B cells produce antibodies, or immuno-globulin molecules, which are able to recognize and indirectly destroy foreign matter by trapping it and calling upon other factors to help complete the job. This process is often referred to as humoral immunity as the substances involved are found in the body fluids (or humors). T cells destroy the enemy directly through a "cellular" immune response in which they directly bind with infected cells, rupture the cellular membrane, and deposit powerful enzymes that cause the viral contents to be destroyed. Viruses are treacherous little devils. They don't have their own DNA, and so these terrorists enter normal cells where they use the cells of our own DNA machinery to replicate themselves. Once these newly multiplied viral attackers have reached a sufficiently large number, they burst from the cell, and each virus is free to start the process again by hijacking the machinery of other cells. Thus, in killing infected cells, T cells destroy whole factories that are engaged in making viruses. Once the job of destroying foreign particles has been completed, a subtype of Th cell, referred to as a Th2 cell, inhibits further immune activity, and in doing so the T and B cells are less likely to attack the self.

In addition to these immune cells, yet another lymphocyte, dubbed a natural killer (NK) cell, can destroy foreign particles. The NK cells have the innate ability to recognize cancer cells or those that are infected with certain viruses and so travel about examining cells for appropriate markers which inform the NK cell whether they should be destroyed. Despite their menacing name, NK cells aren't as powerful as the T and B cells, nor do they seem to have comparable recognition and memory abilities. Their job is to serve as front-line troops that are, in a sense, dispensable, acting primarily to contain an invading enemy, so that other cells of the immune system have the opportunity to mount a strong response to deal with the virus.

Immune memories

One of the most significant aspects of immune cells concerns their capacity to retain a "memory" of invaders they have encountered previously. Once B cells are activated, some will become memory cells that remember an antigen and respond rapidly and vigorously should it be reencountered. They can survive in the body for years, thus providing long-term protection. The B cells secrete large Y-shaped proteins, referred to as antibodies, which can bind with foreign particles. The tips of the Y vary from one antibody to another, and because of this diversity they will be able to bind with virtually any foreign particle that appears. The antibody doesn't need to identify the entire antigen, but only needs to recognize a portion of it, just as we only need to see part of our friend's face to recognize who we're looking at. Once the antibody binds with the antigen it is marked for destruction and removal by other cells. There are five antibody classes, referred to as immunoglobulin (Ig) molecules, namely IgA, IgD,

Watch out

The notion that disease could be transmitted directly from one person to another directly, or through insects acting as intermediaries (vectors), was known well before an understanding of viruses and bacteria came about. But it wasn't until the mid-1800s that a fundamental understanding about diseases, such as cholera, was gained. Once again, when we look back we might conclude that our forbears were primitive in their understanding of diseases, but when you really think about it, we haven't come all that far ourselves. It was only in the 1980s that it was understood that the bacteria helicobacter pylori was the culprit for gastric ulcers, we still don't have a cure for HIV or vaccines to prevent its occurrence, we continue to have trouble treating the common cold, and despite decades of intensive research, most types of cancer still are bewildering.

The bit that was known about disease transmission hundreds of years ago no doubt saved millions of lives. There have been many historical examples where affected individuals were isolated from others. During the black plague (Black Death; bubonic plague) that appeared periodically in Europe, Asia and the Middle East throughout the fourteenth to eighteenth centuries, individuals who were infected were isolated so that the disease would be less likely to spread. During those times, ships that had reached Italian ports were kept out at sea for a period of time to confirm that the plague wasn't on board. Typically, this amounted to a period of 40 days, referred to as quarantena, and it is from this that we now have the term "quarantine." The duration of quarantine ought to vary with the disease being considered, as each virus has its own period during which it can spread. During the time that the United States was sending men to the moon, astronauts from some of the Apollo missions were quarantined for a period after their return to prevent transmission of contagious substances that they might have picked up. I don't know how they came up with the duration of the quarantine period. Moreover, if some sort of virus was brought back, would it kill the host, or would it permit them to survive and then become sick months or years later, allowing them to spread the virus in the interim?

IgE, IgM, and IgG, that have somewhat different functions, and appear at different times after being exposed to a foreign substance.

Once the memory of an antigen has been formed, the reintroduction of the antigen, or something that looks sufficiently similar to it, elicits a secondary immune response in which memory B cells are rapidly activated. Because of the rapidity and magnitude of the secondary immune response being mounted, the foreign substance doesn't have the opportunity to create a full-blown illness. For example, when exposed to the chicken pox virus for the first time, kids usually develop sores over large portions of their body and feel poorly for days. When years later this virus is again encountered, a secondary immune response is mounted so that the virus is destroyed before the illness reappears. This is generally the way it works, but in some instances the virus might not have been entirely eliminated, and remained dormant in the body. In the case of chicken pox, the virus is capable of hiding in nerve cell bodies, and may reappear as shingles, also known as herpes zoster (not be confused with the sexually transmitted herpes simplex), a painful condition characterized by skin rash and blisters on one side of the body.

Cytokines: messenger molecules of the immune system

Just as neurons can communicate with one another through the release of neurotransmitters, immune cells can do so, albeit in a more rudimentary way, through chemicals referred to as cytokines. In response to some stimuli that represent immunological threats, cytokines, such as interleukin -1β (IL-1β), IL-6, tumor necrosis factor-α (TNF-α) and interferons (IFN), are released by macrophages and lymphocytes in the periphery, stimulating the further proliferation of immune cells. These particular cytokines promote inflammation and hence are often referred to as pro-inflammatory cytokines. Although inflammation is usually seen as something that is bad, it actually reflects the efforts of the body to eliminate pathogens, damaged cells or other irritants, and sets the stage for healing to occur. These cytokines clearly have important positive functions, but problems can arise if their increase is excessive. Fortunately, there are other cytokines, such as IL-4 and IL-10, which serve in an anti-inflammatory capacity, and are involved in terminating an immune response once infection has been eliminated. Ideally, a balance exists between the pro- and anti-inflammatory factors so that overreactions don't occur in one direction or the other. Integrated responses are clearly necessary, and these must occur in a proper temporal sequence in order for the organism to be protected from external threats.

Immune–hormone interactions

The immune system has built-in regulatory mechanisms, and is also influenced by hormonal factors. Just as cortisol is released in response to psychological and physical stressors, it is also elevated in response to inflammation, limiting excessive immune activity that might otherwise cause adverse effects. At levels that naturally occur in response to challenges, cortisol sets a cap on how high immune functioning can rise. However, if actual suppression of the immune system is desirable, for instance in an effort to limit autoimmune disorders or to reduce inflammation associated with head injury or stroke, high doses of cortisol can be administered. In the latter instance cytokines present in the brain might have a protective effect on neurons during the period soon after a brain insult, but if cytokine levels increase excessively they can

Gut bacteria: yucky or not

I read the other day that more bacteria get to us from the ice we get with soft drinks in restaurants than they do in our bathrooms at home. I'm totally grossed out by this. Where do these bacteria come from, and can they make us ill? It seems that our bodies aren't all that pristine, no matter how many showers we take. Our intestine, it might not surprise you, is chock-full of bacteria. In fact, the human intestine was estimated to contain 100 trillion microorganisms, derived from somewhere around 500 different species of bacteria. Some of the gut bacteria are bad guys that cause the release of inflammatory factors that can contribute to inflammatory bowel disorder, depressive disorders, and heart disease, and these outcomes can be aggravated by stressful events. But before clean freaks panic over the presence of bacteria and run out for "cleansings," they should reform their perceptions of bacteria. Think of them as cute little puppies that will gobble up anything you put in front of them. In fact, most of the bacteria in your gut are good guys that help metabolize undigested foods, and prevent the development of potentially harmful bacteria.

It turns out that gut microbes, which as a group are referred to as the microbiota, can also influence the effectiveness of drugs used to battle against cancer. This doesn't just apply to intestinal cancers, but also to cancer related to other organs, likely because of inflammatory responses associated with bacteria. Given that antibiotics can affect the microbiome, and can even do so permanently, there is the uncomfortable question as to whether diminishing gut bacteria through repeated antibiotic use might put us in jeopardy in relation to cancer risk?

There are several illnesses that seem to occur as a result of gut bacteria not working properly, and as stressful experiences can adversely affect them, stressors could affect well-being through this route. As well, antibiotic use can overturn the normal balance of bacteria present in the gut, and may result in infection with Clostridium difficile, more commonly referred to as C. difficile, which leads to intense diarrhea and colitis. C. difficile is exceptionally virulent, with about 3 million new cases appearing in the US each year, leading to more than 100,000 deaths. The illness is treated through any of several medications, but its recurrence rate is very high, prompting the search for better treatments. It turns out that altering the bacterial balance within the gut is a particularly effective way of diminishing recurrence of C. difficile. This can be done through fecal microbiota transplantation obtained from a healthy donor. Obviously, if this is the treatment that's necessary, then so be it, although I have to say that this really undermines my whining about bacteria present in ice cubes.

be neurodestructive and elevated cortisol levels may act against these actions, thereby sparing the brain from still greater damage.

Although the effects of stressors on cortisol levels affect immune functioning, some of the immune changes are independent of cortisol. For instance, even mild stressors increase corticosterone release in rodents, but they don't necessarily suppress immune responses, and may even enhance the ability of immune cells to reach the site of physical damage. Furthermore, stressors also influence estrogen and progesterone, as well as epinephrine, thyroid hormones, CRH, and several other hormonal changes that are potent modifiers of immune activity, and hence may have a say in the development of pathology.

It was initially thought that cytokines generated in the periphery during infection didn't have much of an opportunity to affect brain processes. Tight junctions exist between endothelial cells that line the interior surface of blood vessels, so that large molecules, such as cytokines, are unable to reach the brain. This so-called blood–brain barrier varies at different sites and cytokines can gain entry to the brain where the barriers that limit access are less functional. Importantly, under some conditions, such as in the presence of inflammation and possibly in response to stressors, especially when encountered in early life, these barriers may be compromised, allowing greater cytokine access to the brain. Having entered the brain, inflammatory cytokines stimulate neurotransmitter activity, much as psychological stressors have such effects. In a sense, brain neurons interpret a peripheral immune challenge as if it were a systemic stressor and might thus contribute to the development of psychological or neurological disorders.

Cytokines, however, are not just manufactured in the periphery, also being produced in the brain by resident microglial cells. These cytokines aren't just accidental tourists, and it's a fair bet that they serve in some adaptive capacity. In rodents that have experienced physical or chemical insults (e.g., brain injury, concussive injury, seizure, cerebral ischemia, chemically induced brain lesions), as well as systemic or central challenges with a bacterial agent or by viruses, cytokine levels within the brain are typically elevated. Although not nearly as pronounced as those provoked by traumatic events, similar effects were also elicited by moderate psychological stressors, and the ensuing hormonal and neurotransmitter variations might then affect psychopathology. The increase of cytokines in the brain following severe challenges ought to facilitate the repair of damage that might have occurred, but if the cytokine elevations are too great, then a manageable situation may turn ugly.

The real offside of football

Traumatic brain injury (TBI), such as concussion, which doesn't necessarily involve unconsciousness, causes inflammation and an increase of pressure within the skull. The symptoms of concussion comprise headache and disturbances of speech, coordination and sleep patterns, as well as cognitive disturbances that include altered alertness, judgment, decision-making, and memory. Brain damage from brain concussion can increase over time after the head injury, likely stemming from the progressive and marked increase of microglial activation, and the resulting accumulation of inflammatory cytokines, as well as an increase of excitotoxins, such as glutamate, and the accumulation of free radicals. Still more damaging and more persistent effects are elicited among individuals who have experienced multiple concussive injuries, and having particular genes may dispose injuries to be more severe. It also seems that once a concussion has occurred, a lengthy recuperative period may be needed as reoccurrence will otherwise be high. Unfortunately, this period may be longer than the six-month off-season that football players have available.

Stress, brain processes, and immunological changes

As powerful, organized and efficient as the immune system is, it can be influenced by stressors, which can have ramifications on diseases experienced. For instance, stressors could affect the multiplication or killing ability of T, B, and NK cells, and it's possible that immune cells could become deficient in recognizing foreign particles that ought to be attacked. These effects of stressors have been demonstrated in laboratory animals (mice, rats) and in domesticated farm animals (fowl, pigs, cattle). Predator odors, social aggression, or social instability can instigate immune changes in animals, and similar changes are elicited in humans in association with ostracism, relationship difficulties, job strain, and illness. The nature and magnitude of the immune changes are largely affected by the severity and chronicity of the stressor, and may be influenced by many of the experiential, developmental, and organismic factors that were described earlier.

Consistent with the intuition that a highly adaptive immune system would allow for enhanced functioning upon initial exposure to a stressor so that a challenge can be dealt with, mild stressors elicit an immune surge that is accompanied by the redeployment of immune cells so that they appear at tissues where they might be most needed. As in the case of other biological systems, however, sufficiently intense or continued stressor challenges might lead to excessive wear on immunological functioning, so that diminished primary and secondary immune responses ensue.

One of the most potent stressors experienced by humans and social animals consists of negative social interactions. As we've already seen, this takes many forms in humans, and in animals it often comprises social defeat or social disruption where the dominance hierarchy within a colony is altered. The social stressors experienced by animals can be fairly harsh as they may occur on a continuous basis. The animals at the bottom of a social hierarchy have a lot to contend with, being the last to feed and to mate, and they are often bullied by more dominant animals, but the dominant animals don't get away unscathed either, as they have to defend their status repeatedly and need to continually look over their shoulder to see who's climbing up the ladder behind them. As social challenges persist, including being bullied repeatedly, immune disturbances begin to emerge, but once again further adaptive changes develop. Indeed, with continued social disruption over days or weeks, the immunosuppressive effects of glucocorticoids diminish. However, such an adaptation is less likely to develop if the stressor is sufficiently intense and varies over days. There are clearly limits to the adaptive capacity associated with stressors, and when social challenges persist they can promote or exacerbate serious health problems. Thus, it's a good bet that community-level stressors, including poverty, take a toll on immune functioning and increase vulnerability to illness.

In considering the influence of stressors on peripheral immune as well as brain cytokine functioning, it is important to take into account that reactions to immune challenges reflect dynamic processes that vary with the passage of time, as well as in relation to when a stressor was experienced. A stressor encountered soon after an antigenic challenge may cause the immune response to be dampened. However, if the challenge occurred after a moderate stressor was encountered, immune responses may be augmented. It seems that in the latter instance the stressor serves as a priming stimulus so that the immune system is ready to respond if necessary. However, there's an expiry time for this enhancing effect. If the interval between the two events is too long, a stressor may discourage or inhibit effective immune functioning, and during this period the capacity of the immune system to deal with a challenge may be compromised.

Stressful events affect immune functioning in humans much as they do in animals. Modest stressors experienced in laboratory studies promoted an increase of NK cells and IL-6 levels, whereas strong stressors, such as social rejection, altered the availability of some cytokine receptors. Chronic life stressors, such as serving as a caregiver (e.g., for a partner with Alzheimer's), may be accompanied by impaired immune activity in response to challenges. Likewise, ruminative behaviors have been associated with altered immune functioning, and among medical students undergoing the distress of academic examinations, T cell memory and functioning was diminished. As expected, effects of this nature varied in relation to personality characteristics in that the relationship of life stressors to T, B, and NK cell activity was most pronounced among individuals who generally had negative, depressive-like mood states. Paralleling the effects on immune functioning, stressful life experiences were linked to the appearance of respiratory infection, and conversely, resistance to colds was elevated among individuals who reported positive emotions and effective coping methods, especially those that involved social support.

The challenge of surgery

Most people likely view the anticipation of a surgical procedure as being fairly stressful, and the assault of surgery itself challenges multiple biological systems, although there are some people who willfully have themselves sliced and diced in the hope of looking better. Like other strong challenges, surgical stressors can impair immunity, and there is a possibility that this might contribute to postoperative complications related to sepsis and even tumor metastases, although there have been competing claims in the latter regard.

Fortunately, medical procedures have evolved so that some pretty gruesome approaches of the past have been replaced with more humane and effective treatment methods. Anyone who was around in the 1950s or earlier can tell you that a visit to the dentist was a nightmare. There was no such thing as having your tooth "frozen," and even something as simple as getting a filling constituted a visit to hell. The nature of surgery has changed equally dramatically over the years. In the *The Emperor of All Maladies: A Biography of Cancer*, Siddhartha Mukherjee describes the evolution of breast cancer surgery that leaves one shuddering after they read about the procedures used just half a century ago. Likewise, procedures that involved large incisions to reach the abdominal cavity can often be replaced by keyhole (laparoscopic) surgery in which a small cut of 0.5–1.5 cm allows access to organs. As a result, surgery is less traumatic and recovery is much faster. There is the belief that tiny robots the size of just a few cells will eventually be doing the work that's now being done with sharp instruments. Of course, there are skeptics who will say that this is a very long way off, and there are those who will tell you that human judgment is needed for complex decisions. After all, would you rather put your trust in a heartless, dispassionate computer chip or in a compassionate human, even if, for all you know, she or he came last in their graduating class?

Cytokine changes in response to stressors

With the realization that inflammatory factors are important in numerous illnesses, increasingly greater attention was focused on identifying the contribution of specific cytokines to a variety of psychological and physical disorders. Research in animals indicated that moderate stressors increased pro-inflammatory cytokines within the blood and in lymphoid organs, including the spleen and lungs, and levels of the anti-inflammatory cytokines were similarly affected, thus maintaining a balance between the pro- and anti-inflammatories. However, if the stressor was sustained and intense, pro-inflammatory cytokine levels circulating in the blood declined and an imbalance between pro- and anti-inflammatory cytokines was created, which could lead to adverse outcomes.

Paralleling the changes seen in animals, psychological stressors, like those of academic exams, public speaking, exercise, or caregiving, were associated with augmented IL-6 production, as well as increase of the inflammatory marker C-reactive protein. To some extent, the changes observed varied with personality dimensions in that individuals who exhibited cynical distrust exhibited higher IL-6 and C-reactive protein, and like some hormonal responses, the cytokine change was directly linked to the extent that the stressor condition increased shame and anger. Unlike the effects of acute challenges, chronic distress in parents of young cancer patients was accompanied by suppressed IL-6 production, and caregiving was also accompanied by a particularly marked increase of the anti-inflammatory cytokine IL-10, so that the balance between the pro- and anti-inflammatory processes weighed more heavily on the latter. Thus, under strong stressor conditions it generally appeared that the actions of pro-inflammatory factors were compromised.

What happens to cytokines in the brain may be distinctly different from the changes seen in the periphery. Stressor experiences might promote an increase of cytokines within the brain, which as we've seen can have positive or negative effects depending on the extent of the cytokine rise. It may be particularly pertinent that the cytokine increase can be especially marked if an immune challenge has occurred against the backdrop of a stressor, and could thus have negative consequences on psychological and neurological processes. Moreover, as observed in relation to other biological processes, once the cytokine levels have normalized following an initial challenge, the reintroduction of an acute stressor some time later can elicit a marked and rapid rise of brain microglial activity and cytokine levels. Such effects have been evident even when the initial priming involved a physical stressor and the later challenge comprised an immune challenge. Evidently, having previously encountered a stressor that altered immune and brain cytokine activity, vulnerability for future changes was elevated, potentially affecting neuronal functioning and pathological outcomes.

Before you go....

We're only beginning to understand the impact of stressors on immune and cytokine systems, particularly in relation to brain functioning. Nonetheless, it's certain that immune responses and cytokine functioning can be affected in ways that can make us stronger or leave us more vulnerable to pathological outcomes. Over the past couple of decades it has become apparent that inflammatory processes contribute to a

Revisiting Occam's razor

Occam's razor, the rule we're taught as students, is that the "simplest view is likely the one that's most correct." This sounded pretty reasonable during the 1960s and 1970s, but scientists conducting research concerning complex pathologies that involve multiple neural and hormonal circuits often come to realize that the simplest explanation is just that – the simplest explanation – and often simple explanations are uniquely relevant for simple problems. As we learn more about stress processes and newly discovered mechanisms are implicated in disease development, it has become clear that many of the explanations regarding stress-related pathologies that were adopted over the past few decades were far too simplistic. So, instead of Occam's razor, it might be more appropriate to cite Gilbert and Sullivan's *HMS Pinafore*: "Things are seldom what they seem, Skim milk masquerades as cream."

constellation of illnesses that aren't typically thought to be related to immunity. Inflammatory factors have been related to heart disease, diabetes, and dementia, as well as psychological disturbances. Moreover, as immune activation is accompanied by hormonal and neurochemical changes, and conversely, various hormones moderate immune activity, it is believed that stressors my instigate disease states by virtue of the immune, hormonal and brain neurochemical changes provoked.

8

Stress across the Life Span

Chaos

Near one end of the 9 × 4.5 foot felt-top table are 15 balls of various colors, aligned to form a triangle. At the other end is a white cue ball, which will be struck so that it smashes into the 15 colored balls, sending them moving in every direction. Let's imagine that we take two separate shots at this pack. The two hard strokes cause the ball to go down the table with similar trajectories, but the cue ball on the second stroke has a slightly different angle, say 1 degree different from the first. As the second ball leaves the original point, its trajectory increasingly diverges from that of the first ball, so that when it hits the pack it may be off by a small bit. Both strokes result in the 15 balls going in myriad directions, but the movement of the balls and where they come to rest are very different in the two scenarios, and largely unpredictable. One small deviation, just 1 degree at the outset, had markedly different ramifications. This is reminiscent of chaos theory in which minuscule differences at the outset can produce markedly divergent outcomes, and as a result predictions of the future become exceedingly difficult.

Small differences in our early development can have very different consequences on our developmental trajectory, and ultimately how we end up. Often, it's difficult to forecast outcomes, especially when there isn't just one minuscule difference at the starting point, but many differences. Yet, in a general sense, some probabilistic statements can be made regarding the future. Negative early life events will likely, but not necessarily, lead to negative outcomes, whereas positive early life events are more likely to lead to favorable outcomes. But consider that following the early experiences, whether these were positive or negative, there may be other events that alter the course of an individual's life. Some might occur through well-laid plans, and others by happenstance. When the pool balls were careening helter-skelter around the table, one ball might have ended up in a pocket, but it's just as likely that as a ball was heading directly for the pocket, another ball hit it and altered its intended route and the ball wasn't sunk. It's also possible that by chance the cue ball had its course diverted and ended up in the pocket. In pool that's a pretty crummy outcome, but sometimes that's how life is, and we need to be prepared.

Stress and Your Health: From Vulnerability to Resilience, First Edition. Hymie Anisman.
© 2015 John Wiley & Sons, Ltd. Published 2015 by John Wiley & Sons, Ltd.

One more thing. If after hitting the white ball, I were to place my cue diagonally on the table with the narrow end pointing at an end pocket, balls that ran into the cue would roll down it and into the pocket. This would happen irrespective of where the cue ball hit the pack. In effect, there are events that occur after the fact which can alter the course of events. Bad early environments, sickness, poverty, and so many other factors can push individuals in bad directions, but the effects of toxic circumstances can sometimes be undone by proper direction.

Connections over time

Stressors can have negative effects regardless of when they occur, but older people and the very young are particularly vulnerable to the effects of all sorts of life challenges. The very young, in part, because they don't yet have fully developed biological systems that can act against pathophysiological challenges and they typically don't have well-developed coping strategies to deal with stressors. Moreover, they're biologically and psychologically "impressionable" and the effects of stressful events can be carried with them for years. Older folks are vulnerable to the negative effects of stressors as they're in the process of losing their biological ability to contend with challenges and their coping resources dwindle as they age.

Few people would think twice about questioning the notion that stressful events experienced early in life would lead to profound, lifelong negative effects. It's one of those issues that everybody accepts, but rarely wonders about how or why this actually occurs. Yet, it does seem a bit curious that negative events experienced when we were very young, even if we don't remember them, could have the drastic effects that they do. This is the dilemma that Freud grappled with, until he came up with the notion that memories, perhaps in some symbolic form, were buried in the unconscious and struggled to emerge, ultimately influencing well-being. Regardless of whether or not this is the case, we still don't know how these memories got there to begin with. Indeed, these stressors might have occurred before language had been acquired, so that a cohesive and understandable narrative couldn't have been created.

A degree of plasticity or malleability, as we've seen, is a feature of many of our biological systems, and through this neuroplasticity stressor experiences cause the sensitivity or reactivity of biological systems to be permanently altered. In a sense, stressors encountered early in life are the seeds laid down that germinate during adulthood, but in this case the bloom can be either limited or much enhanced, depending on the nature of the early-life stressor experienced. Moderate stressors may result in systems being altered so that individuals become more hardy and more prepared to deal with later stressors, whereas severe or chronic stressors may undermine the organism's ability to contend with later stressors.

Prenatal experiences

Environmental toxins can affect the developing fetus, and what mom eats (or doesn't eat in the case of regions where food supplies are limited) may profoundly affect the offspring. It also seems that stressors experienced by mom when she was pregnant influence the subsequent cognitive, behavioral, and emotional well-being of her children. Of the numerous effects of prenatal stressors, the best documented comprise low birth weight and shortened gestation period, which can increase the likelihood of later childhood disturbances that might carry through to adulthood. Indeed, a daunting number of psychological and physical disturbances have been associated with prenatal stressors, such as increased risk of metabolic syndrome, insulin resistance and Type 1 diabetes, heart disease, allergies and asthma, and even an elevated incidence of cerebral palsy. As if this weren't enough, prenatal stressors were associated with poor mental development and cognitive disturbances, increased risk of attention deficit hyperactivity, anxiety, and language delay, as well as neurodevelopmental disorders, such as schizophrenia and autism spectrum disorders. Intuitively, we might think that such outcomes might only occur in response to traumatic or unique events, such as those related to wartime conditions, but they have also been documented in relation to domestic violence and work-related psychosocial stressors, and experiences of chronic racial discrimination and distress, and such outcomes were particularly common among the offspring of women who experienced multiple stressors.

So, stress makes you old before your years

At the end of each chromosome is a relatively small region, referred to as a telomere, which protects the subsequent sequence of genes from deterioration. As we age, the repeated cell division is accompanied by a progressive shortening in the length of the telomeres, and a similar outcome occurs as a result of chronic stressful experiences and in association with high levels of depression. As well, prenatal stressors and stressful experiences in children, including experiences of verbal or physical assault, or even witnessing domestic disputes, have been found to be accompanied by shortened telomere length. So, just as the rings of a tree can tell us its age and the environmental challenges it has experienced, telomere length can tell us about the cumulative effects of stressors. What regulates the stress-elicited telomere length isn't certain, but it does seem that the occurrence of heart disease and cancer, and even susceptibility to the common cold, increases with shorter telomere length.

Several companies have emerged that can inform customers about their telomere length and, by extension, vulnerability to age- and stress-related diseases. With this information, individuals can make lifestyle changes to thwart illness. I'm uncertain how valid or reliable these tests are, but irrespective of telomere length, the best survival strategy is to adopt healthy lifestyles.

Some years ago the notion was advanced that since certain hormones decline with age, then replacing these hormones ought to make us feel younger. The primary hormones consumed for this purpose are human growth hormone (HGH), which is converted into insulin-like growth factor (IGF-1), as well as dehydroepiandrosterone (DHEA). Unfortunately, these drugs have only modest effects on such things as bone density and have numerous adverse side effects. Recent trials have confirmed that increasing IGF-1 levels may reduce life span and increase the chances of death among patients treated for cancer.

More recently, there have been reports that aspects of aging can be reversed through transfusions of blood from the young, possibly because this blood contains a protein, GDF11, which ordinarily diminishes as we age. This treatment may improve brain functioning and improve the functioning of most body organs. So far, the "vampire therapy" has been used only in mice, but there have been hints that the restorative power of young blood might be useful for illnesses ranging from heart disease through to Alzheimer's, and it is possible that it will be useful for stress-related disorders.

As in the case of drugs that promote disturbances in the fetus, distress during the first trimester of pregnancy, and to a lesser extent the second trimester, were reported to be most closely associated with reduced birth weight, and there have been indications that stressors during late pregnancy were also aligned with psychopathology in the offspring. As we've seen, stressors have a way of festering, and the emotional aftermath of stressors can be persistent and draining, and diminished birth weights and shorter gestation periods even occurred among the offspring of women who experienced strong stressors just prior to pregnancy. Likewise, when a pregnant woman experiences a stressor, its emotional repercussions may carry over to the postnatal period, and thus effects on the offspring may be related to the behavior of mom during this time. The relative contribution of prenatal and postnatal stressors, as well the involvement of genetic factors, is largely influenced by the nature of the pathology at issue. Some disturbances are readily induced by prenatal stressors, whereas others are more pronounced if moms were stressed after giving birth.

Biological correlates of prenatal stress in humans

The fetus's intrauterine environment influences proper brain development, and disturbances of this environment can have consequences that persist through to postnatal periods and into adulthood. Although specific stressor-provoked prenatal neurobiological changes might be linked to particular pathologies, stressors might also create a "general susceptibility" to pathology, and the nature of the pathology that develops depends on the occurrence of still other factors. In this regard, the presence of elevated cortisol might promote preterm labor and reduced birth weight, which increase the likelihood of the development of later behavioral and physical disturbances. In line with this suggestion, prenatal administration of the synthetic corticoid dexamethasone has been found to promote hypertension in the offspring, and the synthetic corticoid betamethasone, which is used to promote lung maturation in fetuses at risk of preterm delivery, has been seen to influence infant temperament and promote elevated behavioral reactivity. It is particularly interesting that the offspring of mothers distressed during pregnancy exhibit a neuroendocrine profile reminiscent of that evident among individuals who have experienced early abuse or chronic stressors provoking PTSD. Specifically, their basal HPA functioning was blunted, but hyperreactivity of HPA functioning was evident in response to stressors. It is possible that prenatal stressors might have elicited their persistent effects by influencing the same neurobiological circuits that are altered by traumatic or chronic stressors.

As informative as studies in humans have been, more detailed analyses of the effects of prenatal stressors have been derived from studies in animals. Among rhesus monkeys and pigs, psychological stressors experienced during pregnancy can be as disruptive to the fetus as physical stressors. When these stressors occur during the development of limbic brain areas and the hypothalamus, neuronal disturbances will subsequently emerge that favor the appearance of anxiety, depressive-like behaviors, and persistent attention disturbances. Such effects may come about because prenatal stressor experiences have caused disturbances in the formation of growth factors, such as BDNF and FGF-2, which can be exacerbated by stressors subsequently encountered during adulthood. In this regard, particularly interesting data have been reported by Mychasiuk et al. (2011), which not only speak to the profound impact of prenatal stressors, but also make us consider stressors in a broader context. They reported that when pregnant rats were bystanders to another rat being stressed, their offspring subsequently exhibited disturbed neural plasticity, diminished neuronal and glial cells in prefrontal cortex and hippocampus, and impaired functional maturation of hippocampal cells. These outcomes persisted into adulthood and were accompanied by depressive-like behaviors and disturbed memory and learning abilities upon encountering further stressors.

Undoing negative prenatal events

The offspring of women who were depressed during pregnancy subsequently exhibited a constellation of behavioral and physiological disturbances. At seven months of age, they displayed elevated fear and anger responses, and their heart-rate response to a mild stressor was unusually high. However, these effects were attenuated among the offspring of mothers who provided a high degree of contact comfort to their children during the initials weeks of life. Likewise, although high cortisol levels in amniotic fluid measured at 17 weeks of gestation predicted poor postnatal cognitive abilities, this outcome was diminished in children with secure parental attachment. It seems that even though prenatal stressors might affect later cognitive and neuroendocrine functioning, these outcomes can be abrogated by a nurturing postnatal environment.

Consequences of prenatal infection in animals and humans

It's been known for ages that viral infection among pregnant woman may profoundly influence the well-being of their offspring. What we hear about most are the effects of a select number of viruses, such as rubella (German measles), in provoking hearing loss, cataracts, heart defects, and brain damage. The course of neurodevelopment in animals is also affected by prenatal infection through herpes simplex, and parasitic diseases, such as toxoplasmosis, so that offspring have exhibited a series of changes consistent with those seen in schizophrenia and anxiety, including deficits of attention, social interaction, and working memory, as well as changes in glutamate and dopamine functioning and diminished cortical and hippocampal size. Just as schizophrenia in humans typically emerges during late adolescence, it is significant that in animals many of the effects of prenatal infection were not evident in offspring soon after birth, but only emerged in adolescence. Moreover, the dopamine changes elicited by prenatal infection developed regardless of whether pups were raised by their biological mother or a foster mom who had not been infected. Thus, the schizophrenia-like symptoms were not attributable to postnatal factors, but instead were tied to prenatal infection. Interestingly, the symptoms could be attenuated by antipsychotic medication, and were diminished by treating animals with such drugs while they were still immature.

Prior to the development of vaccines, viral epidemics weren't uncommon, causing widespread distress and deaths, and even after the outbreaks ran their course, the consequences of the epidemic persisted. Between 1962 and 1965, a rubella outbreak in the United States was accompanied by 30,000 stillbirths, and about 20,000 children were born with some sort of disability. Subsequent studies that examined the link between that outbreak and other pathological conditions indicated that it was associated with a 500 percent increase of psychosis, so that one-fifth of individuals who had been exposed to rubella prenatally were later diagnosed with either schizophrenia or a schizophrenia spectrum disorder. Such incidents were not unique to rubella, as similar effects were also apparent in the offspring of women exposed to influenza during the first trimester of pregnancy, and contracting herpes simplex virus type 2 (HSV-2) can also provoke central nervous system (CNS) abnormalities, although for some reason this was less commonly associated with schizophrenia. The intracellular parasite toxoplasma gondii was also linked to neuropsychiatric disturbances, including a 200 percent increase in

A bad movie

We just can't help ourselves in wanting the underdog to win. Whether it involves a boxer who's a nobody, a group of geeky kids who form a hockey team, or the individual who fights big corporations, we celebrate their unlikely victories even though these feel-good sagas are infrequent outside of movies. Sometimes, the underdog isn't all that scrupulous or might even have an agenda that is self-serving. Based on his "research," Andrew Wakefield purported to have discovered that autism developed as a result of MMR (mumps, measles, and rubella) vaccination. Possibly because his arguments were persuasive, or more likely because people desperately wanted to find a cause for the disorder, his views were widely believed and parents increasingly refused to have their children vaccinated. But this was by no means a feel-good movie, and there was a twist to this real-life story. Wakefield's data were suspected of being fraudulent, and could not be replicated by independent investigators. Some say he manipulated the findings motivated by some sort of inner devil or a need to be the hero. His research report was eventually withdrawn from the *Lancet*, where it was first published, but by then considerable damage had been done: thousands of children had not been vaccinated, leaving them vulnerable to diseases. In fact, even now 1 in 10 moms either delay or fail to have their kids vaccinated, fearing that too many vaccinations cumulatively increase the risk for adverse effects despite the evidence to the contrary. Oddly, it seems that even after parents have come around to seeing vaccination as being okay, when they are provided with accurate information concerning the vaccine's safety they're actually more likely to report a decrease in their intent to have their kids vaccinated, perhaps reflecting a reawakening of their skeptical attitudes.

The anti-vaxxer movement has increased dramatically and has found support from celebrities, who for some odd reason seem to have great credibility, despite having limited knowledge of the subject. The net result of all this has been an increase in the incidence of illnesses such as measles, and the complications that arise from them. Recently, I encountered a woman who informed me that she'd rather her kid gained immunity by simply picking up measles at preschool than have a vaccine administered. "It's just measles," she said, "we all went through it." Impatiently, I explained that measles can actually be pretty severe, to the extent that almost 40 percent of kids might end up in hospital for treatment, and that it can cause brain damage. I added that approximately two out of every thousand children die of the illness, and according to the Center for Disease Control and Prevention, upward of 150,000 children worldwide die yearly, primarily in places where vaccines are not offered. She became increasingly indignant, accusing me of "buying into the establishment's propaganda," an accusation I hadn't heard being foisted on anyone since the 1960s, and so I played my trump card. Vaccination, I told her, doesn't always take. It seems to have little or limited effect in 10 percent of children, and with age the effectiveness of vaccines could diminish as well. So, if her kid developed measles, other kids, who had been vaccinated, might still be infected. As if in a comedy sketch, she sighed, rolled her eyes and said "So, what's your point?" It's sad to see a mind that has liberated itself from common sense.

schizophrenia. Clearly, prenatal challenges, irrespective of whether they comprise psychological, bacterial, or viral challenges, can have profound repercussions on the fetus that can appear soon after birth or might only become apparent years later.

Stress experienced early in life

When we consider the effects of stressful early life events, there is often the reflexive response of thinking in terms of abuse. In fact, however, there are many different forms that stressors can take that have long-term consequences and it has been estimated that by the age of 18, about 12 percent of children in the US have experienced maltreatment in the form of neglect or physical, sexual or emotional abuse. Marital conflict, for instance, can promote distress in children, which affects their subsequent cognitive development. In fact, a baby's brain, being as plastic as it is, can learn from experiences that arguments and angry voices represent stressors, and these events can have lasting effects on brain functioning. As well, stressors secondary to psychological and physical illnesses that children or their parents experience, as well as those that stem from socioeconomic difficulties, can increase vulnerability to adult immune-related disorders, heart disease and diabetes, as well as depression, anxiety and drug addiction.

The persistent effects of early life stressors may come about through any of several processes that are not exclusive of one another. The stressor experiences could promote the sensitization of particular neuronal processes so that later responses to stressors are exaggerated. Alternatively, the initial stressor experiences could alter the plasticity of cells owing to reductions of growth factors in cortical brain regions, resulting in neuronal interconnections being deficient, thereby influencing the development of pathology. The negative effects of early life experiences may also stem from the suppression of gene actions through epigenetic processes so that some neurochemical responses to later stressor experiences are disturbed.

Although one or another mechanism might be particularly important in the evolution of stress-related disorders, early negative experiences alter multiple processes so that the cumulative wear and tear on adaptive neurobiological systems increases the risk for psychopathological outcomes. Such experiences can result in the reprogramming of hormonal and immunological processes, and the nature of the pathological effects that emerge, as described earlier, depend on weak links that exist. For instance, stressors or mild infection encountered early in life can promote diminished receptivity and behavioral responsiveness to later estradiol and progesterone, possibly reflecting enduring changes in estrogen receptors within the brain. Likewise, among women raised in a harsh family environment, the cytokine changes observed in response to a later challenge were markedly increased, and individuals who experienced early life challenges were at increased risk for disorders linked to inflammatory processes as well as pain responsivity that can also involve cytokine functioning.

These neurobiological risk factors aside, the impact of stressors in children can be very different from those that develop in stressed adults for several additional reasons. Children lack the cognitive, emotional, social, and tangible resources necessary to deal with stressors, and typically have limited control over their own destiny, making them that much more vulnerable to the adverse effects of negative experiences. Children also might not appraise challenges the same way that adults do. They may not understand how or why certain stressful events come about, whether these stressful experiences are the norm or something happening only to them, or even what the potential consequence of stressors might be. These early life experiences, particularly if they involve interpersonal

What abuse breeds

Childhood traumatic experiences can markedly influence neuronal functioning of specific brain sites, such as the orbital frontal cortex, which is involved in decision-making and other aspects of executive functioning. In negative social situations this brain region is activated and seems to function to inhibit aggressive responses. However, in rodents that had experienced adverse early life experiences this brain region seemed to be turned off, possibly owing to the silencing of particular gene(s), so that animals were more socially aggressive. We can be pretty certain that negative events in early life also favor the development of violent offences in humans, although it's not certain that this stems from a disturbance of the orbital frontal cortex.

challenges, can influence how stressful events are appraised, which might even lead to warped internal attributions (i.e., self-blaming and self-criticizing) and negative cognitive styles. The trauma can also stunt a child's coping development and the ability to engage new and more effective strategies, so that as adults they might be more apt to use ineffective coping methods. For example, children and adolescents who experienced community violence, sexual abuse, or maltreatment were particularly likely to use emotion-focused and avoidant coping strategies often characterized by risk-taking, confrontation, and the release of frustration, rather than methods that might eliminate the stressor.

Given their limited cognitive abilities and coping methods, a child attempting to understand why abusive or neglectful experiences are happening to them might infer that these adverse events are stable, and attributable to aspects of themselves. As a result, these experiences may engender persistent high threat vigilance, exaggerated perceptions of future harm, heightened stress reactivity, mistrust of others, disrupted social relations, disturbed self-regulation, unhealthy lifestyle choices, and increased likelihood of further stressor encounters. It's not a stretch to suggest that, together, these characteristics could foster the processes that lead to the development of later depression, anxiety, and PTSD, especially when further trauma is encountered.

The negative consequences of early life stressors have been known for decades. Monkeys that were raised in isolated or poor environments subsequently displayed asocial behaviors, and markedly deficient parenting skills. Although they might not be as noticeable as they are in monkeys, the very same outcomes are observed in mice and rats. Rodent pups flourished when they had an attentive mom who cared for them well, and as adults they were relatively resilient in the face of stressors. In contrast, pups who experienced neglect subsequently exhibited disturbed biological functioning and high stress reactivity in adulthood. Indeed, there is considerable evidence that among rodents adversities experienced in early life may have marked effects on serotonin processes, and as we'll see later, epigenetic effects occur in relation to multiple biological systems that result in lifelong behavioral changes. In this respect, if stress-related fear responses were established in early life, they were resistant to being eliminated, and even when fear and anxiety could be reduced, these emotional responses could readily be reinstated, indicating that these animals remained in a highly labile and vulnerable state, and although they might have seemed to "get better," the potential for pathology resided just beneath the surface.

Taking the long view

Psychiatric disorders, diabetes, heart disease, and various immune-related disorders may have their roots in childhood stressor experiences. In fact, childhood
adversity has even been associated with premature death, especially among
those who had experienced multiple childhood challenges. Childhood poverty
has likewise been seen to be accompanied by disturbed development of brain
regions associated with executive functioning and decision-making, with the
problem becoming progressively greater as children matured. Of course, as
we've seen, not every early life stressor has disastrous effects. Those stressors
that are modest or "tolerable" might, with appropriate social support, allow
individuals to learn how to cope with such events, potentially making them
resilient in the face of future stressor encounters. In contrast, "toxic" stressors,
such as extreme poverty, psychological or physical abuse, neglect, maternal
depression, parental substance abuse, and family violence, are more apt to lead
to pathology. These stressful experiences encountered at an early age may have
effects that become biologically "embedded" so that their consequences will be
felt for years.

   Many of us have the unhealthy tendency to accept small rewards today, rather
than waiting for larger rewards down the road. We likewise have a penchant for
reaping benefits today despite the problems that will emerge tomorrow. This may
be true of our responses to potential environmental harms that continue, and
might also speak to why social problems persist in wealthy countries. Shonkoff,
Boyce and McEwen (2009) suggested that several changes of public policy would
be necessary to realize downstream social and financial benefits. Their proposal
involved considerable upfront costs and structural program changes and so it
would take some time before positive effects were realized. As they saw it, the
critical elements required involved reducing toxic childhood environments and
creating more early care and education programs that could serve as safe, stable
and responsive learning environments. This ought to be coupled with the expansion of child welfare services so that comprehensive developmental assessments
are undertaken that would facilitate professional application of appropriate
interventions. Importantly, they proposed greater emphasis on evidence-informed
interventions and treatments to deal with family mental health problems. The
changes proposed are in line with the views of most scientists, educators, and clinicians, but they don't get the last word, which often comes from government
leaders who want quick fixes for which they can take credit.

   Like mice and monkeys, human children who were raised in exceptionally
impoverished environments, with limited stimulation by touch or caress, frequently
suffered psychological and physical disturbances and exceptionally high levels of infant
mortality. In considering the impact of extreme neglect, we often point to the fate of
children who were raised in Romanian orphanages while Nicolae Ceauşescu ruled,
where the care of children was abysmal and the psychological and physical health outcomes were exceptionally sad. However, the attitudes and childrearing behaviors in
orphanages in Western countries during the first half of the twentieth century was fairly

Distinguishing between childhood stressors

Childhood maltreatment, such as abuse or neglect, may engender persistent reductions of oxytocin, which ought to be accompanied by diminished social interactions. Thus, it might seem a bit paradoxical that children who experience neglect related to being institutionalized are more likely to subsequently demonstrate "indiscriminate friendliness" that comprises an inappropriate willingness to approach adults, even those who are strangers. This is not to say that they form friendships more readily, only that they lack the normal inhibitions that most individuals show. These children showed amygdala activation in response to strangers, but this was also evident in response to their adoptive parents. In essence, their brain functioning didn't operate like that of others, but the implications of this for their later behaviors aren't certain, although the nondiscriminating brain changes might foreshadow social difficulties.

It is important to distinguish between different types of childhood trauma in relation to later psychological disturbances. For instance, although the distress of childhood cancer has multiple adverse consequences that carry into later life, the reduction of oxytocin wasn't one of these. Evidently, negative psychosocial experiences may instigate unique consequences that are not evident in relation to medically related stressors. Despite having undergone considerable distress, children who had had cancer might have experienced positive attachments, perhaps more than the norm, which would have protected them from the poor outcomes associated with early neglect or lack of attachment.

pathetic as well, no matter that this occurred unwittingly. The environments were sterile, and physical interaction with infants was limited, and the effects on survival and development were catastrophic. These extreme situations aside, a combination of toxic events and limited parental affection can lead to negative outcomes for psychological and brain development. In fact, the hippocampus of children from a positive, nurturing early-life environment was about 10 percent larger than that of children who were raised in a less nurturing environment, and it is thus predictable that children from poor environments wouldn't fare as well over the long run. On the positive side, even in the presence of toxic environments comprising poverty and poor social surroundings, many of the adverse effects were attenuated if children had received parental warmth and affection.

Transitional periods

Several phases of life involve changes or transitions that call upon our ability to adapt. Entering kindergarten or first grade can be considered a life transition in which mom and dad are temporarily replaced by new adults and a new group of kids, including some who are big and confident, walking around the schoolyard with a macho swagger, kid-sized jean jackets, and sneaker laces purposefully untied. Likewise, entering high

It's not the party you thought it was

Each year, millions of parents with bitter-sweet feelings send their kids off to university, often unaware that many kids run into severe difficulties, including trouble fitting in, loneliness, insecurities and financial distress, which sometimes culminate in intense psychological problems. The occurrence of clinically relevant levels of depression and severe anxiety exceeds 25 percent, and the incidence of suicide in students has been alarming. We can be certain that many more have undiagnosed or subsyndromal symptoms of depression and anxiety that might be risk factors for ensuing major psychological disorders. To be sure, for many young people the transition into adulthood is both exciting and seamless, but for others, especially those who are at the fringes of the "ingroup," it is lonely, challenging and distressing, and every day is filled with more of the same.

school, college, university, or the workforce, retiring or entering a retirement home are major life transitions that can be fraught with insecurities, and in each instance new social groups may be formed and new social identities adopted, and there may be a need for enormous personal coping resources.

Through infancy, childhood and adolescence, the brain continues to undergo considerable reorganization and expansion of neuronal connections. Stressors encountered at these times, including social instability as well as bullying, may influence the development of stress-sensitive brain regions and may increase vulnerability to stressor-provoked neurochemical and behavioral disturbances. Moreover, as observed during early development, fear responses established during this period are especially difficult to overcome, and it is thought that fear-related disorders more often than not stem from adolescent experiences. In fact, adults who had been bullied during childhood not only exhibited greater emotional problems but also physical illnesses that appeared to be linked to increased presence of inflammatory factors.

Adolescence can be an exceptionally difficult period, particularly as kids have an increasing need to "fit in." This means finding a peer group that will accept them and with whom they feel comfortable, and thus developing a proper identity. At this time interest in a sexual partner also takes on a more mature form (physically, if not mentally and emotionally). It's in late adolescence that yet another transition occurs as individuals move from high school to the workforce or on to university. This might involve leaving behind longstanding social networks and forming new ones, changes of personal identity as part of fitting in with others, gaining increased social, economic, and emotional independence, and forming new romantic relationships. All this is happening at a time when aspects of the brain, notably portions of the prefrontal cortex that are involved in appraisals, judgments and decision-making, still don't have all their neural connections fully established. In essence, this is an age during which individuals experience a collision between expectations and desire for autonomy, on the one side, and contending with a series of novel, stressful experiences, on the other. It is also a time when social support is essential, but when it isn't readily obtained, it might be sought in all the wrong places and wrong ways.

Older age

During the early part of the twentieth century the average life span was about 50 years, whereas now it's about 82. What's considered old by today's standards is very different from what it once was. Changes of lifestyle, diet, and working conditions have enhanced life span, and advances in health-related research have prevented or delayed death associated with illnesses. Science and medicine have extended life through heart surgery, control of diabetes, and the development of drugs to deal with viruses and to diminish pain. Further, some cancers are less likely to cause death than they were years ago, and the effects of stroke can be somewhat diminished if they are treated within a couple of hours after its occurrence. Significantly, it's not just a matter of people living longer, but often their quality of life is also improved.

Some "seniors" seem to age successfully, and remain relatively supple and healthy in body and mind. These are the people we see on commercials hanging around sunny beaches or well-manicured golf courses. Unfortunately, despite the medical advances, with increasing life span, frailty develops, possibly due to cortisol dysregulation, diseases of various sorts become more common, and for some individuals aging amounts to long waits in doctors' offices or hospital waiting rooms, day after day. Diabetes and cardiovascular, kidney, liver, and lung diseases affect greater numbers each year, and neurodegenerative illnesses, such as dementia, are especially feared and more common with increasing life span. Mark Twain remarked on this, saying, "When I was younger, I could remember anything, whether it happened or not; but my faculties are decaying now and soon I shall be so I cannot remember any but the things that never happened."

Aging is also accompanied by dispersal of family members to distant places as they find opportunities elsewhere, and with the death of friends the individual's social networks that are important for effective coping become progressively diminished. As family and friends disappear, and an individual's own ability to get around declines, sometimes leaving them housebound, loneliness may become more prominent, which itself is an exceptionally powerful stressor that could favor the development of illness. If all this weren't sufficiently distressing, aged individuals might feel patronized, dismissed, stigmatized, and/or made to feel either a burden or invisible, and as a result self-esteem tumbles, particularly as reliance on others increases and the sense of control decreases. Remarkably, elder abuse isn't all that uncommon as some caregivers redirect their frustrations inappropriately. So, the lives of older individuals aren't necessarily pretty, and the travails associated with aging can exacerbate existent pathological conditions. "Old age," as Bette Davis said, "is no place for sissies."

As much as older folks might wish it weren't so, there's no way around it. Like an older car, the wear and tear on a human body of 70 years plus is far greater than it is on a newer model. Driving on deeply pot-holed roads and failing to conduct periodic repairs make it that much more likely that the bumper or muffler will fall off, but unlike cars, it's more difficult to replace human parts. There has been the view that rather than just focusing on recent stressors in relation to illnesses, we also ought to consider stressful events experienced over a lifetime. Cumulative stressor experiences, in fact, correspond with cognitive deficits and biological factors related to Alzheimer's disease, and a study in which people were followed for 2.5 years (referred to as a prospective study) revealed that mild cognitive decline in older individuals most often converted to moderate levels of dementia in those who had experienced protracted stressful experiences. Even if older people aren't victims of dementia, in most instances a degree of cognitive decline can be expected, making them vulnerable to a different type of virus that comes in the form of telephone and internet scams (even if, as a group, they aren't great internet and email users). Older individuals tend to be more trusting, being less able or less inclined to "doubt" suspicious situations. In this regard, diminished functioning of aspects of the prefrontal cortex might create difficulty in the process that allows for disbelief, making them vulnerable to fraud, particularly among those who have unmet social needs.

Before you go...

Our early experiences, whether we're aware of them or not, can be baggage carried with us throughout life. These experiences can begin in the womb and during the early postnatal years, altering developmental neurobiological trajectories, social experiences, and our perceptions of the world in general. The neglected child or the school kid or adolescent who is bullied won't get by it quickly, and behaviors that emerge later may stem from these experiences. Whether we're young or old, all sorts of stressors can be encountered that adversely affect us. Few of us get through childhood entirely unscathed, but for those who come from a poor early life environment, later stressors have more powerful effects, especially as appraisal and coping methods may have been warped, and the ability to use social resources effectively may be disturbed. Stressors over a lifetime can also have cumulative effects so that the abilities and well-being of older individuals are affected. Regardless of age, having the right social buffers can limit the impact of challenges we confront, and having an appropriate social group with whom we strongly identify can go a long way in diminishing distress and its health consequences. In considering the stress process in relation to an individual's age, it might be useful to avoid simply assessing what's objectively in front of us, but instead see the individual in terms of the cumulative positive and negative events they have experienced.

On Memorial Day, November 11, in Canada, many thousands of people and a great number of veterans of wars congregate at various places to pay homage and respect to those who served. I'm always struck by the oldest vets, many in wheelchairs owing to infirmities, who were once young, virile, and full of beans. Their lives were shaped by experiences of 60 or 70 years ago, and I'm awed by their repetition of the Laurence Binyon poem in honor of those who didn't return.

> They shall grow not old, as we that are left grow old:
> Age shall not weary them, nor the years condemn.
> At the going down of the sun and in the morning
> We will remember them.

9

Cardiovascular Disease

The Little Engine that could

The ability of the heart to do what it does is remarkable. This relatively small organ made up of "involuntary" muscle and connective tissue is regulated by several hormones and is influenced by neurochemical changes within the brain. Its job is fairly simple. It receives deoxygenated or "dirty" blood from the body, and then pumps it to the lungs, where carbon dioxide is removed and oxygen is absorbed. It is then returned to the heart, which pumps the clean oxygenated blood to the body and brain.

This muscle weighs in at about 250–300 grams in females and 300–350 grams in males (9–12 ounces), but punches well above its weight. The first signs of the heart beating are evident a few weeks after conception, and keep on going for years and years. Over a life span of 80 years, at a rate of 72 beats a minute, the heart contracts about 2.5–3 billion times. Put in these terms, the heart is exceptionally durable and reliable. It rarely needs to go in for a tune-up, although it needs to be maintained properly for optimal functioning.

Each of the muscle cells that make up the heart has a beat, but because they touch one another and communicate with one another through pores known as gap junctions, these muscle cells beat in sync with one another. If these cells are thrown off so that they don't beat in unison, heart arrhythmias may occur. Like an orchestra, the natural beat is maintained by following the direction of a conductor or pacemaker that consists of the sinoatrial node. Not only does it make sure that while some cells are pumping others aren't taking a breather, it modulates the rate of beating based on the needs present at any given moment.

There's a lifetime warranty on the heart, and until a certain age, most people don't think much about its health. The heart just does its thing and they do theirs. At a certain point, however, individuals become aware that they run out of steam more readily, needing to rest more often when they do physical work, or feeling a twinge of angina. If it becomes obvious that things aren't quite right, we might become obsessed with thoughts about the waning abilities of our heart, and we might regret not having taken better care of it earlier, so that it could take care of us now.

Stress and Your Health: From Vulnerability to Resilience, First Edition. Hymie Anisman.
© 2015 John Wiley & Sons, Ltd. Published 2015 by John Wiley & Sons, Ltd.

Coronary artery disease (CAD)

Cardiovascular and circulatory diseases are the greatest cause of death worldwide, amounting to about 30 percent in most Western countries. Coronary artery disease (CAD), also known as coronary heart disease (CHD), which is the most common heart ailment, essentially reflects diminished blood flow to the heart leading to ischemia (lack of oxygen). Like CAD, several other heart-related disorders, such as hypertensive heart disease, have been associated with stressful experiences, as has the occurrence of stroke. Other forms of heart disease include congestive heart failure, which occurs when the heart is unable to pump enough blood to meet the needs of the body and organs, and cardiomyopathy, which consists of diseases of the cardiac muscle, as well as inflammatory-based heart problems, such as endocarditis (inflammation of the inner layer of the heart) and myocarditis (inflammation of the muscle portion of the heart).

Over many years, the cell layer within coronary arteries that comes into direct contact with blood, referred to as endothelium, may experience a build-up of plaque made up of cholesterol, fat, calcium, and fibrin. With the narrowing of arteries, slight lesions may form within the arterial wall, resulting in immune cells gathering at the site of damage. The ensuing release of cytokines, presumably in an effort to facilitate healing, promotes inflammation that supports further plaque formation over time, favoring the development of atherosclerosis and hence diminishing the flow of oxygen-rich blood. Coronary artery disease is typically diagnosed in men in their fifties or older, and in women somewhat later, usually in their sixties. The illness develops over many years, but symptoms usually don't appear until the situation is severe and blood flow is fairly restricted. Often, symptoms don't occur unless individuals are engaged in physical exertion or exercise that increases the need for blood supply to the heart. Other symptoms, including shortness of breath, fatigue related to exertion, difficulty sleeping flat in bed, nausea, abdominal pain, or swelling of feet and ankles, are needed to convince individuals of the seriousness of their condition even if their coping style is one in which denial predominates. In fact, individuals might only come under scrutiny when they feel chest pains (angina), or if they experience a heart attack (myocardial infarction, MI). The latter may occur under conditions that promote an increase of blood flow, such as the presence of psychogenic or neurogenic stressors, so that a piece of plaque may break off and this embolus or clot may produce a heart attack. A diagnosis of stable CAD is made when blood flow to the heart improves when exercise is stopped, or through medication, such as nitroglycerine, that increases blood supply. As heart disease progresses, ischemia becomes more persistent and lasts longer and the angina becomes unstable, being present even with minimal energy output, and myocardial infarction, arrhythmias, and sudden cardiac death may occur.

The heart's response to a challenge

Elevated heart rate is among the first biological responses elicited by stressors, being brought on by the release of epinephrine (adrenaline) from sympathetic fibers of the autonomic nervous system. Once the stress has passed the activation of the parasympathetic nervous system causes the heart to slow down. Occasionally, this inhibitory response might be too strong, resulting in bradycardia or diminished heart rate, which can cause fainting, dizziness or light-headed feelings, as well as nausea, sweating, weakness or heart palpitations. These feelings are not uncommon after a sudden stressful experience, such as a near miss in a car, or having to make a presentation in front of an audience.

Blood pressure

Most people have had their blood pressure measured at some time, and the physician has probably looked at them and said something like 120 over 70 with a smile on their face, or looked grimly at them saying 160 over 100. I'd bet that the majority of patients don't quite know precisely what the two numbers mean, but know that lower numbers are better. Blood pressure is usually expressed as systolic blood pressure and diastolic pressure. The former refers to the peak pressure in the arteries, which occurs when the heart (ventricles) contracts and forces blood out, much like the pressure when the garden hose is turned on. As arteries narrow as a result of a partial block, much as if we put our thumb at the end of the hose, blood pressure increases. Diastolic pressure reflects the minimum pressure present, which occurs before the heart contracts.

Systolic pressure increases with age, whereas diastolic pressure drops somewhat, and both these indices vary with gender. Generally, you'd like to have your systolic pressure at about 100–120 and diastolic pressure at 60–80. There seems to be a myth that systolic pressure should be 100 plus your age. That's incorrect. If you're above 140/90, you should probably see your physician, but even at slightly lower levels this action might be advisable so that prehypertension doesn't turn into hypertension.

Psychosocial factors associated with heart disease

Risk factors for heart disease include smoking, too little exercise, having high blood pressure, high levels of bad cholesterol (low-density lipoprotein or LDL) and low levels of good cholesterol (high-density lipoprotein or HDL), and being overweight, particularly in relation to waist–hip ratio. These features largely develop as a result of lifestyle choices, but there are factors that influence the development of CAD that are not of our own making, such as certain stressor experiences, conditions associated with coming from a lower socioeconomic class, or inheriting particular characteristics. Likewise, the progression of CAD has been linked to negative early life experiences, including those related to poverty and the individual's social environment, which includes the level of social support received and feelings of loneliness, isolation and unsupportive relationships, as well as emotional factors such as depression, anxiety, anger, and hostility. These are independent risk factors, and the likelihood of CAD developing increases cumulatively with each of these factors.

The influence of stressors on heart disease

Chronic stressor experiences are closely linked to CAD, which was elevated by as much as 25 percent among individuals who perceived relatively high levels of general distress, and certain situations, such as caregiving, were associated with a marked elevation in the incidence of heart disease. Such outcomes could arise because stressors affect several hormones, growth factors and cytokines, which can promote CAD, or they might come about because stressors influence lifestyle choices, such as smoking, alcohol consumption, reduced sleep, and noncompliance with medications, as well as other self-destructive behaviors.

Positive psychology and a healthy heart

Researchers and clinicians in the field of positive psychology are fond of indicating that the absence of negative events and feelings doesn't necessarily translate into the presence of well-being and happiness. If stressful events and depressive disorders promote CAD, does this also mean that positive events or happiness would enhance heart health? Being optimistic and experiencing high life satisfaction has, indeed, been associated with better cardiovascular health. A 15-year prospective study revealed lower risk for chronic heart disease among individuals who reported greater positive well-being, even after controlling for several other risk factors for CAD. A similar conclusion was derived from studies of individuals before they had signs of illness, possibly because a positive outlook creates a biological environment that actually strengthens the heart, limits the adverse effects that would otherwise be elicited by stressors, or encourages healthier behaviors, such as exercising, sleeping well, and eating properly.

One often hears that happily married couples have health advantages over people who are single, experiencing fewer immune-related disturbances and lower rates of heart disease. Conversely, having a nagging partner, male or female, appreciably cuts down on well-being, and promotes earlier death (what a way to avoid the nagging!). There's a good chance that living with a supportive partner can serve as a stress buffer, but it should also be considered that it might be less being married that attenuates the effects of stressors and more that living alone can create feelings of loneliness that may impair physical health. Loneliness is, after all, a very powerful stressor that has been associated with early death among individuals with a preexistent heart condition. Among people at risk for heart disease, death as a result of a heart attack, stroke or other heart-related problems was more common in those who lived alone relative to those who lived with others.

One would like to believe that in addition to limiting biological disturbances that lead to heart disease, positive mood might create a healthier heart even among individuals already afflicted with CAD. I suppose it may limit further exacerbation of the problem, but despite some suggestive reports, it's unlikely to provide a cure. Put it another way – although drinking poison may kill you, not drinking poison won't make you live longer than you would have naturally.

Although heart problems develop over years, acute traumatic events can have catastrophic effects, especially if an individual's heart is already in poor shape. Following the 1994 earthquake in Los Angeles, a 500 percent increase in cardiac deaths occurred; and the incidence of MI increased following the Iraqi scud missile attacks on Israel during the first Gulf war. Although we might think of these sudden, frightening events to be those most likely to "cause a heart attack," distressing events that aren't frightening, but are depressing, can also promote such an outcome. Mortality rates increase by 200–300 percent in the first month of bereavement, and among at-risk individuals, emotional upset can trigger a heart attack. Reading this, someone might think: "I don't have a heart condition, and so this doesn't apply to me." That's natural enough, but 20 percent of cardiac events brought on by mental or physical challenges occur among individuals without known underlying heart problems. As indicated earlier, most individuals might not know that they have a problem until it's actually fairly advanced.

Broken-hearted

When animals encounter a severe stressor, such as being captured or restrained, they may suffer "capture myopathy" in which they exhibit signs reminiscent of a heart attack. Somewhat similar signs, often mistaken for a heart attack, occur in humans who have experienced an intense emotional or physiologic stressor, including a romantic break-up, death of a loved one, or chronic anxiety related to other factors. Because of its emotional source this is often referred to as broken heart syndrome, although in the medical literature it is commonly referred to as Takotsubo cardiomyopathy, stress-induced cardiomyopathy or apical ballooning syndrome.

This emotionally driven syndrome is characterized by chest tightness and/or dyspnea, electrocardiogram changes and mildly elevated levels of cardiac enzymes (despite the coronary arteries being normal), as well as ballooning of the left ventricle, leading to a decline in the heart's ability to pump blood. The processes responsible for this syndrome are uncertain and its treatment has not been formalized, but it often involves drug treatments, such as beta blockers or those that influence another hormone, angiotensin, or just aspirin. The symptoms usually resolve without permanent damage, but there have been cases of broken heart syndrome leading to death, although this might be most common in the presence of other cardiac risk factors.

In a laboratory context, emotionally laden stressors, such as a speaking publicly about personal faults, provoke rises in blood pressure almost comparable to that elicited by exercise. In response to a psychological stressor, the need for oxygen is increased, and thus blood flow and blood pressure become elevated, especially if CAD is already an issue. In fact, in about half of CAD patients in whom myocardial ischemia (an imbalance between oxygen need and supply) could be provoked by physical exercise, such a response could also be elicited by a psychological stressor. As well, myocardial ischemia during the course of a laboratory stressor was also predictive of ischemia over the course of activity in daily life and was linked to risk of later cardiac events. Thus, it is particularly pertinent that antidepressant medication reduces the occurrence of myocardial ischemia induced by mental stress.

Job strain

To a great extent our job can serve as a way of coping with stressors and can bring considerable satisfaction, but it can also create chronic distress that increases risk for CAD. In fact, the Whitehall studies initiated by Sir Michael Marmot, which involved more than 18,000 British civil servants, and another 10,000 in the ensuing Whitehall II study, revealed that a strong relationship existed between socioeconomic status, rank within an organization, and heart disease (Marmot et al., 1978). Mortality associated with a variety of causes, especially heart disease, was less prominent among individuals in more senior ranks than those in the lower ranks. Subsequent large-scale analyses within several European countries confirmed these outcomes in both genders and across several age groups and socioeconomic strata, and indicated that MI was associated with elevated levels of perceived stress, high levels of depression, belief that individuals had little control over their lives, as well as work and home distress. These studies also revealed that the connection with social rank was not limited to risk for heart disease, but also applied to certain forms of cancer, gastrointestinal illnesses, chronic lung disease, back pain, and diabetes, as well as depression and suicide.

What appeared to be particularly important in predicting heart disease was "job strain," which refers to the psychological consequences of experiencing high job demands but having low decision latitude so that events ordinarily unfold without the individual having much influence or control. As bad as job strain can be, the risk for CAD and other illnesses increased still further if it was also accompanied by the perception of unfairness or injustice within the workplace or of obtaining low rewards for work performed. Not unexpectedly, other life stressors, such as marital discord, was also accompanied by increased CAD, as were chronic stressors that promoted anxiety, irritability, and poor sleep, and when a distressing work life was not met with a supportive home life, but one that was stressful, then the risk for CAD was further elevated.

Depressive illness and heart disease

As if clinical depression and anxiety disorders aren't bad enough on their own, these conditions are also linked to greater CAD, appearing in direct proportion to the severity of depression and feelings of hopelessness and pessimism. In fact, clinically depressed individuals were 2–3 times more likely to die from CAD and the odds of dying of a heart attack was 14 and 3.5 times greater (women and men, respectively) relative to nondepressed individuals. Depression that developed following an MI hindered recovery, was predictive of later MI occurrences, and readmission after apparent recovery was increased.

As interesting as these findings are, the fundamental question is why the depression–CAD comorbidity occurs at all? One possibility is that depression itself is very stressful, and hence may place excessive strain on the heart. Alternatively, both depression and CAD might involve a common element, such as activation of inflammatory processes, which could be aggravated by stressors. As well, the cardiovascular reactivity hypothesis has it that vascular alterations might arise in depressed individuals because they are highly reactive to stressful stimuli. Thus, it is not the depression itself that is responsible for the heart disease, but rather it stems from the high stress reactivity that occurs among depressed individuals. Whatever the mechanism, it appears that psychological and physical illnesses are not independent of one another, and it might be inappropriate to treat them as residing in separate silos. If nothing else, depression, regardless of whether it occurred in childhood, adolescence, or adulthood, might be an important marker for the occurrence of heart disease as well as other disorders, and thus family physicians and psychiatrists might be on guard for these developments.

Despite the strong relations between depression and heart disease, psychological interventions to reduce depression did not diminish the symptoms of CAD. But, then again, why would they? The physiological processes that culminate in CAD will have developed over years, and even if depression and CAD were causally linked, by the time medical attention was sought, damage to the heart had likely already occurred and might not be reversible simply by reducing depression. However, this doesn't imply that treatment would be ineffective in preventing further damage.

Feeling very exhausted?

When a person feels exceptionally fatigued and lacking energy, experiences increasing irritability and feelings of demoralization, a diagnosis of "vital exhaustion" might be made. These features are similar to those stemming from excessive work load or other adverse life events that aren't resolved, and are highly correlated with depressive illness, also often attributed to depletion of biological and coping resources. These symptoms might have broad implications, as vital exhaustion has been found to be predictive of subsequent MI, angina, and sudden cardiac death. Likewise, the presence of "somatic depressive symptoms" comprising fatigability, psychomotor alterations, sleep problems, and appetite changes was predictive of mortality following a heart attack. In contrast, the affective and cognitive disturbances of the disorder were less closely linked to mortality. Thus, the link between depression and CAD may have more to do with peripheral processes than those that involve brain functioning.

In considering potential biological factors that might underlie vital exhaustion, several reports pointed to the possible involvement of an imbalance between pro-inflammatory and anti-inflammatory cytokines, specific viruses, such as cytomeg-alovirus that is part of the herpes simplex family, or an overall increase of viral load. It will be recalled that stressors influence these very same factors, and as we'll see later, they have also been associated with depressive disorders. Together, these data point to the possibility that inflammatory processes represent a common mechanism underlying these conditions.

Socioeconomic status (SES)

The rich are different from the poor in many ways beyond those offered up by F. Scott Fitzgerald in *The Rich Boy*. Indeed, SES has been associated with health disparities, including CAD and several other illnesses. Lifestyle factors, including poor food choices and smoking, might occur more in low than in high SES individuals. As well, low SES is associated with more frequent encounters with psychosocial stressors, social conflict, greater threat of or actual loss or harm, and ineffective ways being learnt of coping with stressors. Low SES might also be accompanied by diminished access to medical care, health knowledge, and preventive care, any of which can lead to greater emotional strain and stressor experiences that conspire to affect heart functioning. As we saw when discussing allostatic overload, our "resource capacity" can be overwhelmed by stressful events, and those of low SES may be particularly prone to the overload that favors the development of CAD.

Sex-dependent trajectories for heart disease

Heart disease is the leading cause of death among women, as it is in men, but among women it is more closely associated with psychosocial stressors, depression, and sex hormones. In considering gender differences related to heart disease, it is important to attend to the course of the disease over the life span. Premenopausal women are less prone to heart disease than men of the same age, but following menopause, women readily catch up so that the incidence of CAD equals that in men. In premenopausal women who do not produce estrogen, and women who experience menstrual irregularities, CAD occurs more frequently. It seems that estrogen contributes to "female protection" against heart disease occurring prior to menopause.

Vulnerability to CAD among women involves factors beyond hormones or might involve interactions of stressors and hormones. Indeed, low SES is a better predictor of CAD in women than in men. Moreover, CAD was found to be lower if women were employed, especially if they were in higher administrative positions. But women often carry a load that men do not, namely that of both working and taking care of a family, and as much as work might serve as a coping outlet for many women, trying to juggle multiple demands may tax their ability to deal with stressors, thereby increasing the risk for depression and CAD.

Personality factors and heart disease

Type A personality

Certain personality characteristics had one time been taken to be predictive of heart disease. Early work suggested that individuals with the so-called "Type A" personality were at twice the risk of developing heart disease relative to Type B individuals. The Type A personality became a buzz-word to the extent that it now appears in our lexicon to describe individuals who are hard-driving, ambitious, competitive, impatient, hostile, and rushed. The type of person who wants you to get to the point quickly and occasionally finishes sentences for you if they perceive you to be too slow. In contrast, the Type B individual is described as living with relatively low stress levels, and while they take pleasure in achievements, they don't get upset when a goal isn't reached, and in competitive situations they're more focused on appreciating the moment than they are on winning. The Type B is also more contemplative and reflective, and they may also be creative; enjoying the act of exploring new ideas. As you read these descriptions you'll be aware that Type A was described in pejorative terms, and if you're Type B you'll be nodding appreciatively, thinking "Yup, yup, yup ... that pretty well describes so-and-so, who drives everyone nuts." If you're Type A, then that description might have bothered you, particularly as you think that you're not too hard-driving, overly ambitious and aggressive, but instead see yourself as dedicated and doing your best to get the job done, taking pride in being able to juggle multiple demands. In fact, Type A might see Type B as precisely the type of person they wouldn't want to be.

The excitement that initially accompanied reports regarding the link between the Type A personality and the development of CAD evaporated as subsequent reports failed to confirm the original observations. However, one component of Type A, that of elevated anger or hostility, was related to CAD. In this regard, there are individuals who express their anger openly (anger-out), and there are those who seal it up, or even castigate themselves for things going wrong (anger-in), and it might be the latter types who are most vulnerable to CAD. Occasionally becoming angry isn't necessarily a bad thing, and in certain situations, as in the case of facing discrimination, it may be a useful coping mechanism that leads to collective action. However, being angry and hostile all or a lot of the time is another thing entirely. As Buddha is thought to have said, "Holding onto anger is like drinking poison and expecting the other person to die."

Linking specific genes to CAD

Coronary artery disease was thought to be related to genetic factors, but only in the past decade have genome-wide studies been conducted to assess which genes might be related to CAD. Numerous gene variants were identified that likely contribute to CAD, with the presence of each variant increasing the odds of heart disease by differing amounts. Importantly, however, they have additive effects so that individuals carrying multiple variants are at progressively greater risk of CAD.

A single nucleotide polymorphism has been discovered in the gene for the 5-HT2C serotonin receptor in about 13 percent of people, which may be linked to heart disease and heart attack. In the presence of this SNP individuals ordinarily did not display altered cortisol levels, but when they were stressed their cortisol levels increased to twice those of individuals who did not carry this polymorphism. The increased cortisol was also related to their anger and depression, both of which are also predictive of heart disease. There is a possibility that cortisol increases a particular enzyme, MMP9, which softens plaque, possibly making it more likely to rupture, thereby creating clots that provoke heart attack.

Type D personality

The disappointment regarding the tie between the Type A personality and CAD didn't diminish the search for other personality types that might predict heart disease. One personality characteristic, the Type D or "distressed" personality, seemed particularly relevant, and was associated with increased occurrence of CAD as well as increased risk of MI, angina, and ischemic heart disease following an initial cardiac event. The Type D personality is characterized by the tendency to frequently experience negative emotions (e.g., depressed mood, anxiety, anger, and hostile feelings), to be particularly attentive to negative stimuli, to have limited ties to others and be inhibited and insecure in social interactions, uncomfortable with strangers, and to worry a lot.

In light of the broadly known effects of stressors on cortisol levels, it has become the bogeyman in relation to all sorts of stress-related illnesses. In fact, the link to CAD is impressive given that stressor-provoked cortisol elevations are persistent in those with a Type D personality, as well as among individuals who express anger. While not denying that cortisol might contribute to heart disease, especially in those with a Type D personality, we need to remember that cortisol is only one of many biological processes affected by stressors, and there may be other neurobiological factors that act in this capacity.

Physiological stress responses associated with heart disease

Sympathetic nervous system reactivity

Sympathetic nervous system activation, which is accompanied by increased blood flow and pressure, is a fundamental stress response that helps us deal with a situation by increasing oxygen availability. However, if sympathetic activation is persistent, hypertension, atherosclerosis, enlargement of the heart, and arrhythmia can develop. This is particularly notable among "hot reactors," who readily exhibit sympathetic hyperreactivity in response to challenges, but less so among "cold reactors." Based on studies in

Changing times, changing treatments

As norepinephrine and epinephrine were associated with sympathetic activation, treatments of some heart-related problems, such as high blood pressure, were focused on drugs that affect the functioning of these transmitters. Thus, beta blockers, so called because they act as antagonists of beta-norepinephrine receptors, became among the most widely use medications in the treatment of high blood pressure.

There are about 20 different drugs on the market which serve as beta blockers, and it has been estimated that until recently 200 million prescriptions were written in the US each year. However, the bloom seems to be off that rose as beta blockers don't get at the root problem responsible for the elevated blood pressure. In fact, they may cause a disservice to patients who might mistakenly believe that since their blood pressure has come down, they can still go on with whatever poor lifestyle factors they had engaged in earlier. Most damningly, a prospective study conducted with 45,000 cardiac patients over three years revealed that beta blockers didn't reduce the risk for MIs, deaths associated with MIs, or stroke. As well, beta blockers used in association with noncardiac surgery had the effect of increasing the possibility of experiencing a cardiac event. There is a sunny side to this. Newer and more effective drugs have been developed and used routinely, including statins to reduce cholesterol levels, as well as newer types of antihypertensives and anticoagulants.

monkeys who were hot reactors (yes, it happens in species other than humans – we're not that special in this regard), atherosclerotic lesions might be especially common among those consuming a high-fat diet.

Although sympathetic nervous system functioning has been a primary focus in relation to CAD, activation of the heart is influenced by norepinephrine and glutamate functioning within the hypothalamus as well as by neuronal activity within brain regions involved in emotional processing and decision-making. In this respect, differences that were observed with respect to stressor-evoked blood pressure reactivity were paralleled by unique activation patterns in cortical and limbic brain areas, and it's likely that brain regions responsible for appraisal or reactivity processes are fundamental for the development of CAD among hot reactors. As well, the locus coeruleus, a brain region known to be involved in vigilance under stressful situations, has been linked to parasympathetic functioning that influences the heart, and might turn out to have considerable relevance in the development of treatments to deal with stress-related disorders.

Inflammatory processes in heart disease

Immune cells, such as macrophages, go to sites of damage in the body, including within blood vessels, in an effort to facilitate healing. But there are occasions where immune-related factors, including cytokines released in response to stressors, end up creating harm. It might be hoped that if inflammatory factors actually contribute to the development of CAD, then altering immune-related processes would influence heart disease. In fact, however, the anti-inflammatory agent celecoxib did not provide

Markers of heart disease

C-reactive protein (CRP) as well as fibrinogen are manufactured in the liver and then released into the blood in response to inflammation. CRP is often used as a marker of whether or not inflammation is present, as well as a biomarker to predict subsequent cardiovascular problems, although it says little about the source of the inflammation. Its usefulness has been reinforced by the finding that statins, such as the drug Lipitor, which is used as a cholesterol buster, are associated with reduced CRP. Other markers of inflammation, such as elevated levels of IL-6 and fibrinogen, have also been found to be associated with fatal heart attack and stroke, but not those of a nonfatal nature. It might be that these inflammatory markers signal that problems have become pronounced, hence the fatal outcomes, or it might be that cardiovascular events that are linked to inflammatory processes are more catastrophic than others.

encouraging results in this regard. Likewise, despite the presumed involvement of TNF-α in heart disease, the anti-TNF-α agents, etanercept or infliximab, did not reduce CAD and even caused further problems. There had at one point been indications that TNF-α antagonists might prove useful in the treatment of cardiac problems related to rheumatoid arthritis, but these efforts have now been abandoned. As indicated in discussing the potential for antidepressants to have an effect on heart disease, inflammatory processes might cause an illness by creating a physical change in the artery, in this case narrowing the arteries. But, once this has occurred, administering an anti-inflammatory might have little positive effect. It essentially amounts to closing the proverbial barn door after the horse is gone. However, anti-inflammatory treatments could be useful in a prophylactic capacity and so your doctor might recommend you take a daily dose of baby aspirin.

Stress, pathogen burden, and heart disease

Heart disease and heart failure occur at a particularly high rate in people with chronic inflammatory disorders, such as inflammatory bowel disorder (IBD). Not only was IBD accompanied by a 37 percent increase of heart disease, but the frequency of hospitalization more than doubled during IBD flare-ups. Increased risk for cardiac illness has also been associated with chronic infection, such as gingivitis, Helicobacter pylori (also associated with ulcers), Chlamydia pneumoniae (which is associated with pneumonia), cytomegalovirus (which is associated with herpes), and some gut microbes which could create inflammation that might affect CAD. It is likely that there isn't a single bacterial or viral agent that is uniquely linked to CAD, but instead, it may be that the total number of infections experienced, referred to as the pathogen burden, was most closely tied to heart problems. It might not be entirely productive to think exclusively of pathogens as the source of inflammation that affects CAD. As we've seen, inflammatory processes can also be activated by stressful events, and when stressors and bacterial agents are present concurrently, they can synergistically influence brain processes and several hormones, including heart-related hormones, such as atrial natriuretic peptide (ANP), which may be markers of cardiovascular disturbance.

Reactive oxygen species, gut bacteria, and your heart

We've seen that the rule for most things related to our well-being is "not too much, not too little," and this also applies to our use of oxygen. All of our cells need oxygen, producing what is called reactive oxygen species (RAS) that are ordinarily beneficial. We have several adaptive mechanisms present that work so that the oxygen can do the work necessary. However, under conditions where cells are stressed by internal factors, overproduction of these radical oxygen species may ensue, which can be damaging to cells. This oxidative stress might contribute to a variety of illnesses, including neurodegenerative disorders, such as Alzheimer's and Parkinson's disease, and autoimmune disorders, such as rheumatoid arthritis, as well as to cancer and cardiovascular disease. As psychologically stressful experiences can have pronounced effects on oxidative processes, negative events and how we deal with them can affect disease processes through this route.

Like certain fruits and vegetables, gut bacteria produce carotenoids that act as antioxidants, and thus might help prevent heart disease and stroke. In fact, individuals who eat foods rich in carotenoids (e.g., sweet potatoes, carrots, pumpkin, spinach, broccoli, cantaloupe melons and apricots) tend to be healthier and live longer than those who eat these foods less often. These notions have been around for years, leading many people to consume dietary supplements containing carotenoids in an effort to improve their health. However, the use of these supplements may not provide health benefits beyond those received from proper eating, and may even have some negative effects, especially in smokers. Rather than using supplements, it might be advantageous to consume bacteria that make carotenoids, as these bacteria could, after all, be doing something beyond simply making the antioxidant. However, I can imagine that marketing bacteria to make you healthier might be a tough sell, unless of course, it's disguised as yogurt. This said, it's likely premature to promote yogurt consumption to prevent heart attack, but as in the case of the chicken soup, "it couldn't hurt."

Obesity, cytokines, and heart disease

Obesity and the presence of body fat are associated with atherosclerosis, although not all cultural groups are equally affected. How and why does this illness develop in those who are obese? Is being overweight a strain that wears down the heart, or does being heavy reduce the propensity for getting involved in exercise that could potentially improve heart functioning? Alternatively, are some health professionals negatively inclined toward obese patients so that their treatment is affected? In fact, these and others factors likely contribute, either directly or indirectly, to the processes that lead to CAD. But, more than these influences, fat cells are a rich source for inflammatory cytokines that contribute to the development of CAD and other forms of heart disease and stroke, and the increased presence of fat cells has also been linked to colorectal cancer, endometrial and postmenopausal breast cancer, Type 2 diabetes, and gall bladder disease. There has been a bit of a myth circulating that obesity might not be bad for all people, and indeed, there may be some individuals for whom this might be the case. Yet, given the long list of potential illnesses that can develop, it's probably better to eat right, exercise, and slim down.

Before you go…

Heart disease is usually a progressive illness that involves numerous antecedent psychological and physiological processes, and is related to age and sex. The occurrence of depressive disorders is highly predictive of later CAD, and as psychosocial stressors markedly influence depression, it is understandable that such experiences would exert negative effects on cardiovascular health. As we've seen repeatedly, however, the response to stressors can be influenced by several other experiential and personality variables, and in the case of heart disease, low socioeconomic status and personality features, such as the Type D personality, hostility, and anxiety, are linked to heart disease.

Heart disease doesn't simply occur overnight, and typically it is influenced by the cumulative effects of several risk factors operating over lengthy periods. In this regard, events that promote inflammatory responses, including stressors, promote changes in the levels and turnover of neurotransmitters and growth factors that influence the development of depression and also influence CAD, and when stressors and inflammatory cytokine activation occur at the same time, the development of these disturbances is synergistically increased. Ultimately, these and other influences, including epigenetic changes related to hormonal and inflammatory processes, culminate in increased plaque formation. As the molecular processes related to heart dysfunction are uncovered, more effective medications can be expected, but as in the case of so many other illnesses, prevention and intervention is much more desirable than attempting to heal a damaged heart. So, as intimated at the beginning of this chapter, "take good care of your heart and it will take good care of you."

10

Diabetes

A brief walk through the history of diabetes

Descriptions of illnesses that seemed like diabetes have been around for many centuries, although its occurrence was likely infrequent. It appeared to be recognized in Egypt as early as 1500 BCE and early Indian physicians described it as an illness that was accompanied by sweet urine, possibly associated with the consumption of rice, flour, and foods high in sugar. Physicians in early Chinese, Greek, Japanese, Indian, Korean, and Persian cultures also seemed to know about diabetes, but it wasn't until the later nineteenth century that serious efforts were devoted to understanding the processes that led to this disorder, and it was at about this time that dietary factors were more formally implicated in the disease. With the discovery of insulin by Sir Edward Albert Sharpey-Schafer in 1910 and its extraction and use by Frederick Banting and Charles Best in 1921, the grim fate of young diabetic individuals was altered. However, this treatment had little effect on those with late onset diabetes, which often developed in middle or late middle age. It was soon recognized that two forms of diabetes existed, one that appeared in the young and the other that appeared in older individuals. The former came to be known as Type 1 diabetes and was managed by insulin injections, whereas late onset or Type 2 diabetes was more aligned with insensitivity to insulin. The latter began to be taken more seriously with the recognition that those affected were much more likely to experience heart and kidney disease as well as several other disorders.

Over the ensuing decades, simpler ways of detecting diabetes were developed, as were several new treatment strategies and ways of administering insulin. A biosynthetic form of insulin was developed, and it was increasingly understood that poor diet, coupled with limited exercise, were major culprits responsible for Type 2 diabetes. Today, the expression that diabetes has reached "epidemic" levels is commonly heard, but the term was used by Elliott Joslin as early as 1921 in reference to diabetes. The growth of diabetes from a rarely occurring illness to one that affects hundreds of millions of people is likely due, in part, to the

Stress and Your Health: From Vulnerability to Resilience, First Edition. Hymie Anisman.
© 2015 John Wiley & Sons, Ltd. Published 2015 by John Wiley & Sons, Ltd.

increased life span that allows diabetes to emerge, coupled with the greater prevalence of poor diet, limited exercise, obesity, poor sleep, and the presence of depression. Essentially, this disease influences how long we live, and develops in great measure on the basis of how we live.

Type 1 diabetes

Type 1 diabetes develops when insulin-producing beta cells in the pancreas are destroyed. Insulin is essential for body cells to take up sugars from the blood, and so while these cells were starving, the elevated sugars in the blood damaged various organs in the body. The typical symptoms of Type 1 diabetes comprise frequent urination, elevated thirst and hunger, and weight loss, which generally disappear when insulin levels are increased by injection of this hormone. However, if it isn't kept under control, diabetes may promote a wide range of health problems, including cardiovascular and circulatory problems, stroke, kidney failure, visual problems, neuropathy that comprises tingling, numbness, or weakness in the hands and feet as a result of problems related to nerves that connect to the spinal cord, and limb amputation, and it might even contribute to hippocampal disturbances and may promote dementia.

Several views have been offered as to how this disorder comes about, the most prominent being that this disease is an autoimmune disorder, stemming from genetic, chemical and environmental factors, including viruses. Even though diabetes can be controlled by insulin injections several times during the day or through a pump that slowly delivers insulin, thereby diminishing the likelihood of kidney failure, it might not be equally effective in reducing the frequency of heart disease and stroke.

Type 2 diabetes

The presence of type 2 diabetes is not due to a complete lack of beta cells, but occurs when there is a relative diminution of insulin or when insulin resistance occurs, essentially meaning that the body is less able to produce and use insulin as it should. The symptoms of Type 2 diabetes are much the same as those of the Type 1 form, but it is usually treated by diets that reduce sugar production, and by exercise, as well as drugs, such as metformin, that limit sugar release from the liver.

Type 2 diabetes has become increasingly common, with about 300 million people worldwide currently being diabetic, and this figure is projected to increase to 400 million within 20 years. Millions more are probably undiagnosed diabetics or prediabetic, which means that their glucose levels haven't yet reached the level that calls for a diagnosis of diabetes or full treatment. The illness appears across developed and underdeveloped countries, in both men and women, and it is especially common among older individuals, but the incidence in young people under the age of 20 has increased by about 30 percent. Too often, Type 2 diabetes may lead to other illnesses, such as kidney failure, heart disease, brain atrophy, and cognitive decline, as well as a doubling in the frequency of Alzheimer's disease and vascular dementia, and early intervention to diminish the occurrence of diabetes may attenuate the course of comorbid illnesses, such as heart disease. Indeed, among individuals at high risk, intervention programs

Metabolic syndrome is a bummer

Metabolic syndrome, a frequent antecedent of Type 2 diabetes, is characterized by disturbed fasting glucose levels (before any food is eaten in the morning) or insulin resistance wherein cells don't respond to insulin as they should. In addition, a diagnosis of metabolic syndrome requires that at least two additional features be present, comprising either elevated blood pressure, high triglycerides, diminished levels of "good" high-density lipoprotein cholesterol (HDL), obesity, or elevation of urinary albumin excretion, the latter possibly being indicative of cardiovascular and kidney disease.

Metabolic syndrome frequently develops as a result of poor lifestyle habits and experiencing chronically stressful events. The syndrome often is accompanied by elevated visceral fat, although not every person who is overweight is plagued by metabolic syndrome. These fat cells release chemicals, related to inflammatory processes that can encourage depression, heart disease and other vascular illnesses, including impaired wound healing that may lead to amputation, as well as rheumatic diseases, such as rheumatoid arthritis and osteoarthritis.

Despite the dangers of metabolic syndrome, it's remarkable that many people simply don't understand its significance. An acquaintance, after a recent medical examination that he gets every year or so, commented that "my doctor told me I've got metabolic syndrome and that I should be dieting. But the good news is that I'm otherwise healthy as an ox."

comprising either lifestyle changes or drug treatments to reduce sugars released from the liver markedly reduced diabetes, with the former of the two interventions being somewhat superior.

Stressor influences in relation to the development of Type 2 diabetes

Although stressor experiences have been linked to the development of Type 2 diabetes, there is some debate as to whether stressors cause diabetes or allow for the features of diabetes to be unmasked in highly vulnerable individuals, particularly when other risk factors are also present, such as obesity. Stressors, by causing the release of cortisol, may hinder the actions of insulin, thereby aggravating the course of the illness. As well, stressors can encourage diabetes by modifying lifestyle factors, such as poor selection of the foods consumed and failure to engage in proper physical exercise. Regardless of how it's seen, stressors have been associated with poorer outcomes and for those who are already diabetic, psychosocial stressors may instigate poor control over the management of diabetes. It is well known, as well, that PTSD and chronic depression are aligned with the occurrence of diabetes. These comorbid conditions may have additive or synergistic actions in that the risk of dying from heart disease has been seen to markedly increase, and among highly stressed diabetic individuals a twofold increase of dementia has been observed, as has faster memory loss among those with Alzheimer's disease.

In testing for pre-diabetes or diabetes, one could simply assess glucose levels in blood, but this represents a static index of what's happening – that is, the level of glucose present at one point in time. It might be more relevant to know what's been happening over the past weeks or months. For this, glycated hemoglobin or A1c levels are measured to indicate the glucose load that has been carried during the preceding two or three months. Evaluating A1c levels in relation to the development of diabetes might also be more informative in defining the role of stressors in affecting the course of diabetes. Usually, when left to their own devices, despite having good intentions, individuals might fall short in managing diabetes, and it's still tougher for those who are at a pre-diabetic stage and hence often view the need for glucose control as being "less urgent." Having a coach to help individuals keep A1c levels in line markedly helps people maintain them within a reasonable range.

The link between chronic stressors and diabetes has received considerable support across different situations. A relation was reported between work stress and diabetes in that burnout was accompanied by an increased risk of diabetes. Further, a 15-year follow-up study indicated a doubling of the incidence of diabetes among women who experienced frequent psychosocial stressors. As in the case of heart disease, a 35-year follow-up study among individuals of five occupational classes indicated that diabetes among unskilled and semiskilled classes was about 50 percent more common than in "high officials," even taking into account factors such as age, body mass index, smoking, physical activity, and current psychological stress. Likewise, having low decision latitude and high job demands were closely related to Type 2 diabetes. These outcomes are generally more

Adaptation to insults that protect against diabetes

Poor lifestyle factors don't always result in the development of diabetes, nor do obese individuals or those with metabolic syndrome necessarily develop Type 2 diabetes. There has been the view that in response to challenges, biological defense mechanisms become engaged to counteract the effects that would otherwise lead to illness. Thus, among some individuals, particular challenges may set in motion compensatory changes that limit the development of illnesses such as diabetes.

In the field of toxicology it was demonstrated that exposure to low levels of a toxin can diminish the response to a subsequent encounter with a higher dose of the toxin, a phenomenon known as hormesis. It was suggested that low dose exposure to metabolic or inflammatory factors or modest levels of radical oxygen species can similarly result in biological changes that act in a protective capacity against the effects that would otherwise be elicited by later exposure to still greater insults. This perspective is not unlike the view that moderate stressors encountered early in life may increase resilience as animals develop strategies to deal with stressors. In the case of hormesis, this "adaptation" would likely be viewed as being a purely biological one, but if the initial challenge involves psychological stressors, then learning how to cope might come into play as well. The fundamental question, however, is how much stress to the system yields an adaptation-like effect and how much instigates sensitization that favors negative outcomes in response to further challenges. Moreover, will knowing the answer to this question allow for the development of new treatment strategies to prevent the development of the illness?

likely to occur in women than in men, and curiously, in some instances, job demands among men were accompanied by fewer incidents of diabetes. It is uncertain whether this is related to sex-specific biological changes exerted by stressors, or whether the job, for men, was more likely to serve as a way of coping rather than as a burden.

Predictably, factors that diminish the impact of stressors, including the availability of effective coping resources, such as emotional support, may limit the effect of adverse events in the appearance of Type 2 diabetes, although this conclusion isn't unanimously endorsed. In some studies, however, high levels of social support were accompanied by greater incidence of diabetes. It is uncertain why this paradoxical outcome occurred, but it is possible that the social support was actually a sign that the individual's distress had come to the point where they reached out for support, but it was obtained when it was a bit too late. As we've seen in the case of other illnesses, Type 2 diabetes takes a long time to develop and retrospective analyses might not provide an adequate portrayal of the link between coping methods and the development of diabetes.

As we saw earlier, events of years ago can have persistent effects on well-being. Studies in humans and in animals have indicated that stressors experienced by the fetus or encountered during early life may influence the development of Type 2 diabetes. For instance, prenatal psychosocial stressors were associated with later insulin resistance in young adults, and women who lost a loved one during pregnancy were more likely to have children that later developed diabetes as adults. Likewise, early life stress, such as that experienced by "war children" from Finland who were sent abroad between 1934 and1944 in an effort to protect them, was associated with an increase of diabetes and heart disease when these individuals were assessed at an older age. Low childhood socio-economic status in some studies was also linked to Type 2 diabetes and the association was apparent even after adjustment for adult socioeconomic status and obesity.

Although insulin is typically considered primarily as a hormone that is essential for sugars to be taken up by cells, its actions ought to be considered more broadly, especially as it serves as a stress hormone that is essential in promoting the mobilization of energy stores and in this sense it facilitates our ability to contend with acute stressors. When the capacity of insulin to function properly is undermined by chronic stressors, it limits individuals in contending with psychological or physical challenges. Thus, it's all

Like an addiction

The consumption of comfort foods in response to stressors, as we've seen, may contribute to stress-induced obesity, possibly through changes in hormones such as ghrelin, leptin and cortisol, as well as brain chemical changes that affect feelings of reward. It's particularly interesting that the positive, soothing aspects of comfort foods might actually become less rewarding when insulin insufficiency or insulin resistance occurs. It might be assumed that if the sugar treats were no longer as rewarding, then the individual would naturally reduce their intake. However, this isn't what occurs. If the rewarding aspects of comfort foods were entirely abolished, then consumption of these foods might well be eliminated entirely, but in this instance the rewarding aspects of the food are only diminished. Thus, like a cocaine or heroin addict, individuals might simply increase their intake in order to gain the same positive feelings as before, potentially aggravating the unhealthy cycle initiated by stressful experiences.

the more important for those with diabetes to develop appropriate ways of dealing with stressors. In fact, stress management training limited the development of elevated glucose levels that otherwise appeared among patients with Type 2 diabetes, and methods such as mindfulness-based stress reduction, which we'll consider in Chapter 20, was useful in having those with diabetes maintain glycemic control.

Immune factors in Type 2 diabetes

A role for immune factors in the development of diabetes is fairly certain, and there is the belief that low-grade inflammation may be a common denominator for the comorbidity that exists between diabetes, heart disease, depression, and other serious conditions. Of particular relevance are the findings that metabolic syndrome, which is promoted by stressful experiences and is a frequent antecedent of diabetes, is typically accompanied by increased presence of inflammatory mediators, such as TNF-α and IL-6, as well as fibrinogen and C-reactive protein. It is believed that macrophages invade the pancreas and surround insulin-secreting beta cells, releasing cytokines that have damaging effects on them. In line with such findings, treatment to diminish the actions of IL-1β can have positive effects on diabetes, although the use of this to treat the disorder is likely some way off.

There are some individuals in whom stressors are more likely to encourage diabetes, notably those in whom stressful events give rise to increased eating, particularly comfort foods, which can engender increased stomach fat. The release of IL-6 and TNF-α from these fat cells might interfere with insulin functioning, thereby favoring the development of diabetes and heart disease. There has been the view that diabetes and not obesity itself increases the risk for developing serious illnesses, such as heart disease. Oddly, this has given fuel to the belief that "I may be overweight, but I'm perfectly healthy" and has permitted individuals to make further poor lifestyle choices. That's a remarkable rationalization, especially when it's heard from those who are 30 or 40 years old, and these individuals may have to wait a few more years before they regret this cavalier attitude.

Brushing for health

Periodontal diseases which comprise the presence of inflammation of the gum around teeth have been linked to diabetes. In fact, the severity of gum disease is directly correlated with glycemic control. The continued inflammation may, through the involvement of cytokines travelling through the blood, reduce pancreatic beta cells and increase insulin resistance, and may influence other complications associated with diabetes.

The American Academy of Periodontal Health has emphasized the importance of periodontal health among pregnant women, as gum disease has been associated with preterm labor or low birth weight, just as these outcomes can be provoked by prenatal stressors. In addition, gum disease has been associated with coronary heart disease, once again being attributed to chronic inflammation. So, besides eating right and exercising, brushing after every meal and flossing regularly can have added benefits.

Genetic contributions

As for so many other illnesses, genetic factors might contribute to the emergence of diabetes. For instance, among individuals with a recent Native American ancestry, which includes Latin Americans, the presence of a particular gene, SLC16A11, confers increased risk for Type 2 diabetes. It is somewhat curious, however, that although humans are thought to have arisen in Africa, this gene variant is absent in Africans or Europeans. Aside from this particular gene, based on a genetic analysis of more than 150,000 individuals an infrequently occurring mutation in a gene SLC30A8 was identified, which was associated with reduced risk for Type 2 diabetes. In the presence of this mutation, the occurrence of Type 2 diabetes among those who ought to have been at risk (e.g., older individuals) was reduced by 65 percent. The trick now is to determine ways of either manipulating this gene or altering the protein that it produces, thereby simulating the impact of the naturally occurring mutation.

Before you go…

Type 2 diabetes has become the plague of the twenty-first century. Poor food choices, lack of exercise, and the resulting obesity, together with increasing experiences of life stressors have all contributed to this disease. Some promising biomarkers of Type 2 diabetes have been reported, including levels of inflammatory factors, as well as high levels of 2-aminoadipic acid (2-AAA), which is involved in glucose metabolism, and they may turn out to be useful warnings of diabetic risk. Once it is present, there aren't easy solutions regarding the treatment of diabetes. It can be managed by lifestyle and drug treatments, but a single magic bullet probably isn't in the offing given that the disorder likely involves multiple processes. Still, glucagon-like peptide 1 (GLP-1), and combination therapies, such as those that influence gastric inhibitory peptide or those that inhibit enzymes that ordinarily degrade insulin, could have better effects than the single-action treatments that have been most commonly used. Alternatively, treatments for diabetes may require manipulations to affect both insulin-related functions together with brain changes that influence energy processes.

Many of us have the tendency to think in the present, and it is fairly difficult to keep our desires and cravings in abeyance for a greater reward that will come later. As Oscar Wilde put it, "I can resist anything except temptation." Indeed, individuals frequently tend not to think too much about the harms that behaviors today might promote 20, 30 or 40 years down the road. It's fairly common for people to have a sense of invulnerability, naively thinking that "bad events like that won't happen to me, but that guy next door might be in trouble." I commiserate with this entirely. The very bad devil sitting on my left shoulder who kept saying "do it, do it" always won out in debates with the kindly little angel on my right shoulder who would say "don't, don't." That angel's voice became softer and softer, and for a time it was hardly audible. Then, when I discovered my levels of blood glucose were on the high side, that angel's voice came shrieking back, but this time saying "I told you so, I told you so," and each time I'm tempted by carb-rich foods, as I often am, that little angel perpetually nags away, saying "go ahead, be a dumbass."

11

Stress, Immunity, and Disease

Wicked little things

There's something really creepy about viral and bacterial illnesses. Some foreign living thing has invaded our bodies, maybe when we were asleep or when we were having a good time with friends, or maybe through recirculated air on the plane when we were returning from vacation. On a day-to-day basis we're bound to run into bacteria and viruses that have the potential to make us ill. We can engage in some preventive behaviors, such as hand-washing, and we can cough or sneeze into the crook of our arm to limit others being affected, but we can't always avoid crowded places, and I don't even want to get near the subject of public toilets, or who last touched the food I get in a restaurant and what that person had touched before that. So there's a lot riding on our immune system operating properly. Unfortunately, when we do encounter a new virus, our immune system won't recognize it and thus it initially offers limited protection, and this deficiency can be exacerbated by stressor-related environmental and biological factors that undermine immune efficacy.

There is also a group of illnesses in which our own immune system revolts and attacks the self. It's like having our best friends turn on us in some potentially drastic ways. Don't our immune cells know what belongs to us versus what's foreign? These cells have had years to learn what's what, and yet, suddenly, for no apparent reason, like a perfidious lover, they turn on us. I suppose that viruses and bacteria do what they do because, like the proverbial scorpion, it's in their nature. But having our own immune system turn on us is just wicked.

Immunity and illness

Whether or not immune-related disturbances emerge is sometimes a matter of chance, occurring if we happen to be in the wrong place when viruses or bacteria are ready to engage in their calculated attack. Of course, illnesses might be particularly apt to occur if an individual's immune system isn't working efficiently, although it may be a bit difficult to define when an immune response should be considered as operating at a substandard level. Stressors could potentially result in impaired immunity, especially if immune functioning had already been impaired, thus increasing the odds of illness developing. As well, stressors might disturb specific aspects of the immune system, and thus might be aligned with the development of particular illnesses. Disturbed NK cell activity could potentially exacerbate or increase the risk for viral illness, impaired T and B cell activity may be associated with human immunodeficiency syndromes, and autoimmune disorders might be aggravated if suppressor cells (or inhibitory cytokines) aren't operating properly. It's important to underscore that in some instances stressors might well influence the development of a pathological condition, whereas in other cases they might not act in this capacity but could nonetheless exacerbate the course or severity of an ongoing illness.

Anecdotal reports linking stressful events and particular illnesses are fairly common. Individuals often ask why they became ill, and in their search for an answer, they might make greater note of unusual or stressful past events, and attribute an illness to them. Formal research has frequently confirmed the link between stress and illness, but many of these early studies involved retrospective analyses in which patients were asked about the stressors they had previously encountered. As we've already seen, patient biases may influence their perception and recall and thus these studies might be seen as offering little concerning the role of stressful events in relation to immune-related disorders. However, prospective studies have also indicated that stressors might have marked actions in relation to pathology. Together, these lines of research provide a strong case linking stressful experiences, compromised immune functioning, and the emergence or exacerbation of illness.

Allergies

Allergic responses occur in about one in three people, and are related to overactivity of certain aspects of the immune system, notably immunoglobulin E responses to antigens. These reactions and related conditions were at one time viewed as psychosomatic illnesses, being brought on by psychological factors, or a mix of psychological and medical problems. For instance, atopic dermatitis, a form of eczema that comprises an inflammatory, relapsing, noncontagious, itchy skin condition, used to be referred to as "neurodermatitis," since it was thought to be related to emotions and "nerves." It had also been believed that asthma in children, which had been called "asthma nervosa," stemmed from a reaction in which neurological symptoms appeared as a result of psychological stressors that came from having a histrionic mother – historically, mothers were blamed for lots of bad stuff.

A glitch on DNA might exist that affects immune functioning so that allergic reactions occur in response to ongoing allergen levels, environmental pollutants, and dietary factors. Once contact with an allergen occurs, the system will react more strongly upon later reexposure to it. When a person with an allergy comes into contact with an allergen, mast cells present in the mouth, nose, inside of the eyelids, mucosa of the lungs, and digestive tract release histamine and several other factors, which promote mucus gland secretions, as well as nasal and/or bronchial congestion. If the reaction is too strong, as might occur among some individuals in response to insect (bee) stings or particular foods, such as peanuts, as well as medications (e.g., penicillin), anaphylaxis may occur, characterized by itchy rash, throat swelling, and low blood pressure, and it can even result in death.

Living in moderate squalor might not be a bad thing after all

Potential allergens and bacteria are everywhere, and there's no escaping them. According to the hygiene hypothesis, allergies develop if individuals live in an environment that is too sterile so that the immune system is insufficiently occupied, and as a result it begins to respond to antigens that are harmless, eventually resulting in excessive immune responsivity. Being exposed to a variety of antigens as kids has the effects of strengthening our immune system and the increase of allergies and autoimmune disorders in Western countries over the past few decades might be due to obsessive cleanliness. The "cleanliness is next to godliness" maxim is clearly juxtaposed to the notion that "one can be too clean."

As stressors can affect inflammatory processes, such experiences could also exacerbate or promote allergic reactions. In fact, eosinophils, a type of white blood cells involved in allergic reactions, increased to a greater extent in response to an allergen during stressful than nonstressful periods of life. Aggravation of the symptoms of atopic dermatitis was likewise related to psychological distress, and the incidence of asthma, as well as asthma-related hospitalization, were linked to life stressors, such as family conflict, negative life events, poor social support, and the presence of ruminative behaviors. Moreover, among individuals with hay fever and seasonal allergies, symptoms were increased by a stressor, particularly among highly anxious individuals. The link between stressors and the exacerbation of symptoms isn't limited to recent negative events, as stressors encountered during childhood may influence allergic reactions, particularly in the presence of a family history of asthma.

Just as stressors can exacerbate allergic reactions, diminishing distress by relaxation therapy or even through expressive writing could have a positive effect on conditions such as asthma. Among depressed asthmatic patients, psychotherapy reduced emergency room visits, and antidepressant medications, such as selective serotonin reuptake inhibitors (SSRIs), also had positive effects, although this might be due to direct immune suppression provoked by the drug, rather than by influencing stress responses.

Infectious illness

Viruses can be transmitted from a carrier to a host, where they can invade existing cells. The spread of a virus depends on how readily it can be passed on, the route by which it's transmitted, such as through the air, by touch, or by body fluids, how readily it can penetrate the host's tissues, and how quickly the virus kills the host. In the latter regard, if a virus causes the death of the host rapidly, then the opportunity for the virus to be passed on is diminished, although in some cases the passage can come about even if the host is dead. Conversely, if the host doesn't die immediately, and especially if viral symptoms aren't evident for some time, then the opportunity for viral transmission is markedly increased. In fact, it is not infrequent for a virus to live inside its host for some time without causing damage, but some viral strains can evolve, either through mutation or a process akin to natural selection, and undergo a break-out so that other cells are infected. As we'll see, stressful events can affect the occurrence of viral illness, and viruses can have some very stressful effects not only on those directly affected, but also those around them (ask anyone

"Don't give a dose to the one you love most (it may get back to you)," sung by Shel Silverstein

Communicable or transmissible diseases have been around for a long time. In fact, the biblical Plague 5 and 6 (pestilence and boils) that rained down on the Egyptians after Pharaoh failed to comply with the request made by Moses, are thought by some historians to actually reflect the natural spread of disease that was common then. Much later, large portions of the European population were wiped out by smallpox epidemics in which about 50 percent of those infected died. However, its origins are believed to date back thousands of years and have been detected on mummified remains from ancient Egypt. This viral illness killed several hundred million people before a vaccine was discovered by Edward Jenner in 1798. Like smallpox, bubonic plague (Black Death) has a long history. This bacterial disease carried by rodents first appeared in Russia in the sixth century, but is most (in)famous for killing upward of 25 million people, perhaps even as many as 100–200 million, once it reached Western Europe in the fourteenth century. Much later, Spanish Flu staggered the world by killing more than 50 million people (and some medical historians suggested it might have been as many as 130 million) from 1918 to 1920, far more than the deaths stemming from World War I that preceded it. Of course, virtually everyone knows about various sexually transmitted diseases (STDs) that are treatable, and about HIV/AIDS, which has affected millions, with cures and vaccines forever being just around the corner.

Most individuals have likely become aware of the potential threats of viral illnesses that could potentially turn into pandemics, especially given the relatively recent threats of bird flu, SARS (severe acute respiratory syndrome), West Nile virus, H1N1 (swine flu), and now there's a threat of MERS (Middle East respiratory syndrome), and Ebola has become more than just a threat. It's even likely that most people have heard the expression often coming from virologists that "it's not a matter of if, but when" in relation to a pandemic. Given this knowledge, it is remarkable that in response to the recent H1N1 pandemic, just 40 percent of people were inoculated, despite the widely publicized warning issued by the World Health Organization (WHO) and government representatives. To a certain extent, we shouldn't be surprised that the turnout was as low as it was, and various factors likely coalesced to yield this outcome. In part, this may have stemmed from the fear that the vaccines might have ill effects, a lack of trust in media agencies that were seen as being overly dramatic, and ineffective communication on the part of government agencies in explaining the vaccines' safety. The conspiracy theorists came out, as usual, proclaiming that this so-called pandemic was nonexistent, actually being a ruse initiated by drug companies that were intent on making a profit from their vaccines. As well, low turnout for vaccination might have stemmed from apathy or "flu fatigue" as a result of frequent alarms of imminent pandemics over the preceding few years. As one researcher put it, the government had "exhausted its quota of scary utterances."

An analysis of 19 countries revealed that 24 percent of people were actually infected by H1N1, and of these individuals 1 in every 5,000 died. The Centers for Disease Control and Prevention (CDC) estimated that in the US somewhere between 43 and 89 million cases of H1N1 occurred, accounting for 300,000–400,000 hospitalizations, and between 8,900 and 18,300 deaths. Clearly, the infection was more widespread than most people thought it was, but all things considered, its lethality was relatively limited. We dodged a bullet as H1N1 turned out to be less of a threat than it could have been, but we might not always be as lucky. In fact, even if we were willing to be vaccinated, it takes a long time for a vaccine to be tested and produced, the vaccine's effectiveness might be limited, and the result could be fairly horrible. Incidentally, H7N9 killed several hundred people in 2013 and 2014, but fortunately wasn't transmitted from human to human. Flu variants appear all of the time, and it's anybody's guess whether and which will be able to make the necessary leap to create a pandemic. As they say in relation to terrorism, we can be successful in our preventive measures on 99 percent of occasions, but these successes will be quickly forgotten if we're unsuccessful even once.

Vaccines have been effective in wiping out diseases that at one time killed millions. Diphtheria and smallpox are almost gone, and polio has been largely eradicated except for a couple of countries that have not endorsed wide use of the vaccine. Some diseases, such as measles, which does kill some people and can have several very adverse effects, seem to be making a comeback as people are not having their children vaccinated. Contrary to any reasonable expectation, even in the face of a looming outbreak of a disease such as whooping cough that can lead to brain damage or death, parents in the state of Washington were no more likely to have children vaccinated than in the period preceding the outbreak. As new viral challenges appear it's inevitable that we'll encounter repeated pandemic threats. Unfortunately, it doesn't seem as if governments are well prepared to release credible information to the public without it being modified by the media, conspiracy theorists and other ill-informed but vocal Twitter advocates. Effective communication networks clearly need to be established, but these efforts are constrained by a lack of trust in governments. The fundamental question that we really face is whom we trust most to provide accurate information. It seems that it's not the media, or the government, or even coworkers, but more often than not, we tend to trust those with whom we identify, such as family members, close friends, coreligionists, and perhaps community newspapers. So, perhaps, health officials need to get the information down to the grass roots where the right people can deliver the appropriate information.

who's been on a cruise ship where Norwalk virus has appeared). To diminish the distress provoked by a virus we might take medicine that either relieves pain or diminishes fever, which also, unfortunately, produces a friendlier environment for the virus to multiply. It's also too bad in the sense that these medications might fool us into thinking we're getting better or close to it, making it more likely that we might wander into the community again or behave like martyrs by going back to work, where we might infect others.

Aside from viruses, our immune system has to deal with a galaxy of different bacteria, fungi, multicellular parasites, protozoa, and prions. Bacteria come in all sizes and shapes, and some like streptococcus can remain on external objects, such as toys and cribs as well as the door handles of washrooms, for weeks and months. Aside from direct or indirect person-to-person contact, bacteria and viruses can also be transmitted through a vector that serves as an intermediary in the transfer of a disease, as in the case of mosquitoes or ticks that transmit malaria or Lyme disease to humans. Likewise, HIV may have been passed to humans through the Simian immunodeficiency virus (SIV)

Smart bacteria? Go figure

We keep hearing about bacteria mutating to evade destruction by antibiotics. Obviously, they're not smart in the traditional way we think of smart. But this doesn't mean that they're not wily and resourceful. It seems that bacteria can actually communicate with one another, and can even do so with other bacterial species. Bacteria can sense the presence of other bacteria, and even whether their number is sufficiently great, referred to as a quorum, to produce the malign effects that they are so skilled in eliciting. Small numbers of bacteria don't produce much harm, but when a quorum is reached, the large number of bacteria will coordinate the release of chemicals that make us ill. There are efforts being made to determine what chemical stimuli are being detected by bacteria to make them engage in a coordinated release of their chemicals, as well as what genes on a bacteria are being activated that cause them to behave as they do. Once this is determined, it may be possible to develop antidotes, so to speak, to prevent or reverse the effects of bacterial infection.

common in some nonhuman primate species. Humans who ate the meat of infected primates, or who had the blood of these critters get onto their hands and then into any wounds that might have been present, might have been infected with SIV, which could have mutated into HIV and then transmitted to other humans through blood, semen, vaginal secretions, and breast milk.

Bacteria can vary in the harm they can do, and have been associated with some common illnesses, as well as some that are fairly uncommon. A given illness could come about through different types of bacterial infections. For instance, bacterial meningitis could be related to infection by streptococcus pneumonia, neisseria meningitidis, or several other bacteria, and this is also the case for pneumonia, skin infections, urinary tract infections, food poisoning and gastritis, upper respiratory tract infections, sinusitis, and eye infections. All of us are at risk of bacterial infection, but individuals whose defensive systems are compromised (as in the case of those with AIDS) are at still greater risk for opportunistic pathogens to have their effects. As compromised immunity can be brought about by traumatic events or chronic stressors, these events might also increase the probability of illness occurring.

Stressors influence vulnerability and the course of infectious illness

Chronic, variable, intermittent stressors may inhibit immune ability, possibly by increasing cortisol levels, and could disrupt an organism's ability to fight off an ongoing infection. In animals, stressors can diminish NK cell activity and promote lymphocyte loss, thereby aggravating the effects of an influenza virus. Likewise, when stressors were applied soon after infection with herpes simplex, the virus was cleared from the body less readily and the course of the illness was worsened, and among people treated with a modest dose of cold virus, those who had experienced greater stressful events in the recent past were more likely to develop upper respiratory illnesses. Stressors similarly increased the recurrence of herpes simplex virus (HSV), cytomegalovirus (CMV), and the antibody response to Epstein Barr virus, and by disturbing helper T cells, stressful events may also increase the progression from HIV to AIDS, particularly among

Stress and staph

Staphylococcus aureus sounds like some sort of bacteria that emanates from a swamp in some far-off place, but might be more recognizable to most people when they hear the term staph infection. It's one of the hospital-acquired infections, along with Acinetobacter and Klebsiella pneumoniae, with the latter being particularly dangerous given its resistance to antibiotics. According to the CDC, bacteria and other micro-organisms account for about 1.7 million hospital-associated infections and contribute to almost 100,000 deaths annually in the US. S. Aureus isn't restricted to hospital settings, being fairly common to the extent that 20 percent of the Western population is affected at some time. It is associated with several life-threatening conditions, being the most frequent cause of postsurgical wound infection, and has been implicated in endocarditis (inflammation of the inner layer of the heart), toxic shock syndrome, meningitis, pneumonia, bacteria in the blood (bacteremia), sepsis and whole body infection. In children, S. Aureus can promote skin infections, pimples, boils, carbuncles (a contagious skin condition associated with an abscess that oozes pus), and scalded skin syndrome (widespread formation of blisters filled with fluid). Stressful events can affect S. Aureus and thus can have implications for physical well-being, especially in vulnerable populations, such as older people. It's not uncommon to hear about various diseases through different media sources, but for some reason we hear little about sepsis, despite the fact that on a yearly basis more people die owing to sepsis than HIV/AIDS, breast cancer and prostate cancer combined.

individuals with negative personality features or in association with ineffective coping styles. In general, stressors were accompanied by increased susceptibility to and frequency of illnesses, delayed recovery, and more frequent complications related to infection.

A person would have had to be isolated on an island not to have heard of herpes, but it's not uncommon to find that the term "herpes" is often misunderstood. There are two forms, herpes simplex virus 1 and 2, sometimes referred to as HSV-1 and HSV-2. Both forms are contagious, but whereas HSV-1 is responsible for most cases of cold sores, HSV-2 accounts for most instances of genital herpes. Both forms have a penchant for becoming latent, hiding out in the cell bodies of neurons where they won't be detected by immune cells. These viruses may again become active, probably at the most inopportune times, transported to the skin, where viral replication and shedding occur, causing new sores and making the individual infectious. There is the belief that stressful events may be a culprit in HSV-1 reactivation.

Autoimmune disorders

About 75 different illness are known or suspected to be autoimmune disorders that come about because the immune system has turned against the self, attacking our own organs or tissues. These illnesses, which appear far more frequently in women than in men, are not caused by stressors, although symptoms of these disorders may be worsened by stressful events. The most common and best known of these disorders are rheumatoid arthritis, lupus erythematosus, and multiple sclerosis. However, there is a long list of other known and suspected autoimmune diseases.

Rheumatoid arthritis, lupus erythematosus, and multiple sclerosis

Multiple sclerosis (MS) is a disease in which immune responses are directed toward a fatty sheath, known as myelin, which surrounds brain and spinal cord axons. Myelin is essential for the rapid propagation of electrical activity within neurons, and if it breaks down, the conduction of electrical signals is slowed, leading to pathological outcomes. The disease is most frequently seen during early adulthood, four times as often in women relative to men, and is characterized by sensory and motor disturbances, such as loss of sensitivity or tingling, pricking or numbness, fatigue, muscle weakness, difficulty moving, and disturbed balance and coordination, and both speech and swallowing may be impaired. As the disease progresses, cognitive impairments and depression may evolve. In the relapsing-remitting type of MS, discrete attacks may be followed by months or years before another incident occurs, and during apparently "well" periods, patients might be tempted to believe that the illness is on hold, or even diminishing, but the neurological disturbances may actually persist and even progress. Primary and secondary progressive MS, two illness subtypes, often appear at about 40 years of age. In primary progressive MS, the initial episode is not accompanied by remission, whereas secondary progressive MS, with the ominous alternative name of "galloping MS," refers to a condition that initially appears like relapsing-remitting MS, but a progressive neurologic decline occurs between episodes.

Systemic lupus erythematosus (SLE) is typically observed among individuals, more often women, 15–35 years of age. It can affect virtually any part of the body, including joints, liver, kidneys, skin, heart, nervous system, blood vessels, and lungs. As the disease progresses, comorbid illnesses may evolve, ranging from cardiovascular disease, infections, osteoporosis, and cancer. The symptoms of the illness are fairly general, comprising joint and muscle pain, fatigue, and recurrent, unpredictable bouts of fever. With illness progression, bouts or flares are usually preceded by signs such as increased fatigue, pain, rash, fever, abdominal discomfort, headache, and dizziness. An early diagnosis of lupus is difficult because of the breadth of symptoms that come and go, and it is not unusual for it to be mistaken for some other illness. SLE can be accompanied by marked neurological and psychiatric manifestations, white matter (referring to glia and myelinated axons) hyperintensities in certain brain areas, as well as hemorrhages, lesions, cell loss, and cell atrophy. The illness can also be accompanied by impaired hippocampal neurogenesis and microstructural abnormalities that affect processing speed, memory, and executive functioning. It is thought that autoantibodies (antibodies directed at our own tissues) may reach the brain and attack cells, leading to the cognitive decline and depression that is often comorbid with SLE.

Arthritis is a fairly common autoimmune disorder that comprises inflammation of a single or of multiple joints, and is accompanied by joint pain, muscle aches and pains, general malaise or feelings of fatigue, weight loss, poor sleep, as well as fever. There are several forms of arthritis that might develop through different processes. Osteoarthritis or degenerative joint disease typically evolves with aging, infection, injury or trauma to the joint. Rheumatoid arthritis shares some characteristics with osteoarthritis as it also involves inflammation of the movable joints that are surrounded by a capsule containing a lubricating synovial fluid. As well, this form of arthritis can also include inflammation of the membrane that lines joints and tendon sheaths as well as cartilage, typically in the fingers, wrists, knees, elbows, and cervical spine. Although less frequent, (juvenile) arthritis can occur in children or young adolescents.

There presently isn't a cure for these particular autoimmune disorders, and only "disease-modifying treatments" are available that delay their downhill course. In some cases, such as the progressive-remitting form of MS, these agents have still more limited effects. These modifying treatments comprise agents that act in an immunosuppressive capacity, modulate immune functioning or directly affect cytokines. These are very powerful agents and they can have some nasty adverse effects, and as a result treatment may be complicated. This said, reducing B cells may diminish signs of MS, and there may be vaccine-like treatments on the horizon for this illness. As well, in mice, treatment with human stem cells eliminated MS symptoms, and perhaps this avenue of research might lead to a cure at some point. There has also been some evidence indicating that marijuana's primary active ingredient, THC, may cause epigenetic changes that act against inflammation that could be beneficial for a variety of autoimmune disorders.

Stressors may promote flares of MS symptoms that may be accompanied by increased frequency of brain lesions. Early studies typically involved only a small number of participants and were conducted retrospectively, making it questionable whether the stressors were, in fact, linked to flares. Later studies, unhampered by retrospective biases, confirmed these findings, but indicated that the frequency of stressful experiences, rather than the severity of these stressors, was most closely related to MS flares. Indeed, whereas repeated intermittent stressors exacerbated symptoms, relapse was diminished following strong acute stressors, such as major surgery or bone fractures. Studies in animals also indicated that when a strong stressor in the form of social defeat coincided with infection being present, the course of the disease was diminished, whereas symptoms worsened if the stressor was encountered after symptoms were already well established. Once more, as similar effects occurred in relation to hormonal and cytokine changes as well as other aspects of immune functioning, the effects of stressors on MS symptoms might stem from time-linked hormonal and immunological changes.

Consistent with a role for stressors in the exaggerated signs of lupus erythematosus, stressor-elicited immune and cytokine responses were more pronounced in patients than controls. Moreover, the symptoms of lupus erythematosus were more likely to be aggravated by day-to-day irritations that increase cytokine activity, rather than by major life stressors that diminish cytokine functioning. The very fact that lupus erythematosus, like other autoimmune disorders, appears predominantly in women leads to the supposition that sex hormones influence the course and severity of this illness. Indeed, estrogen enhances autoantibody production that might contribute to the illness, and the low occurrence of lupus erythematosus in men might be related to testosterone having the opposite effect. As stressful events influence these hormones, which may interact with immune functioning, it is possible that stressor effects on these processes contribute to disturbed cognitive functioning and impaired attention and visual memory performance among those with lupus erythematosus.

For mild symptoms of lupus erythematosus, treatment is usually limited to nonsteroidal anti-inflammatory drugs, but as the illness progresses, drugs that inhibit immune functioning are used. These include cortisol or related agents, and powerful immunosuppressants, such as cyclophosphamide. However, newer and more effective therapies are in the offing, including one that uses synthetic peptides to suppress immune reactions and the production of autoantibodies responsible for the attack on the self. Treatment improvements have also been seen with drugs such as Atacicept and Belimumab that target specific B cells rather than affecting the immune system broadly.

In rheumatoid arthritis, autoantibodies seem to be directed at aspects of the affected person's immune system, namely a portion of the immunoglobulin G molecule, termed rheumatoid factors (RF). As this process occurs in advance of clinical signs of rheumatoid arthritis, it might play a causal role in the illness, or at least could serve as a biomarker to predict illness. Treatment to manage rheumatoid arthritis often includes physiotherapy, lifestyle changes and exercise, but greater effects are realized through anti-inflammatory agents, corticosteroids, and antibodies directed at factors that promote the illness, as well as analgesics. Illness progression can also be slowed through disease-modifying antirheumatic drugs (DMARDs), such as agents to inhibit the cytokine TNF-α (e.g., etanercept, infliximab) or both TNF-α and IL-1β.

Exacerbation of autoimmune disorders by stressful experiences

Not surprisingly, patients with rheumatoid arthritis have frequently attributed their illness to stressful experiences or believed that stressful events worsened their symptoms. Workers with rheumatoid arthritis similarly indicated that their pain levels were particularly elevated on days with more work-related stressors. Pain levels were also highest among individuals with jobs that entailed high "strain," although the symptom aggravation elicited by day-to-day hassles was buffered by having adequate social support. There are numerous routes by which stressors could affect rheumatoid arthritis symptoms, but it might be especially significant that chronic interpersonal stressors increase production of IL-6 and diminish the ability of glucocorticoids to inhibit this inflammatory response, thus implicating IL-6 in the arthritic flares.

Autoimmune disorders are frequently comorbid with depressive illness that might have been instigated by stressful experiences, and it is possible that they share some common underlying mechanisms, including neuroendocrine or cytokine changes that are elicited by stressful experiences. Consistent with this perspective, the negative effects of stressors on MS symptoms were most apparent in individuals who used emotion-focused coping methods, but were less pronounced among those who used avoidance/distraction. Among SLE patients, depression and impaired quality of life were most prominent in those who used disengagement or emotion-focused coping strategies, but least apparent among patients who coped through positive reinterpretation and growth. As expected, cognitive behavioral therapy was useful in diminishing depressive symptoms and enhancing quality of life, but unfortunately it did not have positive effects in relation to organ damage connected to SLE. Consistent with these findings, having social support favored better psychological adjustment in MS patients, but it did not promote symptom remission, indicating that while social support may help individuals deal with their situation, once present the illness is not readily abated.

Before you go...

So, where do we stand regarding the link between stressful experiences and the development of immune-related pathology? There's ample evidence indicating that stressful events can worsen symptoms of autoimmune disorders and aggravate allergies, and could potentially increase vulnerability to the effects of viral and bacterial challenges. These effects could come about through changes of processes that excite or inhibit immune functioning, such as epinephrine and corticoid activation. If the specific factors responsible for stressor-elicited symptom aggravation were identified, coupled with an understanding of why these factors differ across individuals, it might be possible to target specific processes and thus limit the adverse effects of stressors on disease states. In the absence of remedies for illnesses, having individuals learn how to properly appraise and cope with stressors might go a long way in limiting the symptoms and frequent flares of autoimmune disorders. This won't be a cure, but it might make some very distressing aspects of the diseases more manageable.

12

Stress and Cancer: Cancer and Stress

The dreaded diseases

Even if the individual had been expecting the worst, the words "you have cancer" or "the tests came back positive" knock most people sideways. In fact, even that horribly ambiguous phone call saying "can you come back in as the tests showed an anomaly?" can get us to remake our wills. We have special names for cancer, such as "the big C," as if saying it this way will ward off the evil eye. The occurrence of the big C might arise because of genes that were inherited or carcinogens that we were exposed to 20 or 30 years earlier, and thus people often think of the disease as occurring unpredictably and the victim's fate as uncontrollable. The unfortunate fact that it spreads through the body even after brutal treatments have been engaged, reappears without warning, and stymies top oncologists makes for dread and despair.

There was a time when cancer treatment focused on using an array of surgical and chemotherapeutic treatments that gave people an extension of a few months of life, but at considerable physical and mental cost. For some types of cancer, treatment strategies have improved, as have pain medications and interventions to reduce side effects. During the 1960s and 1970s a radical shift developed so that prevention rather than treatment became a major focus in relation to cancer. Individuals were prompted to change their lifestyles, which meant giving up cigarette smoking, cutting back on unhealthy foods, and limiting sun exposure. Still, about 20 percent of people in Western countries smoke cigarettes, and in some countries, such as Russia, more than 50 percent do, with men being the culprits twice as often as women. Those who aren't smokers or those who are former smokers might (self-righteously) wonder why people continue to smoke given the hazards of doing so. Ironically, many of these same individuals likely failed to be vaccinated in the face of potential pandemics, even though they had to be aware that if they did become infected, their family and friends would have been placed at risk. They likely had the same attitude as cigarette smokers and those lying out in the sun: "it won't happen to me."

Stress and Your Health: From Vulnerability to Resilience, First Edition. Hymie Anisman.
© 2015 John Wiley & Sons, Ltd. Published 2015 by John Wiley & Sons, Ltd.

The cancer process

Cancer is a condition, or more appropriately a broad group of conditions or illnesses, in which certain cells undergo uncontrolled growth, leading to the development of tumors. There are about 200 different types of cancer that can come about, involving various organs and different types of cells within these organs. These cancer types may be instigated by different processes and may be differentially responsive to different hormones and various other manipulations. Tissues adjacent to a tumor can be affected, and the cancer cells also have the ability to leave the primary tumor site, get into blood vessels or penetrate the lymphatic walls, travel through the blood or lymphatic system, and eventually find a comfortable home where a new cancer colony can be established. This process, referred to as metastasis, distinguishes malignant from benign tumors. Benign tumors typically don't invade adjacent tissues or metastasize (although there are exceptions to this), whereas most malignant cancers do.

So, how does cancer come about? Why do the first cancer cells occur, and why do they multiply without apparent restraint? One early view, the immune surveillance hypothesis, was that lymphocytes were continuously on guard for cells that had mutated, as they often do, and that cancer was a result of these mutated cells avoiding detection. This could occur as a result of an immune malfunction, such as diminished killing abilities or ineffective recognition processes. However, although an immune dysfunction could potentially increase cancer risk, there are other ways through which a tumor can come about that have less to do with immune disturbances.

As cancer is as common as it is, most of us are bound to have relatives who develop cancer, especially in very large extended families, resulting in the potentially mistaken belief that cancer runs through the family. In fact, only about 10–15% of cancer subtypes are a result of the inheritance of mutated genes. These mutations, referred to as germ line mutations, occur when the mutation is within genes associated with sperm and eggs, and thus vulnerability to cancer can be passed across generations. For instance, women with the BRCA1 or the BRCA2 genes are at a high risk (60–80%) for developing breast and ovarian cancer. The risk for this form of breast cancer varies across cultures, being relatively high among Ashkenazi Jews (about 8% of women), but less so in Hispanic (about 3.5%) and Asian American women (0.5%). Thus women in the high-risk group, especially if there is a family history of breast/ovarian cancer, need to be on alert for signs of cancer and undergo more than usual screening. Some women at high cancer risk might opt for double mastectomy and ovariectomy in order to reduce the possibility of being ravaged by cancer.

Although having the BRCA1 or BRCA2 mutation markedly increases the risk for breast and ovarian cancer, it isn't certain that breast cancer will actually occur, and other factors likely influence the actions of these genes in promoting the illness. As in other illnesses, a "second hit" might take the individual from one level of risk to another. The second hit could be in the form of yet another genetic mutation, immune- or hormone-related factors, or environmental triggers that affect hormones. This has fostered the search for the synergies that could enable cancer-related mutations to become expressed as tumors, and to identify variables, such as pregnancy and lactation, which could limit the development of cancer. In this regard, for instance, individuals carrying the BRCA2 mutation and hence at increased risk for breast cancer also have a one in four chance of developing lung cancer if they're smokers.

More than one way of getting from there to here

Generally, there are two types of genes that might contribute to cancer. The first are oncogenes, which, if they are activated when they shouldn't be, might promote uncontrolled cell growth. The second are suppressor genes, which ordinarily limit the growth rate of cells, but when they are turned off then uncontrolled cell growth can occur. In a sense, activator genes are seen as the gas pedal in a car and suppressor genes are the brake pedal. Regardless of which is dysfunctional, trouble can ensue, more so if both the pedal is pressed to the floor and the brakes are shot.

In the main, mutations aren't inherited from parents, but instead reflect random alterations or those that develop as a result of environmental toxins, pollutants, and hormonal factors. Over the years we've heard about the carcinogenic properties of all sorts of environmental agents that lead to mutations that promote or allow for uncontrolled cell multiplication or disturbed DNA repair processes. There is also the view that lifestyle factors, including exercise and diet, can influence the development of cancers, which might account for differences in the appearance of cancers across countries, regions, and cultures. So, even if cancer did run through families, it might not have anything to do with genetic inheritance, but instead might be due to shared environmental toxins, such as smoking or living downwind from some carcinogen-spewing factory.

The term mutation makes one think of rare occurrences, but as we've seen, mutations occur fairly frequently. Fortunately, during replication of a gene, proofreading and editing occur so that the errors in the transcribed code are repaired. But, even if the errors aren't detected during the editing process, the mutation may show up in a section of DNA that doesn't have notable repercussions. In other instances, in contrast, the mutation can occur on a section of DNA that may create a variety of problems. For instance, genes ordinarily contain a section that, when activated or uncovered, has the effect of promoting cell death, a process referred to as apoptosis. When a cell is severely damaged or could be harmful, then it's of obvious benefit for the cell to die, and so having these apoptotic sites on a gene is advantageous. However, a mutation in this apoptotic region could eliminate the death message, and hence this cell and its progeny would multiply again and again, culminating in a tumor mass.

In addition to carcinogens, viruses have also been implicated in the development of some cancers. Human papillomavirus, which is associated with cervical carcinoma, has received considerable media attention recently because of efforts to have young women immunized against this virus. You have likely also heard of Kaposi's sarcoma herpes virus, an opportunistic infection often seen in patients with HIV/AIDS. Further, Epstein-Barr virus has been related to B-cell lympho-proliferative disease, and human T-cell leukemia virus-1 might instigate leukemia. At this point it's not certain whether stressful events affect one type of cancer more than another, or whether antistress treatments are more beneficial in particular instances than in others. It's actually the case that virus-based treatment strategies have been used to kill cancerous tumors. In this instance, viruses can be modified so that they preferentially infect and kill cancer cells, or they can be directly inserted into solid cancer tumors, ultimately destroying the tumor.

Is there a brighter future for cancer treatments?

As certain tumor types were linked to specific genes, hormones or growth factors, cancer researchers and clinicians recognized the implications for treatment strategies. Advances were thus made in treating some types of cancer, such as the estrogen-sensitive, HER2 positive type of cancer that is responsive to a drug cocktail that includes Herceptin (trastuzumab), although herceptin can also create heart problems. There have similarly been indications that a small molecule that fits precisely into a component of complex androgen receptors might have positive effects in treating prostate cancer, although clinical use of the treatment is still some way off. There have been enormous efforts expended to try to link cancers to gene mutations in the hope that this would inform treatment strategies. However, multiple mutations may be involved in the provocation of cancer, making it difficult to determine precisely the right way of treating it. Furthermore, cancers are wily enemies that can return even after apparently successful treatment, when the characteristics of the cancer may have altered, requiring a shift in strategy to deal with the illness.

Over the past few decades, the battle against some forms of cancer has met with success if the disease was caught relatively early, as in the case of some types of breast cancer. Likewise, certain cancers that once were a death sentence, such as chronic myelogenous leukemia, can now be treated well with Imatinib (Gleevec). This said, the statistics regarding the treatment of other cancers are grim, including lung and bronchial cancer, colon and rectal cancer, non-Hodgkin lymphoma, and pancreatic, liver and intrahepatic bile duct cancer, to name a few. Each has unique molecular genetic features, and as these are identified through the ongoing Cancer Genome Atlas project and the Cancer Genome Project it may become possible to develop treatments to attenuate all sorts of cancers and their recurrence. In this regard, for instance, it may be possible to genetically engineer T cells that will destroy cancer, as recently reported in the case of leukemia.

There are a number of reasons why cancer medicines don't work as well as one would like. One of these concerns the drugs' toxicity, which can have multiple adverse effects, such as diminishing counts of white blood cells, as well as heart failure, frequently requiring that therapy be stopped. In addition, the effectiveness of the drugs may be compromised by the tumor's ability to develop resistance to them. As well, treatments often affect cells in multiple parts of the body beyond those affected by the cancer. Thus, there have been increasing efforts to use nanotechnologies to deliver medicines to where they are needed. By being so specific, low doses can be used to avoid toxic side effects and limit tolerance to the drugs' actions.

The stress–cancer link

This brings us to the issue of whether or not stressful events, like other environmental factors, affect the cancer process. Is it possible that stressors, through their effects on hormonal or growth factor processes that promote DNA mutations, encourage or cause tumor growth? In fact, the evidence supporting a role for stress in causing cancer is unimpressive, although there's a fair likelihood that stressors can exacerbate already existing cancers. It may be that stressors can influence the growth of induced or transplanted tumors in rodents, possibly by affecting endocrine functioning or diminishing the strength of the immune system's responses. It also seems that social stressors in early life can be associated with subsequent growth of carcinogen-induced tumors, although it isn't known whether this is secondary to hormonal changes, epigenetic processes or some other mechanism.

Studies in humans indicated that stressful life events were linked to cancer progression and cancer-related mortality, increased aggressiveness of some forms of cancer, such as breast cancer, and were even associated with a poor prognosis following stem-cell transplantation carried out to treat the illness. Furthermore, depression and anxiety secondary to a stressor experience were also related to the course of tumor growth, and these mood states were accompanied by a poorer response to neoadjuvant chemotherapy, which consisted of the administration of therapeutic agents, such as hormone treatment, prior to the start of the primary treatment. Overall, the relevant literature has supported the view that cancer survival declines as stressful events increase, and higher cancer mortality occurred among those with stress-prone personality styles, poorer coping styles, negative emotional responses, or diminished quality of life.

Stressors could potentially affect tumor growth and metastases through hormonal changes, such as corticosterone release, that diminish immune functioning, thus permitting less restrained tumor growth. Alternatively, stressors could disrupt DNA repair, thus allowing mutated cells to multiply. It is also possible that the stressor-induced release of epinephrine and norepinephrine in the body, along with changes of β-norepinephrine receptor functioning, could influence the migration and invasion of cancer cells, and could affect the growth of new blood vessels that might be important in order for the growing tumor to survive.

It seems that stressors can also influence the effectiveness of drug treatments used in cancer therapy. For instance, corticoids could potentially undermine the effectiveness of chemotherapy by inhibiting processes that would ordinarily cause death of the cancer cells. Similarly, norepinephrine changes elicited by stressors could influence the response to cancer therapy. Ordinarily, administering the anticancer treatment bicalutamide to mice reduced prostate tumor size. However, these positive drug

Foresight and hindsight

The Million Women Study in the UK was initiated to address, among other things, questions concerning the effects of hormone replacement therapy (HRT) on the development of several cancers in women aged 50 and over. It included analyses of cancer development in relation to dosage factors, type of HRT used, and earlier use of oral contraceptives. The results were fairly unambiguous, indicating that women currently using HRT, particularly a combination of estrogen and progesterone, were at increased risk of developing breast cancer. Findings such as these might prompt us to consider that since stressors can influence multiple hormonal processes, including estrogen, stressors could have their effects on the progression of breast cancer through actions on these hormones, and these actions might be more pronounced among women using HRT.

effects were diminished if mice were chronically stressed, and this outcome could be attenuated by treatment with a β-norepinephrine blocker. As patients with cancer are understandably stressed, it is possible that the beneficial effects of their treatment are diminished by stressor-elicited epinephrine changes, and it is possible that a beta blocker would help them to reduce stress and thus enhance the effectiveness of their cancer treatment.

One function of NK cells is to destroy tumor cells, and it was supposed that since stressors impaired NK cell functioning, this might have contributed to stressor-provoked enhancement of tumor growth. Indeed, among breast cancer patients with high levels of psychological stress, NK cell functioning was disturbed relative to that seen in patients with lower stress levels. As well, in patients diagnosed with breast cancer, coping ability, social support, benefit finding, and optimism were related to enhanced NK cell activity and lymphocyte multiplication. This outcome was not unique to breast cancer patients, having been observed in patients with gynecologic, prostate, gastrointestinal, digestive tract, and liver malignancies. Moreover, immune functioning was augmented in men who were provided with stress management tools prior to radical prostatectomy.

The studies in humans that assessed the stress–cancer relationship have largely been of a correlational nature, often relying on retrospective analyses that attempted to tie a current cancer state to past stressful events. Although some of these studies suggested that stressor experiences and cancer might be linked, they suffer from the usual biases inherent in retrospective analyses. Thus, it is especially interesting that when a patient's stressor history was assessed when a tumor was suspected, but prior to the results of the biopsy having been received, reports of distress, as well as plasma IL-6 and cortisol, were greater among individuals who were later found to have malignant tumors than in those who turned out to have benign tumors. If the increased stressor experiences that have been reported stemmed from patient biases secondary to their worry that they had cancer, then negative life events ought to have been equally frequent irrespective of whether the tumor was malignant or benign as all women would have been equally concerned about the tumor being malignant. If these findings had gone unchallenged, then the link between stress and cancer would be fairly impressive. However, there have been reports that irrespective of whether the biopsy revealed a benign or malignant condition, comparable anxiety and tension, disturbed NK functioning, and elevated levels of pro- and anti-inflammatory cytokines were evident.

Several studies evaluated the stress–cancer link prospectively, and although they are an advance over retrospective analyses, they aren't without their own problems. For instance, it is important to know when certain life stressors occurred in relation to cancer development, and it is essential to evaluate individuals on the basis of whether or not they were at risk for certain forms of cancer. As well, given the multiple factors that might play into the development of cancer, including several lifestyle factors, these too need to be considered in conjunction with other variables. For instance, a 20-year prospective study of Israeli individuals who had lost a son in war or by accident indicated that the relationship to cancer was a weak one. However, one can't be certain whether the inclusion of other factors into the equation would have yielded a different result. As we've seen, stressors and stress responses are complicated, being affected by a constellation of psychosocial factors such as appraisals, coping, and early life events, making it unlikely that simply correlating stress experiences and cancer occurrence would provide especially meaningful or impressive results.

Stress and metastasis

There's a sense of order among our cells. Brain cells don't migrate to the liver, and kidney cells don't suddenly decide that they'd rather be in the pancreas or intestine. Cancer cells, in contrast, seem to be motivated to travel to distant sites, where they set up a new colony. So, what is it about them that supports their inclination to migrate and still survive? Do they have some sort of protective coating, an invisibility cloak of sorts, which protects them from immune cells or from specialized factors, such as proteins known as metastasis suppressors? Alternatively, are they being politically wise, buddying-up to regular cells, thus fooling the immune system into thinking that they're just part of the good old gang, and you know how that works – "a friend of my friend is also my friend." Or, are they using substances in the body, such as neurotransmitters, in order to disguise themselves once they get to particular locations, such as the brain. These alternatives are presented here in a fairly cavalier fashion, but each has at some time been offered as a possible factor that could affect metastasis.

Cancer metastasis is accompanied by the growth of a new network of blood vessels, a process known as angiogenesis, which feed the tumor cells. As not every environment is necessarily hospitable, being able to attract a blood supply increases the likelihood of the cancer cells' survival. In this regard, it is conceivable that stressor-elicited hormonal release, including sympathetic activation and the release of epinephrine, might create an environment conducive for cancer cells to flourish. In fact, among mice that had been exposed to a social stressor and later reexposed to this stressor shortly after tumor cell inoculation, pulmonary metastases increased five fold, particularly in mice that engaged a passive coping style in response to the stressor. Significantly, if mice had been pretreated with a drug that blocked the actions of epinephrine, the cancer-promoting effects of the stressor were attenuated. It's still too early to say whether such findings will be relevant in preventing metastasis in humans, but it warrants assessment.

A gene, ATF3, has been identified that may be the fundamental mediator between stressor events and cancer progression and metastases. Ordinarily, when this gene is turned on it causes damaged cells to undergo apoptosis (cell suicide). However, in some instances, the response to ATF3 might be counterproductive. When immune cells gather at a tumor cite, the tumor cells get them to express ATF3, which has the effect of allowing cancerous cells the opportunity to escape from the main tumor mass and then to migrate to other parts of the body. In fact, in mice engineered to lack the ATF3 gene, breast cancer cells lost the propensity to metastasize. As physical, biochemical or psychological stressors can cause the ATF3 gene to be turned on, this might exacerbate metastases.

Implication for cancer treatment

Cancer treatments have evolved considerably over the decades, and would hardly even be recognizable to patients treated just 30 years ago. Cancer treatment and management include powerful combinations of chemotherapeutic agents, better and more focused chemotherapy and radiation therapy, monoclonal antibody therapy, and superior surgical approaches. In recent years considerable headway has been made through immunotherapy which entails the enhancement of our immune system's ability to attack a wide range of cancer types. This can be accomplished by uncovering aspects of the stealth cloak that cancer cells use to disguise themselves as part of the body, or by extracting T cells from individuals, strengthening them or making them better able to distinguish subtle differences between cancer cells and those that are healthy, and then returning them to the patient's circulation. Of course, the effectiveness of individual treatments will likely vary according to the type of tumor, its aggressiveness, stage, and location, as well as the genetic characteristics of that cancer. Despite these improvements, the road to recovery is arduous, with numerous obstacles, stumbles, and backward steps frequently being encountered, and as already indicated, the stress of treatment itself could potentially influence the course of the illness. Predictably, patient satisfaction with services obtained has been associated with extended survival time. It is widely accepted that treatment of cancers requires an individualized approach, and perhaps it would be appropriate to include stress reduction as part of the treatment strategy.

Stress stemming from cancer

With the appearance of suspicious symptoms, anxiety, fear, fretting, and rumination evolve, which is just the lead-up to still more distress, as individuals need to undergo a series of invasive tests. During this time, considerable uncertainty and unpredictability prevails regarding outcomes, and the procedures experienced can create feelings of helplessness. Not long after the cancer diagnosis is confirmed, the individual, now in their new identity as a cancer patient, may experience a set of dehumanizing procedures, including chemotherapy, radiation, and in some instances the removal of certain organs

And it ain't no use in sit and wonder why

When something bad happens unexpectedly, people often want answers concerning why it has happened. Was it a result of something they did or something someone else did? After all, this is a just world, and bad things shouldn't happen to good people, and so they might engage in a search concerning who or what is to blame for their unfortunate condition. In one study, women frequently attributed their breast cancer to stress (58%), engagement in hormone therapy (17%), or to genetic factors (10%). Of course, these explanations might not have borne any resemblance to the actual causes of their illness. Sometimes there simply isn't an obvious answer; we simply can't identify any factors that made one person become ill, whereas others with similar experiences stayed healthy.

Not understanding why they became ill, or perhaps because it's part of human nature to feel that they've been exceptionally unlucky, it isn't unusual for affected individuals to say to themselves or to others, "why me?" Really, there's no suitable reply to this, but for every statistic there are some people above the mean and some below, and so, as cold as it might seem, the answer really is "why not you?" Obviously, this isn't something one says to a person afflicted with some form of cancer, and instead the job for most of us is to rally round to diminish the distress they're feeling.

or parts of organs. The treatments themselves can promote physical symptoms, such as sickness, nausea and vomiting, extreme fatigue, and chemo-brain, which includes cognitive disturbances. As well, damage to the heart and brain may occur secondary to the treatments. Yet, an individual's endurance is fairly remarkable, provided that the hurdles encountered are taken one day at a time.

Among some individuals the treatment they receive eliminates the cancer, for it never to return. For other patients the treatment provides only a brief stay, perhaps a couple of months are added to their life, or symptoms may disappear for years

Stress management and social support following cancer treatment

Severe illnesses, such as cancer or its treatment, can lead to PTSD symptoms in some individuals. It is estimated that one in four women with breast cancer, and one in five children with other forms of cancer, develop PTSD symptoms, and an approximately equal number of children treated for cancer will develop PTSD upon later stressor encounters. Clearly, it's exceptionally important that cancer treatments include stress reduction procedures, especially for children who might not have a full understanding of what is occurring, and for whom there have been few effective PTSD treatment strategies established, although cognitive behavioural therapy (CBT) may be effective. Owing to the understandable concern of oncologists to deal with the physical illnesses, an individual's mental health might receive insufficient attention. Yet, it is possible that the cancer treatment might be more effective if mental health issues related to the current distress and trauma were dealt with concurrently. In this regard, women who received psychological intervention to reduce distress related to breast surgery displayed enhanced mood, improved health behaviors, and augmented adherence to cancer treatment and care, and the recurrence of the disease was reduced relative to that seen in women who had not received the psychological intervention. In line with such findings, having support from a married partner was exceptionally important. An analysis of over 700,000 patients diagnosed with the 10 leading types of cancer found that metastases occurred 17 percent less often among individuals who were married than in those who were not.

It's common for a person affected by cancer to find that friends rally to help out. A friend told me how thoughtful and kind her buddies were when she was first diagnosed with breast cancer. However, once her chemo and radiation therapy was completed, virtually all of them, who now referred to her as a "cancer survivor," assumed she was cured, and their attention toward her waned. So, to her friends, the ordeal was over, but for her, distressing uncertainties continued. She learned not to mention her fears to acquaintances as the responses received on a couple of occasions were unsupportive, amounting to "You beat it, so stop being so neurotic." She also learned that there were certain people with whom she wanted to hang out, and others whom she felt weren't worth the effort.

before returning in a metastasized form. If the treatment ends up having little positive effect, or if the cancer returns and can't be dealt with effectively, then the patient may have additional needs, including those from a palliative care team and other health professionals, as well as from family members and friends. Home care, unfortunately, may become difficult and consequently hospice care might be required to permit the person to die with as little pain and with as much dignity as possible.

Among fortunate individuals who seem to have beaten the illness, at least initially, aspects of the stressor might persist. Having reclaimed their identity by this point, the individual may still have to spend time in physical or occupational rehabilitation, and they might require frequent medical testing to confirm that all is right, as well as to determine whether other illnesses secondary to the cancer treatment might have developed. Understandably, each of these tests could potentially bring bad news, and may thus create anticipatory distress. Clearly, being a cancer survivor doesn't mean that life returns to normal, but instead it might be viewed as life returning to a new normal. Cancer survivors may develop a better appreciation for the good aspects of life, but they may also experience enormous strain and uncertainty about the future, and the distress will be that much greater among those who deal poorly with uncertainty.

Treating cancer-related distress

Some individuals dealing with cancer are able to find meaning or find something positive in their misfortune. They might develop a greater appreciation of life, or they might devote themselves to helping others. In general, those who experienced "benefit finding" or "posttraumatic growth" reported reduced distress and psychological disturbances were diminished. However, for many individuals there was nothing positive about their experience and it was something that simply had to be endured. People can't be pushed to find meaning, and for some the best strategy might be one of defiance in which they "rage against the dying of the light."

Knowing that cancer causes stress and that stress could aggravate the illness or promote other disorders has obvious relevance regarding what should be done for cancer patients. You'd think that it would be possible to have patients learn methods of diminishing their stress, which would also aid in attenuating disease progression promoted by distress. In fact, CBT and mindfulness-based stress reduction (MBSR), which are described in Chapter 20, can diminish the distress associated with cancer, enhance psychological well-being, and influence neuroendocrine functioning, lymphocyte proliferation and cytokine production. Supportive group therapy likewise has been found to increase natural killer cell activity and enhance survival time among patients with either gastrointestinal or metastatic breast cancer. However, there have also been reports indicating that psychological intervention did not have positive effects on the course of the illness. As much as one would have hoped for positive effects, it isn't surprising that this wasn't the case. The proposition that psychological interventions might enhance the effectiveness of traditional cancer treatments was a long shot. The influences of these treatments are no doubt dependent on the type and stage of the cancer, as well as the effectiveness of the procedure in diminishing distress, anxiety and depression. Thus, these treatments, at best, would only be expected to have positive effects in a subset of patients.

Wacky stuff or real concerns

Quite a number of years ago, my doctoral student Lawrence Sklar and I sent a theoretical paper regarding the stress–cancer link to a fairly influential journal in psychology called *Psychological Bulletin*. Although it received very good reviews, the editor decided to reject the paper, saying that the topic was "at the outer fringe of psychology." When a new editor was appointed shortly afterward, he wrote an editorial expressing surprise at how few physiologically based papers were being submitted to this premier journal in psychology. So, being young and brash, I wrote him saying that he shouldn't be surprised, especially when papers were rejected for being "at the outer fringe of psychology" instead of being viewed as "at the cutting edge." Being reasonable, or because he was a linguist who liked that turn of phrase, he decided to have the paper published in *Psychological Bulletin*.

At that time the notion that stressful events might influence the cancer process wasn't only seen as wacky stuff within the realm of psychology, but was thought of even more negatively by the oncology community. Well, that was a long time ago, and it is fortunate that today the collaboration between the oncologist, surgeon, anesthesiologist, nurses, and specialists to deal with pain medications and other discomforts experienced by the patient have expanded to include psychologists and social workers. In fact, it's not all that unusual to find acceptance of the notion that stressful events, lifestyle, and patient comfort could influence cancer progression and the efficacy of treatments. Besides, even if these factors had no bearing on survival, it is comforting that attention is being devoted not just to the patient's physical needs, but also to their psychological well-being.

Before you go...

There is appreciable evidence that stressors could influence the progression of some cancer types, and there have been reports that diminishing cancer-related distress can enhance survival time however briefly. In contrast, support for the belief that stressful experiences cause cancer has been close to negligible. Still, one uncomfortable thought about this conclusion has been nagging at me for years. Specifically, several decades may pass between the first mutated cells developing and cancer's subsequent frank appearance. Is it possible that the first cancer cells appeared as a result of stressor-induced mutations or secondary to epigenetic changes, and a second hit generated uncontrolled cell growth? So, although the evidence for stressors playing an active role in the emergence of cancer has not been supported, it is likely premature to close off this possibility entirely, especially as most studies have focused on stressors experienced during a few years preceding detection of the cancer. Perhaps, in attempting to link stress and cancer we haven't looked in the right places or times. In fact, there have been indications that early adverse experiences, such as loss of a parent, poverty, and physical or emotional abuse, have been accompanied by an increased incidence of breast cancer, although admittedly their role in cancer production could be related to any number of poor lifestyle factors bred by distress.

13

Depressive Illnesses and Cognitive Mistakes

Mental illness affects all of us

Even as our knowledge about mental illness has been increasing, it's unfortunate that attitudes about it haven't changed nearly enough. There's still considerable stigma surrounding mental illnesses despite the fact that they're so common that there's hardly an extended family that isn't affected by some sort of psychological disorder.

Mental illness is the plague of the twentieth and twenty-first centuries, affecting about 20–30% of individuals at one time or another. Depressive disorders occur in more than 10–15% of the population, anxiety disorders of several forms are thought to similarly affect 10–15% of people, schizophrenia occurs in about 1.1% of the population, and approximately 1.5–2% suffer from bulimia or anorexia nervosa. Many of these disorders, even when treated successfully, have a high recurrence rate and might be considered to be lifelong disorders. What seems to be less well known is that mental illnesses of several types reduce life expectancy and do so to a greater extent than heavy smoking.

Depression doesn't discriminate (much), but it does occur about twice as often in females relative to males. It also appears at an astonishingly high rate among college-aged students, frequently going untreated, and suicide, which is often related to depression, is second only to auto accidents as the leading cause of death in this age group. The prevalence of depression in middle-aged and elderly people had long been underestimated as well, and is exceptionally high in older individuals, with almost half of those in residential care homes being affected.

Aside from the human cost, mental illness has staggering effects on healthcare systems and the costs associated with them. Even during well periods, depressed people are much more likely than others to use medical facilities. As well, depression is associated with a marked loss of potential labor supply through sick leave and reduced work productivity. In some countries, in fact, more than 50 percent of new claims to disability benefit are related to mental health, with depression being at the top of the list. A recent report in Ontario, Canada indicated that the burden of mental illness and addiction eclipsed any other medical costs, exceeding

Stress and Your Health: From Vulnerability to Resilience, First Edition. Hymie Anisman.
© 2015 John Wiley & Sons, Ltd. Published 2015 by John Wiley & Sons, Ltd.

that of all cancers by 50 percent, and was 700 percent greater than all infectious diseases combined. At the expected growth rate, depression is projected to become the leading burden of disease worldwide by 2030. Obviously, intervention strategies and more effective treatment methods are needed, and the stigmatization of those with mental health problems needs to be eliminated so that they are more likely to seek treatment early.

What is depression?

Most of us have experienced let-downs that left us feeling miserable and perhaps depressed. Relationship problems or those associated with work are fairly common, likely producing a down mood that passes fairly quickly, but in some instances the poor mood is more than just a poor mood, persisting for an extended period, and significantly disturbing daily functioning. The specific symptoms expressed can vary appreciably across individuals, often fluctuating over time, and new symptoms can be incorporated into the illness.

Classification systems have been developed for the various symptoms of mental illnesses. One of these, the Diagnostic and Statistical Manual (DSM) has undergone several revisions over the years, with the most recent fifth edition (DSM-5) being released in 2013. A similar instrument, the World Health Organization's International Statistical Classification of Diseases and Related Health Problems (ICD-10) is in many respects similar to the DSM, but is more commonly used in Europe. Having a compendium that outlines specific illnesses for a range of diseases is useful, if for no other reason than to make sure clinicians are working from the same set of criteria. However, as we'll see, these criteria also create problems, including some that might hamper treatment. My own preference is to describe depression on the basis of what the National Institute of Mental Health (NIMH) in the US describes as Research Domain Criteria (rDoC), focused on linking symptoms to neurobiological processes and then relating these to particular treatments.

Major depressive disorder, according to the DSM-5, is diagnosed when an individual presents with either depressed mood or anhedonia (diminished feelings of reward), for at least two weeks. Additionally, individuals must present with at least four of the following symptoms: (a) significant weight loss or weight gain; (b) insomnia or hypersomnia; (c) psychomotor agitation or retardation; (d) fatigue, loss of energy; (e) feelings of worthlessness or excessive, inappropriate guilt; (f) diminished cognitive abilities, such as impaired concentration and difficulty making decisions; and (g) recurrent thoughts of death or recurrent suicidal ideation. In some individuals one or more episodes of mania may also occur. This might comprise hypomania in which manic symptoms are limited, but it can also manifest as hypermania. In either event a diagnosis of bipolar disorder might be appropriate, which requires treatment that is different from that of depressive disorders.

You might have realized based on this list of symptoms that there's something very fishy about the way major depressive disorder is defined. Two individuals may present with entirely different symptoms, to the extent that even symptoms opposite to one another may be present, yet both will be diagnosed with depression. This sort of difficulty has reinforced the view that the appropriate way to treat patients should be based on the specific symptoms that patients exhibit rather than on some amorphous concept referred to as depression. Patients with high levels of anxiety might be affected by neurochemical processes that are different from those seen in individuals with low anxiety. Likewise, increased eating and reduced eating, increased sleep and reduced sleep, and the presence of suicidal ideation or not, may each reflect differences of underlying biological processes. The appropriate treatment for depression may vary with the specific symptoms of the disorder as well as potential differences of the genes and biological substrates that are present in any given individual.

So, how come so little has been done to tackle the suicide epidemic?

Suicide may result from the individual's desire to die on their own terms instead of being victimized by dementia or some other illness. Mental illness in the form of schizophrenia and bipolar disorders are also associated with suicide, but severe depression and PTSD are the most common motivators of this behavior. It is estimated that deaths by suicide worldwide approach 1 million people a year, and promise to increase further; in Canada alone about 3,600 individuals die by suicide each year, in the UK it's 4,400, and in Australia it's about 2,000, whereas in the US, 30,000, some say 40,000, people die in this fashion yearly. Those occurrences are about the same as the deaths that occur through automobile accidents, but while those deaths have declined by about 50 percent over the past few years owing to increased safety measures, suicide rates have increased. In fact, it's estimated that about 60 percent of individuals contemplating suicide do not receive the professional help required.

There are several elements that favor suicide: feelings of loneliness and disconnection from others, feeling as if one were a burden owing to poor health or joblessness, and the diminution of fear that comes from being tired of unhappiness or becoming habituated to the thoughts of engaging in self-harm. The risk of suicide is high if an individual has the desire to die and the ability and means to end their own life. It's sad whenever anyone dies, and especially so when the person dies by suicide. But even when the person makes an attempt that is unsuccessful it's obviously a sign that things are very bad, and it raises flags about the future. Young individuals who attempt suicide are apt to encounter bad times down the road, ranging from financial and physical problems, through to those involving mental health issues.

Among depressed individuals treated with SSRIs, the risk for suicide increases, especially among adolescents who ordinarily are more impulsive than older individuals. However, it's exceptionally difficult to know which individuals will be those who are affected in this way. A new test may be on the horizon in this regard. A set of multiple genetic biomarkers has been identified that is estimated to predict with about 90 percent accuracy which individuals would be at risk of suicide associated with antidepressant use. While there has been reluctance to prescribe antidepressants to adolescents, there is still the question that needs to be addressed as to what fate awaited those who did not receive treatment?

Depressive subtypes

Rather than referring to depression in the singular, the term sometimes preferred is that of depressive disorders, since we're probably not dealing with a singular disease, but instead, diverse disorders exist that have some overlapping symptoms. Subtypes of depression have long been distinguished from one another, and it has been considered

Subtypes of depression

Melancholic depression is characterized by severely depressed mood and pronounced anhedonia. Symptoms are often worst in the early mornings, and psychomotor agitation, early morning awakening, excessive weight loss, or excessive guilt are common.

Typical versus atypical major depressive disorders differ markedly in their symptom profiles. In both instances the depression is less severe than in melancholic depression, but whereas typical depression is associated with reduced eating, weight loss and diminished sleep, atypical depression is characterized by increased eating, weight gain, and increased sleep, coupled with a tendency toward persistent rejection sensitivity that may promote disturbed social functioning.

Dysthymia comprises chronic but moderate depressive symptoms that persist for at least two years, although symptoms often wax and wane. If not effectively treated, major depression may develop, superimposed on a dysthymia background, wherein the symptoms of this so-called "double depression" are much more difficult to treat.

Seasonal affective disorder (SAD) is a form of depression that is tied to duration of light over the course of a day, typically appearing in the autumn or winter, and resolving in the spring.

Recurrent brief depression is characterized by intermittent depressive episodes that occur, on average, once a month over at least one year, but are not tied to any particular cycles (e.g., menstrual cycle). The symptoms persist for brief periods, typically 2–4 days, but can be very intense and can be accompanied by suicidal ideation and suicide attempts.

Postpartum depression as the name applies, occurs after childbirth. The symptoms are much like those of major depression, likely linked to hormonal changes that accompany pregnancy or those that occur in association with childbirth. In this regard, childbirth may give rise to PTSD, and it is possible that in some women the depression is a comorbid feature of the PTSD.

Treatment resistant depression is the term used to describe patients who haven't shown a positive response to at least three different treatments. Often, such patients show lifelong depression despite having undergone numerous treatment efforts. As we'll see, newer medications have been making significant inroads in treatment of this condition.

that these illnesses have very different etiologies and underlying mechanisms, and might also call for distinct treatments.

Cognitive theories of depressive disorders

Several theoretical perspectives have been offered to account for the development of depression. Some of these, such as psychoanalytic theories, have largely dropped by the wayside, being replaced with either cognitive models of depression or those that involve biochemical and/or genetic explanations. According to cognitive models, depression arises as a result of disturbed or negative ways that individuals think about themselves, whereas the neurochemical explanations of depression assert that changes of hormones, growth factors or neurotransmitters are responsible for the development of depressive disorders. Of course, the two may go hand-in-hand, as neurochemical changes might promote the cognitive disturbances, which can further exacerbate the biological disturbances.

Helplessness

It might be recalled that Seligman and his associates suggested that when animals or humans encounter uncontrollable stressful situations they learn that they have no control over their destiny, essentially being "helpless" in determining events. If these cognitions persist and are strong enough, individuals might fall into a state of depression. These feelings and cognitions would not only be accompanied by a failure of the individual to make efforts to alter their destinies, but responses to positive or rewarding events would be altered as well. This is reminiscent of the negative biases that depressed individuals display when they encounter difficulty in achieving goals ("I can try to do what's required, but I know that it just won't work out"), and may encourage anhedonia in which the rewarding value of stimuli and events is diminished. Of course, the helplessness expressed by depressed patients might be a feature of their illness, rather than being a causal factor, but the helplessness view is intuitively appealing and was widely adopted as being responsible for the development of the illness.

Although most people, at one time or another, encounter stressful events over which they might not have control, only a modest proportion actually become clinically depressed. What is it about some individuals that makes them vulnerable to psychopathology, whereas others escape relatively unscathed? Helplessness theorists suggested that the specific attributions formed regarding failure or stressor experiences were fundamental in determining the development of cognitive disturbances. When individuals fail in reaching their goals they might ask themselves why this occurred, and their specific attributional style may have a lot to do with their propensity for depression. Individuals differ on three appraisal (attribution) dimensions that in particular combinations would favor the emergence of helplessness and hence depression. They can make internal attributions ("I'm not very good at stuff related to computers") or external attributions ("I might not be very good at computer stuff, but who could work in that noisy environment?"); the attributions can be stable or unstable ("I'm never any good with computers and never will be" versus "at times, I'm not very good with computers, but it depends on a bunch of things"); the attributions can also be either global or specific ("I'm neither good with computers, nor any of the other new-fangled stuff" versus "I'm not very good at anything that has to do with computers, but I'm fine with other things"). If they are the type who makes internal, stable, global attributions regarding their inabilities, they will develop negative expectations of the future, coupled with feelings of inadequacy and poor self-esteem, culminating in feelings of helplessness, which encourages depressive disorders. It's fine to make assertions regarding the link between attributional style and the development of depression, but we might also want to know how these dysfunctional ways of thinking evolved. As we've already seen, many factors that influence our stress responses, including early experiences, genetic dispositions, and several personality variables, might play into this cognitive mindset.

Hopelessness

A view that preceded the helplessness perspective was the perspective advanced by Beck (1970) that feelings of "hopelessness" were a primary feature of depressed individuals. According to this view, among some individuals streams of negative automatic thoughts

Imaging the brain and other organs

The discovery that X-rays could be used to image bones and abnormalities in soft tissues, such as the lung and bowel, eventually led to the development of powerful imaging methods that could be useful in deciphering what was happening in other soft tissues, including the brain and muscles such as the heart. With computer innovations, computed tomography (CT) scanning was developed so that a series of two-dimensional X-ray images from different directions could be combined to render a three-dimensional image of tissues that could be used for diagnostic purposes. Another widely used technique is that of fluoroscopy, which provides real-time moving images of particular organs, permitting detection of coronary artery blockages. Some of these procedures, such as CT scanning, involve high levels of X-ray doses that ought to have limited their use, but from 1996 to 2005 the use of CT scans more than doubled in children younger than 14 years of age.

The methods used to evaluate what might be happening in the brain in association with cognitive processes have evolved to an astonishing extent. Researchers and clinicians can now evaluate neuronal activity that occurs within particular brain regions and circuits during specific thoughts or exposure to particular stimuli, and considerable research has been conducted to identify neuronal processes associated with psychopathological conditions. Among the most widely used imaging techniques in experimental settings are functional magnetic resonance imaging (or fMRI) and positron emission tomography (PET). The fMRI method indirectly assesses brain activity by measuring changes of blood flow and particularly the changes dependent on blood oxygen level. Essentially, the more oxygenation that occurs, the greater the neuronal activity presumed to be present. By measuring changes that occur at two points in time (e.g., before versus after a stimulus is presented) one can get some idea of what brain regions are being affected by particular stimuli or events. However, they don't inform us which types of neurons or transmitters are essential for a particular behavior. By analogy, they tell us that the suspect of a crime is situated in a particular part of a city, but it says little about what he or she looks like. PET deals with this to some extent. This kind of imaging offers a view of activity within the brain, revealing the type of neuronal receptors that are activated. Recently, PET has been combined with fMRI to show changes of activity over small time-frames, allowing the identification of both neuronal activity and receptor changes in response to specific stimuli.

frequently emerge that center on negative aspects of the past, the present, and the future. In response to negative events, one or two disturbed thoughts might initially appear, but with the passage of time and more stressful experiences, individuals may develop a negative framework in which they see themselves as being inadequate, worthless, and a failure. With these biases reinforced through further experiences, memories of past events take on a more negative tone, and individuals may come to have poorer expectations that the future will be any better. In fact, these individuals might selectively attend to those stimuli that are consistent with their negative perspectives, and will filter or ignore evidence inconsistent with this schema, thereby strengthening their warped cognitive views, and furthering the depression.

The strengthening of negative schemas involves a degree of automaticity, so that instead of coping with stressors through effective, situation-dependent methods, individuals may resort to negative ruminations, which feed on themselves. Although cognitive systems might ordinarily keep excessive rumination in check, when these control systems are not operating properly, ruminative behaviors may proceed unabated. Essentially, depressive features are reinforced and maintained by a combination of negative ruminative thoughts, as well as negative self-referential cognitions. In fact, this form of rumination is an excellent predictor of later depression, as well as the deteriorating and chronic course of some physical illnesses.

In an effort to bring together the biological and cognitive frameworks of depression, Disner and his associates (2011) offered a biological model of hopelessness that involved

Better, but not cured – recurrence of depression

Individuals who have been depressed are at high risk of becoming ill again. They might simply have a personality that renders them more prone to depression, or it might be that having experienced multiple stressors, their biological systems have become sensitized or primed, so that when stressors reoccur, neurochemical responses will push them toward depression. Imaging studies revealed that among currently depressed patients and those in remission, inducing an unhappy mood by exposing them to sad autobiographical memory scripts resulted in neuronal activity being reduced in the medial orbitofrontal cortex and anterior cingulate cortex, an outcome that did not occur among those who had never been depressed. Likewise, among patients with a history of recurrent depression, viewing a sad film clip altered neuronal activity within the medial prefrontal cortex, and that, in turn, predicted ruminative propensities and increased risk for relapse. In contrast, these neuronal disturbances were not observed among individuals who showed sustained remission from depression. Thus, even though some individuals had recovered from depression, their brain reactions to unhappy stimuli were just as they might have been when they were depressed, signifying that their vulnerability to illness persisted. Essentially, the absence of symptoms didn't necessarily mean that the mechanisms responsible for depression were "cured." Instead, processes responsible for depression might provisionally be modified, but in the face of a challenge they reappeared and could prompt further depression. Parenthetically, these data also lead to the possibility that brain activity variations in response to a challenge might be useful in predicting recurrence of illness and might be clinically relevant, possibly indicating the need for continued cognitive therapy to thwart further depressive episodes.

a series of interconnected brain pathways. They suggested that emotions are regulated through bottom-up processing in which negative events may cause activation of limbic brain regions that promote strong emotional responses. At the same time, cortical processes may act in a top-down control manner to inhibit or limit certain thoughts related to emotions. Thus, aspects of the prefrontal cortex that ordinarily control self-referential schemas, rumination and biased attention and processing could influence limbic brain regions, such as the amygdala, and hence emotional responses. When prefrontal cortical functioning is disturbed, control over emotion-related brain regions may be abdicated so that automatic, negative processing predominates. The resulting negative appraisals, attributions and rumination would thus persist, causing still other brain changes, including those important for recognizing and responding to positive stimuli, culminating in anhedonia and pessimism. Eventually, depressed individuals or those at risk for the illness not only react strongly to negative events, but also exhibit attention and memory biases directed toward negative stimuli and inappropriate information processing ensues. Once a depressive state has been established, breaking through the persistent negative wall can be exceedingly difficult, although the development of cognitive behavioral therapy (CBT) as well as variants of this procedure have achieved considerable success.

Depression from an evolutionary perspective

Based on natural selection, those characteristics that are useful and allow for the species to propagate should be maintained, whereas selection should have worked against disadvantageous characteristics. Indeed, it is with considerable hubris that many of us believe that we're at the peak of natural selection processes, despite the fact that we know of many phenotypes that have persisted even though they're seemingly not useful and may even be destructive. Actually, given so many millennia of natural selection, why does depression exist at all? As mentioned earlier, a gene can be altered by a random mutation or by an epigenetic change that favors the occurrence of depression in a given individual even if there is no selective advantage in this occurring. There are also genetic characteristics that seemingly don't have negative consequences, only becoming apparent under certain conditions, such as when particularly stressful experiences are encountered. In this instance the selection pressure against these genes being passed on may be relaxed under non-threatening conditions and thus the phenotype may persist, although at a relatively low frequency. There are also instances in which the negative consequences of a particular gene might not become apparent until somewhat later in life, well after carriers have already passed on these genes. Huntington's disease is an example of this, as are forms of heart disease and certain types of cancer, including breast cancer. Despite the very terrible consequences of these diseases, they have been passed from parent to child simply because people hadn't recognized that they carried the gene that could put their offspring in jeopardy.

Some of our emotions and cognitions, particularly those that are negative, might not seem to have much value. But, like pain and nausea, their presence lets us know that there's something physically amiss that needs to be dealt with. Of course, nature could have been kinder to us and provided a nonpainful method of signaling us to take protective measures. Individuals who have experienced severe depression could testify to the distress they endured, and might confess to their all-consuming days of rumination and thoughts of suicide simply to escape from the dark, gloomy place they were in. It's unlikely that we can find any value in this experience, except perhaps the relief that comes with its alleviation. However, in the case of mild depression there might be another type of advantage, so long as it doesn't mature to severe depression.

In the 1950s, kids in grade school were educated in many ways that were different than they are today. Certain maxims were delivered as absolute truths. Speaking out of turn was met by a teacher saying "empty barrels make the most sound," and breaking away from the mold and trying new ideas would be constrained by "a bird in the hand is worth two in the bush." But there was nothing more annoying than "if at first you don't succeed, then try, try, try again," which basically meant that homework would have to be redone until we got it right. "Stick-with-it-ness," pronounced as a single word, was considered a virtue. I suppose that might have been good for some kids, but for others it might have been demoralizing and promoted hatred of school, especially when kids were shamed for not attaining the goal that the teacher insisted on. It's unfortunate that having certain goals simply doesn't mean that the individual has the ability to reach these goals, and teachers and parents need to come to terms with what is attainable and what is not for a particular child.

Have you watched early phases of *American Idol*, or one of its imitators? How did this poor kid who can't hold a tune come to believe that if he or she tries hard enough they'll be the next idol? Likewise a person might have the desire and drive to become a professional hockey player or a physicist, but they might lack in other ways, and encouraging them to try, try, try again might be counterproductive. The mild depression that comes from a failure experience could increase motivation and promote positive outcomes, but in some instances repeated failures might encourage the abandonment of unattainable goals, and perhaps the discovery of those that are more realistic. As expected, it has been reported that with such shifts of goals, health improved and physiological signs of distress diminished. Of course, there are many occasions when defining what reflects appropriate versus inappropriate goals can be difficult, and squelching hopes can have demoralizing effects that lead to still other negative consequences. Nobody said that being a parent or teacher is easy. Is there any chance that Justyna once said to her son, Fryderyk Chopin, something like "Freddie, Freddie, there is no future in this. Besides, you seem confused by the sharps and flats, and you're so clumsy you can hardly play chopsticks. Put away this music writing and go play outside with the other children."

Forecasting illness

Depressive features often appear with a variety of other illnesses, such as heart disease. But this doesn't necessarily mean that individuals become depressed because they learn that they have a heart problem, and it similarly doesn't necessarily imply that feelings of depression promote heart disease. Instead, one illness might be predictive of a second because they share common environmental or experience-based triggers or underlying neurobiological processes. As it happens, depressive disorders are associated with numerous illnesses in addition to heart disease, occurring in association with stroke, inflammatory disorders, autoimmune conditions, PTSD, anxiety disorders, addiction, metabolic syndrome and diabetes, and delayed recovery from concussion, as well as neurodegenerative diseases, such as Alzheimer's and Parkinson's disease. Moreover, the presence of depression in association with an illness, such as stroke, usually is indicative of a poorer prognosis. In view of these various comorbidities, depression ought to be considered as a marker that forewarns physicians about the potential for the later emergence of other illnesses.

Depression from a neurochemical vantage

The basic premise of all neurobiological perspectives of depression is that for some reason neurochemical, hormonal or growth factor processes in particular brain regions have changed in some fashion which then influence the development of illness. In addition to other approaches, scientists often rely on animal models of human disorders in an effort to determine the mechanisms underlying these conditions and to develop treatment strategies to attenuate them. Although it could be surmised that depressive illness is a uniquely human condition, those close to their pets will say that they can sense depressed feelings in their animal companions. Pig farmers can also tell you that when piglets are separated from their moms it's fairly typical for both to become distressed, often showing signs of depression much like those seen in humans. The same thing seems to happen in rodents that express their dismay through ultrasonic vocalizations, and so we don't hear their distress. Of course, it's still questionable whether the multiple dimensions of human psychological disorders can be fully captured through animal models. Rodents presumably don't have the cognitive capacity that humans do, nor do they necessarily have the complex emotions that we do, and it's hardly likely that their behaviors and moods are governed by attributions like those associated with depression in humans (e.g., my self-esteem is low; I can never get anything done right; I'm no good at finding cheese). Furthermore, do animals feel shame and humiliation as humans do? Do they have hopes and aspirations for the future, or do they even know that there is a future? Despite the limitations, animal models have been developed that recapitulate many of the symptoms of human depression and they could be modified by standard antidepressant treatments.

Neurobiological explanations of depressive disorders

Knowing what we do about the effects of uncontrollable stressors on neurobiological processes, particularly if they comprise chronic, variable events, it's highly likely that they contribute to the development of psychological disorders. Indeed, pharmacological studies indicated that antidepressants and other drugs could alter stressor-induced behavioral disturbances. In humans, electrical brain activity as well as neuronal or receptor disturbances could be detected in specific brain regions of depressed individuals. Brain neurochemicals and receptors in postmortem tissues of depressed people who had died by suicide revealed several distinct differences relative to those who were not depressed and had died through causes other than suicide. Finally, genetic analyses have linked particular genes or gene polymorphisms to symptoms of illness. Together, the data obtained through these various approaches have provided important clues regarding the processes responsible for mental health disorders and helped in developing new treatment strategies.

Coping with stressors is shared by cognitive, behavioral, and neurochemical process, but in the absence of cognitive and behavioral methods of dealing with external challenges, the coping burden rests heavily on neurochemical processes. As a result, these systems might become excessively taxed, especially if the stressors were encountered on a chronic and unpredictable basis, and thus psychopathology might ensue. Based on the neurochemical consequences of stressors, several candidates were identified that could account for the effects of stressors on depression. There isn't all that much to be gained by providing an exhaustive list of neurotransmitters and how they might be related to depression. So, the focus here will be limited to only a few of these, providing indications of their potential roles in mood-related illnesses.

Predicting pathology

In view of the diversity of symptoms and the array of neurobiological processes that might underlie psychiatric disorders, and the individual differences that occur regarding the effectiveness of pharmacological and cognitive strategies, their treatment might not be best served by assessing them as syndromes. Instead, there has been a push to adopt an "endophenotype" approach in which specific characteristics or symptoms of the illness (or clusters of symptoms that tend to fall together) are linked to genetic and biological factors, which then determine the choice of treatment. This is the approach used in the treatment of cancer, and it is beginning to be adopted in the diagnosis and treatment of psychological disorders.

Inferences regarding the cause of an illness are often made based on biological changes detected in blood or saliva. These neurobiological changes might not be causally related to the illness, but they still might be useful as "biomarkers" of illness. They can tell us about pathological outcomes that are imminent or present, and can potentially be useful in predicting which treatments might be best suited for an existing pathology, or whether an individual is at risk for illness recurrence after the initial disturbances have resolved. More than a single marker may be necessary to provide a full story, but when considered as a group, these markers might be indicative of a system in distress that calls for rapid and marked lifestyle changes or other treatment interventions. There's some question concerning the ethics of trying to figure out who will or who won't develop pathology at some time in the future. However, no one would argue about the usefulness of having biomarkers that are indicative of which treatment strategies would be most effective for individuals who have been struck by illness.

Serotonin, norepinephrine and dopamine in relation to depressive disorders

Analyses of the biochemical factors responsible for depressive illness have been concerned more with serotonin than other neurotransmitters. In animals, the instigation of depressive-like features by stressors was accompanied by variations of serotonin and its receptors, and treatments that attenuated the serotonin disturbances reduced the signs of depression. Similarly, in healthy human volunteers, treatments that temporarily diminished serotonin levels could induce a transient sad mood, and repeated use of selective serotonin reuptake inhibitors (SSRIs), which increase serotonin availability, frequently diminished depressive symptoms.

Such findings supported the view that serotonin was involved in depressive disorders, but once again, it turned out not to be as simple as it first appeared. As a whole, studies involving imaging procedures and those that assessed neuronal changes among depressed individuals who had died by suicide haven't provided overly impressive findings. Some studies supported the involvement of particular receptors in mediating depressive illness, but others told an entirely different story. There were also reports that although certain receptors weren't causally related to the development of illness, they could be used as markers to predict the response to antidepressant medications. For instance, mutations were uncovered in a gene coding for an enzyme responsible for serotonin synthesis as well as within genes that regulate the $5\text{-}HT_{1A}$ receptor, which seemed to be related to how individuals responded to pharmacotherapy.

With improved understanding of receptor functioning, greater attention focused on whether certain receptor subtypes or other factors related to receptors, such as the processes involved in transporting receptors to the neuron's surface, might be cogent in relation to depressive illnesses. When many of the early studies concerning the link between depression and specific receptors were conducted, most researchers weren't thinking in terms of personalized medical treatments, or that specific biological changes ought to be linked to particular aspects of a given pathology. However, as greater attention was devoted to these relations, particular serotonin receptor variations were found to be associated with specific aspects of depression. Increased activity of particular serotonin receptors in discrete portions of the prefrontal cortex, for instance, occurred primarily in patients with especially elevated feelings of pessimism and hopelessness. Likewise, other receptor subtypes were associated with depression among individuals who had displayed high levels of hostility or aggressiveness.

Gene and environmental interactions

This brings us to yet another component of the serotonergic system that might be important for depressive disorders. Having been released from a neuron, serotonin will stimulate receptors on an adjacent neuron, after which the action of the neurotransmitter will be terminated by particular enzymes present at the synapse, or the transmitter will be taken back up into the neuron through a mechanism referred to as the serotonin transporter (5-HTT). The SSRIs were initially presumed to have their positive effects by inhibiting the reuptake of serotonin into the neuron so that it would remain in the synaptic cleft longer and thus have a greater opportunity to stimulate receptors. Thus, the possibility was considered that depression might arise owing to a dysfunction in the serotonin transporter process, but initial studies were inconsistent concerning this linkage.

Exciting data were subsequently reported regarding the connection between depression and a polymorphism related to the gene controlling the serotonin transporter. As most readers know, we ordinarily have two forms (alleles) of each gene, one coming from mom and the other from dad, and variations can appear on either one or both alleles. In the case of the gene coding for the serotonin transporter, the alleles may comprise either a short or a long form, with the latter containing a sequence of amino acids absent in the short format. The incidence of depression did not differ in relation to whether the short or long form of the gene was present. However, depression was elevated if individuals carried the short alleles of the serotonin transporter gene and also encountered major life stressors, early life trauma, or a stressful family environment. The interaction between a specific gene and environmental factors created considerable excitement, prompting many similar studies. Those studies that relied on interviews and objective measures of stressor experiences confirmed that depression was elevated among individuals with the short serotonin transporter allele who also experienced a strong stressor during adulthood, and this outcome was still more pronounced if the stressor comprised childhood maltreatment.

These findings are not only informative in their own right, but also make one wonder how likely it is that genes involved in other neurochemical systems might also be acting additively or interactively with environmental factors in promoting depression. For that matter, what other syndromes made up of many complex factors also involve interactions between the environment and genetic factors? As we've seen, scientific inquiry often moves

A gene for depression or a gene for stress sensitivity

Why would having the serotonin transporter gene polymorphism make individuals particularly vulnerable to depressive illness provided that a strong stressor was experienced? One could invoke all sorts of complex processes, but it might simply be that the presence of the short alleles might dispose individuals to altered serotonin neuronal activity that makes them more sensitive to stressor experience. Those with the short alleles might be more sensitive to stressors, appraise stressors differently, or might not cope well with stressors, and thus when aversive events are encountered they might have greater repercussions. It was similarly suggested that this polymorphism influenced neuronal plasticity, so that environmental experiences would be more apt to shape later reactions to stressors, and hence individuals with the short allele would be particularly likely to develop stressor-provoked depressive disorders. These perspectives seem to be sensible as the gene associated with the serotonin transporter is not uniquely related to depression, but also to PTSD and obsessive compulsive disorder (OCD). In essence, by influencing stress sensitivity or neuronal plasticity, this gene could affect the emergence of a variety of stress-related pathological conditions.

It seems that among carriers of the short allele, amygdala and hippocampal neuronal activity could be distinguished from neuronal functioning among those with the long alleles. Among short allele carriers, neuronal activity in these brain regions was continuously activated and the response to negative events was exaggerated. In a sense, continuous activation of neurons might have had effects akin to a chronic state of distress, which may be accompanied by hypervigilance and rumination. If individuals carrying the short alleles for the serotonin transporter are, in fact, more sensitive or reactive to stressors, teaching them how to properly appraise stressors, avoid automatic negative thought processes, and cope effectively might be particularly useful in limiting the negative influence of this gene.

in small incremental steps, and a couple of steps forward can be interrupted by a step back. Thus, processes that hadn't seemed to be related to depression in earlier studies might need to be reevaluated as they might interact with other genes or environmental factors.

Reward processes in depression: dopamine and anhedonia

Depressed individuals, as we've seen, frequently exhibit diminished feelings of reward or pleasure from things that ordinarily would have made them feel good. Given that dopamine functioning is fundamentally involved in reward processes, the presumed involvement of diminished dopamine in depression was almost a forgone conclusion. But this wasn't how it worked out at first. It's remarkable how many drugs used to treat psychological disorders were discovered serendipitously, which could mean that their discovery was a fluke, but it could also mean that the researchers put themselves in the right place at the right time. On the other side are possible instances, many of which we likely still aren't aware of (unknown unknowns), in which drug discoveries failed to be realized because of misleading evidence or because researchers were too quick to abandon potentially positive treatment strategies. The involvement of dopamine in depression falls squarely into the latter category.

It was expected that administering the drug l-DOPA, which is converted into dopamine once it gets to the brain, ought to alleviate depression, or at least diminish the anhedonia associated with the illness. However, its effectiveness as an antidepressant was limited, and as a result, and perhaps because dopamine was overshadowed by serotonin as the main suspect in depression, detailed analyses of dopamine in relation to depression didn't materialize. It took several decades, and a great deal of preclinical evidence implicating dopamine involvement in depression, before drugs that affect dopamine were used as antidepressants.

A role for dopamine in reward processes is fairly certain, but there are still some aspects of dopamine functioning that are puzzling. Increased dopamine release certainly occurred within the nucleus accumbens in response to positive, rewarding events, but a similar outcome also developed in response to stressful stimuli. It seemed paradoxical that two such different events would affect dopamine in a similar way. To account for this, it was suggested that instead of thinking of dopamine as being involved in reward processes, it would be more profitable to consider dopamine neurons within the nucleus accumbens as being responsible for stimuli or events appearing especially salient, irrespective of whether they are viewed positively or negatively. In a sense, dopamine activity in the nucleus accumbens might serve as a signal that something significant is happening, and it is the job of other regions to provide further instructions concerning what behavioral responses are needed. Yet another alternative is that positive and negative events may activate different types of dopamine neurons within a given brain region, or these stimuli may instigate different firing patterns and neuronal rhythms, which lend themselves to different emotional and behavioral responses. Whatever the case, stressors do influence dopamine functioning within brain regions associated with reward processes, and disturbances of dopamine functioning in these regions might contribute to the anhedonia that so often is characteristic of depressive disorders.

Depression and anxiety: corticotropin releasing hormone (CRH) as a player in depression

As anxiety is a frequent comorbid feature of depression, and variations of CRH in several brain regions are associated with anxiety, CRH might contribute to depressive disorders. The potential involvement of CRH in depression was encouraged by the fact that HPA axis functioning, which involves CRH activation, is often disturbed among depressed patients. As well, CRH_1 receptor functioning within aspects of the prefrontal cortex was disturbed among depressed individuals who had died by suicide. In addition, depression has been associated with polymorphisms of the gene that codes for CRH_1 receptors, and has been linked to a relatively poor therapeutic response to SSRI treatment, especially among depressed patients who presented with high levels of anxiety.

There has been progress in developing pharmacological strategies involving CRH antagonism to diminish depression, although this has been modest. Several novel CRH_1 antagonists reduced the symptoms of depression and altered the depressive electroencephalography (EEG) sleep profile in a subset of patients. However, it may still be premature to accept agents acting through CRH as effective antidepressants, but it's also too soon to reject them. The usefulness of CRH-based therapeutics may come down to finding biomarkers that inform clinicians about the nature of the biochemical disturbances present so that treatment strategies can be tailored accordingly.

Coordination and discoordination of neuronal process: gamma-aminobutyric acid (GABA)

It will be recalled that GABA in the brain serves in an inhibitory capacity, thus regulating the functioning of other neurons. Without this function, neuronal chaos could occur as every neuron attempted to have an input. Over the years, interest in $GABA_A$ functioning in relation to depression has appeared sporadically. The levels of GABA in depressed individuals were reported to be particularly low in some parts of the prefrontal and occipital cortex, and treatments that influence GABA functioning had positive effects on depressive mood. As well, GABA-related genes of individuals who died by suicide were altered in the prefrontal cortex and hippocampus. However, this was also evident among individuals who died by suicide but had not been depressed, and thus factors uniquely associated with suicide, rather than depression, were linked to these genes.

Depression and anxiety might not simply be related to how much GABA is present, but might reflect the actions on receptors or altered characteristics of these receptors. The GABA receptor is made up of five subunits or components from a fairly broad set of subunits. How these receptors behave in response to environmental stimuli, including stressors and drug treatments, might be determined by the specific combination of

Flexibility and inflexibility of neural connections in depressive disorders

Even if you knew very little about neuronal activity and mental illness, you might imagine that considerable coordination ordinarily occurred between brain neurons across broad neural networks. You might also think that the focused negativity and rumination associated with depression might be accompanied by neural networks that would be limited in their breadth. However, this isn't quite what was found. Instead, depression was associated with increased neural connections across many brain regions, and this connectivity was marked in the frontopolar cortex of depressed individuals, a brain region important for information processing, and was diminished following electroconvulsive therapy (ECT) that reduced depression. Although efficient brain functioning, including proper appraisals, decision-making, and coping responses, requires connections and cross-talk across many brain regions, a degree of selectivity is also needed. No matter that having broad neural networks can be useful, if they uniformly lead to negative thoughts and rumination, their actions will be counterproductive. Among depressed individuals the neural highway and its interconnections may be wide, but all neural roads lead to negativity and rumination.

As described earlier, flexibility with respect to how we appraise and cope with stressors is essential to deal with negative situations. The loss of this flexibility results in a diminished ability to move from one strategy to another as the situation demands, and in depressed individuals this inflexibility in the frontal cortex might be manifested as persistent negative thinking about the past, present, and future. It is conceivable that inhibition of neuronal functioning ordinarily offered by GABA is critical so that thoughts and ruminations don't go off in nonproductive directions.

subunits present. What might be particularly significant in relation to depression is that the behavior might not be linked to the density of the receptors, but instead might involve the coordination of different subunits that make up receptors. Specifically, among nondepressed individuals who had died suddenly, the expressions of the different $GABA_A$ subunits within several brain regions were highly correlated. Coordination between the subunits seemed to exist so that as one subunit went up, so did the expression of others. In contrast to this seemingly coordinated profile, in brain samples of the depressed individuals who had died by suicide, as in mice that experienced chronic stressors, the interrelationships between the $GABA_A$ subunits were largely absent. It was as if a conductor was present who orchestrated the subunits to respond in a synchronous manner, whereas in the brain of a depressed person who had committed suicide and in the chronically stressed mouse brain, there was nobody present to do this, resulting in a cacophony of random patterns. We don't know how these disturbances occurred, or precisely what they mean. However, coordination between the subunits may be essential for operation of neural networks and for neuronal rhythms that ordinarily occur in different brain regions. When these rhythms are disrupted our cognitive and emotional processes might be impaired.

Growth factors and depression

Structural and functional brain variations appear among depressed individuals, especially those who have experienced repeated episodes of depression or in whom depression is persistent. The brain changes include reduced hippocampal volume and reduced neural cell bodies within cortical brain regions, but these findings often don't speak to whether stressor events led to depression which caused this outcome, or whether stressors caused hippocampal or cortical changes that, in turn, provoked mood disturbances. It is also possible that genetic factors might have endowed some individuals with some brain regions that are relatively small, which might have disposed them to depression in the face of stressors. It is significant, as well, that reduced hippocampal volume doesn't occur solely among depressed individuals, but also in those with schizophrenia or posttraumatic stress disorder, raising the possibility that diminished hippocampal and cortical volume may be cogent risk factors for the development of psychopathology, and that additional factors determine which pathology will emerge.

Although the processes responsible for the diminished brain size associated with depressive disorders aren't certain, it's a good bet that growth factors play some role in this regard. Considerable evidence has linked growth factors to hippocampal neurogenesis, and the emergence of depression. For instance, BDNF and FGF-2, which sustain and encourage neural growth, are diminished in limbic brain regions in response to stressors, and in rodents the positive effects of antidepressants and electroconvulsive therapy were accompanied by elevated hippocampal cell growth. As well, signs of depression were evident among mice with deletion of genes for BDNF, and in the absence of BDNF or FGF-2 the positive effects derived from antidepressant medications were diminished. It seems that although antidepressants can increase BDNF and neurogenesis, if BDNF or FGF-2 fall below some critical level or cannot be manufactured, then the positive effects of antidepressants are precluded.

In addition to the brain changes, reduced BDNF levels were also observed in blood (serum) in different subtypes of depression, particularly among patients with severe or recurrent depressive illness, and in the presence of comorbid anxiety. As expected, growth factor levels in blood increased among patients who exhibited a positive antidepressant response after several weeks of treatment. However, this finding takes us back to the elephant in the room in relation to the effects of antidepressant drugs. Specifically, why is it that the level of serotonin goes up very quickly following SSRI treatment, but a 2–3 week drug regimen is needed for the mood changes to occur? As the effects of antidepressants on BDNF also require several weeks of treatment, it is possible that the antidepressants operate on depression through actions on BDNF rather than effects on serotonin, but this process takes some time to occur.

Another line of inquiry regarding the BDNF–depression link evolved following the discovery of a particular polymorphism on the BDNF gene. The presence of this poly-morphism was accompanied by diminished BDNF, which manifested behaviorally as a propensity toward negative affect, biases toward recalling negative events, as well as vulnerability to depression. This was especially notable if individuals had also encoun-tered adverse life experiences and if this BDNF mutation was accompanied by still other polymorphisms that predicted depression, such as the short alleles of the gene for 5-HTT. It is particularly interesting that early life abuse coupled with the BDNF polymorphism was associated with low grey matter volume within the anterior cingulate cortex, although this was not apparent within other aspects of the prefrontal cortex and the hippocampus. These findings point to the functioning of the anterior cingulate cortex, a region critical in appraisal and decision-making processes, as a mechanistic link between stressful early life experiences, the BDNF polymorphism, and adult depression.

As strong as the case has been supporting a role for BDNF in depression, stressful events don't always result in diminished BDNF, and acute and chronic stressors may actually be accompanied by elevated levels of this growth factor in some brain regions. Furthermore, despite reports that serum BDNF levels increased following antidepressant treatment, there have been failures to observe this outcome. Why these differences occurred across studies is somewhat baffling, but as indicated earlier, if BDNF levels fall too low it might be that the positive effects of antidepressants won't develop. This aside, even if blood levels of BDNF were related to brain changes of BDNF, it's not clear that BDNF changes in blood are representative of what's happening within the specific regions of the brain that are responsible for depressive symptoms. It seems that there is still much that we don't know concerning the link between growth factors and depres-sion which needs to be resolved before effective treatment strategies can be formulated based on BDNF functioning.

Inflammatory processes and depressive disorders

Researchers in the field of psychoneuroimmunology are fond of indicating that multidi-rectional communication occurs between the immune system and other processes, including hormones and central neurotransmitters. Moreover, just as stressful events can influence immune functioning, variations of immune factors, such as cytokines, can have profound effects on stress hormones and brain neurotransmitters, and may promote depressive symptoms.

Immunological challenges, as we've seen, may influence brain neurochemical processes, much as psychological stressors do. In mice, these outcomes are still more pronounced if the immune challenges occur when they have been stressed. These neurobi-ological changes are accompanied by depressive-like behaviors characterized by anhedonia and disrupted social interactions, as well as a constellation of other features, such as anorexia, fatigue, reduced motor activity, curled body posture, ruffled fur and drooping eyes, that collectively are referred to as "sickness behaviors." The latter symptoms are, in

Getting a jump on illness

Immunologically related illnesses can affect neurochemical processes that influence our mood, cognitions, and behaviors. Indeed, brain neurochemical changes can be engendered by immune challenges, such as viral or bacterial insults, even before overt signs of illness are present. You might not have made the connection, or even noticed it, but on the day preceding the appearance of a viral illness, you may be a bit lethargic and perhaps a bit out of sorts. A friend might pick up on this, saying "you seem to be a bit off today," and might even add that "maybe you're coming down with something." It is possible that your immune system, being aware of the viral presence, has informed the brain of this, and so unbeknownst to you, your brain has instructed your body to slow down to conserve the energy that will be necessary to deal with the cold or flu that you might soon experience. Such a smart brain!

Ungrateful cat

Incidentally, cat bites have been associated with very high rates of depression, more so in women than men. Indeed, of 750 patients treated for cat bites 41.3 percent were later found to be depressed. It's not likely that little Mitzy, having turned on its owner, caused feelings of rejection that resulted in the tailspin into depression. Instead it could be that the cat bite, which can deposit a variety of bacteria, may have promoted inflammatory responses that led to depression.

some respects, reminiscent of the neurovegetative features associated with atypical depression as well as fatigue-related illnesses, such as chronic fatigue syndrome. Consistent with the involvement of inflammatory factors in relation to depression, repeated treatment with antidepressant drugs attenuated the depressive-like behavioral disturbances in rodents. Paralleling these animal studies, depressive disorders in humans were often accompanied by high levels of acute phase proteins, such as C-reactive protein, as well as blood levels of cytokines, notably IL-6 and TNF-α. Moreover, the presence of immune-related disorders, viruses and common parasites in humans were associated with the appearance of depressive disorders, and among patients experiencing strong depression for the first time, almost one-third had been admitted to hospital previously with an infectious illness.

The fact that inflammatory factors and depression occur together doesn't mean that one caused the other. In some patients, cytokine levels were reported to normalize with successful antidepressant treatment, but in others, cytokine elevations persisted even after "recovery" from depression, possibly indicating that inflammation has little to do with promoting or maintaining the depression. In this regard, the cytokine changes associated with depression might come about owing to factors secondary to depressive disorders, such as disturbed sleep, poor health-related behaviors, weight changes, drug use, and institutionalization, as opposed to being directly linked to the mood disorder. Yet, it is equally possible that despite the improved mood, the continued cytokine elevation might be indicative of something still being amiss within the inflammatory immune system, which could potentially predict recurrence of depression.

Although many studies showed that cytokine elevations and depression occurred contemporaneously, this doesn't mean that the cytokines actually caused depression. The best way to determine whether a causal connection exists between the two is through experimental manipulations that elicit inflammation, followed by evaluations of changes of mood state. Indeed, in humans, treatment with a low dose of a bacterial agent that increases cytokine levels promoted mild depressive symptoms as well as a feeling of "social disconnection." Similarly, vaccination that ordinarily triggers an immune reaction elicited depressive-like mood, fatigue, and impaired concentration, coupled with altered neuronal activity within the anterior cingulate cortex, just as is evident in clinical depression.

In line with the view that inflammatory factors are involved in depression, the effectiveness of antidepressant medication was enhanced by treatment with nonsteroidal, anti-inflammatory agents. It was similarly found that diminished depressive symptoms were reported among individuals with arthritis or with a skin condition who were treated with the TNF-α antagonist Etanercept. These findings are consistent with a role for inflammatory factors in depression, but it's certainly possible that the signs of depression abated as a result of the reduced pain or diminished skin problems that patients experienced.

Some of the strongest evidence implicating inflammatory factors in depression has come from clinical studies using the cytokine interferon-α. This particular form of interferon is used in the treatment of some forms of cancer, such as melanomas, leukemia and lymphomas, and when combined with antiviral agents, it is used in the treatment of hepatitis C. Like many cancer treatments, interferon-α can have fairly nasty side effects. Cognitive disturbances can be marked, and depression occurs in 30–50 percent of patients, sometimes necessitating discontinuation of treatment. The development of depressive symptoms in response to this immunotherapy was most pronounced among patients with a disposition toward a mood disorder and in individuals with poor social support, as well as those with relatively high levels of IL-6 prior to therapy. It is of practical and theoretical significance as well that when patients were treated with an SSRI the depressive-like effects of the immunotherapy were abated.

Several explanations have been offered concerning how interferon-α comes to induce depressive features. In response to immunotherapy, as in the case of stressors, several cytokines are released from brain microglia, leading to serotonin, CRH and growth

Obesity and inflammatory process

There is a stereotype of the obese person being jolly and always joking. In fact, however, obesity is related to depressive illness. Even if you were aware of this, you might have attributed it to heavier people having issues involving stigma or shame, and bullying. As we discussed in our consideration of heart disease, adipose tissue (fat) is an exceptionally rich source of several cytokines and thus the more frequent depression in overweight people might have to do with greater release of cytokines from fat deposits. Unfortunately, a vicious circle may exist wherein adiposity contributes to depression, and in some individuals the depression promotes elevated eating.

factor changes that could promote depressive illness. Alternatively, these cytokines might cause cell damage that favors depression or they may indirectly cause the appearance of products that can be toxic to neurons and might thus favor the development of depressive illness.

Before leaving the topic of IFN-α therapy in the provocation of depression, it is significant that in rodents IFN-α and stressors synergistically influence neurochemical functioning and the induction of depressive features. Patients who receive immunotherapy to ameliorate cancer or hepatitis C are likely very stressed owing to their medical condition, and when combined with immunotherapy the propensity for depression might increase. Accordingly, treatment of cancer and hepatitis C might benefit from broad approaches that consider the patient's psychological health and their ability to deal with stressors.

Although there has been an emphasis on linking immune and peripheral cytokine changes to depression, cytokines aren't only produced by peripheral immune cells, but can also be generated by microglia present within the brain. These cytokines are markedly increased in association with brain insults comprising traumatic head injury, stroke and seizure, and they can also be affected by stressors. In small amounts these cytokines might facilitate healing of microdamage, but at high levels these molecules could be neurodestructive so that they favor psychological disturbances, such as depression, which might signal a poor functional recovery. It is also possible that the depression

Gut microbes and depression

The importance of gut bacteria in relation to our health has been cropping up a fair bit in recent years. Earlier, we saw that it was important in relation to immune-related conditions and heart disease, but we usually don't think of our intestine as having much to do with depressive disorders. However, gut microbiota might contribute to mood disorders by virtue of their involvement in inflammatory processes. In fact, antibiotics seem to have positive effects in relation to mood states, and the depressive-like behavior in rats that had experienced early-life separation from their moms was attenuated by treatment with the probiotic Bifidobacterium infantis. Likewise, chronic treatment with lactic acid bacteria Lactobacillus rhamnosus limited stress-induced corticosterone elevations, influenced GABA expression within the amygdala, hippocampus and cortical regions, and diminished behaviors that reflect anxiety and depression. In rodents born germ-free, several brain neurotransmitters were altered and anxiety elevated, but when microbiota were introduced to their gut, the anxiety was attenuated, even though some neurochemical disturbances persisted. The point is that microbiota can profoundly affect brain processes, and because these can be lasting changes, vulnerability to later behavioral disturbances can be increased in response to stressors.

Probiotics have become one of the buzzwords for healthy living. These probiotics comprise living bacteria that enhance digestive processes and are being marketed as good bacteria. The data concerning their usefulness for psychological treatments are still limited, but probiotics could potentially have positive effects on psychological health, presumably by altering inflammatory processes.

Another perspective on depression

Although microglia haven't received the attention of neurons in relation to depression, they might play a pivotal role in this illness. Raz Yirmiya and his collaborators at Hebrew University (Kreisel et al., 2014) demonstrated that in mice a stressor administered over a few days provoked a marked increase in the proliferation and size of microglia, possibly reflecting an attempt to adapt to the challenge. However, with a more prolonged stressor regimen, microglia began to die off so that their numbers were appreciably reduced in the hippocampus, coinciding with the appearance of depressive-like behaviors. If the initial rise of microglia was prevented, so were the depressive symptoms and the death of microglia that accompanied further stressor experiences. Once the depressed state was present, however, this same treatment was ineffective, but when mice were treated with drugs that enhanced the growth of microglia, a very rapid reversal of the depressive-like features followed. These findings point to the important role of microglia in the evolution of depression, and a promise of new lines in the treatment of this disorder.

Incidentally, concussive injury in mice can lead to increased vulnerability to behavioral disturbances long after the initial insult. When mice that experienced concussive injury were later challenged, their microglial response was greatly exaggerated and they expressed symptoms of depression. It seems that following the initial hit, microglia are primed to respond so that when a second hit comes along a still greater inflammatory response is elicited that has negative consequences.

develops as a result of the incapacitating effects of stroke and the lifestyle changes that follow, or with the realization of an individual's mortality. Studies in rodents have suggested a neurobiological explanation as experimental procedures that mimicked ischemic stroke in humans led to anhedonia, a key aspect of depression, which could be attenuated by diminishing the actions of IL-1β.

Before you go...

If nothing else, what should be clear from this chapter is that there are several different behavioral, cognitive and biological routes that favor the development, continuation and recurrence of depressive disorders. On the one side are cognitive theories, which propose that life experiences might culminate in negative biases that favor depression. On the other side are the perspectives that neurobiological processes are responsible for the emergence of depression. These positions aren't exclusive of one another, and both are consistent with the view that the confluence of genetic dispositions, earlier experiences, personality factors and stressful events may come together to engender particular neurobiological and cognitive outcomes that promote depression. Likewise, it's likely that multiple neurobiological processes, acting in series or in parallel, ultimately are responsible for depressive disorders. For instance, serotonin changes could come about because of stressor-elicited CRH activation, or it might occur because of stressor-provoked disturbance involving growth factors. Alternatively, through a series of steps, stressors or infection could affect cytokine processes that influence serotonin and hence depressive states. What determines whether an individual will become depressed could reflect whether the strain on a biological system becomes excessive so that it fails to function as well as it should. As indicated earlier, the weak link in the chain of neurochemical variations associated with stressors will be the one that fails most readily, and presumably it will be associated with illness. However, the weak link will differ across individuals and hence there may not be a single process that applies to every depressed individual, nor would there be a single treatment that is effective for each person. Of course, this is a simplistic version of what probably occurs, as it is unlikely that any single neurotransmitter, neuropeptide, growth or inflammatory factor is responsible for all of the symptoms associated with depressive disorders.

14

Fretting over Anxiety Disorders

Fear of flying

There's not much I don't know about the fear of flying. At one time my own flying phobia prevented me from doing lots of things that I would have liked to do. I'm uncertain how it developed as I never had any stressful experiences related to airplanes, but my hypothesis is that the phobia stemmed from my not having control over the situation. Although I have no supporting evidence for this, I believe that the phobic symptoms would never have evolved if I had been actually flying the plane. How hard could it be? It's like driving a car except for the up and down part, and there isn't even the need for reverse, parallel parking or three-point turns.

When people know that you have a plane phobia, they seem to feel obliged to offer advice as to why you should be flying. Great information is repeatedly provided that they think that I, an expert on every relevant negative statistic regarding airplanes, might not know. "More people die in cars than in planes" – Oh gee, really? I'd never heard that before. Now I'm cured. "More people die by lightning strikes than in airplanes" – Well, I don't see how that's relevant, unless the message is that I should also stop going out in the rain? One of the most common comments was that "your phobia is irrational" – Duh ... that's why they call it a phobia. Incidentally, though, if it's so irrational, then why did so many people stop flying after 9/11? Another frequent comment was that "the fear was all in my head" – Another good point, as I had thought it was in my bladder given the sensations that took hold in the period before the flight. I'm no longer phobic about planes. Maybe it's because my kids are older and I'm less concerned about leaving them on their own, or maybe it's related to age-related brain cell deterioration.

Phobias aren't difficult to get rid of through procedures such as cognitive behavior therapy or exposure therapy. However, you need to believe that the therapy will work and be committed to it. This means periodic confrontations with the phobic stimuli, such as taking more plane flights rather than avoiding them.

Stress and Your Health: From Vulnerability to Resilience, First Edition. Hymie Anisman.
© 2015 John Wiley & Sons, Ltd. Published 2015 by John Wiley & Sons, Ltd.

A plague of anxiety disorders

Anxiety is a common emotion that most of us have experienced, typically in anticipation of negative or uncertain events, such as waiting for the results of medical tests, taking an academic examination, preparing for a job interview, or in anticipation of public speaking. Typically, the anxiety is manageable and since it occurs under only certain conditions, it usually doesn't have life-altering consequences. As uncomfortable as these feelings are, they might have adaptive characteristics, keeping us alert and vigilant so that we're prepared to deal with potential threats as they arise. However, anxiety can also be intense, persistent, and excessively disturbing, and for some individuals these feelings are present much of the time, even when specific anxiety-provoking stimuli aren't actually present. Anxiety disorder can refer to several related conditions that differ with respect to their features, course, underlying processes, and treatment. These disorders, which can begin in childhood, affect about 15–20 percent of individuals, being about twice as common in females relative to males.

Generalized anxiety disorder (GAD)

Excessive, uncontrollable or irrational anxiety or worry regarding usual day-to-day events, which persists for at least six months and isn't focused on any single subject, object, or situation, might reflect a syndrome referred to as generalized anxiety disorder (GAD). Along with anxiety or worry, for a GAD diagnosis to be made, individuals must

Getting bored without something to worry about

Worry is often put in the same package as anxiety, as the two are obviously closely related. Having to wait for critical medical results is obviously worrisome and creates anxiety. It seems that under such conditions, some individuals "watch and wait," whereas others "watch and worry." You've likely noticed that in times of anticipatory stress, some individuals are relatively serene, and although they might have concerns, they take events in their stride. Others may become nervous Nellies, calamity Carls, or fretting Franks, who sit around contemplating and ruminating about anything that could go wrong, and even feel that if there is anything at all that can go amiss they would be negligent if they weren't alert to these threats. As one worrier told me, "There's so much that can go wrong. If I don't do the worrying, then who will?"

There is the view that the worrier evolves because of overprotective parents who might instill the idea that the world isn't a safe place and so there is good cause to be alert and fretful. However, other factors may have promoted the development of the worrier, having nothing to do with parents. The fact is that the world often isn't a safe place, and perhaps it's realistic to be a worrier. The worrier is more likely to take protective steps, and might be alert to realistic dangers that life imposes. Worriers will likely use seat belts and push their passengers to do so, they're more likely to get the recommended vaccinations, and they avoid many of the hazards that might otherwise be encountered. The issue, of course, is how much worry is appropriate versus how much is just over the top.

exhibit features such as difficulty concentrating, irritability, restlessness or feeling on edge, sleep disturbances, muscle tension, and being readily fatigued. It's not an uncommon condition, affecting about 1 in 20 individuals over their lifetime, usually developing slowly during young adulthood and tending to be fairly persistent. It's likely that GAD may be influenced by genetic factors, and is elevated among those who have previously encountered strong stressors, especially if these occurred early in life.

The neurobiological processes responsible for GAD haven't been fully identified, but as the anxiety persists even in the absence of danger, it might reflect a failure of certain brain circuits to shut down appropriately. In response to potentially stressful events the prefrontal cortex is responsible for judging the situation and then, should the external stimuli be deemed not to be threatening, it instructs the amygdala to calm down. However, if the pathway that carries this message is disturbed, then anxiety will persist. Given the involvement of CRH, serotonin and GABA in animal models of anxiety, it's a good bet that these neurotransmitters might also contribute to GAD in humans. Treatment strategies for stress-related problems will be considered in Chapters 20 and 21, so we'll leave this topic for the moment, with the understanding that there are numerous behavioral and pharmacological methods of treating this illness with varying degrees of success.

Panic disorder

Of the various anxiety disorders, one that seems particularly puzzling is panic disorder. Unlike a condition where anxiety is generally present, ebbing and waning to some extent, panic attacks appear suddenly and unpredictably, making it strange to observers and frightening for those experiencing the symptoms. These may comprise intense apprehension or terror that comes out of the blue, typically accompanied by fear of losing control, as well as physical signs such as shortness of breath, chest pain, heart palpitations, and feelings of choking or smothering. These symptoms peak within a few minutes, although bouts can occasionally be longer. Once individuals have had several such attacks, their recurrence can become problematic, sometimes occurring weekly or even daily.

Although the source for the initial attack is uncertain, it is telling that attacks are often first seen following a stressful event, after physical illnesses or illicit drug use that caused adverse emotional or cognitive reactions. The subsequent occurrence of panic attacks may be a result of sensitized biological systems or classically conditioned responses where particular cues elicit the attacks. In this regard, arousal related to anxiety may be associated with internal sensations, the reappearance of which can elicit a panic attack. In a sense, feedback from the body might be "catastrophically" misinterpreted as being especially threatening, leading to high levels of perceived threat, arousal, and greater physical changes. Eventually, even the fear of having another attack can elicit one, sometimes in very public venues.

Although panic attacks seem to come out of nowhere, it may be that some people are disposed toward this disorder owing to genetic factors or previously encountered uncontrollable and unpredictable stressors, particularly if they were experienced in early life or adolescence. As with so many other psychological illnesses, however, identifying the mechanisms responsible for panic disorder has been difficult because of the multiple brain regions that could potentially be involved. Nevertheless, when panic patients are exposed to anxiety-provoking visual stimuli or threatening words, neuronal activity is elevated in the anterior cingulate cortex, which is involved in appraisal and executive processes, and normalizes following psychotherapy that has diminished panic disorder symptoms. Yet, when successfully treated patients were evaluated in a situation where emotional conflict was elicited, elevated neuronal activity was still evident, suggesting that symptoms had been suppressed but that inappropriate neuronal responses might nevertheless be "ready" to be reinstated in response to particular situations.

The neurochemical processes thought to be associated with panic disorder are the same as those associated with other anxiety-related disorders. In this regard, it was supposed that anxiety emerges when inhibitory GABA signaling is diminished so that neuronal activity of particular systems can persist unabated. Among panic disorder patients, GABA concentrations are relatively low in the anterior cingulate cortex and basal ganglia, particularly among patients with a family history of mood and anxiety disorders, pointing to the possibility that genetic factors related to GABA functioning might be at play in determining vulnerability to panic disorder. Several GABA-related genes have been identified that may be relevant in this regard, but translating their presence into treatment methods or useful biomarkers has yet to be achieved.

In addition to GABA, norepinephrine has been associated with panic disorder, and drugs that block certain norepinephrine receptors, notably α2 receptors, can diminish symptoms. Some success in treating panic disorder was also achieved through the use of SSRIs and related compounds, although they may occasionally promote panic symptoms at the start of treatment. Neuropeptide factors, such as CRH, arginine vasopressin, and one that we haven't yet discussed, cholecystokinin (CCK), might also contribute to panic disorder. There clearly is a bit of a mish-mash concerning the mechanisms underlying panic disorder, but antidepressant drugs and cognitive behavioral therapy have proven fairly effective in controlling the disorder, although there's still considerable room for improvement.

Obsessive-compulsive disorder (OCD)

Obsessive-compulsive disorder is characterized by repetitive obsessions that may comprise persistent, distressing and intrusive thoughts or images, together with compulsions or urges to perform specific acts or rituals. The nature of the obsessive thoughts a person may have can range from thoughts of dirt permeating everything around them, the perception that someone close to them might become infected by a disease, or the conviction that they're the victim of conspiracies. The compulsive behaviors can similarly vary, comprising actions such as repeated hoarding, aggressive or sexual impulses, hair pulling, hand washing, repeated checking (e.g., whether the door is locked, the stove is off), or preoccupation with sexual, religious or aggressive impulses. When the disorder first begins to appear, the obsessive thoughts are mild, vague and unformed, but nonetheless create discomfort or anxiety. Relief occurs once the obsessive feelings have been dealt with through a particular behavior. But the relief is transient and the obsessive thoughts and the accompanying anxiety may reappear, and again a given behavior relieves the anxiety. With continued repetitions, individuals might become preoccupied with the anxiety-inducing thoughts as well as the behaviors necessary to diminish the anxiety.

The obsessive and compulsive aspects can be independent of one another, as some individuals may present with obsessions that are not expressed as compulsive behaviors. The OCD-related behaviors likely appear more than a little unusual to others, promoting social alienation. Recognizing this, the person with OCD might push the compulsive behaviors underground, so that individuals engage in mental compulsive rituals instead of overt odd behaviors.

Numerous formulations and reformulations have been offered concerning the brain processes involved in OCD. One perspective was that the illness stemmed from dysfunction

Depends on how you see it

OCD has a lifetime prevalence of about 2 percent, and there's a possibility that someone within your circle of friends, or perhaps someone who lives on your block, is affected by this condition. The disorder might seem a bit strange, particularly when the compulsive behaviors comprise self-injurious acts, such as repeated cutting of body parts or repeated hair pulling (trichotillosis).

I can recall being obsessed when a high-school teacher erased the blackboard but failed to get a small, 6-inch, scraggly line. I could hardly contain the impulse to run up to the board and obliterate the line. Of course, I didn't, but I can distinctly recapitulate the relief I felt once that line was eventually erased. I've since learned that this reaction is hardly uncommon. There are also many people who need to start a draft of an essay on a new clean page, and if the opening line isn't quite right, it's not enough to cross it out, but instead they need to scrunch up the offensive page and start on a new one. The current option of just highlighting and deleting may have preserved forests.

Like most kids, you might have engaged in games on the walk to school, such as stepping on sidewalk cracks, or alternatively avoiding them, or touching each parking signpost as you passed it. Did you also feel a degree of discomfort if you missed a sign or a crack, and just had to go back to "get it"? Not doing so ate at you, and the relief created by "getting" that sign was palpable, even though you understood that your behavior was dopey. As an adult you no longer do that touch-the-sign stuff or avoid walking on cracks, but you might still feel some discomfort when you feel that you've left something undone. You probably know how uncomfortable it is as it continues to gnaw, until you finally give in and scratch that itch. An international study indicated that 94 percent of people will have unwanted, intrusive thoughts and impulses, but typically they don't cause serious problems. At the end of the day, these thoughts aren't the problem, but instead it's what we make of them and ultimately how we deal them that's most important. In effect, compulsive behaviors might not be all that unique, and perhaps the person with OCD is simply engaging in these thoughts and behaviors to a greater extent than the rest of us. For that matter, some seemingly odd behaviors, including those that involve self-injurious acts, might encourage the release of certain brain chemicals, such as dopamine and endorphins, thus eliciting a reward or a high that encourages the behavior's reoccurrence. Alternatively, self-injurious behaviors might stem from an individual, for whatever reason, feeling emotionally numb, and behaviors such as cutting provide emotional stimulation that was otherwise deadened.

within a complex loop that comprised cortical brain regions responsible for executive functioning and decision-making, those associated with reward processes, and brain regions involved in voluntary motor control, learning routine behaviors, and decisions regarding which of several behaviors to execute in response to a particular stimulus. Disturbances at points in this series of brain processes, including ineffective feedback to the cortex regarding the appropriateness of the responses that were made, could cause repetitive behavior. Variations of this view have been advanced incorporating the appraisal and resolution of fear responses as contributing to OCD. We might encounter situations that could potentially elicit fear or anxiety responses on a regular basis, but with experience we learn that a situation is safe, and the fear response extinguishes. However, if aspects of the orbital frontal cortex aren't operating properly, then information needed for the extinction of the danger signals won't be passed on to other frontal cortical regions, and consequently certain obsessive thoughts will persist.

While not denying the importance of the orbital frontal cortex in mediating OCD, the anterior cingulate cortex, which may be especially relevant in the context of depression, might also contribute to OCD by virtue of its involvement in error monitoring and decision-making. It's not unusual to find ourselves in situations where we might receive inconsistent messages, or when we have to interpret situations where one signal tells us to "go" and a second says "stop." There are also occasions in which decision-making processes are hampered by external sources of interference, and in such complex situations the anterior cingulate cortex is engaged for decision-making. Once a decision has been made, the activity within this brain region diminishes, essentially relaxing when the job's done. However, when OCD patients were placed in decision-making situations, their anterior cingulate cortex was persistently activated, suggesting that it was having difficulty making appropriate appraisals and decisions. In a sense, individuals might not receive proper neuronal feedback, so that inappropriate repetitive responding would develop, such as that prominent in OCD.

A somewhat related formulation has it that we are endowed with a "security motivation system" that is activated when situations call for us to be alert for danger, and then calms down when a situation is deemed to be safe. However, if the brain safety signals aren't operating properly, then we might obsessively think about particular issues and repeatedly engage in behaviors in an effort to obtain security. At one time or another, it's likely that you've had a thought such as "Did I turn off the iron (or stove)?" or "Did I shut

Using TV and movies

Some years ago, my son asked me whether panic attacks were as "freaky" as he'd heard. "I don't know," I said, "but you've got to figure that if Tony Soprano is going for help to deal with his symptoms, it's gotta be pretty bad." With television programs such as *The Sopranos* and movies such as *Analyze This* in which the disorder is showcased, panic disorder has come out of the closet, and hopefully the stigma associated with this illness has diminished.

It's interesting how television and movies shape our perceptions of mental illness. In the case of panic disorder, even hoodlums affected with the illness are portrayed as basically nice guys, albeit killers, and having the disorder actually makes them seem more human. The TV and movie portrayal of OCD, in contrast, is that of a really creepy illness, and the person with OCD offers up clues that portend their ill intent. The evil-doer has OCD-like traits that involve turning a handle three times or repeatedly opening and closing refrigerator doors just a crack. There's also a scene that has been used frequently, in which the innocent victim realizes she's in trouble when she opens her kitchen cabinet and sees the soup cans lined up neatly, a behavior her jealous ex-husband was compulsive about. So, we as viewers might come to feel sorry for the patient with panic disorder, but less sympathetic toward those with OCD. This makes for good movies and television, but doesn't do much for those with OCD.

the garage?" and we need the "feeling of knowing" that we've done the right thing for anxiety to be abated. Thus, despite the inconvenience, we often go back and check, only to find that we hadn't, in fact, forgotten to do what we had worried about, likely because it was part of our repertoire of behaviors that had become like a habit. Yet, because there are occasions where we have blundered and forgotten to do something important, we know that we should go back. If we elect not to do this, the worry and anxiety might haunt us all day, depending on our ability to tolerate uncertainty. Perhaps the person affected by OCD feels this way all or much of the time.

Phobias and social anxiety

There's hardly a person who doesn't know that phobias generally refer to persistent, irrational fears of certain situations, activities, people or things, such as snakes, heights, or enclosed spaces, to name only a few of many that exist. Even if the individual is aware that their fears are irrational, this doesn't diminish their anxiety, nor does it attenuate the unreasonable avoidance of the feared stimulus. Fortunately, most phobias don't have the stigma attached to them that other anxiety disorders might, perhaps because so many people, about 8–18 percent, have one sort of phobia or another. Unlike anxiety, which can be aligned with threats that are neither specific nor predictable, fear responses are generated quickly in response to a threat or specific cue, and then abate quickly once the threat is removed. In this sense, the "fear" response is perfectly adaptive provided that there's an actual threat present.

Some phobic stimuli are rarely encountered or individuals are blissfully unaware that the feared objects, such as spiders, are actually more common than they think. However, other phobias might involve daily confrontations with the feared object or event. Many of us feel discomfort in relation to social situations, especially those that are new, but for some individuals this discomfort can be so intense that it hinders their day-to-day functioning. Social phobias, or social anxiety, are usually related to a fear of public scrutiny, and affected individuals are loath to walk into a room full of people for fear that they are being observed, and they likewise tend not to make public statements that draw attention to themselves. A social phobia can be specific to particular situations, or it may be a broad, generalized social phobia that becomes so severe that individuals fear leaving home or places where they feel safe. The brain functioning of those with social anxiety, as in other anxiety disorders, is characterized by the orbital frontal cortex and amygdala being excited in response to social-emotional cues, without much of an inhibitory influence coming from other cortical brain regions to diminish the anxiety.

Social anxiety frequently begins during childhood and then declines with age. However, in a good number of children it may remain stable and can become incapacitating, to the extent that they might become fearful of playing with others or even speaking to teachers. It is not entirely certain what processes contribute to the initial provocation of a social anxiety, but negative social experiences might be a factor. The anxiety could be maintained because the person affected might engage in behaviors that confirm this bias. For instance, individuals afraid of public presentations might be especially sensitive and highly vigilant for negative reactions from others, and they might actually focus on audience members who appear the least receptive or who seem the most critical of the presentation.

Phobias might develop through simple conditioning processes so that when a stimulus occurs in association with a negative experience, feeling or emotion, it may come to elicit autonomic responses, such as increased heart rate, ordinarily associated with anxiety. As indicated earlier, different stressors may call different neurochemical processes into play, and this also applies to phobias. A social phobia, for instance, might develop as a result of experiences or neurochemical changes that are different from what happens with a phobia that involves, say, a fear of spiders or elevators, and thus may call for different treatment strategies.

Before you go...

Anxiety responses are fairly common, and likely have adaptive value in keeping us alert, focused and ready to respond. Whether you're about to perform on stage or at a professional sporting event, or you're simply dealing with moderate daily stressful events, a modest amount of anxiety keeps you at peak levels of readiness. However, there are times when anxiety can become excessive and as a result performance is impaired, but this too is a perfectly normal response. It becomes a problem if it happens all or most of the time so that the individual isn't able to function properly.

Anxiety disorders come in a variety of forms, and as different as they are, they share some common features. Phobias are distinct from GAD, which can readily be dissociated from OCD, but each is considered an anxiety disorder, which may share common features and underlying biological processes, and they may be responsive to some of the same treatments. Given the great number of individuals affected by an anxiety disorder, it's somewhat surprising that these disorders generally haven't received the attention or generated the concern that other disorders have. This could turn out to have serious repercussions not only because of their potentially debilitating effects, but also because anxiety is a common comorbid feature of other disorders that complicates their treatment. In this regard, anxiety is a feature of PTSD, is frequent among drug abusers, and is a comorbid feature in most cases of depression, and among some individuals the anxiety is perceived as being more aversive than the depression.

15

Acute Stress Disorder and Posttraumatic Stress Disorder

A perspective on PTSD

Wars have been spurred by a variety of different causes, but they all create a common outcome – misery. The misery may comprise grief related to loss, physical injuries, and psychological trauma, as well as the spread of famine and diseases. Trauma or chronic stressor experiences of any sort can provoke pathological outcomes, including posttraumatic stress disorder (PTSD), but this condition only came to the fore when it was realized how many soldiers returning from battle were affected by this illness. Although the inclusion of PTSD as a mental disorder is relatively recent, the symptoms of PTSD appeared in the writings of the Greek historian Herodotus (ca. 484–425 BCE), and in numerous subsequent documents that recount the consequences of wars and natural disasters. In the early part of the twentieth century there were frequent accounts of the persistent emotionally damaging consequences of traumatic events. Later, during World War I, shell-shock was fairly common in soldiers, but unfortunately they were exceptionally stigmatized because it was often seen as a shortcoming of the victim, who was considered to be either weak or a malingerer. Eventually, PTSD found its way into the DSM-III, but it was some time before scientists and clinicians could get their act together to conduct the research that was necessary to fully describe the disorder, let alone properly delve into the mechanisms that might provide clues regarding treatment of the illness.

The focus on PTSD escalated once it was understood that it could appear as a result of virtually any situation in which traumatic stressors were experienced, as well as with repeated stressors of a nontraumatic nature. The importance of being able to deal with PTSD became exceptionally clear with the realization that traumatic events are experienced by 50–70 percent of people, and within Western countries the incidence of PTSD is as high as 10 percent. PTSD is no longer considered in the way it was decades ago, but instead is viewed as an unfortunate response to abnormal experiences.

Stress and Your Health: From Vulnerability to Resilience, First Edition. Hymie Anisman.
© 2015 John Wiley & Sons, Ltd. Published 2015 by John Wiley & Sons, Ltd.

We usually think about PTSD in terms of its immediate toll on an individual's well-being, including the depression that is frequently comorbid with it and the many instances of suicide that have been reported among soldiers returning from war. However, there are other long-term disturbances associated with PTSD, such as an increased incidence of dementia, more likely heart disease, elevations of inflammation in cardiac patients, and Type 2 diabetes. Indeed, a 10 year prospective study of combat veterans with PTSD indicated that they were 2.4 times more likely to die prematurely than individuals without PTSD.

Acute stress disorder

Acute stress disorder (ASD) was introduced in the DSM-IV, and modified in the DSM-5, where it, along with PTSD, was included in a new category, "Trauma and stressor-related disorders," rather than in the category of anxiety disorders. It is common for intense emotional reactions to begin to appear soon after a catastrophic event, but in most cases they diminish with time. A diagnosis of ASD is considered if symptoms appear within three days after the trauma and persist for up to a month. In addition, for a diagnosis of ASD, three or more "dissociative" symptoms from a set of five must be present. These peritraumatic (at the time of the trauma) dissociative features comprise (a) a sense of numbing, detachment or absence of emotional responses; (b) diminished awareness of surroundings, essentially feeling as if in a daze; (c) derealization, in which an individual's perception or experience of the external world seems unreal; (d) depersonalization, wherein an individual has the feeling of watching himself or herself act, but feels as if they have no control over the situation; and (e) dissociative amnesia, characterized by memory gaps in which an individual cannot recall information concerning events of a traumatic or stressful nature.

One of the key reasons for originally having this category of illness was based on the belief that it might predict the subsequent development of PTSD. As it turns out, although ASD was frequently related to the subsequent development of PTSD, it also appeared that PTSD could emerge without individuals ever having exhibited ASD. Thus, there is some question as to the usefulness of ASD as a separate category of illness.

Posttraumatic stress disorder

The triggers for PTSD include threatened death, serious injury or sexual violation, personally witnessing such an event or death itself, or learning of a violent or accidental trauma to a close family member or close friend. Second-hand reports through the media aren't considered to be precipitating factors for PTSD, but among those with ASD or PTSD, media repetitions of traumatic events can serve as reminders that maintain or aggravate symptoms. The nature of the trauma events that have been associated with PTSD vary widely, not only involving war experiences, but also natural disasters (earthquake, hurricane, tsunami), car accidents, rape, being held hostage, medical complications, being told about a severe medical condition, bullying, common assault, witnessing traumatic events (e.g., abuse), and chronic stressors, such as repeated racial discrimination. It is significant that although in the past PTSD was only diagnosed if the trauma elicited fear, helplessness or horror, these requirements have been dropped in the DSM-5 as they weren't useful in predicting later symptoms.

The general symptoms that individuals express fall into four categories: (a) avoidance of distressing memories, thoughts, feelings or reminders of the traumatic event; (b) negative cognitions and mood that might comprise a persistent and distorted sense of self, blame or estrangement from others, diminished interest in usual activities, or an inability to remember key aspects of the event; (c) arousal that is characterized by aggressive, reckless or self-destructive behavior, as well as sleep disturbances, hypervigilance or related disturbances; and finally (d) reexperiencing the event, reflected by the occurrence of spontaneous memories of the traumatic episode, recurrent dreams related to it, flashbacks, and prolonged, intense psychological distress.

Vulnerability and resilience

As with most stress-related disorders, the basic question that we often come down to concerns why only some will actually develop PTSD whereas most of us might encounter traumatic events of one sort or another? We have covered many of the primary factors that determine how and under what conditions stressors will affect us most, and these also figure into whether PTSD will develop. For instance, trauma experiences early in life, such as abuse or neglect, could potentially influence later appraisal and coping methods that favor the development of PTSD in response to stressors. Individuals who experienced childhood trauma and who expressed high levels of self-blame and guilt (I was responsible for the abuse), or who blamed their family for not protecting them adequately, were most likely to develop PTSD.

An individual's coping abilities have considerable sway in the development of PTSD. Although problem-solving is frequently seen as the most effective way of coping, this isn't always the case, as we've seen, and adopting an avoidance strategy might be

Predicting PTSD

A cogent predictor of PTSD is whether a psychological disorder was present prior to the recent traumatic experience that seemed to instigate the disorder. Women with a previous mood disorder were at increased risk of PTSD in response to trauma, and soldiers with modest mental health problems before their deployment to Afghanistan were more likely to return suffering from PTSD. Likewise, those who exhibited neuroticism, characterized by overreaction to daily stressors, as well as constant worry and anxiety, were also more likely to develop PTSD.

Previous traumatic experiences might also increase vulnerability to the development of PTSD in response to later trauma. Soldiers who had experienced earlier trauma were at increased risk of developing combat-related PTSD, and women were at increased of developing PTSD following childbirth if they had encountered a trauma previously. Such effects could occur owing to altered appraisal and coping processes, or the sensitization of neurobiological systems might promote excessive reactions upon later encounters with stressors. Likewise, traumatic brain injury can prime the amygdala so that PTSD is more likely to develop in response to later stressors.

effective, especially as the memory of a traumatic event and the cues that stimulate these memories tend to exacerbate symptoms. For other individuals, however, emotional expression may be more effective in diminishing the severity of PTSD symptoms. It is interesting that soldiers who had experienced early life trauma frequently exhibited high levels of anxiety prior to deployment, but this anxiety diminished during the initial months of deployment, only to resurface when they returned home. It is hard to know precisely what processes were operative to promote these changes, but it is possible that the usual factors that might lead to PTSD were attenuated while soldiers were receiving strong social support from their buddies during deployment. In essence, different types of coping strategies might be useful in dealing with PTSD, but these differ between individuals and the circumstances in which they find themselves.

Neuroanatomical underpinnings of PTSD

The symptoms of PTSD are diverse and hence its development likely involves multiple biological processes. Identifying these mechanisms is complicated by the frequent comorbidity between PTSD and other pathological conditions, such as depression. In particular, biological disturbances present among those with PTSD might not be specifically linked with this disorder, but instead might be caused by the comorbid condition or other stress-related processes.

A particularly important finding regarding PTSD was that it was associated with reduced hippocampal size. But how did this come about? Did it reflect atrophy that developed as a consequence of the trauma or the development of the symptoms, or were individuals with a relatively small hippocampus at increased risk for developing PTSD? It was reported that co-twins of individuals who had experienced war-related PTSD had a relatively small hippocampus, even though they had neither been traumatized nor suffered from PTSD. The obvious conclusion was that diminished size of the hippocampus was not a result of the trauma, but likely existed prior to deployment and somehow influenced the development of the disorder. It similarly appeared that the presence of diminished amygdala size was associated with vulnerability to PTSD, although it should be said that the presence of diminished amygdala was not always observed. This said, however, studies in animals have made it clear that chronic distress caused diminished BDNF functioning that led to neuronal loss and reduced brain size. Moreover, the brain size of PTSD patients who recovered from the illness, including individuals who recovered through CBT treatment, was larger than that of those who hadn't recovered. Thus, there are data which indicate that stressful events or alleviation of PTSD could affect brain size.

What is it about the hippocampus and amygdala that makes them particularly cogent for the development of PTSD? The hippocampus is associated with memory processes and, given its connections with the amygdala, these regions are likely fundamental to the creation and maintenance of emotional memories. In fact, among individuals diagnosed with PTSD, the amygdala is exceptionally responsive to vague cues related to a traumatic experience, and the hyperreactivity of neurons within the amygdala persisted even when threats were absent and the individuals weren't thinking about them. It might be expected that with time memories would fade, even those that involve traumatic events, but the persistence of PTSD symptoms might reflect a disturbance related to the processes that ordinarily allow for fear to diminish as time passes. In essence, PTSD might be a reflection of disturbed normal forgetting in which the amygdala never rests.

Another aspect of learning and memory might contribute to PTSD. If an individual experienced a trauma within a particular situation, it would be perfectly reasonable and

Danger: brain at work – use other path

"Time heals all wounds" might be better put as "Time heals a lot of wounds." It is not unusual for people to assume that once a trauma has passed, individuals should be able to recover and go on with life. Some wounds might heal with time, or it might simply make them less salient, and thus these wounds might be mistakenly thought to have healed. You might not remember ordinary day-to-day events, and even significant past events might not be recalled every day, although they might appear on the radar every so often. Trauma memories, however, might linger and so might the psychological and physical consequences of the trauma. Some individuals, for instance, who were survivors of an effort at genocide might never speak about their experiences (a conspiracy of silence), whereas others can hardly stop speaking about it. Either way, the memories are there, intact, and ready to surface.

Freud made enormous contributions to the brain sciences. Of course, not every theoretical viewpoint he advanced has been widely adopted, but his thoughts on defense mechanisms and other processes that protect our egos are remarkably astute. Freud was also prescient in postulating that stressful early experiences can affect individuals for life, although it was premature for him to define precisely how this came about. Nevertheless, he didn't see stressors as having static effects. To the contrary, to Freud, traumatic memory represented a causative "agent still at work," and as we've seen, replaying traumatic incidents and ruminating about them might encourage the development of PTSD.

adaptive for strong reactions to be elicited when that same situation or even reminders of it were encountered again. However, it would be counterproductive for such reactions to appear in response to cues that were only vaguely similar to those which were associated with the initial trauma. Ordinarily, when a memory is firmly established, the response to the primary learned stimulus is strong, and some generalization might be expected in response to somewhat similar stimuli. However, when the memory is less well entrenched and focused, the response to the primary stimulus might be somewhat weaker, but might be accompanied by greater generalization. After all, if the brain isn't absolutely certain what cue is most important, it might respond to a broader range of cues. Individuals with PTSD seem to fall into both classes, reacting very strongly to cues highly reminiscent of the original trauma, and also reacting strongly to relatively vague cues.

As in the case of the hippocampus, the volume of the anterior cingulate cortex is also diminished among individuals with PTSD, likely stemming from the trauma experience rather than serving as a factor that influenced vulnerability to PTSD. In view of this brain region's involvement in various executive functions and decision-making, its interactions with the amygdala and hippocampus in the emergence and continuation of PTSD can be exceptionally significant. As described in our discussion of anxiety disorders, aspects of the prefrontal cortex ordinarily moderate the activity of the amygdala, so that excessive activation doesn't occur in response to inconsequential stimuli. Thus, dysfunction of prefrontal cortex circuits may result in this regulation being forfeited so that amygdala reactivity would proceed unabated when individuals are confronted with negative stimuli, even those unrelated to their trauma experience. For instance, written

Getting there before it's too late

With any disorder, prevention is preferable to cure. Thus, it would be beneficial to know whether some individuals are especially likely to develop an illness, so that prophylactic measures could be taken to limit its occurrence. It may turn out to be significant that fMRI analysis of the amygdala conducted when soldiers first enter the armed forces could be used to predict the likelihood of PTSD developing in combat conditions. If nothing else, this could potentially be useful in deciding where individuals would be best deployed given their vulnerability to the disorder, and if they did become ill, it might also guide treatment strategies.

There have been clues from genetic studies that might also be relevant in limiting the occurrence of PTSD among individuals who might otherwise be placed in high-risk situations. Individuals carrying a particular polymorphism for BDNF, which it will be recalled is associated with neuronal growth, were especially vulnerable to PTSD, and were less amenable to treatments aimed at reducing fear and anxiety. As well, a gene for Oprl1, a member of a family of opioid receptors associated with processing pain, was also associated with PTSD in rodent models, and was dysregulated in humans with PTSD, thus making it a viable candidate in predicting PTSD vulnerability and informing treatment approaches.

scripts that contain traumatic imagery, images of fearful faces, and a test that elicited an emotional response unrelated to the trauma provoked excessive neuronal reactions among those with PTSD, and with successful treatment, prefrontal cortex functioning returned to its normal state. Together, these findings suggest that the neural circuit comprising the anterior cingulate cortex, amygdala, and hippocampus, representing appraisals and regulation of the amygdala, is responsible for many of the symptoms of PTSD, including emotional reactivity, fear and avoidance, generalized responses, as well as reexperiencing the trauma.

Biochemical determinants of PTSD

Identifying the biochemical determinants of PTSD is fundamental for the development of drug-based therapeutic strategies to treat this illness, and as in the case of other brain-related disturbances, animal models ought to have figured largely in such analyses. As we've seen, there is some question whether complex human pathologies can be simulated in rodents, but this becomes especially notable in the case of PTSD. It's a simple matter to assess some PTSD-related behaviors, such as hyper-arousal or avoidance of particular stimuli. However, how do we know when a mouse or rat is spontaneously "reexperiencing" the trauma, or encountering cognitive distortions? Nonetheless, the triangulation achieved through human drug and imaging studies, together with animal-based models, has spawned some early success that could be a harbinger for the development of effective methods of dealing with this disorder. Like most mental illnesses, PTSD might involve multiple components governed by different neurochemical processes. Some might be fundamental in the initial establishment of symptoms, whereas others might contribute to the maintenance of symptoms over time. As well,

Epigenetic influences in PTSD

Stress-related psychological disturbances, including PTSD, have been linked to epigenetic changes. A broad gene analysis revealed that individuals with or without PTSD differed with respect to hundreds of genes being turned off or on. Interestingly, among those with PTSD who had experienced childhood abuse, epigenetic changes were more common and there were more variations of genes linked to development of the nervous system and regulation of immune functioning than among individuals with PTSD who had not experienced early life abuse. In effect, although these individuals might display many common symptoms, their different epigenetic profiles raises the possibility that their symptoms are governed by different (although overlapping) neurobiological processes, and they might not be equally responsive to the same treatments.

some neurochemical processes might contribute to the fear or anxiety that is associated with PTSD, or to the comorbidities that are commonly observed, whereas others likely contribute to traumatic memories. In the ensuing section we'll cover some of the neurochemical factors that have been implicated in these aspects of PTSD, but it's likely that they represent only a modest fraction of the processes that will eventually be uncovered.

CRH and corticoids in relation to PTSD-related memories

In view of the pronounced effects of stressors on CRH and cortisol, there has been considerable interest in determining whether treatments that affect these hormones would influence the development or course of PTSD. As expected, when a drug that specifically blocks CRH_1 receptors was administered to rodents just before or 30 minutes after a traumatic experience, stressor-induced anxiety measured days later was diminished. The obvious conclusion is that the treatment diminished anxiety directly associated with the trauma and hence later symptoms were abrogated. Furthermore, it was suggested that the treatment didn't simply act as a Band-Aid to mask anxiety, but actually affected the formation of the anxiety-related memory. Specifically, when a memory is older and well entrenched it is relatively difficult to disrupt. However, when the memory is first being formed, or when it is in the process of being consolidated for later use, it is fragile and easily disrupted. Thus, blocking CRH_1 receptors might have disturbed traumatic memories before they had the opportunity to take hold, and in this way precluded the development of strong fear responses and PTSD. Paralleling these findings, a high dose of cortisone, which is closely tied to cortisol, administered during a 6-hour window following trauma attenuated the development of PTSD, as did a 10-day low-dose regimen of cortisone beginning within 12 hours of trauma. In contrast, when cortisol treatments were administered long after the initial trauma experience, the PTSD symptoms were not readily affected. It would seem that if the CRH or corticoid treatment was given during the "golden hours" soon after a trauma, they interfered with the synaptic connectivity within the amygdala, thereby short-circuiting the consolidation of traumatic memories and hence interfering with the development of PTSD.

There are occasions when one might expect correspondence between a particular neurochemical and the presence of pathology, only to be surprised that the expected

Altering emotional memory

Although a memory that has been consolidated and is in long-term storage isn't readily disrupted, there are ways that this can be done. Specifically, when an event is recalled from long-term memory, and the relevant neuronal processes are actively engaged, that memory again becomes more susceptible to being altered. In fact, even subtle suggestions or questions that are asked during this time can be incorporated into the individual's narrative. We've known this for some time, and it became a source of notoriety as some therapists might have inadvertently or, perhaps purposefully, caused "false memories" to be incorporated into patients' recall of events, leading to considerable harm to many innocent caregivers and parents. It also appears that when a memory is being recalled ("retrieved") it is also subject to being modified by particular drug treatments. Cortisol might be able to affect the reconsolidation of a memory that is being "retrieved," and thus it has been one of several treatments explored in an effort to diminish the aversiveness of negative memories.

outcomes aren't apparent. When this occurs it forces us to reevaluate our basic perspectives on how particular biological systems operate, and sometimes they provide clues that would otherwise have been missed regarding the processes through which pathology arises. As acute stressors ordinarily increase cortisol levels, it might have been predicted that the hormone levels would be still higher among individuals with PTSD. However, among individuals with PTSD, cortisol levels may be diminished, even falling below those observed in the absence of PTSD. This might seem counterintuitive, but not if we consider this from an adaptive perspective. Ordinarily, under conditions where cortisol release occurs at a high and sustained level, as in response to severe or chronic stressors, corticoids might be damaging, promoting the loss of receptors on the hippocampus, potentially leading to pathological outcomes. Thus, an adaptive change may occur so that cortisol release diminishes in an effort to preserve the integrity of the hippocampus and HPA functioning.

Given cortisol's essential role in dealing with stressful events, it might be thought that the diminished HPA functioning associated with PTSD might render individuals less well prepared to deal with further challenges. However, our neurobiological systems are flexible so that selectivity exists concerning activation of HPA functioning. By example, when depressed women who had previously been abused were pharmacologically challenged with a drug treatment that ordinarily increases HPA activity, this response was muted. Yet, if women were tested in a socially stressful situation, the down-regulation of HPA functioning wasn't evident. To the contrary, an exaggerated response was apparent (Heim and Nemeroff, 2001). My colleague, Kim Matheson and I (2012) similarly observed that among women who had experienced abuse in a dating relationship and in whom PTSD symptoms were evident, cortisol levels were lower than in women who showed low or moderate PTSD symptoms. But, when these women were asked to recall and write about their abusive experiences, those with the highest PTSD levels displayed a particularly marked increase of cortisol levels despite the inordinately low basal levels of the hormone.

Evidently, among traumatized individuals HPA activity is down-regulated so that excessive cortisol activity won't occur in response to just any event, thereby precluding hippocampal damage that might otherwise develop as a result of excessive cortisol levels. However, override systems exist so that in the context of particular stressors, such as those that are personally meaningful, HPA activation can be elicited. Essentially, top-down management exists in which aspects of the prefrontal cortex might be responsible for the decisions regarding which stimuli are not particularly important and thus can be overlooked and those that are meaningful, requiring elevated HPA functioning.

Norepinephrine and serotonin and PTSD-related memories

There have been suspicions that both norepinephrine and serotonin might contribute to PTSD, and indeed it seems that among humans engaged in high-risk jobs, such as law enforcement, elevated norepinephrine levels in the blood following a critical incident was predictive of later development of PTSD symptoms. Studies in mice suggest that the norepinephrine changes might not simply be correlates of PTSD. If mice are exposed to a series of different insults, and then over the ensuing weeks exposed to reminders of the stressor experience, they subsequently exhibit heightened reactivity to environmental stimuli, diminished social interaction, unusual aggressiveness directed toward an intruder, and resistance to the extinction of fear responses. These behavioral signs, which are reminiscent of PTSD, were accompanied by increased neuronal activation involving norepinephrine within brain regions associated with vigilance, fear, and anxiety. Of particular relevance to our understanding of the mechanisms supporting PTSD is that the behavioral effects of the stressor regimen could be attenuated by the administration of a drug that disrupted norepinephrine functioning. As we'll see in Chapter 21 when we deal with therapeutic strategies, the link with norepinephrine in relation to PTSD will take on greater significance.

There is reason to believe that serotonin-related processes might also contribute to PTSD. As in the case of depressive disorders, serotonin contributes to anxiety, and individuals carrying the short allele of the 5-HTT gene were more apt to develop PTSD in response to trauma than those carrying the long allele, especially if individuals had also encountered a childhood stressor. It seems that the development of PTSD involves the confluence of several of the same factors that come to provoke depressive disorders. This isn't surprising given the comorbidity that exists between depression and PTSD, but these disorders also have unique behavioral characteristics and effective treatment will likely necessitate determination of the specific neurochemical signatures aligned with depression and those which are more closely linked to PTSD.

GABA and the extinction of fear responses in PTSD

GABA and its receptors, as we've seen, are key players in the stress process, and as it is an inhibitory transmitter that puts the brakes on neuronal functioning, low levels of GABA in certain brain regions would result in particular neuronal processes not being inhibited. From this perspective, low GABA levels could hinder extinction of fear responses so that PTSD symptoms would persist and even be strengthened with recall of the traumatic event. Based on this explanation, GABA might not be directly responsible for the initial development of PTSD, but instead might influence the maintenance of PTSD once it has developed. Despite the potential involvement of GABA in PTSD, benzodiazepine treatments, which have their effects through GABA processes, are not effective in treating PTSD, and could even exacerbate the negative effects of subsequently encountered stressors. Yet, as we'll see later, there are indications that other treatments that influence GABA functioning can diminish PTSD symptoms.

Cannabinoids

Given the potential relaxing effects of agents that stimulate cannabinoid (CB1) receptors, such as marijuana, they have been considered in the treatment of PTSD. In fact, among individuals with PTSD, levels of the naturally occurring substance anandamide, which ordinarily stimulates CB1 receptors, are particularly low. This was accompanied by a greater number of CB1 receptors, which may have evolved to compensate for the low levels of anandamide. Such findings have raised the possibility that treatments that influence this system might be useful in treating PTSD symptoms. Although cannabis creates a relaxing effect in some individuals, in others it may cause paranoid-like reactions. As it's currently difficult to predict in whom particular outcomes will be evident, experimenting with cannabis in an effort to self-medicate is not a good idea.

Neuropeptide Y (NPY) and resilience

One of the more interesting aspects related to PTSD is the suspicion that NPY might be a resilience factor that can limit the development of PTSD. This attribute of NPY has been seen in several situations. Among a group of soldiers engaged in a survival course that simulated conditions of being a prisoner of war, including intensive interrogation and sleep deprivation, NPY levels in blood increased fairly quickly. However, this increase was particularly dramatic among those in the Special Forces who had been trained to be resilient in the face of stressors. Subsequent studies in rodents indicated that stressor-elicited PTSD-like symptoms could be diminished by NPY administered directly into the brain. It is of practical significance that NPY administered as an intra-nasal spray to rats prior to experiencing a prolonged stressor likewise limited the development of PTSD symptoms. There has thus been interest in developing a nasal spray containing NPY as a method of ameliorating PTSD symptoms in humans.

A gene polymorphism was identified that was relevant to NPY and which was associated with altered stress responses, including disturbed corticoid changes among individuals who experienced early life stressors, and particularly marked amygdala and hippocampal activity in response to threating stimuli. As NPY-related polymorphisms might contribute to the individual differences observed in relation to PTSD, this polymorphism could potentially serve as a biomarker to identify individuals most likely to develop this disorder, and could thus be used to predict which individuals would be suitable as first responders, emergency workers, or soldiers.

Before you go...

There are aspects of PTSD that are perfectly understandable at one level, but difficult to really get a grip on when trying to understand them from other perspectives. For instance, why would the symptoms of PTSD become increasingly more pronounced with the passage of time following a traumatic experience, and why is it that an individual who seemingly dealt well with a traumatic event might subsequently develop PTSD, even years after the trauma was first experienced? From a psychodynamic perspective it might be that the distress associated with trauma could result in persistent rumination and replaying of events producing additive effects so that PTSD eventually emerges. Rumination could reinforce PTSD symptoms and could prevent the person from letting go so that healing can occur.

As we've seen repeatedly, the neurobiological effects of stressors don't end when the stressor disappears. Traumatic events could potentially change the characteristics of neurons so that they are primed or sensitized to respond excessively to further stressors, even if they are relatively mild. Moreover, intermittent reminders of the trauma or rumination related to the trauma can strengthen the neuronal networks responsible for the related emotional memories, or they might serve to prevent forgetting of such memories. The strengthening of synaptic processes may involve growth factors that affect the sensitization of neuronal processes related to several neurotransmitters, such as norepinephrine, serotonin, GABA, and CRH, which could then instigate the symptoms of the disorder.

We often assume that certain biological disturbances can either cause an illness or sustain it over the long run, and that modifying these processes will necessarily alleviate the symptoms of illness. However, like other conditions such as drug addictions, the evolution of PTSD might involve different processes kicking in over the course of the illness. The factors that initiated the illness might involve one system, but the maintenance of the illness might be governed by others. It follows that the effectiveness of treatment strategies might similarly vary over the different phases of the disorder. This is largely speculation on my part, so it's not surprising that this option isn't often discussed in the treatment of psychological disorders, except perhaps in the case of addiction. Yet, the limited effectiveness of treatments might be due to their use at each phase of the illness as if they all have a common underlying mechanism.

16

Addictions and Forbidden Fruits

Is that an addiction?

Drug addicts don't get much sympathy. Heroin or cocaine addicts certainly don't, although a bit more might be obtained by those affected by alcoholism, perhaps because so many people like to have a drink or two, and sometimes more. Cigarette smokers only get sympathy from other smokers. In fact, they're reviled because their secondhand smoke affects others, and like those with alcohol addictions, they're seen as being weak for not being able to kick the habit. One also hears the terms addict and addiction bandied about in relation to other behaviors – sex, email, internet, pornography, and eating have all been framed as being addictions, and indeed, the DSM-5 now includes internet and sex addictions under the class of "Behavioral addictions." Are workaholics addicted, too, or does this amount to compulsive behaviors engaged in as a way to reduce anxiety or discomfort?

Smoking, drinking, or abuse of other drugs reflect choices that individuals make. Poor choices, to be sure, but to what extent should we blame the addict for their behaviors? Do we say that drug addictions reflect biological processes that are ready to be messed up given particular genes or stressful early life events over which the individual has had no control? Should we add that despite the individual's free will, the "system" was complicit in creating addictions by allowing or facilitating the sale and distribution of alcohol and cigarettes, and even becoming a major partner in various gambling ventures? Let's face it, for several levels of government, booze, smokes, and gambling have become cash cows to which they're addicted.

What's an addiction

There was a time when the development of "tolerance" to a drug was viewed as a key element in the addiction process, as it meant that increasingly larger doses were needed to obtain a desired effect, and without a fix, "withdrawal" symptoms would appear. Today, individuals are more often characterized as exhibiting abuse, addiction,

---

Stress and Your Health: From Vulnerability to Resilience, First Edition. Hymie Anisman.
© 2015 John Wiley & Sons, Ltd. Published 2015 by John Wiley & Sons, Ltd.

or dependence. Abuse refers to excessive use of a substance on a regular basis, even in the face of legal problems, danger to themselves, jeopardizing relationships, or falling through on major responsibilities. However, these individuals haven't yet formed an addiction and are not dependent on the drug. Addiction comprises an intense craving for a particular substance, coupled with an inability to control its use, despite negative consequences. Dependence is diagnosed when individuals have exhibited three of the following features during the preceding year: greater tolerance for the substance, withdrawal symptoms upon cessation of drug use, loss of control regarding drug use, preoccupation with the substance, diminished attention devoted to other meaningful activities or commitments, and continued drug use even when it brings negative consequences.

Stress as a provocateur in the addiction process

Initial drug consumption may occur owing to social influences or as an element of experimentation during adolescence or early adulthood. For some individuals these early experiences might amount to nothing more than a social occurrence, but for others these experiences "take" and dispose them to further use, potentially leading to addiction. As frequently depicted in the movies, strong stressors may also be associated with alcohol consumption, and even expressions such as "and so he buried himself in a bottle" tell us that the notion that stressors might contribute to addiction isn't particularly new. These stressors often involve psychosocial challenges, including the loss of a child, the death of someone close, unfaithfulness by others, rape, being a victim of other violence or observing victimization. Based on our earlier discussions, it should come as no surprise that drug abuse has also been linked to stressors experienced early in life, including events such as emotional abuse or neglect, parental loss, divorce or conflict, isolation, physical abuse, and the impact of these stressors are magnified by further stressors encountered in adulthood.

A common perspective is that drug consumption might reflect an attempt at self-medication to help individuals deal with emotional pain and bad memories. Like many escape coping methods, the effectiveness of drug-based coping works only for a certain amount of time and to a certain degree, and alcohol or use of other drugs can promote further stressors, including problems with friends, family, job and health, which might encourage still further substance use.

Reward and aversion in relation to addiction: a multistep process

The factors that initially promote drug consumption might differ appreciably from those responsible for maintaining the addiction. Stressful events, social pressures, engaging in risky behaviors, or simply curiosity and experimentation might have been pivotal in getting some people on the road to addiction. During this early phase, individuals might gain pleasure from the drug owing to the engagement of dopamine reward processes. Later use of the drug might occur in an effort to reexperience earlier positive feelings, and with continued use a craving for the drug emerges, possibly driven by cues related to the drug that have taken on the quality of being able stimulate dopamine activity. At the same time, or shortly afterward, another motive for continuing this behavior emerges. For the addicted individual, not being high is perceived as

Alcohol as a pandemic

Alcohol addiction is rampant throughout the world, and in some countries, such as Russia, the alcohol problem has contributed to increased interpersonal violence, suicide, and various antisocial behaviors, and it has severely cut down life span, primarily among males, who are traditionally much heavier vodka users than are females. I'd bet that because of the alcohol problem there is a high likelihood of Russia's international ascendancy being stayed in its tracks, and thus Putin's dreams of a greater Russia might not be realized. In his book *The Last Man in Russia*, Oliver Bullough makes the very prescient statement: "One man's alcoholism is his own tragedy. A whole nation's alcoholism is a tragedy too, but also a symptom of something far larger, of a collective breakdown." Amazingly, Russia isn't even at the top of the list of the biggest drinkers, as that status belongs to Moldova, followed by the Czech Republic and Hungary, and only then does Russia appear, followed closely by Ukraine.

Across countries, males out-drink females, and the proportionate difference in some parts of the world is remarkable. In the United States this difference isn't nearly as pronounced. About 20 percent of men abuse alcohol, whereas about 7–12 percent of women do so. However, this difference is diminishing as drinking in women becomes more acceptable. Although social factors have favored alcoholism in males, females might actually be more biologically vulnerable to this form of addiction. On a pound for pound basis, a woman's body contains less water and more fatty tissue than a man's body, and as fat can store alcohol whereas water dilutes it, women are actually exposed to more alcohol than are men. This is further fueled by the fact that the enzymes that ordinarily degrade alcohol in the body, alcohol dehydrogenase and aldehyde dehydrogenase, are lower in women than in men, and thus the alcohol will stick around longer in women and will be taken up into the blood more readily, and thus they ought to be physiologically more prone to addiction. Then again, in response to stressors, women are likely to engage in internalizing behavior (e.g., rumination), whereas men are more prone to adopting externalizing behaviors, such as impulsivity, antisocial personality and substance abuse. Perhaps treatment in many women ought to emphasize coping and cognitive skills, thereby limiting the rumination that favors drug use, whereas treatment for most men might focus more on limiting impulsive behaviors.

unpleasant, and they might continue to use the drug in an effort to diminish the lousy feelings or discomfort that otherwise occur. These phases in the addiction process might involve different brain regions and neurochemical processes, and thus call for different treatments.

Dopamine in relation to stress and reward

Many drugs with addiction potential share the feature that their rewarding effects diminish with repeated use (tolerance). However, a prominent feature of cocaine and amphetamine is that with repeated use some of their effects actually become more pronounced. Even a single treatment of amphetamine or cocaine can result in a sensitization so that intake of the drug on a second occasion provokes greater behavioral

Impairments of pleasure associated with addiction

Long-term cocaine use was accompanied by reduced neural cell bodies within the hippocampus and within several cortical regions, and the normal brain electrical response to particular stimuli was disturbed. Ordinarily, when electrophysiological responses are measured while participants engage in a task where they have the opportunity of earning varying amounts of money for making responses, brain electrical activity increases with the monetary value. However, among cocaine users the differential responses associated with varying amounts of reward weren't apparent, even though the drug users were able to tell the difference between the rewards, and indeed expressed the view that the task became more interesting and exciting as the potential winnings increased. Moreover, the brain electrical activity elicited by the reward situation corresponded with the amount of prefrontal cortex grey matter that was present. It seems that at a physiological level, chronic cocaine use undermines the ability of addicted individuals to react to different levels of reward and pleasure obtained, and it is possible that once individuals get to this point they might also be incapable of regulating their increased drug intake. It might also have some bearing on what pleasure these individuals receive from other aspects of their lives, and thus might be relevant to the frequent comorbidity that occurs with depressive disorders.

change, accompanied by augmented dopamine activity. With repeated drug treatment these effects become still more pronounced, so much so that dopamine neurons within the ventral tegmentum and prefrontal cortex, which are involved in reward and pleasure processes and executive functioning, undergo long-lasting neuroanatomical and electrophysiological changes, possibly driven by growth factors, such as FGF-2. As a result, when these neurons are subsequently excited, even by drug-related cues rather than the drugs themselves, much greater responses are elicited. Of particular significance is that the drug-related cues can act on dopamine functioning to promote drug intake in a previously addicted animal and cause the reinstatement of the addiction long after the habit has been kicked. As indicated by Jane Stewart (2000), stressful events excite these very same growth factor and dopamine processes, and are thus cogent in reinstating a previous addiction.

Corticotropin hormone in relation to stress and addiction

If stressful experiences contribute to addiction, then those biological substrates affected by stressors might in some way influence this process. There has, indeed, been considerable evidence pointing to CRH as being a fundamental aspect of drug addiction. For instance, in animals, treatments that blocked CRH_1 receptors reduced the intake of drugs, such as alcohol, amphetamine and cocaine, and attenuated drug relapse that was otherwise provoked by stressors. It also seems that CRH may cooperate with dopamine activity in affecting addiction.

Occasionally one runs into the view that all addictions involve the same processes or that all addictions share at least some common elements. To some extent this might be true, but it's fairly certain that cocaine, heroin and alcohol also have distinguishable aspects, so that treatments effective in attenuating one form of addiction are ineffective in

Remembering addiction

One can view addiction from the perspective of memory processes and the formation of habits. At the neuronal level, learning occurs when the signal through which one neuron excites an adjacent neuron is facilitated and strengthened. Once this connection is firm, it will remain so for extended periods. Complex behaviors involve neural circuits that are formed in just this way, and upon one component of this network becoming excited, the whole network will follow. In this fashion, networks of neurons can be established that can be activated in a synchronous fashion in response to significant stimuli. This same process may be responsible for the development of addiction, in that synaptic connections between drugs' neuronal and behavioral actions are strengthened with drug consumption, and the network of neurons involved widens with repeated drug experiences, including links to specific environmental cues. Eventually, the cues associated with the reward provided by the drug may themselves influence craving, which encourages further drug use.

Just as stressful experiences enhance the response to later stressors, cross-sensitization effects can be elicited so that stressor experiences enhance the later dopamine response elicited by cocaine or amphetamine. Thus, when a recovered addict encounters a stressor, the sensitized "neuronal addiction network" will be activated, provoking reinstatement of the addiction. Interestingly, the link between drug and stressor effects is bidirectional so that the use of cocaine or amphetamine may result in responses to later stressors being exaggerated. Thus, drug intake may have persistent ramifications in exaggerating stress responses and might thus further promote the development of stress-related pathological conditions.

It's interesting that common neural circuits are associated with natural rewards and addiction, but there are also several distinct differences possibly related to epigenetic changes associated with addictions. Stressful events, including those encountered early in life, could affect addiction processes through epigenetic changes related to dopamine functioning within the nucleus accumbens. As epigenetic changes can be long-lasting, their presence might account for why addictions are as sustained as they are. However, as different classes of abused drugs may also differ with respect to the epigenetic changes accrued, neurobiologically based treatments of the disorder might require targeting of distinct factors.

diminishing others. For example, the reinstatement that follows the presentation of alcohol-related cues could be attenuated by naltrexone, a drug that acts as an opioid receptor antagonist. Yet, reinstatement elicited by a stressor was not affected by naltrexone, but was reduced by a CRH antagonist. As well, reinstatement of an addiction induced by cues or stressors might involve different aspects of reward circuitry. Finally, relapse engendered by "priming" injections of either cocaine or heroin likely involve dopamine neuronal functioning, whereas relapse elicited by a stressor involved CRH and norepinephrine neuronal activity. As different processes govern reinstatement of different addictions, it may be necessary to use different strategies to curb the array of addictions that exist.

Can eating become an addiction?

The very systems that have been implicated in stress responses and drug addiction, including CRH and dopamine, have also been linked to eating processes. It is thought that for some individuals eating has the effect of limiting negative emotions, and might thus serve as a form of self-medication, just as drug-taking can act in this capacity. A hormone, orexin, which we haven't considered to this point, has been implicated in these common processes. Orexin is likely best known for its role in food intake, but stressors also stimulate the activity of orexin cells, which cause the release of dopamine at the nucleus accumbens and the prefrontal cortex, and thus promote behaviors associated with addiction. Like orexin, the hormone ghrelin, which promotes increased eating, might also play a role in addiction. It too stimulates activation of dopamine brain reward pathways, and potentiates the positive effects obtained from rewarding stimuli, and could contribute to addiction-related behaviors, especially under stressor conditions where an individual might crave a quick fix. In line with this, in rodents, ghrelin administered directly to a brain region fundamental for reward processes increased alcohol intake, whereas a treatment that antagonized the actions of ghrelin had the opposite effect. The notion that eating and addiction processes are linked has been receiving increasing attention, and the data at hand are sufficiently compelling to prompt further research targeting eating mechanisms in the treatment of addictions.

An integrated perspective

The addiction process consists of multiple steps, each of which seems to involve different processes. The work of Koob and Le Moal (2008) and that of Volkow and her associates (2010) have been especially significant, and they have laid out a series of steps and factors that contribute to the course of addiction. As we've seen, different reasons may exist as to why individuals first start using drugs, including self-medication to abate the impact of ongoing stressors. Not all individuals who encounter strong stressors will resort to drugs, but when stressors and personality factors favor rumination, drug use is often elevated. These drugs typically activate dopamine reward pathways and increase the salience of rewarding stimuli, furthering the expectation of feeling better with subsequent drug use, and thereby increasing the potential for addiction.

With continued drug use, receptors in some brain regions are repeatedly stimulated, leading to a decline in their sensitivity. As a result, a correspondingly greater drug dose is needed to achieve the neural stimulation and pleasure/reward that the drug once provided. As mentioned earlier, biological systems prefer to maintain balance, and although a state of euphoria is elicited by drugs such as cocaine, presumably by stimulating dopamine release, other processes are also activated against the dopamine excitation in an effort to maintain a biological balance. With continued drug use these opponent processes become progressively stronger, so that increasingly greater doses are needed to achieve the positive effect ordinarily induced by the drug. In this respect, the euphoric effects elicited by the drug not only decline over time following a hit, but are replaced by dysphoria, so that drug intake may eventually occur largely to thwart the dysphoric feelings, rather than to gain the pleasure that had once been elicited.

It's at this point that trouble really begins. Cues associated with the drug may have gained their own positive value and ability to prime neural reward circuits, and may prompt cravings for the drug. Individuals, particularly if they are impulsive, might give in to the craving even though they are fully aware of the problems that are being created

Hijacking flight control

Surely, those addicted to drugs should be able to maintain self-control and banish temptations created by environmental cues. We do, after all, have free will and should be able to judge what's good or bad for us and then behave in our own best interest. Volkow, however, has suggested that disturbances within aspects of the prefrontal cortex can be instigated by certain drugs, contributing immeasurably to the addiction process. She indicated that these drugs may provoke disturbed functioning of the cingulate and orbital frontal cortices, so that attention to goals and the ability to develop action plans become impaired and impulsivity increases, as do disturbances of reward processes. As a result, addicted individuals are not only desirous of obtaining reward through drugs, but are also more likely to be impulsive and want immediate gratification. In effect, Volkow and others have maintained that drugs can hijack the process involved in rationale thinking and impulse control.

In considering this aspect of addiction, what likely comes to mind are drug addictions involving alcohol, cocaine, amphetamine, heroin, or Percocet. It seems, however, that even smoking has the effect of biasing perceptions regarding the dangers of tobacco in that emotional reactions and areas of the brain that are activated differ between smokers and nonsmokers in response to positive and negative portrayals of smoking.

by doing so. Indeed, the neural circuits responsible for the craving might be so strong that even after people have abstained for a lengthy period, reminder cues and stressors can actively promote the reinstatement of the addiction.

Treatment for addictions

Beating an addiction, like breaking up (in a romantic relationship), is hard to do. The cure rates are low, and although favorable treatments are forever on the horizon, the horizon seems to move as we approach it. There has been a continuous search for drug therapies to treat addictions, or ones that could be used as adjuncts to behavioral therapies. Methadone or buprenorphine have served as replacement therapy in the treatment of opioid dependence, benzodiazepines (e.g., Valium) have been used to minimize the negative side effects of alcohol withdrawal, and antiepileptic medications, such as gabapentin and valproate, have been employed to deal with barbiturate or benzodiazepine withdrawal. Naltrexone has been utilized to treat alcoholism as it reduces the rewarding aspects of drunkenness, and it has even been recommended that addicts on naltrexone be permitted to consume alcohol so that the association between alcohol and positive feelings will be extinguished.

Although success with various pharmacological approaches hasn't been stellar, there seems to be a change in the wind with newer medications. In this regard, baclofen (marketed as Kemstro and Lioresal), which stimulates $GABA_B$ receptors, has been used to reduce drug cravings, and hence diminish relapse among those with problems related to amphetamines and alcohol. Patients who were treated with baclofen reported that they experienced a general indifference to the drug to which they were addicted, leading to the suggestion that baclofen affects a general reward/craving system, rather than one uniquely associated with any given compound, although it might be still more effective in combination with treatments that target a specific type of addictive agent. Like baclofen, the drug topiramate, which has been used to diminish epilepsy in children, seems to diminish cravings and use of cocaine and alcohol. There have also been rumblings that ibogaine, a psychoactive compound derived from Tabernanthe iboga, a plant used in particular rituals in West Central Africa, may be effective in diminishing addiction related to narcotic substances. This compound may create a hallucinogenic state that lasts for several days, after which addictions may be markedly diminished. Although it had been marketed for some time, in the 1960s it was placed on a list of restricted drugs owing to its own addictive properties and because of the risk for death, and consequently research to determine its antiaddiction properties have been limited. Nonetheless, compounds similar to ibogaine are in development and might eventually prove to have greater value in treating addictions.

The 12-step and residential treatment programs are likely the best known of the addiction treatments. Programs such as Alcoholics Anonymous and Narcotics Anonymous include social support as a fundamental component, thereby capitalizing on one of the most important ways of coping. Substance-abuse rehabilitation, more commonly referred to as "checking into rehab," also involves a social support component, and allows individuals to be away from the cues related to their addiction while they go through particular therapies that could potentially facilitate the engagement of behaviors to kick the habit. If the individual can afford it, then this obviously has some positive attributes, so long as they accept that they have a problem, want to beat the addiction, and believe that they can. For individuals who are still at the point where they're using Amy Winehouse's refrain "They tried to make me go to rehab, but I said no, no, no," there's probably little point in checking in.

A CBT-based approach in treating addition, the Transtheoretical Model of Behavior Change (TTM), has a considerable following. Assuming that a person accepts that they have a problem and they're ready to act on it, this program provides strategies that guide individuals through a series of stages to deal with their addiction. Often, when addicts fall back into their old ways, even slightly, their reaction might be "oh forget it. I'm a loser, and I might as well just do what I've always been doing." However, the TTM approach accepts that accidents happen, and the individual is encouraged to stick with the program despite the setbacks. Despite having many proponents, it has also been argued that a stage-based intervention strategy in the elimination of smoking and eating disorders is no more effective than a non-stage based approach. The final word concerning this issue remains to be said, but consider that, as in the case of any other mental disorder, a given treatment might be effective in treating addiction in some individuals, but different approaches might be more appropriate and effective for others.

Before you go...

The view of addiction proposed by Volkow et al. has been enormously influential, particularly as it has put a humane understanding on what addiction is about. In effect, one shouldn't see addiction as a character flaw or a weakness in the individual's personality, but an unfortunate change in their physiology that has made it much more difficult for them to help themselves. Because of the disturbances within the prefrontal cortex, the addicted individual experiences cravings that will be difficult to override through cognitive control mechanisms that have become impaired. In fact, at some point in the addiction process, a drug might not provide the pleasure that it once did. Instead the addiction is driven by the motivation to diminish cravings, which has for all intents become an automatic response, just as this automaticity appears with other habits and the negative thinking characteristic of depressed individuals. At the same time, the inhibitions that ordinarily allow individuals to pause may be subverted, making it difficult to stop using drugs and to stay clean once individuals have kicked the habit. This isn't just a matter of the abdication of common sense, but instead, the neurochemical disturbances created by repeated drug use hijack the ability of addicts to consider their behaviors appropriately.

17

Coping with Illness, Caregiving, and Loss

What do you really know about your illness and how it's about to be treated?

In some places finding a personal or family physician is easy-peasy. Get a name from a friend and phone for an appointment. In other countries or regions, it can be difficult as there's a shortage of physicians. Furthermore, if it's a place that has socialized medicine or individuals are part of a managed care program, a person might not get to select their physician. They get whoever happens to be available at a given time.

In one of his early stand-up routines, Jerry Seinfeld described a scene that involves two guys talking, in which one, let's call him Murray, says to Jerry, who had been kvetching over some pain, "Go see my doctor, Dr X. He's incredible, graduated first in his class. Tell him I sent you." This leaves Jerry thinking, "Okay, if I tell the doctor that Murray sent me, then what's he supposed to say? 'Oooohhhh, Murray sent you! Terrific. So, I'll give you the real medicine. Other people get the placebo.'" He goes on to speculate further: "if there's a first in the class, then there's also a last in the class!"

There's a serious side to this anecdote. When we encounter a health problem, for example one that will require surgery, we want particular information from our physician or from the surgeon to whom our doctor sent us. Most of all we want to know the probability of the procedure leading to death during or soon after surgery, the chances of complications in the days or weeks following surgery, the probability that the procedure will cure us, and the degree of pain and discomfort we can expect and for how long. Population statistics are helpful, but they don't really give an accurate portrayal. Let's take a hypothetical case where we're told that death or disability occurs during or soon after surgery in 10 percent of patients. Are these deaths spread across the entire population or do they occur primarily in certain people? Do they occur more often in people who are obese, or don't work out regularly, or those who smoke? Moreover, do they occur at a rate of 10 percent across all surgeons, or are there some with a 19 percent failure

Stress and Your Health: From Vulnerability to Resilience, First Edition. Hymie Anisman.
© 2015 John Wiley & Sons, Ltd. Published 2015 by John Wiley & Sons, Ltd.

rate, but others who experience problems in only 1 percent of cases? In effect, did my surgeon graduate at the top of the class or was he last? Furthermore, has my family doctor or cardiologist actually looked into the success rate of the surgeon they recommended? Sadly, the research suggests that most physicians likely haven't done this! To some extent, information can be obtained about doctors on internet sites, but few of us actually do this. Most often we ask a couple of friends if they know much about a given surgeon and typically their information is third-hand. It strikes me that when we go out to buy a car we might make all sorts of inquiries about which is best, and what the advantages are of different brands and models. We should engage, as much as possible, in finding the physician that suits each of us best.

How might illness come to affect health?

Intuitively, you might think that fairly strong stressors and those that have been experienced relatively recently are the most likely to affect our health. This is true to some extent, but in other respects both conclusions are wrong. Although recent strong stressor experiences can certainly put us into a tailspin and can quickly lead to any number of disturbances, many illnesses take years to develop and the effects of stressors on these pathological conditions might have been experienced well before the disorder actually emerged. Indeed, the course for some illnesses, as we've seen, may have been set by stressors encountered prenatally or during childhood. Moreover, some illnesses can occur as a result of what has been referred to as a "double-hit," in which an initial challenge weakens or primes a system so that a second hit, even one very different from the first, might be more likely to produce a negative outcome.

Experiencing many hits over an extended period of time may also have cumulative effects that erode an individual's psychological and biological abilities to contend with challenges. Understandably, there haven't been many studies that have examined the cumulative effects of stressors experienced over years, but prospective studies conducted over several decades have indicated that among women midlife events such as divorce, widowhood, unemployment, and illness cumulatively increased irritability, fear, and sleep disturbances. More than this, the compounding effects of midlife stressful events that stemmed from work, family, health, or other problems predicted a reduced volume of cortical brain regions responsible for decision-making, impulsivity, emotion and reward

For richer or poorer

... in sickness and in health. You certainly know where those vows come from, but do you actually believe them? In fact, when a partner becomes seriously ill, the chances of the marriage breaking up increases appreciably and women are at greater risk than men if they become ill. The risk of a split also increases if they have a child who becomes ill. Needless to say, this is a double whammy. It's bad enough to have to deal with an illness without having a primary source of support abandon you.

regulation. These same factors also influenced immunologically based disorders, heart disease, diabetes, and the risk for Alzheimer's disease. Interestingly, it wasn't just severe stressors that were associated with pathology, as ordinary day-to-day stressors were pivotal in determining health risk. To be sure, stressors interact with and can engender other lifestyle factors (diet, sleep, work–life balance, happiness in marriage, food choices, drug consumption, and smoking) in determining the evolution of disease states.

Major physical illnesses

The global burden of disease, which refers to the average number of years lost by individuals as a result of disease, has changed considerably over the past few decades. Childhood illnesses related to malnutrition and infectious diseases still represent a significant burden, but with improved health technologies, medicines, and delivery systems, the picture has changed. At one time, the global disease burden was primarily viewed from the perspective of mortality, but it is now more commonly viewed in terms of the frequency and impact of particular illnesses, as well as the factors that serve to disturb health. From this vantage, the greatest health burdens, varying across countries, are currently chronic diseases and those related to aging, musculoskeletal problems, and neuropsychiatric disorders. The trick isn't just to stay alive, but to live well, and largely this means living with as few illnesses as possible.

Many of us go through life rarely thinking about encountering diseases even though their prevalence makes it likely that we'll be affected by one or more of them. These conditions come to mind primarily when we suddenly develop particular symptoms, but even then we might delay seeing a doctor, hoping that the symptoms will disappear, although we know that this might not be a good strategy. If we end up visiting the doctor, sometimes with the worst thoughts imaginable, it's pretty common to hear the hoped for "It's nothing, don't worry," and we then leave the doctor's office, a new skip to our step, and feeling as if it were spring and we're reborn. However, there are occasions where things don't work out quite as well. Sometimes we're sent for "more tests," which almost unfailingly heightens our distress, and it's not unusual for symptoms (perhaps false symptoms) to intensify as we continue to focus on them obsessively.

What patients know and what they need to know

There was a time when there was debate as to what a patient should be told about their illness. If the picture was grim, then there might not be any point in telling them as this would only create distress. In my immigrant community of the 1950s it wasn't unusual to hear a statement such as "Did you hear? Mr X has the real thing." To which the second person might reply, "Does he know?" As you'll have quickly realized, "the real thing" was "the Big C" but nobody would say the word because, obviously, uttering it might somehow bring down a curse. At any event, the belief was that the affected person would be better off if they didn't know they had the Big C. Those were the days before "early detection" and once the symptoms were sufficiently severe to initiate a visit to the doctor, it's unlikely that they wouldn't know for long.

This view sounds fairly antiquated, but to some extent it still persists, as there continues to be some question about what the patient needs to know, the patient's right to know, and whether patients have the right to not know. Open communication between a patient and doctor is the norm, but issues regarding treatment efficacy and prognosis are sometimes a bit blurred, and one might even get the feeling that there's a bit of obfuscation going on. Prognoses regarding illness trajectories for individual patients are difficult to make as the physician usually can only respond on the basis of population statistics. Yes, 50 or 75 out of every 100 patients will survive a particular illness, but there may be individual characteristics that need to be considered, and the physician can't always make accurate predictions, and thus might be reluctant to get too deeply into this with patients. As well, some patients might not actually want full disclosure from their physician. As long as the prognosis isn't an absolute death warrant, not knowing everything might permit them to feel a sense of control over their destiny, and may allow them some hope for a cure, as much as that might be possible. Likewise, following genetic testing, a patient might desire not to know of some anomaly that might or might not affect them. Thus, a physician might be faced with a juggling act in which they wish to maintain their integrity and provide accurate information to patients, but at the same time it might be acceptable, even advantageous, to maintain a degree of ambiguity about the future, provided that this is consistent with what the patient might want.

Appraising and coping with illness

Uncertainty, ambiguity and the anticipation of stressors tend to breed anxiety, and this is particularly evident in relation to illnesses – what treatments are planned, when will these be initiated, and what is the probability of a successful outcome? Reducing

Worse than the illness itself

Not every illness is considered or treated in the same way, and some illnesses have gotten a pretty bad rap. In psychiatric circles there's a reluctance to deal with conditions in which personality disorders (e.g., narcissistic, borderline, histrionic) are present, largely because these patients are often viewed as demanding and hard to deal with, and treatments are typically ineffective in modifying these traits. Patients with chronic fatigue syndrome (CFS) or fibromyalgia may likewise end up with considerable frustration. Both these illnesses are unexplained medical conditions with similar symptomatology (e.g., fatigue, widespread pain, depression). However, their diagnosis is difficult as there are no objective tests that can be used, their etiologies have not been established and there are no clear-cut treatments. Indeed, there are a great many people, including some practitioners, who view affected individuals suspiciously, thinking that they're a bit off or that they're malingering. As a result, those living with the pain and fatigue associated with the illnesses have also been burdened with the stigma that often accompanies these conditions. It's been thought for some time that CFS might be engendered by inflammatory processes that affect muscles and sleep, and that among CFS-affected individuals stress-response systems are always on alert, reflected by elevated and protracted cardiac responses to cognitive challenges. Recent evidence gleaned from CFS sufferers has pointed to inflammatory processes potentially leading to altered activation of a brain region, the basal ganglia, which is involved in reward processes, cognitive functions, and motor acts. It seems we're getting to the point that the etiology for CFS will be determined and firm diagnostic criteria established, and the stigma burden might thus be diminished.

unpredictability by being informed of the precise date for imminent surgery and what to expect following surgery allows individuals the opportunity to prepare themselves, spend time with loved ones, and deal with other issues that need tending. Suspense can be exhilarating when it comes to murder mysteries, but not when it involves imminent invasive medical procedures. Women waiting for breast cancer surgery indicated that this period was difficult, painful, long and especially frightening, but this anticipatory distress could be diminished through psychological interventions, which had the additional benefit of improving immune responses and enhancing survival. Likewise, psychological interventions during recovery can enhance general well-being and the benefits of the medical treatments administered.

Personal control, decision-making, and trust

When seriously ill, we might be given options about treatment strategies that can be used, but our limited knowledge might hinder decision-making, especially if the options available are daunting (e.g., surgery, radiation, chemotherapy). In such circumstances some patients prefer not to engage in making treatment-related decisions, leaving this to the physician, whereas others desire shared decision-making, often spending considerable time getting information regarding the best options and then making decisions in consultation with their physician. Often, they'll end up agreeing with what the physician might have thought was their best option, but sometimes they might not take the physician's advice, and might even opt for some pretty bad alternatives, such as one of many shlock cancer cures, instead of those based on the available hard data. As illusory as it might be, patients might simply desire a sense of control over the situation, or they might want to prevent or dispel the feeling of being a victim. When they have a say in relation to treatment options, as in the case of the selection of treatments to alleviate pain, such as that experienced after surgery, their satisfaction with care improves, as does their sense of improvement in their healing, although pain perception itself might not change.

My best friend, the doctor

We often have an interesting relationship with our family physician. Typically, we like them and even seem, in some sense, to be possessive about them, using terms such as "my" doctor, whereas we refer to others as "the" plumber, "the" moving guy, or "the" snow plow guy. We trust that our doctor has our best interest in mind, and hence follow their advice to the extent that we can. Although patient compliance is often a problem, it would be still more difficult if the advice came from someone who wasn't trusted. Furthermore, the trust inspired by the doctor, wearing a white coat, looking very professional, knowledgeable and confident, serves as a powerful placebo that can make us feel better. That said, you might want to skip the next couple of paragraphs as they could potentially undermine the trust you have in the medical system, even though your own doctor might be excellent.

Sometimes negative outcomes come about that are more serious than the initially treated condition, and there are times when unexpected errors or even gross negligence occurs. To be sure, not every bad event that occurs in complex surgical procedures is the fault of the surgeon, and some treatments often come with negative side effects. There are instances when there's nobody who can or should be blamed for negative outcomes of medical procedures, but there are occasions when certain difficulties could (or should) have been foreseen, and there are occasions when the adverse outcomes were solely due to negligence.

Iatrogenic illness, which refers to negative outcomes or illnesses that occur as a result of the performance of those who are supposed to heal the sick (the physician, pharmacist, therapist, anesthetist, the hospital itself), is not uncommon. Iatrogenic illness has been estimated to occur in as many as 25–30 percent of patients in hospital, with 10 percent being considered serious, and death occurring in about 2 percent. More conservative estimates of "medical misadventure" put the number at slightly less than 2 percent, but even this amounts to millions of cases each year within Western medical systems. These negative outcomes can stem from inaccurate diagnoses, surgical error, secondary infection, secondary effects of anesthetics, incorrect drug doses, allergic reactions, viruses or bacteria present in hospitals, and psychiatric illness brought on by medical procedures. There are also many "never events" that comprise inexcusable procedures or outcomes. In the US, Canada and Europe deaths related to such errors amount to hundreds of thousands and long-term negative effects are still more frequent. With so many instruments being used during any complicated surgery, it is perhaps not all that surprising that surgical instruments have been left behind in patients' bodies. These can include clamps, tweezers, forceps, needles, safety pins, scalpels, knife blades, scissors, sponges, towels, suction tips and tubes, to name the most common, but even scopes and, ultrasound tissue disruptors can meet this fate. Every week on average, surgeons in the US leave a sponge or towel in a patient 39 times, undertake the wrong procedure on a patient 20 times, and operate on the wrong person 20 times. These are obviously extreme cases, but they occur too often, and other types of medical iatrogenic problems are still more common. In fact, one study in Great Britain that focused on treatments in mental health facilities indicated that more than half the patients received incorrect medications for other illnesses they might have been suffering. Diagnostic errors appear to be among the most common difficulties, thought to be as high as 5 percent in outpatient clinics, and it has been estimated that such errors are responsible for 80,000–160,000 deaths or disabilities each year in the US. These errors most often concern missed diagnoses, rather than incorrect diagnoses. The intent here isn't to diminish patient trust and confidence, especially as this could undermine the potential benefits that accompany trust in physicians. Still, as errors happen more frequently than one would like, transparency is important and patients ought to be prepared, especially if a few days or even weeks after surgery odd or new symptoms occur.

Social support and unsupportive interactions in the face of illness

The positive attributes of social support are not only apparent in the context of psychological illness, such as depression, but also in the ability to adjust to physical illnesses. Effective support is often obtained from family members, particularly when family cohesion is high and when emphasis is placed on self-reliance and personal achievement. Conversely, negative patient outcomes have been common in the presence of critical, overprotective, controlling, and distracting family responses to illness management. Aside from family members, especially potent support is frequently obtained from our ingroup, which can take the form of work friends and colleagues, coreligionists, or our ethnic or racial group. If we share a bond with them, if we share certain visions, if we share goals and aspirations and hope, then their support will be particularly welcome. In the context of illness, the ingroup that might be particularly useful are those individuals who have had or are currently dealing with similar illnesses. These individuals are more likely to "understand my pain" and the shared beliefs between support group members make them especially valued.

There seems to be a degree of selectivity as to which illnesses engender the most social support. People with cancer usually receive considerable support, whereas those with progressive, chronic illnesses, such as MS or lupus erythematosus, as devastating as they might be, likely receive somewhat less social support, possibly because the risk of death isn't as imminent. Sadly, there are far fewer people who gather to the side of those with a mental illness, almost as if it were contagious. Regardless of the illness, when social support does appear, it has its limits. It can only go on for so long before supporters feel that they need to get on with their own lives. Unfortunately, the ill person who comes to rely on the support of friends may interpret even modest withdrawal as an unsupportive response, saying "you know who your friends are when the chips are down."

As we've seen, unsupportive interactions can be devastating to an individual's psychological and physical health. Unsupportive behaviors are experienced by those with mental health problems and with diseases such as HIV/AIDS, and family members are also victims of unsupportive responses, especially the children of those with mental disorders. Unsupportive interactions are frequently experienced by the elderly with a variety of neurological problems, such as impaired cognitive functioning and Alzheimer's disease. In some instances this might escalate into elder abuse owing to frustrations experienced by caregivers. As ugly as it is, this situation is sufficiently frequent to have prompted the American Academy of Neurology to advise clinical neurologists to screen older patients for abusive experiences.

Mood changes associated with illness

It's hardly surprising that depressed mood might develop in some individuals with physical illnesses, because pain, discomfort, uncertainty, and a lack of control over their life can strain their psychological and physical resources. This distress can have far-reaching effects, not only in limiting recovery from illness, but also by contributing to the appearance of still other illnesses. For instance, the development of depression following a stroke or a cardiac episode was a grim predictor of future well-being, whereas patients who received individualized psychological treatments as part of their rehabilitation fared better. Indeed, in older depressed individuals who were treated through "collaborative care" that comprised drug treatment and psychotherapy, half as many heart problems were encountered over the ensuing five years relative to individuals who had received standard treatment. Such outcomes point to the importance of coping resources and methods to deal with the stress of illness, and suggest that illnesses, including depression, stroke and heart disease, share common underlying biological processes. The relations between illnesses are so common that depression might be considered an important marker for the occurrence of other disorders and might point to the need for appropriate intervention strategies.

The other side of the story

There's long been the notion that raging against an illness might increase survival, whereas despair would have the opposite effect. Dylan Thomas famously advised not to "go gentle into that good night," but instead to "rage against the dying of the light." In fact, a relationship exists between feelings of helplessness and hopelessness and five- and ten-year survival rates following breast cancer treatment, and there is evidence that a positive outlook and the availability of social support can enhance survival. It's unlikely that anyone would argue against the importance of maintaining a positive perspective, but at some point it's also important that we see this from the patient's perspective as opposed to the knee-jerk "stay positive – fight this" reaction. Consider the individual's physical and psychological state, how long they've been ill, their pain, discomfort or loss of self, what the prognosis might be, and what quality of life they can expect even with the best of outcomes. There are certainly times and situations where one might question whether the struggle is worth it, and whether a family's encouragement to rage against the illness is always the right thing. Is it ever the case that the dying person would prefer to go gentle into that good night, and wishes for their family's consent to do so?

Adjustment to chronic illnesses: psychological resilience in the face of illness

Those who have gone through a traumatic illness, even if it occurred much earlier, might be psychologically exhausted, making it difficult for them to deal with still further encounters with illness. As well, for a substantial number of patients, particularly those sufficiently ill to end up in an intensive care unit, cognitive disturbances may occur much like those seen following traumatic brain injury. There are other individuals, in contrast, who are particularly resilient so that they're able to maintain or regain their mental health in the face of fiercely strong illnesses. They might have gone through a form of cognitive restructuring, such as finding meaning, so that when they encountered illness again they were better prepared to appraise and cope with that event. Finding meaning in the face of trauma can be an effective way of coming to terms with a chronic and severe illness, but for some individuals finding meaning isn't in the cards, and other methods need to be relied upon. Essentially, while some people start smelling the coffee, for others it leaves a bitter taste. For them, adjustment to illness might be facilitated by the endorsement of proper coping methods and the ability to manage stressors not related to illness, and the effective use of support systems.

Acceptance of the diagnosis and treatment of an illness can be difficult, often being undermined by uncertainty regarding the course of the illness, rumination, pain, and sleep disturbances. Yet, more often than not, affected individuals turn out to be more resilient than they might have expected. As we've seen, many factors contribute to resilience in the face of illness, including varied personality characteristics, such as self-efficacy, self-esteem, determination, internal locus of control, optimism, mastery, hardiness, hopefulness, self-empowerment, and acceptance of illness. These are relatively fixed characteristics that can't readily be acquired through some sort of treatment. However, proper therapy can influence other characteristics associated with resilience, such as appropriate cognitive appraisals, effective coping methods, acknowledging and expressing emotions, spirituality, engaging in self-management whenever possible, and even making every effort to focus on potential positive outcomes of their illness.

Stress associated with caregiving

When a person becomes severely ill, others may also have their lives tilted or turned entirely upside down. Family members are obviously going to be most affected, especially as they might be called upon to take on new and difficult responsibilities. The caregiving role is common in Western countries, where about 30 percent of people will serve in such a capacity at some point in their lives. This might comprise caregiving for children with varied problems or for people who have been in debilitating accidents or are experiencing mental health problems, and with increasing life spans the need for elder care has increased.

In response to a severe illness or accident it isn't unusual for family members to become enmeshed in every aspect of the patient's life. Sometimes family members might be over-wrought and all members try to do everything at once, rather than pacing themselves and dividing the burden, often because they don't realize that this might be a long journey and the load ought to be shared. Occasionally a family member may go a bit over the top, even attempting to take over the decision-making role in the patient's medical care. They may be well intentioned, but through their dogmatic and even aggressive behaviors they may also become troublesome to the treatment team, annoying to other family members who are trying their best to cope and remain respectful, and an appreciable burden to the patient. Their "bossy" behavior might serve as a fundamental coping mechanism for them so that they feel a semblance of control over their own lives, but they frequently cause distress for everyone else.

Once the initial crisis regarding the patient's illness has passed, the ensuing months can take any of several routes. Recovery can be good, even if it involves a lengthy recuperative period, or this period might comprise a slow, dismal, inexorable decline with occasional "up" periods that create false hope. This might mean that a family member steps up or is recruited for the caregiving role, even though they may be entirely unprepared to act in this capacity and the load might be too heavy. For example, the caregiver may be an elderly spouse who isn't physically able to do the job, or it may be a member of the sand-wich generation who is already caring for children so that full-time care of a parent can be excessively difficult.

The hardships of the caregiving role vary with the nature of the patient's illness, and the relationship between the caregiver and the recipient. For the caregiver who watches the strains on the patient unfold, the distress can be considerable, likely aggravated by setbacks that patients might experience, uncertainties regarding the course of the illness, and the dehumanizing treatments their loved one undergoes. These negative feelings can be exacerbated by the frustration of feeling alone in the caregiving role and feeling hard done by, as other family members always seem to be unavailable to help. The strain on family members can be so chronic and profound that it causes anxiety, depression, and PTSD, and disturbances related to endocrine and immune functioning. Older caregivers are at particular risk for stroke and heart disease, and the incidence of dementia increases sixfold.

Despite the hardships, some people are able to handle the caregiving role, and it seems that characteristics such as personal mastery, optimism, self-efficacy, and the use of particular coping methods are especially pertinent. As well, better adjustment on the part of the caregiver is related to greater social support and the quality of the caregiver–recipient relationship. For some individuals, religion and spirituality were instrumental in dealing with the distress associated with caregiving, as were lower threat appraisals and the use of problem-oriented coping strategies. As fundamental as these individual characteristics are, the positive attributes of social support and the opportunity to take breaks from the situation can't be overstated. For the caregiver, one day runs into the next and the load they're carrying is often unremitting. Caregivers need time away to recuperate, they need social support, and others need to step in to help. Too often, those who ought to be helping let the willing horse do the work and feel that their duty is done by visiting on odd occasions.

Individuals who are driven primarily by the intrinsic reward derived from caregiving, or those who find meaning from this experience, tend to be least likely to experience negative outcomes, such as depression, anxiety and anger. Those who engage in caregiving obviously need to do so for the right reasons, rather than taking on unwanted obligations or succumbing to the perceived demands of others.

Loss and grief

The death of a loved one may have varied consequences on those left behind, depending on the circumstances surrounding the loss. For example, who was it who died (parent, child, sibling, friend), how old was the person, and was the death expected following a long illness, or was it sudden and unexpected? Was death due to natural causes, accident, suicide, homicide? Was there an opportunity to say good-bye? And, as crass as it may sound, what financial burdens will survivors endure? Each of these issues has obvious relevance for the physical and mental health of the bereaved. Although, there are general features that apply to coping with loss, in some instances, such as how to deal with loss due to suicide or loss of a child, obtaining advice from a professional or support group members is advised.

If loss occurs suddenly and unexpectedly, it can be shattering, but if it occurs after a long illness we often have the opportunity to prepare, and there may even be relief in seeing an end to the misery of the sufferer, and an end to the distress engendered by the caregiving burden. The loss of a child is always horrendous, irrespective of its cause. However, each situation can engender different consequences for survivors. Parents who lost a child owing to factors not related to drugs and those who experienced a drug-related loss of a child were both seen to exhibit grief responses and mental health difficulties, but the grief and mental health problems were complicated among parents who had lost a child through a drug-related death. These parents might be experiencing guilt ("If only I had done something else, something more effective"), and to a considerable extent the stigma associated with drug use and mental illness might undermine their ability to recover, particularly if they encountered unsupportive responses from others. When the death occurred as a result of suicide a somewhat different set of factors might affect parents. What triggered the suicide? Did it stem from severe depression or another form of mental illness, or did it emerge as a result of bullying, and to what extent, if any, was the parent aware of their child's situation and the accompanying despair? Given the multiple factors that play into the grieving process, coupled with the individual differences that influence emotional and behavioral responses to loss, people will react differently and diverse strategies for coping with loss may be necessary. There isn't an easy solution for dealing with these diverse events, and any recommendation that can be offered certainly varies across individuals. For some people enduring these experiences, support groups of similarly affected individuals is often recommended, and to be sure social support can offer a social cure, as Jolanda Jetten, Cath Haslam and Alex Haslam (2012) have indicated. We are, after all, social animals and take great comfort from supportive group members. Yet, as we've seen with so many stress responses, for some individuals, finding meaning, staying active, or simply being alone to sort out their thoughts is remedial.

The initial intense grief that follows loss typically diminishes with the passage of time and through the use of effective methods of coping. It's not a rapid process and adjustment to loss often happens over several years, and despair can readily be reinstated by significant stimuli even decades later. The period soon after loss, extending to about two years, is exceptionally difficult, and among mothers who have lost a child, this period is marked by a 130 percent increase in death. Typically, grief does not call for clinical intervention, but there are occasions when acute grief can transform into "complicated grief," a chronic and debilitating condition that requires specialized treatment, especially as it can result in psychological and physical illnesses. Whether or not such grief outcomes occur may be difficult to predict, but the presence of mental illness prior to the loss and the presence of a poor attachment style seem to be associated with particularly poor outcomes. Predictably, the influence of these factors might be modified by the availability and perception of social support, religious and cultural beliefs and practices, financial factors, the coping methods used, positive emotions, and by the comfort gained from positive memories, as bitter-sweet as these might be.

The processes of grieving were at one time seen as individuals working through a series of stages to achieve comfort and closure. These perspectives have increasingly come under scrutiny, and alternative positions have been offered. One especially influential perspective, the dual process model, proposes that individuals can engage in two types of bereavement-related coping processes. The first, loss-orientation, comprises a cognitive behavioral coping method in which an individual's internal experiences regarding the loss are at the forefront, usually focusing on the attachment the individual had with the deceased person, together with the emotional responses elicited by the loss, such as rumination, yearning, despair, loneliness and positive reminiscing, and sometimes feelings of being strangled by their grief. The second, termed restoration-orientation, is more concerned with the new challenges and adjustments that emerge as a result of the loss. These can range from financial issues, changes in quality of life and living style, and developing an identity that is independent of the person who was lost. Initially, loss-orientation predominates, but with time, this ought to shift to more effective restoration-orientation. How other coping strategies are used also contributes to the emergence of well-being following loss, and having social support may be fundamental in determining the extent to which individuals successfully transition from a loss-orientation to a restoration-orientation perspective.

Before you go...

Most of us can count on becoming ill at some time, and it is then that we might realize how foolish we were in fretting over trivial events that we had previously taken so seriously. Illnesses we endure can also affect those around us to varying degrees, and in some instances the distress experienced by family members can lead them to become ill. Making appropriate appraisals and having effective coping methods, as well as offering and receiving support from ingroup members, are obviously essential for everyone. We'll be discussing methods of dealing with strong stressors in ensuing chapters, but

So, what's on the other side?

Although it isn't meant for everyone, some people find relief by coping through religion, which comes with the bonus that individuals might find a social group who can offer advice and support. For those with a religious slant, the thought of an afterlife, or the thought of going to heaven, can be a great comfort. However, for many others it represents nothing more than superstition and wishful thinking.

As we age, some of us might be inclined to wonder about what happens after we die. Do we get to see the things reported by those who've had near-death experiences? Or, do we just get buried and then lie there, day after day, bored. Atheists clearly don't use religion as a coping strategy to deal with their own potential death, and even those who aren't atheists in a strict sense aren't likely to turn to a god as a means of coping. On a few occasions over the years, in talking to agnostic friends who were at late stages of a terminal illness, I have pointed out that some physicists believe that multiple universes exist, possibly lying in parallel with this one, even taking up the same physical space. Moreover, these universes could potentially be connected by wormholes. If this is the case, then who's to say whether or not a soul could have access to these alternate universes through these wormholes. An alternate universe might be the final resting places of our souls and those who came before us. Perhaps because it sounds as if there is some science behind it, some of my science-minded friends were ready to accept string theory and multiuniverse theories in relation to a hereafter, even though they had little knowledge about this topic. To be sure, I haven't had this discussion with many people, but of those with whom I discussed it, not a single one rejected the notion, and several were very positive, even hopeful, about the slim possibility of something being on the other side.

for the moment one additional piece of advice might be appropriate. In coping with illness, your own or that of a close other, deal with it one day at a time. Limit yourself to thinking in the moment and don't guess and second-guess the future. It will come and you'll deal with it then.

18

The Workplace for Better or Worse

Casting stones

For most of us, about a quarter of our adult life is spent at work, and with the explosion of internet communication and cell phones, it's fairly usual to have our home lives enmeshed with our work lives. For some of us, our job isn't just what we do, it's who we are. It's part of our identity and the workplace is a place of great satisfaction, and even serves as one of our most effective ways of coping with stressful experiences. For others, work is a chore that's undertaken simply to earn a living and they wait impatiently for weekends or days off when the drudgery stops for a while. The workplace can also be a source of considerable distress that can even intrude on a person's outside life. Regardless of our general disposition toward our job, we might encounter workplace stressors that comprise minor annoying events or unremitting challenges that persist for days on end, calling for self-control, patience and tenacity.

There are some organizations or managers within organizations that do not foster a healthy work environment, and often enough they learn the hard way that this is entirely counterproductive. There are, on the other side, some employees who feel that problems that exist with the corporation are exclusively a consequence of characteristics of the organization or management. It's likely that most of us know dissatisfied people who never find anything good enough and undermine the organization from their very first day on the job. They don't get the attention or promotions they feel they're entitled to, or they might simply have a negative view of virtually anything to do with the organization, or maybe they're just bitter, negative people who also have too much spare time on their hands and thus spend it sowing bitter seeds wherever they go. It's too simple to get enmeshed in their disturbed thinking, which can create *folie à deux*, and then *folie à trois*, and eventually *folie à plusieurs* – the madness of many.

Stress and Your Health: From Vulnerability to Resilience, First Edition. Hymie Anisman.
© 2015 John Wiley & Sons, Ltd. Published 2015 by John Wiley & Sons, Ltd.

Job-related distress

Stressors are almost invariably encountered in the workplace. Some stressors are created by the employer, others stem from employees, and sometimes poo just happens. Regardless of the source, workplace stressors can have enormous ramifications on our well-being, and we'll address some of these, after which recommendations will be offered to limit the adverse consequences that can occur. However, as we go, it should be fairly obvious what employees and employers need to do to improve the workplace, and in so doing enhance performance.

Status and job strain

As we've seen, individuals in lower social tiers are at increased risk of illness, possibly owing to lifestyle factors, such as high levels of smoking, less leisure-time physical activity, lousy food choices, obesity, or a poor work–leisure balance, as well as diminished access to medical services. But there's more to it than just these factors, as aspects of the job have a lot to do with well-being. The risk for illness was most notable among individuals experiencing job strain, which consists of having low decision latitude coupled with high job demands. Basically, having lots on your plate, but little control over how and when to deal with it, can be exceptionally distressing, especially if it is accompanied by the perception of unfairness or injustice. Individuals have a basic need for self-worth and respect, and when they find themselves in situations that diminish them, then their mental and physical health may be compromised and, understandably, their morale declines and commitment to the organization falls.

Burnout

The term "burnout" is used so commonly it's become a cliché, although the term is often used incorrectly. Burnout refers to feelings of persistent exhaustion coupled with diminished interest or anhedonia in relation to one's job, sometimes coupled with cynicism. In several ways, these characteristics are what one sees in clinical depression, and burnout is, indeed, not far removed from depressive disorders. There are characteristics of the individual that feed into burnout, just as organizational factors play a prominent role in this regard. Whereas the presence of depressive symptoms together with low levels of organizational support predict later burnout, personal and organizational support tends to bolster an individual's accomplishments and buffer them against emotional exhaustion. Using cognitive coping strategies, as we'll discuss shortly, can also go a long way in diminishing this form of distress.

Absenteeism and presenteeism

Frequent absence from duties or obligations is sometimes thought to reflect poor individual performance and is taken as a breach in the implicit contract that exists between an employee and employer. It may reflect malingering, laziness, or outright dishonesty, but it could also reflect health deterioration brought about by events in the workplace. In fact, psychosocial stressors or low expectations regarding the near future are predictive of sick days from work and general work dissatisfaction. This aside, based on insurance claims it has been estimated that about two-thirds of disability cases involve a psychiatric diagnosis, with the overwhelming majority being linked to stressful experiences. Clearly, it's in the employer's best interest to create an environment that limits job strain and other stressors,

Glad to see that you're better; now can you possibly get your butt moving?

With the recent increase of suicides related to head injury among professional athletes, as well as occasions when players have had to sit out the season owing to concussion, we've come to appreciate that these injuries need to be taken much more seriously than they were in the past. At the behest of management, or because they were so inclined, players would rejoin their team when they weren't quite ready to do so, and even a small jolt could set them back. We now know that a concussion has downstream ramifications that are apparent months and months after the injury was first sustained. These same risks exist for workers who take sick leave for psychological reasons. They're likely pretty fragile when they get back to work, and getting back into the job can't be expected to occur instantly. It can be a slow process, and the individual will likely be counting on others to help them readjust. Unfortunately, there may be stigma and suspicion regarding sick time taken for mental health issues, which may be compounded when others have had to take up the slack for the sick employee. So, when they do return they might not be received with genuine good wishes and happy faces, but with the glare and lack of support that translates as "have you noticed that your selfish behavior has cost the rest of us?"

thereby maintaining employee morale and good health. Of course, there are employees who just can't be satisfied, and there are those who will use sick leave as a means of punishing the employer whenever they feel they have been wronged.

An issue as important as absenteeism, but talked about less frequently, is that of presenteeism. This generally refers to an individual coming to work when they are sick or beyond the point where they are effective, as happens when employees are overly fatigued or when they feel burned out. The employee might show up when they are ill because they feel intense loyalty and dedication to the company, or feel that nobody else can do their job properly, or because their self-esteem is tied to their job performance. They might also show up to work because they can't financially afford not to be there, or they might feel that they are dispensable and thus had better be at work, or they might reason that the work will eventually have to be done in any case. It's unlikely that distressed and demotivated individuals who work under these conditions will be engaged or effective.

Bullying in the workplace

Employees within a firm may all be on the same team, but this doesn't mean they all play nice. They might not only fail to be supportive of one another, but could actually be very unsupportive, which might undermine group morale and individual well-being. The extreme form of an unsupportive relationship within a job setting is that of workplace bullying that comprises prolonged harassment or violence emanating from an individual or from a group, the latter being referred to as mobbing. Although bullying is most frequently discussed in relation to school environments, it's fairly common in the workplace. It can come from a boss or a fellow employee and is manifested in a variety of ways, such as threats, belittling others, sarcasm, rudeness, name calling, sexual harassment, scapegoating, violence, overworking an employee, or criticism directed at the individual for no motive other than self-aggrandizement. Estimates of bullying frequency vary widely, ranging between 2% and 8%, but a report from the Workplace Bullying Institute in the US in 2007 indicated that 13% of workers felt that they were currently being bullied, and 37 % indicated that they had been bullied at some time. Of these workers, 40% had not informed their employers, and of those who had, 62% indicated that the issue was not resolved as employers might not have known what to do or seemed to simply hope that the problem would dissipate on its own.

Common to most studies was that bullying had multiple adverse health-related outcomes. It's no great wonder that victims of bullying may express extreme distress, showing the classical symptoms of anxiety, depression, sleep problems, and even PTSD, and these outcomes could even appear years later. However, it's not just the bullied person who is affected, as the ill effects are also apparent among witnesses to the bullying. This may reflect an empathetic reaction, or it might develop owing to guilt or despair created by not being able to do anything about the bullying, or the fear of the same thing happening to them. Whatever the case, it ought to be particularly relevant to employers that witnessing others being bullied increases the individual's intention to leave the organization. Whether it's in the schoolyard, through the internet or in the workplace, bullying can be humiliating and exceptionally distressing, and creates a poisoned environment filled with destructive psychological bacteria that spread.

Bullies in the workplace and bullies in the classroom

We've all heard about the boss who is exceptionally egotistical and demanding, and is said "not to brook fools lightly." Amazingly, that last phrase is often made to sound as if it's a positive attribute. This might well be the boss who not only bullies his employees, but makes a habit or game of humiliating them publicly. The very same behavior sometimes comes from university professors who humiliate students, particularly at thesis oral exams where they can do so in front of colleagues while hiding behind the illusion that since this is an exam, anything goes.

It has been estimated that more than 26 percent of workplace bullying is conducted by corporate psychopaths, although they number only 1 percent of the workforce. As well, their nasty behaviors might be emulated by managers somewhat lower in the hierarchy. Psychopaths might be highly placed in the business world because of their ruthlessness and fixation on personal power, and they are often appreciated in their organizations. In fact, it has been suggested that the corporate culture has not only enabled these individuals, but actually fostered the promotion of psychopathy in higher levels of the corporate structure, particularly at the time when greed, corporate fraud, and financial misrepresentation became increasingly more widespread, and eventually led to the economic meltdown a few years back.

We can go through all sorts of analyses as to why bully bosses behave the way they do. Bullying might reflect an effort to maintain power and control over others, or it might be that job demands and the lack of job-related support foster bullying. Alternatively, bully bosses (or other bullies) might well be psychopaths or they might simply be jerks. We can only hope that the bully on the way down the ladder will again encounter the young employees they bullied, on their way up.

It isn't my intent to delve into what sociological and biological processes make callous bullies become what they are. However, I can't resist making a comment that seems to be particularly germane. Although we usually have a perspective of the psychopath based on what we see on television or what we read in newspapers in relation to serial killers, it would be an error to limit our view in this way. It has been estimated that 1 percent of the population falls into this category, and these psychopaths are encountered across various professions, including business and politics, and I think I can identify a few university professors that fall into that category. Babiak and Hare (2006) have described psychopathy as an "emotional deafness." The psychopath is unable to appreciate or experience empathy for others, but more than this, they focus on their own interests and perceive others simply as suckers who can be preyed upon. With this type of attitude, coupled with above-average intelligence, the psychopath might advance in corporate hierarchies, where they will continue their bad behaviors.

There has been an increasing move toward explaining this pathology on the basis of a dysfunction in some brain regions, and there have, in fact, been suggestions made that these individuals shouldn't be blamed for their sickness! But it's hard to feel sorry for a psychopathic boss who delights in humiliating employees. In their aptly titled book *Snakes in Suits: When Psychopaths Go to Work*, Babiak and Hare (2006) provide an extensive description of the corporate psychopath. It seems that there are distinct sub-types of corporate psychopaths that comprise the "manipulator," the "bully," and the "puppetmaster," each of whom has horrible qualities with each being more vile than the last. Of interest, Babiak and Hare provide tips on how to spot these psychopaths, and what to do if they target you.

Social support in the workplace

As in other situations, social support is fundamental to diminish stress in workplace settings, and as described earlier the provision of social support might be manifested in multiple ways (e.g., emotional support, practical support). Beyond serving as a way of coping, social behaviors may be adopted in an effort to further a social identity that is shared with other organization members. As in other situations, having a particular social identity can minimize distress otherwise provoked by workplace

If I had a hammer

Social identity has numerous important implications, and is a fundamental ingredient for workplace well-being and the development of good leadership. I was discussing this perspective with my friend Zul Merali, focusing on how one's identity might be influential in affecting appraisals and in dealing with stressors. We ended up talking about why employees' perceptions of corporate management are so often negative, even though they might never have had any experience with management. This negativity is fairly pervasive, appearing in the corporate world, in government and in universities, frequently being expressed from an "us versus them" perspective. We concluded that to a significant extent this stems from the identity that individuals carry with them and the identity they ascribe to members of management. As Zul's late mother used to say, "to a hammer, everything looks like a nail."

stressors, and can minimize illnesses, such as diabetes, that have been associated with workplace distress. As well, sticking together to create a team helps to maintain the camaraderie of group members and enhances motivation. This is frequently apparent when the work situation is a positive one and when resources are plentiful. When the workplace environment begins to deteriorate, positive social attitudes may be important in keeping group members connected and for morale to be maintained. However, as things continue to sour, individuals might be less inclusive in considering who belongs to their group.

Trust in the workplace

As in many other venues, trust in bosses and the workplace, as well as in other workers, has lots to do with well-being and satisfaction with the organization. Ordinarily, "trust-worthiness" refers to the integrity, benevolence, and ability of a person or organization, and "trust" comprises the intention or willingness to allow oneself to become vulnerable with the expectation that the trustee will behave appropriately. Of course, having exposed our vulnerabilities and having this trust trampled upon can be exceptionally distressing. Thus, within a corporate setting trust can become a very important commodity. A value of trust that occurs in the workplace has been translated into a monetary equivalent. If the average worker has the opportunity of a new job with a salary increase of some amount less than 30 percent or the opportunity to work in a trusting environment, people would likely pick the latter.

Many suggestions have been offered by psychologists and economists to improve workplace trust, but several seem to stand out. Integrity of the individual or the corporation, along with competence, loyalty, consistency and openness, are thought to be essential. These might seem fairly obvious, but their implementation can be difficult. What may be particularly important in the workplace, as it is in other domains, is that all these fancy-shmantzy words are just that, words. We all know that talk is cheap, and trust will not be dependent on what is said, but on what is done.

Unemployment

History doesn't always repeat itself, but it can take on some similar forms. Economic bubbles burst fairly regularly. In the 1630s it was the tulipomania during which the price of tulip bulbs went up by 6,000 percent before crashing, and in more recent times we've seen similar things happen with housing, hi-tech, and gold, although many might now wish that they had hung on to gold stocks and bought into some hi-tech firms despite their volatility. The bursting bubbles have led to recessions such as those we saw in the 1970s, 1980s, and 1990s, as well as the severe recessions in just the last few years. As always, recessions are accompanied by many job losses, and the uncertainty of maintaining a job can be exceptionally stressful. The distress created by actual job loss is linked to the financial strain it imposes, but that's not the end of it. The psychological distress might also be exacerbated by shame and feelings of inadequacy, and having to face coworkers when you leave, having to go home and tell a partner and other family members that you've been fired or laid off is a bitter pill that can undermine self-esteem and self-respect. The well-being of those who have lost their jobs is also related to their cognitive appraisals of the situation, the personal, social and financial coping resources available, and whether their work role was a central element of their identity.

For many, the job is not just the job. It's central to their identity, it engenders great pride, it's part of their social life, and defines them in intangible ways. Thus, the threat of job loss is a threat to core elements of the individual. In fact, social dynamics, including identification with the company, may play a prominent role in how individuals behave in response to threats of unemployment. Consider, for instance, the behavior of those working for a company that is in jeopardy of going under. Workers might initially rally to save the company with the mantra that "we're a team, and if we work together, then this great company will survive." They share an identity, they're an ingroup, and they support each other and the company. But, as the situation continues to go downhill, the attitudes and the actions of the group fizzle and individuals may become apathetic, replacing their initial pumped behavior with thinking "what's the point?" They still might receive social support from one another, even as their numbers dwindle with continued cutbacks, but this support may be undermined by the fact that they might view themselves as in competition with one another – "if some other person loses their job, it might allow mine to be preserved," even though in the end there might be no last man standing.

Like other strong stressors, the distress related to job loss may be sufficiently intense to disrupt immune, endocrine and neurotransmitter functioning, potentially leaving individuals at increased risk of immunologically related disorders and depression, particularly among older individuals whose prospects of finding another position are slim. Unemployment has been associated with increased mortality, particularly in those in the early or middle stages of their career. Furthermore, periods of unemployment may be tied to the spread of influenza to the extent that a 1 percent increase in unemployment has been associated with a rise of regional influenza that has ranged from 17 to 44 percent across several studies. As well, unemployment has been linked to high levels of C-reactive protein in the blood, the inflammatory biomarker for the development of heart disease.

Time management and juggling

Some people simply can't deal with multiple demands being placed on them, whereas others thrive on being able to juggle and are even able to prioritize jobs based on deadlines and levels of importance. Others might also be capable of juggling tasks but prioritize on the basis of what they like best or what's easiest, rather than what's most important. Time or project management is obviously essential when individuals are required to do multiple tasks, but too often individuals lose perspective or are simply unable to prioritize or manage their time and some important things don't get done or are done in a less than acceptable fashion. Once again it isn't surprising to see someone's distress and panic as a deadline approaches, and as an observer you're left saying to them: "deep breath, deep breath, now focus. No, no ... deep breath and focus, not breath or focus."

Related to time and project management is attention management, which means the allocation of cognitive resources to particular tasks. Of course, each of these is needed in getting jobs done, especially when multiple demands haunt us. One would think that time, resource and attention management would be fairly simple: identify tasks to be achieved, prioritize them in terms of importance and/or deadlines, set limits on how much time will be spent on certain tasks, don't assume that certain jobs can be achieved during spare moments or late in the evening, and be sure that there is a buffer period scheduled in the event that emergencies come up. As simple as this might sound, too often things don't work out the way we'd like. Events creep up or surprise us so that our plans fall apart in moments.

So, is there anything that can be done to facilitate juggling and time management? Several methods have been suggested that might be useful, and although they all differ from one another in some way, they are in line with what has been referred to as the POSEC method, which is an acronym for prioritize, organize, streamline, economize (on things you like to do versus those you ought to do) and contribute (to those things that are important to the individual, including social and familial obligations). In a perfect world this ought to work. Too bad that the world isn't perfect, but given this reality I'm a great believer in adding a "B for buffer" to this acronym, which means keep some time aside for unexpected eventualities. I know this won't catch on. POSEC isn't all that catchy an acronym and POSECB slides off the tongue even less well.

Before you go...

The workplace is replete with potential stressors and finding methods to deal with them or prevent them from occurring isn't simple, and at the least requires efforts by individual workers, groups and the organization itself. As for many other stressor situations, individuals need to make proper appraisals and have effective coping strategies, and there are methods that can be adopted to facilitate this. Beyond the individual's own efforts to deal with stressors, there's much that an organization can do in this regard. However, this requires that good leaders be present. I highly recommend *The New Psychology of Leadership* written by Alex Haslam and his associates (2011) for an extensive understanding of what it means to be an effective leader, and how to become one. For the moment, a brief listing of some important elements of management devices is provided here.

Some useful managerial tips

Identity: Individuals within an organization need to work together in order for optimal output and satisfaction to be realized. This occurs when they feel they are part of a team, and to this end an ingroup identity should be established.

Loyalty and commitment: Although a company or boss can buy employees, their commitment and loyalty requires much more. Among other things, it is necessary for job strain to be reduced, identity and trust to be increased, and the employee to understand that they are appreciated and respected.

Wide vista: Employees ought to be made aware of the bigger picture regarding company goals and, importantly, how they fit into this picture, including what their individual contributions are in attaining these goals.

Clear leadership and expectations: Uncertainty is a kiss of death within a work environment. The leader ought to diminish uncertainty, being explicit about employees' duties and responsibilities, as well as expectations of them.

Trust and organizational culture: Trust should exist between employees and management, as well as among employees. The relationships must be honest and transparent, and the environment should foster fairness and allow employees to have input concerning how their work is accomplished.

Job strain: As job stress leads to poor health and poor productivity, there is a need for employees to feel that they have some decision latitude and that job demands are reasonable.

Workload expectancies and job fitness: Employees ought to be assigned tasks and responsibilities that are in line with their skills and emotional abilities.

Engagement and recognition: Individuals ought to feel connected with the job, and to feel positive about the work. To this end, employees ought to receive appropriate acknowledgment, reward and appreciation.

Support: Employees may have psychological and physical needs so that support resources from within and outside the work environment need to be in place. This means more than simply having a human resource division that hands out brochures.

Civility and respect: Rudeness, bullying and unsupportive interactions are as hazardous to an organization and its employees as the plague. As bad as bullying can be, ostracism can be worse for a person's health. The environment must be one that fosters respect and consideration among employees and management. As disputes inevitably arise, a clear, equitable and transparent mechanism for conflict resolution is necessary.

Growth and development: Employees ought to feel that their job is not a dead end, and that there's room for growth and self-fulfillment. Thus, encouragement and support should be provided, as well as programs that foster interpersonal and job skills.

Flexibility: Some employees are at a phase in life when they need to manage multiple demands, such as children at one end and aging parents at the other. For most workers, but especially this sandwich generation, having flexibility is very important to their well-being.

Balance: Healthy bodies and healthy minds might be tied to events and experiences away from the workplace. Management should not just acknowledge, but actually facilitate the employee's need to maintain a balance between work demands, family and personal life.

Catching flies: More flies are caught with honey than with vinegar, and a good word likewise goes a long way.

Incentivization: It's better catching people doing things right than catching them doing things wrong.

19

Transmission of Trauma across Generations

Replacing shame with anger

Humans are blessed with extraordinary memories, and as much as this might be a blessing, the recollection of negative events can also be a curse. In dealing with stressors, our memory and emotional processes can either make individuals stronger and more resilient or they can engender greater vulnerabilities. The same holds true in relation to trauma that we experienced, as well as the historical, collective traumas encountered by members of some groups. The direct victims of a cultural trauma sometimes express feelings sadness and anxiety, and they might also express feelings of guilt and shame – guilt for surviving, and shame for not being able to do anything to help others, as well as shame for being a victim. This is perfectly understandable, even if it might not be reasonable. But can attitudes and emotions of collective traumas have effects on ensuing generations? Do they experience feelings of shame for their forbears because they did not adequately defend themselves? And, do they harbor anger for the egregious behavior directed at their group, and if so does this influence their own behaviors? Often, when descendants of trauma encounter new episodes of discrimination, they might not feel shame, which would prompt them to simply play turtle at the back of the bus. Instead, the shame will be replaced by anger that catalyzes active group resistance.

Those who haven't had their culture victimized by dominant, hateful groups sometimes seem not to understand the feelings and behaviors of those who have had these unfortunate experiences. When indigenous peoples resist having their lands or fishing rights taken away, or when they block a road because it traverses ancestral lands, it's not simply the behavior of a small group of hot-heads acting out. Instead, it might reflect behavior that emanates from a history of abusive behaviors directed at them, and more than a few individuals are saying "Never again." Members of the outgroup may be sympathetic to the cause, at least in a general sense, but this quickly dissipates if they get held up in a long traffic line-up as a result of the blocked road. Empathy is quickly replaced with unsupportive and even racist attitudes. The fact is, however, that collective action generated by anger and frustration is a powerful method of coping, certainly better than succumbing to collective shame or guilt, and it's not likely that they'll "just get over it."

Traveling across generations

One might be under the misimpression that trauma only affects the people who directly experienced the events, and those close to them. In fact, however, traumatic events can profoundly influence psychological and physical well-being across generations. Such intergenerational consequences of stressors have been observed in response to genocide, war, famine or natural disasters, as well as events of a nontraumatic nature, including illness, financial problems or work-related distress.

Intergenerational consequences of stressors may come about through various routes. The behavior of parents may be disturbed by traumatic events that they experienced, which can have damaging effects on their children. Likewise, traumatic events can have epigenetic consequences, and these silenced genes can be inherited by an individual's children, which they, in turn, could pass on to their children. The impact of traumatic experiences might also depend on what occurred during the period following the stressor experience. Were support resources available, did the individual have the opportunity or ability to maintain their group identity, and did opportunities exist for healing? Alternatively, did the survivors and the children of survivors of trauma later experience toxic conditions, such as poverty or famine? Moreover, was the traumatic event a unique experience, or was it one in a long chain of collective, historical traumas experienced by the group?

Parental stress influences on children

Survivors of wars, attempted genocides, chronic discrimination, and natural disasters aren't just affected as events unfold or in the immediate aftermath of the event, but instead the consequences may persist for years or decades. Following severe trauma some parents might become more protective in the wish to spare their children from adversities. However, it isn't unusual for those who have experienced trauma, especially if it persisted over a lengthy period, to exhibit disturbed parental behaviors. This is most notable if they have developed mental disturbances or drug-related problems, which are frequently accompanied by neglect, disengagement and disorganization, hostility, coercion, and abuse. Further, trauma might cause parents to develop impaired coping strategies, which are emulated by their children, rendering them less equipped to deal with stressors. It is especially significant that children who have experienced poor parenting may themselves subsequently exhibit inadequate parenting behaviors. To be sure, having been the recipient of poor parenting, some individuals try to extricate themselves and their own children from the vicious circle that exists, and make every effort to be great parents. Escaping this cycle is exceptionally difficult without external assistance, a proper role model, or very good luck.

222 *Transmission of Trauma across Generations*

Silence

What subtitle could be more telling than "My father bleeds history," the subtitle of Art Spiegelman's book *Maus*, which concerns survival of the Holocaust? Some children of survivors recount that their parents recapitulated their experiences over and over, whereas others indicate that their parents were more likely to withhold any communication about their experiences, possibly because they didn't want to remember or revisit them. This latter communication pattern, which is fairly common among survivors, was termed a "conspiracy of silence." A silence that can speak much louder than any words, especially as it leaves children to imagine events that they've only heard about in vague terms. As a result the children who experienced this silence generally seemed to be more vulnerable to intergenerational transmission of trauma. This same profile was not unique to survivors of the Holocaust, and in research with Amy Bombay and Kim Matheson we found that it was evident among First Nations individuals who were survivors of Indian Residential Schools (IRSs) (Bombay, Matheson, and Anisman, 2014).

In her stunning and very sad book *After Such Knowledge; Memory, History and the Legacy of the Holocaust*, Eva Hoffman sums this up as follows:

A few survivors were determined never to talk about what they had lived through ... In my home, as in so many others, the past broke through in the sounds of nightmares, the idioms of sighs and illness, of tears and acute aches that were the legacy of the damp attic and of the conditions my parents endured during their hiding.

Intergenerational effects of trauma: beyond poor parenting

In her poignant work related to genocide, Marianne Hirsch (2001) uses the term "postmemory" or a "reclaiming of memory" to describe the consequences of trauma. She suggests that the children of those who survived the Holocaust or other genocides will form memories of narratives that they had grown up with. These narratives and the associated imageries of the trauma their parents and others of their group endured may be so powerful as to become incorporated into their own schemas, essentially part of their collective memory, which they might pass on to their children. As much as there are some who say or wish that "the past is the past," it often isn't so. The consequences of traumatic experiences can wane over generations, but they're not abolished, and reminders of the trauma might make them vivid.

The intergenerational effects of traumatic events observed among children of Holocaust survivors or Aboriginal peoples who were mistreated in Indian Residential Schools were also reported in Japanese Americans subjected to internment during World War II and survivors of the Armenian genocide conducted by Turks, as well as in other groups. We can likely count on similar outcomes appearing among the children of survivors from Syria, Somalia, Darfur, Bosnia, and Rwanda. However, the experience of survivors across different collective traumas can't be easily compared to one another given the differences in hatreds and motivations that led to them, in the magnitude, ferocity, and durations of the events, as well as in the support received by survivors both from their own groups and from others. As much as we in the West are disinclined to acknowledge it, most countries, as well as the United Nations, failed to intervene in response to genocides, or relentlessly dawdled in doing so. How will the children of the genocide survivors perceive the governments of other countries when it is understood, as Elie Wiesel has put it, that in their silence these countries condoned the acts of the aggressor?

Environments modify gene actions

Old conceptions concerning nature versus nurture in relation to a broad range of phenotypes have appropriately been abandoned. Although our genes may dispose us toward certain characteristics, their ultimate expression may be determined by environments and experiences. In our discussion of depression we saw that inheriting the short form of the gene for the serotonin transporter might not cause depression under normal circumstances, but having that polymorphism and encountering a stressor in adulthood and/or during childhood appreciably increased the chances of individuals becoming depressed. In effect, having certain genes might make individuals susceptible to the influence of environmental or experiential factors so that a second hit in the form of negative early life events might increase the likelihood of bad outcomes. Other genes, in contrast, might limit the influence of environmental events or facilitate coping responses, such as the ability to gain social support, which could act against the negative effects otherwise encouraged by stressful events.

The case of epigenetic effects

There are different things we can inherit from our parents. We can inherit their wealth, we can inherit their behavioral styles, we can inherit their genes, and we can also inherit epigenetic changes (silencing of a gene's functioning) that resulted from stressors they encountered. As described in earlier chapters, stressful events, endocrine challenges, toxicants, and poor diet can result in certain genetic characteristics being silenced, without actually causing a change of the gene. Epigenetic changes can readily be induced by stressors in utero or when an organism is very young, and can also be engendered in response to challenges experienced in adulthood. This can occur either through a process referred to as "methylation," or through "chromatin remodeling," but for our purposes the essential point is that environmental events can influence the expression of genes present on a DNA strand, and thus can have neurobiological and behavioral consequences.

What has made epigenetics particularly interesting to behavioral scientists is that having particular genes doesn't necessarily mean that behavioral phenotypes are fixed in stone. Instead, for better or for worse, an organism's experiences can promote epigenetic changes so that behavior and mood is affected throughout life. Poor parenting among rodents, for instance, can result in the silencing of particular genes, such as those that code for glucocorticoid receptors within the hippocampus, so that as adults these pups are more likely to exhibit increased stress responses. Similarly, repeated introduction of a stressor during the first trimester of pregnancy in mice resulted in epigenetic changes in the fetus so that later stress responses associated with HPA functioning were altered. It is especially significant, however, that the presence of a particular epigenetic change doesn't necessarily doom individuals to this gene being silenced forever, as epigenetic effects are potentially reversible, and drugs that target DNA methylation and enzymes involved in this process have been tested in clinical trials (Szyf, 2009).

If an epigenetic change occurs in a germ cell (sperm or ovum), then this silenced gene could be passed from parent to offspring and thus produce behavioral or physiological effects in the next generation. Thus, as a result of poor maternal care or multiple stressor encounters, epigenetic changes can evolve that can be passed on to offspring. In rodents, epigenetic changes were documented with respect to estradiol, corticosterone, oxytocin, and CRH receptors, any of which can influence behaviors, including parenting styles. In some instances these epigenetic outcomes might not have particularly marked behavioral consequences on the offspring under quiet conditions, but should a stressor be encountered, then behavioral disturbances may emerge.

Despite the fact that environmental factors can influence gene functioning and hence affect behavioral processes, defining the link between particular epigenetic changes and specific outcomes has been difficult. A very great number of epigenetic changes are present at any given time, making it difficult to determine which of these might be causally related to particular neurobiological processes and behaviors. Some investigators, for instance, have placed their bets on epigenetic effects related to glucocorticoid receptors as being responsible for behavioral changes, but this doesn't rule out a role for other epigenetic modifications in determining later outcomes. For instance, poor maternal care in rodents wasn't just associated with silencing of genes for glucocorticoid receptors, but was also accompanied by changes of the gene promoter of estrogen receptor alpha (ERα) in the hypothalamus of female rodents. As this receptor is related to estrogen and oxytocin functioning, which contribute to social behaviors and maternal styles, the silencing of these genes might contribute to subsequent poor maternal behavior among rodents raised in impoverished environments. In monkeys, negative early life events influenced DNA methylation of the gene involving serotonin uptake (5-HTT) as well as CRH_1 receptors, which it will be recalled, might contribute to maintaining or provoking depressive disorders, which in turn could also affect parenting styles. Likewise, stressors may affect the genes controlling growth factors, such as BDNF, and might thus come to affect stress-related behavioral outcomes. In a particularly interesting study, Roth and his associates (2009) raised rat pups with an adult caretaker that had been stressed and thus displayed abusive behaviors. When these abused pups were assessed in adulthood, epigenetic suppression of the gene for BDNF was apparent within the prefrontal cortex. Of particular interest was that when these abused rats later had their own pups, the silencing of the BDNF gene was apparent in their offspring. These findings point to the importance of BDNF in regulating behavior, and also implicate its involvement in the intergenerational effects of early life stressors. The good news again is that these effects aren't necessarily permanent, as rats that were later raised in an enriched environment, a manipulation that itself increases BDNF, attenuated the negative transgenerational stress effects.

The transmission of epigenetic effects is typically assessed in females, but there have been attempts to determine whether they could be transmitted to the offspring through the father. In fact, when male rat pups experienced a stressor in the form of chronic maternal separation, they subsequently displayed depressive-like behaviors and altered behavioral responses to aversive stimuli that were linked to epigenetic changes. When these male pups, as adults, sired offspring, those too exhibited epigenetic changes even though they had never been in contact with their dad. In effect, it seemed that epigenetic changes can be passed on through the father, just as they can through the mother. This, however, wasn't the final word on the topic as the possibility existed that the anxiety present among stressed male mice might have transferred to females during the course of mating, and her distress might have affected the pup's in utero development. Admittedly, this seems to be a bit of a stretch, yet if female mice were impregnated through in vitro fertilization using sperm "donated" by a stressed male mouse, the epigenetic and behavioral effects otherwise passed down from parent to offspring were largely absent. Thus, it's less certain that stressor-related epigenetic changes within the male were passed on to the offspring, although the debate on this continues, especially as epigenetic marks have been detected in the sperm RNA of stressed mice. In fact, male mice raised by a stressed mom not only carried these marks in the RNA of sperm cells, but also passed these on to their own progeny, which then passed these on to a third generation.

Epigenetic marks associated with stressors have been detected in humans, and maternal depressed/anxious mood present during the third trimester of pregnancy can also promote such an outcome. In this regard, distress in mothers was accompanied by silencing of genes related to corticoids and altered stress responses in their offspring when they were three months of age. As well, among individuals who died by suicide, and who had a history of early childhood neglect/abuse, the promoter region of the gene for the glucocorticoid receptor was silenced. These data are in keeping with the view that early experiences may have long-term consequences through variations of glucocorticoid receptor functioning. Yet, among depressed individuals who died by suicide, epigenetic changes were also detected in relation to GABA as well as BDNF, making it clear that depression/suicide is accompanied by several epigenetic changes, and linking depression uniquely to the glucocorticoid receptor changes is premature. In fact, one report indicated that within the hippocampus of individuals who died by suicide, several hundred epigenetic changes were apparent. Thus, we're left with the question as to which of these silenced genes was causally tied to the suicidal behavior or secondary to suicidal ideation and which were simply bystanders.

Plus ça change, plus c'est la même chose

"The more it changes, the more it's the same thing." The Darwinian view of evolution was that species arise and develop on the basis of inherited variations of behavior or biology that increase the individual's ability to compete, survive, and importantly, to reproduce (fitness). However, this wasn't the first view of how certain characteristics or behaviors came about. In the pre-Darwinian era there seemed to be a great number of scientists who expounded the Lamarckian view of heritability, which essentially was that an organism could pass on to its offspring those characteristics that it had acquired during its lifetime. This "heritability of acquired characteristics" essentially suggested that if a person had acquired particular skills through learning or practice, then this individual's children would inherit these features.

The Darwinian view had greater explanatory power and was generally adopted, although Lamarckian diehards were around for many years. A Russian agronomist and high-level politician, Trofim Lysenko, apparently accepted Lamarckian inheritance, which led him to adopt "environmentally acquired inheritance" in the development of agricultural policies and practices, and the result of his counterfactual thinking drove the agricultural productivity of the country into the ground (literally). Despite the famines Lysenko helped to produce, and his unwitting success in diminishing the Lamarckian view, the results of epigenetic studies make it appear that this perspective might not have been entirely incorrect. Although we might not inherit genes based on what dad or mom did in the past, from an epigenetic perspective certain life experiences can influence whether particular genes are turned off or on, and some of these features can be transmitted to the next generation.

Collective and historic trauma

In dealing with the impact of trauma, it's important to consider the period after trauma, including the relationships that exist with other members of a group, especially as social identity and social support may go a long way in affecting resilience. Having a particular identity and affiliation with a group serves multiple functions that can influence well-being, especially when there is a challenge to the viability of the group. In the case of some identities, such as those that involve religion or culture, members of the group might see their own lives as being impermanent, but the traditions, values, morals, beliefs, and symbols representing the group itself are seen as being passed on from one generation to the next. The more that members invest themselves into the group, the greater their identification with it, and hence threats to the group will yield greater individual and collective anxiety about the group's future well-being.

One thing after another

Most countries that colonized others don't have impressive track records regarding their treatment of indigenous peoples, and Euro-Caucasian colonizers fit the mold. As part of a forced assimilation policy aimed at "taking the Indian out of the Indian," from the mid-1800s to 1996 the Canadian government either encouraged or allowed large numbers of Aboriginal children to be removed from their homes and placed in distant Indian Residential Schools. Children in these IRSs experienced strict discipline, neglect, all manner of abuse, loss of identity, and the suppression of cultural expressions through language, dress, food, or beliefs, and as a result the health of children declined. A substantial number of children died at IRSs, and in many instances their fate is still unknown.

But the abuse didn't end at the doorsteps of the IRSs. Upon being released, it wasn't uncommon for the children of survivors to live in substandard conditions within communities that had disintegrated. A period of recuperation and healing wasn't possible, and psychological and physical pathologies became increasingly frequent. The children's educational levels were low, their practical skills were primarily applicable to menial jobs, unemployment was high, and whatever other disadvantages could be visited on them, likely were. What they often did learn was abusive behavior that was modeled after those who punished them at the IRSs, and lateral violence has been a perpetual scourge that has hindered forward movement.

The removal of children from their homes caused deep wounds to parents and communities as a whole. Parents were beset by feelings of powerlessness, as well as guilt and shame for not saving their children, and familial bonds were often irreparably broken. The consequences of the IRSs continue to be felt. First Nations adults who had a parent, or even grandparents, who attended an IRS experience higher levels of depressive symptoms and thoughts of suicide, more frequent adverse childhood experiences and adult traumas, and higher perceived levels of discrimination relative to First Nations adults whose parents did not attend an IRS.

As horrible as the IRSs were, they represent only one trauma in a lengthy series encountered by Aboriginal peoples. Since first contact with Euro-Caucasians, Aboriginal peoples in Canada have experienced numerous traumas and had suffered an 80 percent decline in their population by the early 1800s. Within Canada, as in the United States, First Nations people were frequently kept on reserves where they experienced poverty, poor education, exceptionally poor health, corruption and unsupportive interactions with the government as well as with non-Aboriginal people. Understandably, the IRSs became a symbol of the poor relationship that existed between the government of Canada and its indigenous peoples. Postmemory concerning IRSs among the children and grandchildren of survivors is ever present and current encounters with discrimination serve as reminders of collective injustices. When these reminders occur repeatedly they likely contribute to psychological and physical pathologies that are witnessed today. However, reminders of historical traumas also encourage organized protests that are meant to reclaim more than just lands, but also a reclamation of identity, making it clear that they will no longer be "victims" and nor will they carry the burdens that the IRSs instilled, especially that of being ashamed of their culture.

It isn't unusual for emotional and psychological wounding to be experienced by groups, and this "collective trauma" may have consequences that are manifested over successive generations. Survivors of the Holocaust, as well as their children, recognize that the events of 1939 to 1945 were part of a long series of cumulative traumas that date back to the pre-Christian era. The survivors of Indian Residential Schools, as well as their children and grandchildren, similarly recognize that the indignities experienced in these schools were not historically isolated events, but reflected one long terrible event among many that recurred over generations, to the extent that their culture, language, and identity were jeopardized. These negative experiences are brought to the surface, and symbolically recapitulated through grievances with governments.

Traumatic incidents that threaten the survival of the group as a whole can instigate collective distress and anxiety that is evident in response to threats in subsequent generations that did not directly experience trauma. For that matter, these reactions may even be displayed among individuals who simply feel a connection to the victimized group as opposed to being part of the group itself. Understandably, a history of collective abuse, traumatization, and threats of extermination might render groups sensitive or vigilant regarding perceived threats and the evil or malign intents of others. Heightened vigilance regarding such threats doesn't represent paranoid behavior; if history is any teacher, then elevated vigilance is not only reasonable and adaptive, but to do otherwise would invite treachery.

Collectively experienced traumas might instigate unique social and psychological trajectories, and their consequences may be aligned with collective responses and interpretations of past indignities. As observed in Aboriginal groups, experiences of discrimination have had the predictable effect of enhancing group identity, particularly if these discrimination experiences remind individuals of historical, collective traumas that had been experienced by their group. Although the consequences of traumatic experiences might never be eliminated entirely, the adverse effects across generations might be diminished by encouraging the development of appropriate social identities, effective social networks, and support from ingroup members. To be sure, this isn't the case for all individuals. Some have alternate superordinate identities, others might choose to cease to identify, possibly from a desire to assimilate with the majority out-group, or they might have different issues that lead them to distance themselves from their group.

"Let me tell you about the very rich. They are different from you and me"

You've heard it repeatedly, "Money doesn't buy happiness." Right. They think we've all just fallen off a turnip truck. Money doesn't buy happiness! Isn't that just about the dumbest thing you ever heard? It's something poor people say to make themselves feel better about not having money, and something that rich people say either to appease the poor who might otherwise rise up against them or because they feel guilty for having so much when others have so little. We occasionally hear that beyond a certain income, $76,000 a year seems to be the current favorite, there isn't much gain in happiness. That, too, is a bunch of baloney. I can't really say how much happier you'd be if you were twice as wealthy as you are now, but given that so many people line up to buy lottery tickets, I'd guess that there are lots who think the money will buy them happiness, lots and lots of happiness. There's the perspective that having too much money can have negative ramifications in that it might foster spoiled children, and the "shirtsleeves-to-shirtsleeves in just three generations" syndrome is a characteristic example of this. That's definitely true in some instances, but not in others, and I suspect that it might be a cop-out for poor or negligent parenting.

Let's leave the rich aside for the moment and focus on the poor. Poverty has been associated with impaired cognitive functioning, including impaired decision-making abilities that can further promote poverty. When poverty is persistent and begins early in life, then the effects observed are far more dramatic. Individuals in the lowest 20 percent of the population in economic terms were six times more likely to be teenage mothers and school drop-outs, far less likely to seek prenatal care relative to individuals in high economic brackets, and they were apt to die a decade earlier than the wealthiest 20 percent. Moreover, among those on the lowest social-economic rung, infant death, emergency department visits, hospital visits owing to self-harm and other mental health issues were at least twice as likely compared to the wealthy. As disturbing as these figures might be, what do you suppose would have been found if these data hadn't been collected from the average poor person, but instead had been collected from survivors – or their children – who had experienced a cultural trauma and were then raised in poverty.

We can probably agree that money doesn't necessarily buy happiness (note that the phrase has the word "necessarily" inserted), and there are many things that don't cost money that can make you happy. Importantly, not having money, being impoverished, will more often than not make you fairly unhappy, and this will be still more notable when other aspects of your life are diminished.

Nyla Branscombe, a leading scientist in the field, has not only considered the conse-quences of severe discrimination on victims, but has also considered collective guilt and collective shame among members of a group consisting of perpetrators of bad behavior (Branscombe et al., 2004). As she indicated in a discussion we had,

> Collective guilt and shame are both moral emotions, but guilt is primarily a perpetrator emotion, whereas shame is primarily a victim emotion. To experience collective guilt, it is necessary that people self-categorize as a member of a group that is seen as responsible for committing illegitimate harm to another group. With the experience of collective shame, people perceive their group as having been victimized, belittled, or devalued. The group's public image is often at stake with collective shame because it reflects an appraisal of one's group as weak, incompetent, or inferior in the eyes of others. When people feel collective guilt they are often motivated to make reparations for their group's illegitimate harm-doing. When they feel collective shame they are often motivated to improve their group's image if that is possible, but when that is not feasible they may try to distance from or hide the weakness that has been exposed.

Before you go…

Many individuals will at one time or another experience a traumatic event, which might haunt them for decades. Often the event wasn't one where an individual was specifically targeted, but in other instances, because of their race, ethnicity, gender, or some other

Not just surviving, but thriving

Analyses of the intergenerational effects of trauma have largely focused on the neg-ative consequences that occur among the children and grandchildren of survivors. Many children of Holocaust survivors find this disturbing, as do some who are the children of IRS survivors. I certainly abhor the idea of being perceived as a child of victims who has somehow gotten through life despite the inadequacies or distur-bances that might have been inherited in some biological or psychosocial way.

Having survived an attempted genocide, survivors might be that much more caring for their children, and might have developed perspectives, especially those related to social and educational values ("they can take away your material pos-sessions, but you'll still have your brain"), that were beneficial for the children. In line with this, some trauma survivors report closer friend and family relations, elevated appreciation of life, more spirituality and greater personal strength, as well as new priorities in life. In some instances the children of trauma survivors are not more likely to experience PTSD, and to the contrary, they might be less likely to develop this illness. It is uncertain why this is so, but it is possible that positive early care made them more resilient in the face of a traumatic event. Alternatively, the experiences of their parents or grandparents may have in some way allowed members of the next generation to accommodate the distress associated with their own negative experiences ("this is nothing compared to what my parents endured"), essentially hardening them so that they were better able to deal with trauma.

Many groups have experienced collective, historical trauma, but the destinies of these groups, as we've seen, differed in many ways. It is inappropriate to draw parallels between the collective, historical trauma experienced across groups, as each is unique and each has its own consequences. The experiences of Jews at the hands of the Nazis and their collaborators are beyond imagination, and often can't be fully absorbed by those who weren't witness to the events. Despite the abhorrent aggression directed toward them, and despite being the recipient of unsupportive responses from other countries, being turned away from their borders again and again, the survivors of the Holocaust, in part through a strong collective identity, thrived and flourished. Aboriginal peoples had a very different set of experiences. They too encountered repeated abuses, and the Indian Residential Schools represented only one of many occasions when their communities and culture were undermined and their pride demolished and replaced with shame. Unfortunately, owing to poor government policies, planning and financing, in an ill-conceived effort to reestablish communities, coupled with internal divisions and poor community government, the lifestyles of Aboriginal peoples only improved marginally, and thus they might not have experienced proper healing.

Reminders of trauma to an individual's group are potent in provoking emotional responses in those who highly identify with the group. These can take the form of shame and humiliation, and also "soul wound" as Brave Heart (2003) put it in the context of Aboriginal trauma. However, with the realization of just how profound previous injustices were, anger and social activism have replaced shame and humiliation, and fostered efforts of members of the group to take control of their own destinies. The children who are survivors of collective, historical abuses are not inclined to be herded into concentration camps, IRSs, or gulags and they're not likely to be silent or muzzled in the face of blatant discrimination, and instead they share the mantra of "never again."

characteristics, they are singled out to bear the burden of traumatic discriminatory events. These targeted experiences might comprise an isolated event, or they might reflect one of many catastrophes historically encountered by their group, and collective trauma can influence behavior and attitudes across generations.

Past egregious actions not only affect individuals through collective memories, but also through biological processes, such as epigenetic changes. However, the epigenome is dynamic and the influence of prenatal and postnatal stressors on gene processes and the behavioral disturbances that accompany them can be modified. Given a positive and supportive environment, the adverse consequences of earlier trauma can be limited. In the case of epigenetic changes, the "bell can be unrung" through the adoption of positive support or therapeutic methods, but when traumatized individuals and groups also have to deal with a psychologically toxic environment, we can realistically expect that the outcome will lead to the worst of all possible cases.

20

Stress Reduction through Cognitive and Behavioral Strategies

Selling snake oil

Over the centuries there have been many unproven or fraudulent practices that promised to bring relief from a huge variety of ailments. Some could be used to treat just about anything, whereas others were meant for specific ailments. Quacks, a term that comes from the Dutch "quacksalver" which refers to individuals who falsely maintain that they have medical skills or varied potions to eliminate illness, have for centuries shamelessly taken advantage of desperate people. It could be argued that if there's no actual cure for an illness, then some ointment and lotion that itself causes no harm might serve as an excellent placebo to diminish the strain of illness, provided that it doesn't strain the patient's finances. However, there are occasions when these phony remedies are selected instead of conventional remedies that might provide an escape from an illness.

With the notion that stressful events can cause psychological and physical illness, the "stress industry" has proliferated markedly, and there's more crud on the market than you'd find in a cow pasture. Showers with high-pressure nozzles promise to reduce the aches and pains that come with stress, squeezing soft rubber balls has replaced counting religious beads to diminish anxiety. The natural products market has moved in as well, offering herbal products, neutraceuticals, which are certain to give you what you need to combat life's challenges. Neuroscience has also been bandied about to promote products, and you can't get away from ads that emphatically assure us that their product enhances well-being, including our failing memory through "the science of neuroplasticity." There are also recommendations that we join a gym, drink one tea or another, get a hobby, engage in deep breathing, meditation, different forms of yoga, artistic expression, spa treatments, or somatic training, spend time in nature, listen to relaxing music, and spend quality time with pets or loved ones. Together, they've done an excellent job in attracting a market share from the products of earlier days when nothing could get rid of stress more readily than "a good smoke" or "a double on the rocks." But how effective are these purported remedies to prevent or diminish stress?

Stress and Your Health: From Vulnerability to Resilience, First Edition. Hymie Anisman.
© 2015 John Wiley & Sons, Ltd. Published 2015 by John Wiley & Sons, Ltd.

Prelude to dealing with stress

Some stressors that are encountered seem to be relatively mild and often insignificant in the big scheme. But to the person experiencing these stressors they might be as big as it gets. They might be overreacting, possibly because it's just part of their personality, or they react to stressors this way because they simply don't know how to deal with it in any better way. Other stressors are of the "you might as well bang your head against the wall" variety. The situation seems hopeless, and you're cornered with no place to go, and you're forced to accept that "it is what it is."

We'll consider potentially better methods of dealing with stressors, but several issues ought to be considered from the very start. Foremost of these is that individuals encountering stressors and not handling them well need to recognize that they have a problem, and once this is accepted, they ought to be prepared to seek help. But the failure to seek help has been one of the major hindrances to mental health treatment. In some instances, such as severe depression, it has been estimated that only half of affected individuals contact a help provider. However, even if treatment is sought, the effectiveness of treatments might depend on the specific stressors being encountered, and this could vary yet again over the time following the stressor's appearance. Furthermore, it's all well and good to identify a potentially useful strategy to deal with distress, but implementing the strategy and doing so at the right time is another thing entirely. This is especially the case when the individual is exceptionally distressed so that their mental state might prevent them from understanding, planning or taking the initiatives necessary to diminish their own distress.

Out of the shadows

Some traumatic events are so powerful that they affect individuals throughout their life and their effects can be passed down to subsequent generations. In these circumstances we often turn to others to receive their advice and support, but there are occasions when people are reluctant to seek help, whether from friends, family or professionals. This is precisely the situation that individuals find themselves in when they are experiencing problems related to mental health, and this failure to seek help is among the greatest deterrents to achieving mental well-being.

The shame created by stigma is exceptionally destructive and plays a major role in limiting help-seeking. As indicated by the Czech novelist and poet Milan Kundera: "The basis of shame is not some personal mistake of ours, but the ignominy, the humiliation we feel that we must be what we are without any choice in the matter, and that this humiliation is seen by everyone." As we've seen, shame can be sufficiently powerful to cause individuals to feel diminished and worthless in the eyes of others, and even in their own eyes. It can also instigate neurobiological responses that act to exacerbate illness, limit recovery, and undermine the ability to cope with further stressors. Clearly, resolving mental health problems requires that those affected be encouraged to come forward, and that those without problems shed their stigmatizing attitudes and behaviors.

Relaxation training

Several relaxation training methods have been used to diminish tension. Autogenic training, which has been around for about 80 years, has individuals adopt a comfortable, relaxing position, and then for brief periods repeat a set of visualizations that promote relaxation. Another method, mind-body relaxation, is based on the premise that anxiety and muscle tension appear together, and so relaxing muscle tension might also reduce anxiety. This method advocates alternate tensing and relaxation of muscles, coupled with a mental component wherein individuals focus and feel the difference between the sensations associated with tension versus those that accompany relaxation, hopefully promoting somatic calmness. A somewhat related approach, biofeedback, is based on conditioning procedures in which a person is made aware of their physiological responses through feedback from the body using devices such as those that measure body temperature, skin or brain conductance, heart functioning, blood flow or CO_2 changes. By monitoring these changes and matching emotions and cognitions to them, individuals might learn to alter their levels of anxiety in favor of relaxation. There are now sensors that are combined with mobile applications (apps) that inform individuals that they are stressed based on their physiological changes, and remind them of appropriate methods of dealing with stressors.

There's nothing inherently wrong with these approaches, and they might get people to diminish their day-to-day discomforts, essentially altering their baseline levels of reactivity. These techniques can also be useful in relation to discomforts that appear in the aftermath of stressor experiences. Migraine headache was, for instance, long suspected to be linked to eating particular foods and to stressor experiences. In the latter instance, it seems that migraine may occur hours or even a day after a stressor has passed. It's almost as if during the stress itself it's too important to avoid a headache and we're successful in doing so, but during the subsequent "let down" period, headaches can emerge. It's been suggested that this can be prevented by engaging in a period of relaxation after a stressor experience, thereby precluding the activation of processes that would otherwise lead to migraine. It's less likely, however, that relaxation strategies are as effective in dealing with major life stressors. They probably don't do any harm, but there are better and more powerful, systematic methods of dealing with these stressors. So, while relaxation approaches are not to be disparaged, they should be used in conjunction with other methods.

Exposure therapy

If we reward an animal after it makes a particular response, then that response will be more likely to reoccur. When students took their first psychology course, this was introduced as "the law of effect" and was ascribed to Thorndike, never mind that it's been around as long as kids have had dogs. It also seems that when we expose animals to particular events, either positive or negative, these experiences can elicit unlearned responses (salivating in response to food or feeling pain and anxiety in response to painful stimuli), and when a stressor occurs in the presence of specific cues, then these cues will elicit learned emotional responses, such as fear and anxiety. Pavlov was the first to publish related findings in the scientific literature, a phenomenon known as classical conditioning, but it's again hard to imagine that farmers and little kids hadn't figured this out on their own, but they likely never thought of publishing these observations.

If, in contrast to having a response established, we want to get rid of a response learned by an animal, then we can simply adopt an extinction procedure in which particular responses are not rewarded, and gradually that response will drop out. If we cease giving Rover scraps of food at the kitchen table, he will eventually stop his begging. Extinction, however, is a bit more difficult to achieve when we want fear or anxiety responses to be eliminated. If animals were trained to make a response to avoid receiving a noxious stimulus, in later extinction we would expose the animal to the fear-eliciting situation without anything bad happening. However, animals will nevertheless make the previously established avoidance response, and so might remain unaware that the negative stimuli wouldn't have appeared even if they hadn't made the response. Essentially, if I believe that I'll always be uncomfortable in social situations, and thus continuously avoid them, I'll never know whether or not these social situations are still as uncomfortable as they once were. Thus, for extinction of the anxiety response to occur it might be necessary for me to experience the negative cues or situations and learn that nothing bad will transpire. However, suddenly "flooding" individuals with these anxiety-provoking stimuli might be a bit much for them to handle. So, we might want to conduct this "forced exposure" in graded steps, a procedure known as "systematic desensitization." Exposure therapy of this sort is effective in diminishing the influence of fearful stimuli, and can be combined with cognitive approaches to obtain still better results. Although its greatest use has come in stress-reduction programs and to diminish phobias, success of exposure and response prevention has also been achieved for OCD, as patients learn to tolerate the anxiety associated with not engaging in the compulsive behavior. A related approach focuses on teaching individuals to appraise external objects less negatively, essentially by pairing their obsessive thoughts with neutral emotions.

Another form of these methods, prolonged exposure therapy, has been used with traumatized individuals. In this instance the distressed person is asked repeatedly to cognitively relive their trauma experiences, but they are instructed to "go to" safe places or are asked to imagine positive activities. With frequent retelling, individuals may get used to thinking and talking about their horrific experiences, and by pairing them with positive thoughts, they may come to understand that the trauma events are in the past and the future will be different. To be sure, even in the absence of therapy, victims of trauma often engage in telling and retelling their experience, and for some it may have effects like that of prolonged exposure therapy. However, when this persists for extended periods, sometimes for years, it's obvious that the person can't let go and move on and they likely need formal therapy.

Cognitive behavioral therapy (CBT)

In discussing depression, Beck's view was that our cognitive systems comprise both primitive and mature components (Beck, 1970). The primitive aspects may involve unrealistic expectations and beliefs, and when they predominate, various psychological disturbances might evolve. This view blends with that described by Kahneman (2011) in relation to decision-making. Many of our behaviors are said to be based on a fast or automatic, primitive system that is greatly influenced by priming or expectancies developed on the basis of subtle cues or experiences. But on some occasions these fast responses need to be regulated or modified by the more mature or thoughtful slow system. Among highly stressed or depressed people, however, the mature system may be overwhelmed or hijacked by the automatic fast-thinking system, to the extent

Cognitive distortions

Cognitive distortions may come about owing to automaticity that largely reflects the individual's negative appraisal style in which everything and anything is seen from a bleak perspective, while the mature aspects of the cognitive system seem to be on an extended holiday. Cognitive distortions come in several flavors, some or all of which are often adopted by depressed individuals, and there are also many people who aren't depressed who engage in some of these same biases, potentially making them vulnerable to illness.

Dichotomous thinking comprises an individual adopting either of two extreme positions without consideration of the multiple shades of grey that exist in-between. When questioned about this, they assert that they're not biased or all black and white, but instead they see themselves as being "realistic" or "principled."

Arbitrary inference refers to arriving at a conclusion when there is, in fact, limited evidence supporting it, and there may actually be appreciable evidence to the contrary.

Selective abstraction happens when only particular aspects of a situation are recalled or emphasized. This can even occur as mind reading when inferences are made regarding another individual's thoughts or state of mind without any evidence to support the conclusions.

Magnification or an exaggeration of the importance or meaning of a particular event can lead to poor appraisals. Likewise, problems are apt to arise when over-generalization occurs in which the results of selective abstraction are applied to multiple different situations.

Cognitive deficiency refers to the situation when negative patterns become all-encompassing, so that individuals ignore information that could inform them about the likelihood of particular outcomes, and thus they become unable to integrate the information into their basic schema.

that aberrant forms of thinking become a habit. In depressed individuals these primitive elements might be expressed as cognitive distortions, automatic thoughts or images concerned with deprivation, self-debasement, and thoughts of hopelessness. Anxious individuals also experience these primitive distortions, but their cognitions might focus on stimuli that are inappropriately seen as signaling imminent threat.

It's not a great leap to suppose that treatment of depression and other psychological problems that are a reflection of habitual cognitive distortions ought to focus on changing automatic negative thoughts. The fundamental goals of cognitive therapy are to have the patient become aware of these automatic thoughts, and then challenge and replace them with more appropriate and realistic appraisals, attitudes and functional thoughts, and to develop appropriate ways of coping with stressful events (Beck et al., 1979).

During therapy patients quickly recognize the counterproductive nature of their responses to threats, but knowing this is just a first step in fixing the problem. It is more difficult and time-consuming to replace disturbed cognitive processes with those that are functionally effective. This entails the "quieting" of the primitive (automatic), fast-responding cognitive processes, which is initially achieved through Socratic questioning in which the patient is helped to identify negative automatic thoughts, and finding alternatives that are not only more likely, but also more favorable. Later, patients practice identifying cognitive distortions in their thinking and are encouraged to question and test their counterproductive appraisals, assumptions, and beliefs. During this phase, "exposure" to the irrational ideas or objects might only occur cognitively, so that the patient is able to practice countering the irrational ideas before confronting actual life situations. This requires homework assignments so that therapy is not limited to one-hour sessions in the therapist's office. As well, patients are asked to keep a diary of significant events, as well as the related feelings, thoughts, and behaviors, and are encouraged to deal directly with uncomfortable issues and finding new approaches to counter them. The newly acquired cognitions will then be carried to real-world situations, allowing patients to "reality test" their thoughts. The changes in thoughts are expected to precipitate a change in both feelings and actions, and fundamentally change the individual's belief systems.

Generally, the procedures used are not entirely fixed and a degree of flexibility permits other methods to be incorporated into a CBT program, including distraction techniques, relaxation training, and drug treatments. Indeed, the combination of CBT with drug therapy often yields better results than either treatment alone. The drug treatment might get a person to the point where they are amenable to receiving CBT. The basic CBT procedure has also been modified so that it can be used for specific conditions, and it has had success in reducing symptoms of PTSD, obsessive compulsive disorder, substance abuse, and psychotic disorders. As well, it has been viewed as an effective adjunctive treatment to diminish the distress and depression that frequently accompany physical illnesses, such as multiple sclerosis, cancer and breast cancer rehabilitation, epilepsy, and HIV/AIDS. Typically, CBT is administered on a one-on-one basis with a clinician, in which a degree of flexibility is possible on the part of the clinician so that they can place emphasis on certain cognitive or behavioral aspects of the therapy. However, it can also be administered on a group basis where it is effective for some disorders. Guided self-help approaches have also been developed, although there has been some question concerning the effectiveness of these methods.

Cognitive behavioral therapy isn't a procedure that can be applied over a brief period, typically requiring weekly sessions of an hour over about 12–16 weeks, and patients need to have a strong commitment to engaging and following the procedures outlined. As a result many individuals opt for alternative treatment strategies. As well, high drop-out rates are encountered in CBT and as with most forms of psychotherapy some patients don't exhibit a positive response to the treatment. In the view of some clinicians, CBT is effective primarily for those patients who have the belief that CBT can help them and are prepared and able to invest in this approach. Many patients who want an easy fix might be okay with taking meds, but aren't prepared for the work involved in CBT.

Sharing those emotions

Cognitive therapies involve patients sharing their emotions with others, but for some people sharing thoughts and private feelings can be very difficult. Thus, it's especially interesting that administration of oxytocin, the prosocial hormone that promotes trust, has also been found to increase willingness to share experience and emotions. It might turn out that for some individuals oxytocin treatments could facilitate the patient–therapist alliance that is needed for successful cognitive behavioral strategies.

Interpersonal psychotherapy (IPT)

Interpersonal therapy, or IPT, was initially developed to treat depression in adults, but it has since been found to be especially effective in children and adolescents, and has been useful in the treatment of other psychological illnesses, such as bipolar disorder and bulimia, as well as substance abuse disorder. IPT is delivered over a period of 12–16 weeks, during which the therapist helps the patient to feel understood, and aids them in resolving difficult interpersonal issues by offering a clearly defined, rational treatment ritual. Patients learn that their depressed mood might have developed within an interpersonal context wherein relationships with others were affected. To be sure, disputes between individuals are fairly common, often developing as a result of different expectations that ultimately create considerable distress and sometimes even loss of relationships. These interpersonal challenges are often distressing enough to promote depressed mood, especially among ruminative people.

The IPT method involves the therapist working collaboratively with the patient in an effort to identify just one or two significant problems in their social interactions. By limiting the interactions to just a few topics, these can be dealt with in detail so that the patient will understand the situation and then make necessary adjustments regarding their interpersonal relations. For instance, the issues covered might entail disputes that can occur within family, marital, social, school, or work situations. Over the course of therapy, the patient will come to learn that changes in mood are tied to their relationships, and they will be able to communicate feelings effectively, express their expectations regarding the relationships, and when difficulties arise they will be able to solve these effectively. Because of how important interpersonal relationships are to us, repairing damaged relations can be exceptionally effective in diminishing distress and provide individuals with an essential coping resource to deal with other situations. Once patients learn how to make adjustments in one situation they can then apply these skills to other situations. In general, IPT is as effective as CBT in treating depression, and because it doesn't involve homework or the jargon so common in clinical psychology milieus, IPT is often preferred over CBT.

Meditation

Meditation generally refers to the practice in which individuals train their mind and body to reach an alternative level of consciousness and calmness. Meditative practices can promote physiological outcomes consistent with a stress-reducing effect, including diminished cortisol levels, brain electrophysiological responses, and even brain changes detected through neuroimaging. In the latter instance, for example, nondirective meditation (where individuals focus on such things as breathing and the mind is otherwise left to wander) was accompanied by elevated brain activity relative to "at rest" periods in brain regions associated with thoughts and feelings. In a sense, nondirective meditation might allow for feelings and thoughts to emerge that would otherwise be held back.

Meditation might also be accompanied by positive physiological changes. Among those in highly stressful occupations, such as caregiving, meditation was accompanied by alterations in psychological distress, reduced blood pressure and attenuation of inflammatory immune disturbances. Unfortunately, data from some studies need to be considered cautiously as many were not well controlled and were affected by confounding factors. For example, meditation practices are often accompanied by lifestyles which also affect well-being, including those related to sleep, eating, smoking, and exercise.

Sleep to cope

The mind needs rest and rejuvenation and it needs it often. Meditation might well reflect a form of brain rest, but we need more than just that. Like eating and drinking, sleep is driven by internal biological processes and is necessary for survival. Sleep has multiple restorative functions, permitting repair of the damage that occurred through wear and tear on the body and the brain, and lack of sleep has been associated with acute illnesses, such as flu and common colds as well as hypertension and heart disease, and in this regard signs of problems can even be detected in adolescence. Getting enough sleep can limit signs of metabolic syndrome and Type 2 diabetes. It is also essential for protein synthesis and hence muscle and tissue repair, and it contributes to the replenishment of hormonal and immune functions. As sleep facilitates processes related to brain neuroplasticity, it enhances learning and memory abilities as well as the capacity to make proper stressor appraisals and coping responses.

Even though attention has usually focused on the consequences of obtaining too little sleep, too much sleep doesn't necessarily imply good quality sleep, and hence might be linked to illness. It is also possible that the presence of inflammatory factors appearing early in a disease might be responsible for encouraging increased sleep. In effect, altered sleep patterns may be an early index of something being amiss, and can also be a causal agent for illness.

Not all people need the same amount of sleep or cherish it in the same way. There are individuals who say they enjoy sleep and that there's nothing better than sleeping in. Others, however, have trouble understanding why anyone would enjoy sleeping. A very cranky and often haggard-looking acquaintance once commented: "I appreciate that we need sleep, but I just don't see lying there in a sort of semi-comatose state as being much fun and it takes away from the things I'd rather be doing. Frankly, I see it as a practice run for being dead."

Furthermore, people who engage in meditation might differ in personality from those who aren't the meditative type, and so the differences in calmness and stress levels might have reflected personality characteristics, rather than stemming from meditative practices. This said, even a single session aimed at creating relaxation among individuals with no previous experience relevant to relaxation training had short-term positive effects in relation to inflammatory processes and insulin secretion. Despite the cautious tone taken here, this isn't meant to discourage the use of meditation, but simply to indicate that the data concerning the effectiveness of meditation isn't as strong as it could be if the research, in many instances, had been conducted better. As well, even if meditation did have positive effects, it might be useful only for some people, and definitely not for others.

Mindfulness

One of the new breed of therapies to reduce stress and stress-related illness is mindfulness, also referred to as mindful meditation. This approach comes jointly from meditation-centered practices and CBT (Kabat-Zinn, 1990). Mindfulness is meant to draw attention away from unpleasant or stressful external thoughts, redirecting the individual's focus toward moment-to-moment internal processes. This entails being aware of events in the present moment, but not being judgmental about them, making it less likely that individuals will ruminate or fixate on nonproductive thoughts. In this way, they will be able to observe events as they are unfolding, and to experience physical and emotional responses to these situations, but without making attributions that involve blame, judgment or motivation. Essentially, thinking in the moment in a non-judgmental manner can disrupt the self-perpetuating "imprisoning" loop through which negative appraisals come to promote or exacerbate rumination, anxiety and depressive symptoms.

To a significant extent, mindfulness can be considered a characteristic trait wherein individuals naturally differ. This trait, which can be measured through the Mindful Attention Awareness Scale (MAAS), or the Five Facet Mindfulness Questionnaire (FFMQ), has been linked to optimism, the use of problem-oriented coping strategies, and positive self-perception. Mindfulness can also be acquired, and its use to reduce stress and related psychological illnesses has increased exponentially in recent years, to the extent that mindfulness-based stress reduction (MBSR), developed by Kabat-Zinn (1990), and mindfulness-based cognitive therapy (MBCT) (Segal, Williams, and Teasdale, 2002) have become mainstream methods to diminish distress. Indeed, the stress-reducing capacity of mindfulness-based treatment has been effective in a remarkably wide set of situations. The intent here isn't simply to provide a catalogue of uses for mindfulness training, but given the number of stress-related disorders that exist, and the usefulness of mindfulness in achieving positive outcomes, it is productive to mention some of these. Among other things, mindfulness has been used in the treatment of substance abuse, chronic pain, binge eating, employee distress and burnout, anxiety, recurrent depression, OCD, distress related to cancer, sleep disturbances related to cancer treatment, cardiovascular health, and anxiety among women in late stages of pregnancy; it has been used to help reduce loneliness in the elderly, and to increase gray matter within several brain regions, including those associated with cognitive functioning, perspective taking, and emotion regulation. Its effectiveness has also been accompanied by attenuation of physiological stress responses. For instance, these treatments reduced blood pressure, diminished levels of the inflammatory marker C-reactive protein, and attenuated inflammatory responses and cortisol levels ordinarily produced by a laboratory stressor, as well as the cytokine elevations otherwise evident in patients being treated for cancer.

Just as appraisals can be automatic and negative, coping methods can also comprise automatic, reflexive-like responses that sometimes are entirely ineffective in attenuating the impact of stressors. It is thought that mindfulness training can enhance the individual's focus on those aspects of a situation that are most pertinent, and can thereby promote the use of appropriate coping methods. Essentially, by properly appraising stressors, together with an awareness of thoughts and emotions, individuals might be able to tailor their coping strategies to suit specific situations, promote creative problem-solving and maintain cognitive flexibility. Not only might this be evident in relation to relatively severe stressor situations, but mindfulness may be particularly effective in dealing with day-to-day annoyances that can undermine well-being. Typically, we are able to appraise daily hassles for what they are, and then, with proper deliberation, effective coping strategies can be used. As simple as this sounds, mild stressors can thwart our abilities to engage in cognitive coping methods that might be useful in dealing with both mild and strong stressors. Through its capacity to allow individuals to nonjudgmentally watch stressors unfold, mindfulness may be the ticket for dealing with moderate day-to-day hassles.

Several other approaches have evolved that incorporate elements from CBT and mindfulness. These so called third generation therapies, such as Acceptance and Commitment Therapy (ACT), seem to be gaining traction. Admittedly, being old-school, I wasn't prepared for the jargon and heavy philosophical components involved in ACT. I've since come to appreciate that there may be elements of ACT that are useful, particularly as it emphasizes cognitive flexibility. I suspect that the language and concepts associated with this form of therapy might not be ideal for a meat-and-potatoes type of person, but it might be right for others and is mentioned here as a possible alternative to more usual treatments.

The default mode network

You might have had the experience of driving some place familiar, such as work, and suddenly finding yourself at the destination, largely oblivious of the events that had transpired on the way there. Somehow, while on autopilot and not all that aware of what was going on, you were able to avoid hazards, navigate red or green lights, make turns, and presumably drive under the speed limit. Evidently, we can move through simple tasks in an automatic mode while our brain seems to be in some sort of other state – not quite at the point where the screensaver has turned on, but not really in action either.

There is the common misperception that when we're at rest or not purposefully engaged in active information processing, our brain is essentially offline. However, during these resting states a particular neural network comprising several cortical regions and the hippocampus is active. This so called default mode network (DMN) is involved in mind wandering, self-referential thought and introspection, a component of creativity, and may be fundamental for our conception of consciousness. During periods of active information-processing the DMN is deactivated and neuronal activity predominates in a different set of cortical structures, collectively referred to as the task-positive network (TPN). The TPN and the DMN act in an opposing fashion, maintaining a balance based on our alertness and goal-directed or purposeful behaviors. In fact, for engagement in cognitive tasks it is not only necessary that the TPN become engaged, but it is also important for the DMN to be tuned down.

Disturbances of the TPN–DMN balance in which the DMN dominates has been associated with elevated negative rumination and low levels of more adaptive, reflective rumination, as well as depressive illness. What was especially interesting was that the neural network activity that accompanied these two forms of rumination was also differentially engaged in depressed and nondepressed individuals. The DMN was primarily evident during "bad" rumination, emotional-cognitive disturbances and an increase of self-focus in patients with depressive disorders, whereas TPN activation was more prominent during reflective rumination among those who were not depressed. But more than this, unlike nondepressed individuals, those who were depressed didn't display shifts from DMN or TPN when they were reappraising negative images. The patients seemed to lack the ability to move from a self-referential state to one that requires other thought processes. In a sense, the flexible brain functioning required for adaptation was limited in depressed patients, and their thinking networks were locked in place, with DMN being predominant. It has been suggested that mindfulness training might have its positive effects by diminishing the activity of the DMN network engaged in rumination and self-focus, thereby facilitating appropriate appraisals of stressors, thus reducing emotional intensity and permitting proper coping.

Fear of happiness

You'd think that being happy is a basic right that we all would cherish. Yet, among some people and some cultures, happiness (or at least being too happy) isn't something that people strive for. Much like the biblical Job, being too happy will eventually result in negative outcomes. Some deity or supernatural devil, seeing that we're a bit too content, will bring down their wrath to put us in our place. Thus, after relishing a positive event, some people protect themselves from the evil eye and future harm by knocking on wood, tossing salt over their shoulder, or spitting three times. Having done this, supernatural phantoms presumably shrug their shoulders in dismay and pass over a potential victim. Warding off bad luck in this way is oddly reminiscent of calling for the five-second rule when your jam-covered toast hits the floor.

In addition to considering the balance between the DMN and TPN, Georg Northoff (2014), a leading figure in the field, has indicated that the characteristics of the DMN are fundamental in other ways. In an email conversation we had, he suggested that

> the default-mode network may exert specific modulatory effects on other brain regions. In this respect, it may set the threshold and resting state activity for other regions and networks that, in turn, may be relevant for how these networks react in response to stressors. Hence, the DMN acts in the background but, as we know, sometimes the background provides the key to what happens in the foreground and thus how stressful stimuli and situations are perceived and experienced.

Although the potential importance of disturbance of the TPN–DMN balance has often been considered in the context of depressive illness, it has become clear that it may be imperative for our understanding of a variety of psychopathological conditions, including PTSD, anxiety, autism, attention deficit/hyperactivity disorder, and schizophrenia.

Positive psychotherapy (PPT)

Just as negative events can adversely affect well-being, positive events and having a positive outlook can also have profound effects on health. In fact, traditional methods of psychological treatments which focus on getting rid of negative symptoms fall short in the sense that the absence of symptoms doesn't necessarily mean that individuals are happy or content. Several "positive" therapeutic approaches were adopted in an effort to have individuals change their ways of seeing the world and seeing themselves. One method that tended to reduce levels of depression was a "happiness" intervention in which individuals received training to help them socialize more, form closer and deeper relationships with loved ones, engage in meaningful work, and lower expectations. Related approaches that likewise produced positive outcomes focused on such things as personal growth, purpose in life, autonomy, self-acceptance, and positive relations with others.

A method that has been receiving progressively broader attention, termed positive psychotherapy (PPT), was introduced in an effort to diminish the negativity that presages depression, to build positive emotions and character strengths, and to create meaning for individuals. Over the course of about 14 sessions, individuals are first introduced to a variety of issues related to the recognition of their own emotions, their resources and character strengths, and how these might influence them in particular situations. Later, they cover topics related to bad or hurtful memories, feelings of anger, and how to use forgiveness to overcome counterproductive feelings, as well as the cultivation of positive emotions, including thankfulness, optimism, hope, and recognition of the character strengths of others. Finally, individuals are encouraged to savor positive events and to integrate pleasure, engagement and meaning in daily life. Several experimental tests of PPT in the treatment of depression revealed it to be as effective as pharmacotherapy or CBT in the treatment of the disorder.

Giving and receiving

It might sound a bit hokey, but it seems that happiness may also be contagious. When we are happy and display it, it's more likely that others will be drawn to us, making us that much happier. It also results in the other person being happy, which also affects that person's friend so they are happier as well.

On behalf of the Canadian Institutes of Health Research, which supported my research for many years, I am sometimes asked to provide information to the media regarding topical issues. One that seems to be of interest year after year concerns why some people become very sad at Christmastime, and what can be done about it. The topic doesn't allow for a great deal of creativity and new ideas, and my answers to the questions were much the same every year. I typically would mention the bit about seasonal affective disorder and light therapy, and cover the issue of being lonely when everybody else seems to be having fun with loads of friends, and suggest that mindfulness might help some people, focusing on the importance of thinking in the moment and stopping worrying about small stuff. Not long ago, looking for something new to say, I suggested that volunteering (e.g., at a soup kitchen, collecting funds for disaster relief, donating time and money to animal welfare societies) might have beneficial effects, especially if the behavior brings the individual into a supportive social group that serves as a distraction or as a stress buffer. Besides, a charitable act might in itself be rewarding. Whether it involves "random acts of kindness," targeted giving, or volunteering for a specific cause, it might create a feeling of well-being. I was so impressed by my own insight that I decided to follow up on this and see whether there were published data available concerning this topic. It turns out there was a fair bit, all pointing in the same direction. For instance, Lara Aknin, an economist at Simon Fraser University, has indicated that charitable giving not only makes individuals feel better, but also diminishes distress, including biological responses to stressors (Aknin et al., 2011). She has since found that the positive effects of giving are evident across cultures, even those that are isolated and relatively primitive. Moreover, she has suggested that we have evolved so that giving is rewarding, and even in young children the act of giving seems to make them happy. As much as the concept of helping is nice, there needs to be a concrete component to giving. For example, if my charity goes to a nonspecific cause (e.g., "every dollar you give will help a person in need") it's not as rewarding as a concrete goal ("every dollar you give will help a child left homeless in the Congo"). If I can see the child smile it will have more impact than the abstract notion that the child will smile.

Let them eat cake

I have, for a very long time, had great trouble passing street people asking for money without making some contribution. Sometimes I'd feel guilty for not doing so, and then discovered that it made me feel good when I did, as I could see the person being helped. So I just continued making myself feel good. One day, while walking with a friend I gave a homeless person a small donation, but my friend scoffed, saying "he'll only spend it on booze." "That's fine with me if that'll make him feel good," I responded. I then told him an old story, a fable, which I'll share.

A beggar came to the house of a well-known and respected rabbi. Feeling empathy, the rabbi gave him some money so that he didn't starve. The next day, while walking in the center of town, he spotted the beggar sitting at an outdoor café, about to indulge in coffee and a piece of cake. He quickly rushed to the beggar and lit into him, saying, "you came to me starving and so I gave you money. And, what do you do with it, you toss it away on a frivolity, some cake!" Deeply hurt, the beggar replied, "Rabbi, yesterday I was starving and, of course, I had no bread, let alone cake. Today, you chastise me for spending a little money to have some cake. Rabbi, will there ever be a time that I will be sufficiently blessed so that I, like others, can eat some cake?"

It also seems that volunteerism has benefits for the heart by reducing bad cholesterol and levels of inflammatory factors. It is especially interesting that among individuals with altruistic tendencies the brain region involved in reward processes, the nucleus accumbens, lit up appreciably when they made a charitable donation, but this happened less among individuals who were more self-interested (egoists). This same region, it will be recalled, is also associated with the intake of drugs such as cocaine, and with sex and food rewards. In a sense, charitable acts may give individuals pleasure, just as other behaviors do, but charitable acts don't have the negative consequences of cocaine. In fact, the effect of helping is so well known it's been given the name "helper's high."

There can be a downside to being too charitable. When people engage in repeated prosocial behaviors, relentlessly engaging efforts to make changes, but don't see returns as quickly as they'd like, "helper burnout" can be engendered, which can have adverse effects on well-being. There is also the possibility that helping efforts will be misunderstood. One fellow was arrested in Quebec in 2012 during a cross-Canada run for cancer for doing his running on a major highway. As well, a Halifax man found himself in a psychiatric ward for "suspiciously" handing out $50 and $100 bills. Go figure.

The social cure

You've repeatedly heard how important social support is for our well-being, and conversely that the absence of social support, social connectedness (reflected by the number and quality of an individual's relations), and increasing loneliness are associated with very poor well-being. What it amounts to is that having strong social relationships is accompanied by longer life, greater ability to contend with illnesses ranging from the aftermath of stroke, through to depression and addictions, improved recovery from illness, and enhanced immune functioning. It was suggested that forming even a single strong connection can reduce the risk of dying in the ensuing year, and the risk diminishes still further with an increasing number of social connections. Of course, not every social relationship will be useful, but having a "shared identity" with other members of a group is the essential element of social connectedness that makes us stronger in the face of adversity (Best et al., 2014). In this regard, support groups that have been established to get individuals through difficult times are effective when its members share an identity in the sense that they are all there because they have similar problems, whether it's drug addiction, a physical illness, or the loss of a child. Furthermore, interventions that get people to engage with social networks can promote the development of identities that can enhance recovery from illnesses or treatment, such as heart surgery, stroke, or depressive illness, and can even delay the expression of degenerative disorders. In this sense, sharing an identity with other group members and using it appropriately can offer a "social cure." Predictably, those with a shared identity are also in a better position to offer advice and consolation, and it has even been suggested that in relatively large social groups individuals can learn from one another in a way that facilitates cultural knowledge and the acquisition of sophisticated technical skills that can be passed on across generations.

If social connectedness based on shared identity can be an awesome coping strategy that enhances well-being, then the obvious question is whether we can take advantage of this so that identity formation can be facilitated. In fact, Jetten et al. (2014) addressed these and related issues, and offered guidelines to determine whether and when social initiatives should be undertaken to enhance well-being, and they described some of the costs of doing so. In some instances, such as among older individuals, maintaining contacts can be difficult owing to physical or mental disturbances, or simply because of the difficulties inherent in staying connected with people residing in far-off locations. There may also be social elements, such as shyness or insecurities, which act as barriers to maintaining meaningful connections. Perhaps there are occasions when therapists or caregivers can enhance an individual's well-being by the development of ways to facilitate the maintenance of connections as well as in the formation of new, empowering shared identities.

Before you go...

Stressful events and the pathologies that arise can be dealt with through several behavioral or cognitive approaches. Without question, CBT has been among the most prominent of the cognitive therapies, and although initially established to treat depression, it has found its way into the treatment of many other disorders, as well as the psychological ramifications stemming from stressful medical illnesses. Mindfulness training, interpersonal therapy, positive psychology, and social identity and connectedness all can be used to diminish distress. As we'll see shortly, there are still other options in the realm of pharmaceuticals. As I've said repeatedly, there's no single strategy that fits everyone, and it's good to have alternatives.

As my friend Nyla Branscombe says, "suffering is plentiful," and we can all count on getting our share. So, a fundamental strategy might be to operate on the assumption that bad things can happen, and thus we might be best served by having proper interventions in place. To be sure, it wouldn't be healthy to think, on a daily basis, that lightning is going to strike us, but we can take measures to avoid bad events or use intervention strategies that limit their impact. First, the individual has to be psychologically ready to in engage proper ways of dealing with stressful events, and this includes appropriate ways of appraising events, maintaining coping flexibility to counter adverse events, and having social connections that enhance the resilience. At the same time, the body must also be ready to deal with stressors. Exercise might be useful in dealing with stressors as it may help the individual block out certain problems, or allow the mind to rest as it goes into a DMN-like state, and even influence growth factors in the brain that facilitate neural connections. Similarly, eating properly may be essential to allow the individual the physical resources to behave and think effectively, and sleep is essential as its absence can have multiple negative physical and mental health repercussions, including hindrance of recovery from illness.

21

Drug Remedies to Attenuate Stress and Stress-Related Disorders

A brief history of pharmacotherapy in treating depression

The history of psychiatry is replete with "should haves," "could haves," and "if only I hads," but there have also been a few lucky breaks. One of the best known of these came about in 1951 when Irving Selikoff and Edward Robitzek, who had been treating patients with iproniazid in an effort to beat tuberculosis, observed that the mood of patients improved. The wards that were filled with sad, lethargic patients were transformed to more active, happier places. An explanation for the surprising effects of the drug wasn't at hand as scientists didn't fully understand how brain chemicals operated, but it was eventually understood that drugs, such as iproniazid, acted by inhibiting an enzyme, monoamine oxidase, which ordinarily degraded norepinephrine and serotonin, and thus increased the levels of these transmitters.

At about the same time, while treating patients in an effort to combat schizophrenia, it was discovered that a drug, imipramine, had positive effects in attenuating depressive symptoms. The remedy appeared to be effective for about 60 percent of patients, but it came with side effects that made their use uncomfortable. Still, given the limited arsenal to deal with depression, it became the treatment of choice. It was eventually concluded that disturbed serotonin was the important element underlying depression, and so increased efforts were devoted to the development of treatments that specifically focused on this neurotransmitter. With the introduction of the selective serotonin reuptake inhibitors (SSRIs) in the late 1980s, which had fewer side effects than their older cousins, the media quickly became obsessed and numerous reports appeared concerning this new miracle drug that had replaced the old miracle drug that was suddenly deemed to be much less miraculous.

As it turned out, the effectiveness of these drugs didn't match the hype. As with earlier drugs, only 50–60 percent of patients were successfully treated with any given drug. To achieve positive effects the drug had to be taken for 2–3 weeks, and if improvement wasn't evident after a month, then another drug was administered,

Stress and Your Health: From Vulnerability to Resilience, First Edition. Hymie Anisman.
© 2015 John Wiley & Sons, Ltd. Published 2015 by John Wiley & Sons, Ltd.

and another delay experienced, with the hope that this treatment would be better than the first. Equally disconcerting was that even when the drugs had a positive effect, the depression might not be entirely eliminated, as residual symptoms frequently persisted. Finally, when patients realized a positive outcome, it seems that the treatment frequently didn't have permanent effects, as recurrence of illness was exceptionally high, reaching 50–70 percent over five years, reoccurring more frequently among those treated with drugs than among individuals treated with CBT.

During this time, scientists realized that perhaps a drug that focused on serotonin might not be the answer that was sought. So, the clock was turned back and drugs were developed that affected serotonin along with other neurotransmitters, such as serotonin and norepinephrine, or those that affected both serotonin and dopamine. These drugs have been taking up an increasing portion of the market share, but their advantages over earlier drugs are marginal.

So, this is where we stood for quite a time, but we do need a "happily ever after" part to this story. In fact, there are several new drugs in the pipeline, and it seems as if novel targets for drugs are being defined, some of which can have their effects within hours rather than weeks.

Something about drug treatments

Some clinicians swear by the usefulness of antidepressants and antianxiety medications, whereas others see them as a scourge. There is considerable controversy regarding the efficacy of drug treatments, and it is widely accepted that of the numerous drug trials that are conducted, many of those that find positive outcomes are published in the scientific literature, whereas negative results are infrequently published as the journals tend not to be interested in treatments that aren't effective. So, a search through the drug literature would lead to the possibly erroneous conclusion that positive outcomes in response to drug treatments are found in most studies. There is also the issue that many trials are funded by drug companies, and thus inherent biases might be present that favor positive drug outcomes, and the spin put on the data might also be related to who funded the project. We can go back and forth on such issues, but even the most diehard drug advocates would agree that we can do better than we have to date, and those most negative about drugs might agree that they have worked well for some patients.

Placebo and nocebo responses

How we respond to stressors is largely based on our appraisals, which can be influenced by expectancies that were generated. The very same thing applies to our responses to medications to deal with pain or psychological distress. If we are primed to believe that our psychological state will improve as a result of some treatment, then it's more likely that it will. A placebo effect emerges if there is the expectancy or belief that a treatment will have a positive effect, even though the inert substance being administered can't directly influence physiological processes associated with symptoms. A "nocebo" response, in contrast, refers to the lack of a positive outcome by a potentially effective treatment, owing to the individual's expectation that it won't lead to any benefit.

Aside from placebos in the form of inert drugs, positive effects can also be obtained through electrical or mechanical devices, acupuncture needles inserted into inappropriate locations, and even faith healing can reasonably fit into this category. Physicians themselves are part of the placebo treatment, and trust in a person wearing a white coat who looks professional may be an essential element in whether prescribed treatments will be followed and whether positive effects will be realized. The efficacy of many drug treatments might involve a placebo component, and the expectancies they create can be expressed within brain processes associated with pain perception in addition to activation of brain regions associated with emotional, cognitive, and executive functioning, as well as reward processes. So, if placebo responders are told that it's all in their head, this likely is true.

The effects of placebos and nocebos are particularly evident in relation to pain perception where the strength of the placebo response approached that of low doses of morphine. Patients told that they had received morphine treatment reported greater pain relief than did patients who hadn't been told when treatment began. Even when patients saw another person receiving pain medicine that worked, they were more likely to show a similar response. Conversely, if patients receiving analgesic treatments were led to believe that they were no longer receiving pain medication, they reported increased pain perception. Although, placebo treatments don't influence severe physical or viral illnesses, they might nevertheless diminish the anxiety that accompanies these conditions. In fact, objective measures of lung functioning among asthma patients indicated that although placebos were ineffective, patients indicated that they received as much relief from the placebo as they had from active broncodilation.

So long as it catches mice

There are a lot of people who can't help rolling their eyes, and maybe muttering something unintelligible, whenever they watch the "miracles" created by strident faith healers. These poor saps might have come miles and actually trust this guy to heal them. We probably shouldn't be so skeptical since this trust isn't that much different from that placed in organized religions. So long as it isn't preventing the afflicted individuals from seeking more traditional methods of healing that could have some benefit, then perhaps we shouldn't really be critical of it. So what if it's "just" a placebo effect? If it gets rid of pain, then it's a good treatment?

Deng Xiaoping, the leading figure in the People's Republic of China from 1978 to 1992, was largely responsible for dragging China into the global market and creating the environment that permitted the successes seen over the past few years. However, he wasn't always viewed so positively, being sent off for "rehabilitation" by Mao. Defending a daring break in agricultural policy by quoting an old Sichuan saying, he declared: "No matter if it is a white cat or a black cat; as long as it can catch mice, it is a good cat." The comments Deng Xiaoping made regarding white and black cats seem to be particularly apt in relation to placebos. For the patient experiencing distress, it might not matter in the slightest why drugs work, so long as they do the job.

Selecting the right treatment and related caveats

A drug's efficacy is typically assessed through randomized controlled trials (RCTs). Criteria are established concerning who can and who cannot be enrolled in a particular drug trial, and if they meet the "inclusion criteria" and aren't excluded because of factors that make them ineligible, such as the presence of other illnesses or the use of particular medications, participants in the study will be assigned on a random basis to one or another drug or to a placebo. In some trials, the treatments are administered in a double-blind manner so that neither the patient nor the treating physician knows what the patient actually received. In a single-blind procedure the physician knows which drug was administered, but the patient doesn't. In other trials an open label procedure is used so that patients receive one of several possible treatments, and their relative effectiveness is determined with respect to how many patients get better, to what extent they improve, how long it took to realize positive effects, the severity of side effects, and the treatment's lasting actions.

Good drug, bad patient

Some patients seem to be treatment resistant and don't respond to any available drug. In other instances, the drug used is simply the wrong one and a trial and error procedure is used to find the most effective drug. Hopefully, this sort of fishing expedition will diminish as better biomarkers become available that inform clinicians about the best treatment strategy. There are also occasions when the drug treatment might be perfectly fine, but the problem is the patient. In fact, failure regarding patient compliance is among the greatest obstacles to effective treatment. This is true among diabetics and those with heart problems, and it's also the case for those with mental issues. Patients sometimes simply forget to take the drug or renew their prescriptions, or willfully choose not to take a drug. They might not like abdicating control over their brain, or they might be bothered by the side effects of the drug. Indeed, one the most difficult aspects of SSRI treatments comes from the sexual side effects that are often present, including diminished libido and difficulty reaching orgasm, and as a result some patients decide to go on drug holidays, or cease taking the drug entirely.

There are also occasions when patients, having a superficial understanding of the drugs, often based on what they obtain from internet sources, decide that they can experiment to enhance the effects of prescribed treatments. When my mom was about 70 years old, she temporarily had some bad side effects after taking a prescription drug. The drug was actually a good one, but she apparently took a few tablets too many. Being concerned about her cognitive abilities, I asked her whether she was confused about the number of pills she was supposed to take. She picked up on what I was suggesting and became indignant, saying: "No, the bottle said take 2 pills every 4 hours. You think I'm an idiot? You think I need a PhD to read a pill bottle?" "So, ma, how did you end up taking too many pills?" "Well," she said, "I thought that if 2 pills every 4 hours would work, then 4 pills every 2 hours would work still better." Seeing my surprised expression, she added: " I'm an old woman; you think I can just sit around waiting to get better?"

These randomized drug trials follow scientifically appropriate protocols. However, what they haven't typically been doing is distinguishing between patients on the basis of the specific symptoms presented and the presence of particular biomarkers. Strictly speaking, the view that antidepressants have limited effects is correct, but they have the potential of having much more positive actions if used appropriately. As mentioned on several occasions, this would mean determining behavioral and biological markers that tell us more about the nature of the pathology, which would inform the optimal treatment strategy. While we're on this topic, the effects of drugs may also vary with the sex and age of patients, as well as ethnic and cultural factors, but these are infrequently considered in clinical trials or by treating physicians.

As it happens, an increasing number of biomarkers are being discovered that can provide clues concerning best practices. Some are based on genetic markers and others involve the identification of specific hormones that are assessed relatively simply. Other markers can be obtained, but they come with a price, literally. For instance, based on PET analysis it was reported that if neuronal activity was low in the right hemisphere of a frontal brain region known as the insula, the patients were better off when treated with CBT than with an SSRI. Conversely, if that region was overly active, then an SSRI treatment was more efficacious. If this pans out in further studies it will mean a major breakthrough in treatment, but cost, access to imaging, and having expert personnel available may set limits on its clinical utility.

Treating depression

Selective serotonin reuptake inhibitors (SSRIs)

Drug treatments that comprise SSRIs were especially popular during the latter part of the 1980s and the1990s and became the most prescribed drug in the US and other Western countries. As of 2011, antidepressant drug use among women in the US reached 23 percent and about 10 percent in men, the difference largely being a result of women becoming depressed twice as often as men. As already mentioned, the effectiveness of drug treatments has been unimpressive for a large number of people. But the statistics often cited by the antidrug side are a bit over the top. When someone is treated for cancer they don't receive just a single drug or a single procedure with the expectation that the disease will be eliminated. Instead, they receive drug cocktails and multiple procedures that include surgery, chemotherapy and radiation therapy. Better effects for antidepressant agents might also be obtained through combination treatments. Pierre Blier, a leading figure in the assessment and development of drug treatment strategies, observed that positive outcomes could be doubled through the use of combination therapies (Blier et al., 2010). This is not to say that SSRIs are an optimal treatment strategy, but in the absence of better approaches we could do better than we do with what is already available.

Following the development of fluoxetine (Prozac) and paroxetine (Paxil), other SSRIs came to market, including citalopram (Celexa), escitalopram (Lexapro, Cipralex), fluvoxamine (Luvox) and sertraline (Zoloft), most of which were moderately effective in diminishing depressive disorders. If positive effects aren't produced by a given treatment, other antidepressants within this class can be used, as subtle differences between drugs may result in a positive treatment response. Alternatively, the treating psychiatrist may prescribe a second drug as an adjunct. For instance, depressed patients

Band-Aid or cure?

How do drugs come to have effects on symptoms of mental illness? Are these drugs acting on the mechanisms responsible for promoting the illness, or are they simply "masking" the symptoms, much like sticking your hand in cold water might alleviate pain from a superficial burn? If the treatments only mask symptoms, patients might do well while taking their meds, but promptly fall ill again when the meds are stopped. It would obviously be desirable to fix the underlying processes for any illness, but most often we aren't even certain what those biological processes are. So, when this isn't possible we simply have to accept that we have what we have. Anyone who has experienced severe, unremitting pain will tell you that at the time they didn't care about the underlying mechanism responsible for their pain, they were simply grateful to experience relief. For those experiencing stress-related psychological difficulties, as well as their families, there is considerable relief to have the symptoms vanquished, even if only for the moment.

with lots of anxiety might receive a particular antidepressant together with trazodone (sold as Desirel, Trazorel and under several other names), which has strong anxiolytic and sedative effects. Likewise, high anxiety or irritability may call for a standard antidepressant being administered together with quetiapine (Seroquel), and in some instances the influence of antidepressants is enhanced by augmenter drugs, such as buspirone (Buspar) or bupropion (Wellbutrin, Zyban). So, individuals often receive more than just a single drug, but this depends on the patient's symptoms and the knowledge and experience of the treating physician. Although we hear most about these agents in relation to their effects on depressive disorders, alone or in combination with other treatments they can be useful in the treatment of generalized anxiety disorder, obsessive compulsive disorder and PTSD.

A serious limitation of all currently marketed antidepressant drugs is that relief from depression doesn't come quickly, and 2–4 weeks of treatment is usually necessary before positive effects are evident. The delay in obtaining relief can be wrenching for patients, especially if the first drug used isn't effective, and they have to go through a second or third regimen in an effort to obtain relief. Moreover, if patients are at risk for suicide and have the means to carry this out, then drug treatments aren't the best strategy, and instead electroconvulsive therapy may be called for in light of its faster action. The delay before the drugs become effective has important implications regarding the process through which they have their positive effects. If symptom amelioration develops as a result of increased serotonin at the synapse, which occurs quickly, then why would it take weeks of treatment for the depressive symptoms to abate? Obviously, there's more to the effect of the drugs than just the increased availability of serotonin. This could entail progressive changes of receptors or other processes that occur within neurons stimulated by serotonin, or through actions on other systems, such as growth factors, which take time to develop.

One advantage of SSRIs over the older "tricyclic" antidepressants, such as imipramine, amitriptyline, and desipramine, is that they are accompanied by fewer and less

One step forward and another back

Osteoporosis, which comprises progressive decline of bone mass and density, is frequently comorbid with depression and chronic stress. Although SSRIs may diminish depression, they may also have the effect of reducing bone density. Thus, some of the benefits of the brain effects of SSRIs may be outweighed by its skeletal effects. In vulnerable groups, such as the aged, caution needs to be taken in relation to prescription of SSRIs. As well, it's not widely circulated information, but SSRI use has been associated with a 10 percent increase of adverse events following surgery, even after accounting for the presence of depression and various factors that go with it.

What about the other side of the equation? What happens when antidepressant use is curtailed? There were a number of reports indicating that SSRIs could promote suicidal ideation, especially among adolescents and young adults. In 2004 such findings prompted the Food and Drug Administration in the US to issue a warning on antidepressant packaging concerning the risk for suicide, and countries such as Canada also issued warnings. These policies were not meant to eliminate antidepressant use, but were intended to caution physicians about the potential for these drugs to encourage suicide, and perhaps for them to consider alternative treatment strategies for their young patients, because the young are typically much more likely to engage in suicide than are older groups. Good intentions notwithstanding, to a considerable extent the strategy has backfired. By 2008, there were reports from Canada indicating an increase in suicide attempts. Moreover, over the past 10 years the use of antidepressants in the US declined by 31 percent among those in their teens, and concurrently, overdoses on psychiatric meds increased by 22 percent. Moreover, among 18–29 year olds suicide attempts rose about 37 percent. Predictably, everyone blamed everyone else for the outcome. However, what is clear is that the policy was likely initiated without full consideration of potential negative downstream effects, and the media likely sensationalized the earlier reports of SSRIs being linked to suicide. As mentioned when we discussed pandemic threats, there needs to be better communication between public health officials and the media.

intense side effects. Nevertheless, these agents still have side effects, such as promoting suicidal ideation, loss of appetite, nausea, weight loss (or gain), sleep disturbance, and reduced libido or ability to reach orgasm. As already indicated, this is no small matter, as weight gain or sexual dysfunction might lead patients to elect to discontinue the treatment. Fortunately, remedies are being found to counteract these actions. As well, side effects differ across antidepressant agents, and some, such as bupropion (Wellbutrin), moclobemide (Aurorix, Manerix), and mirtazapine (Remeron, Avanza, Zispin), have few sexual side effects. Finally, it should be mentioned that in some instances coming off the drug can be difficult, requiring progressive small reductions in the dose taken. Too rapid a decline of dose can result in "SSRI discontinuation syndrome," which is characterized by "brain zaps," electric shock-like sensations, and may cause dizziness, confusion, nausea, insomnia, tremor, nightmares, and vertigo.

Two is better than one

If CBT is somewhat effective, and so are SSRIs, then the combination of the two treatments might be expected to yield still better outcomes. There have been many reports showing exactly this, but is this a matter of the two treatments having additive effects on a particular process or is something going on? One possibility is that the drug restores an appropriate biological state, making it easier for CBT to be used to establish proper appraisals and coping methods that act against depression. A related alternative is that the drug treatment, by acting on growth factors, influences the individual's "neuroplasticity" or "malleability," enabling CBT to have better effects.

Regardless of why the improvement occurs, if the two treatments are better than one, then why isn't this combination used more often? My longtime friend and collaborator Dr Arun Ravindran, a psychiatrist at the Center for Addiction and Mental Health in Toronto, told me that there are several factors that contribute to this. He says that

> many patients want CBT alone, and some want only medications. Regular time commitments for CBT are a factor that limits its use, which could play into the preference for medications alone. As well, CBT is not covered by medical insurance when it is obtained through a private practitioner, and most hospitals only provide a skeleton service with long wait times and often only for groups, as opposed to individual therapy.

He also indicated that

> although the combination is generally more effective that single treatments, it is sometimes difficult for more severely ill patients to tolerate and complete assignments (homework) for CBT. As such, many of them find it stressful and don't want to continue. The current consensus seems to be that sequential application with medications first, followed by CBT after some amelioration of symptoms, may be more beneficial. Finally, most depressions are treated in the community by GPs who don't do psychotherapy, and often don't bother to offer referral for CBT unless the patient requests it.

A cocktail of acronyms: SNRI, NDRI, NaSSA, MAOI

As we've seen, focusing on just serotonin didn't yield optimal antidepressant actions, and so efforts were made to develop treatments that targeted specific receptors or concurrently affected other transmitters. There has been a bit of interest in the possibility that targeting particular serotonin receptors, such as the 5-HT2C receptor, can have positive effects within a few days rather than several weeks. Drugs affecting several neurotransmitters were developed, such as the serotonin-norepinephrine reuptake inhibitors (SNRIs), which, as the name suggests, inhibited the reuptake of both serotonin and norepinephrine, and they have become increasingly popular. As well, because dopamine is involved in reward processes and depression is accompanied by diminished

Cross-fertilization in the drug world

It isn't unusual for a drug developed for one purpose to end up having multiple effects and then being patented for other uses. Thus, drugs to reduce eating might end up being used to treat depression, and antidepressants can be a first line of defense against PTSD, eating disorders, migraine headaches, and anxiety and anxiety-related disorders, as well as chronic pain conditions. The SSRI paroxetine may also have beneficial effects in the treatment of diabetes, owing to factors unrelated to its antidepressant properties, and Warfarin, a rat poison, has been used since the 1950s as an anticoagulant, and is best known as Coumadin, one of the names under which it is marketed. As it happens, warfarin might be effective for long-term remission of schizophrenia. There has also been some indication that drugs used to treat schizophrenia might be useful in treating glioblastoma tumors, the most deadly form of brain cancer.

Early trials using a modified form of the polio vaccine had success in this regard as well, and there was a report of a megadose of modified measles vaccine having an anticancer effect. One of the most horrid drugs, thalidomide, which was used to diminish morning sickness early in pregnancy, ended up inducing birth deformities before it was removed from the market. However, it has resurfaced as part of the treatment of multiple myeloma, and for some time it was thought that it might also have positive effects in the treatment of leprosy, but this has been dropped.

Recycling drugs has multiple advantages. It can reduce the cost of the drug, provided that the manufacturer passes the savings on to the patient. As well, since these drugs have been in use for a relatively long time, there has been the opportunity to determine whether long-term adverse actions can occur. Typically when drugs are brought to market the manufacturer will be aware of short-term negative consequences, but rarely will they be aware of effects that might crop up a decade or two later.

feelings of reward from ordinarily positive events, a class of drugs was developed that acted as norepinephrine-dopamine reuptake inhibitors (NDRI).

The SNRIs now being marketed are not only used in the treatment of depressive disorders, but serve in the treatment of generalized anxiety disorder, social anxiety disorder, OCD, attention deficit hyperactivity disorder (ADHD), chronic neuropathic pain, fibromyalgia , and relief of menopausal symptoms. The first of these agents, venlafaxine (Effexor), was quickly followed by others, such as duloxetine (Cymbalta), which was also used to diminish chronic musculoskeletal pain, including pain associated with chronic osteoarthritis and chronic low back pain. Not to be outdone, other drug companies introduced their versions of SNRIs, such as desvenlafaxine (Pristiq), which is the active metabolite of venlafaxine, as well as milnacipran (e.g., Dalcipran) and sibutramine (e.g., Meridia), which was initially developed to curb appetite, but turned out to have antidepressant properties.

Other agents, referred to as norepinephrine and specific serotonergic antidepressants (NaSSAs) have seen increased use. These drugs indirectly increase the production of norepinephrine, and concurrently block certain serotonin receptors that would otherwise favor the appearance of depression. These agents, which include mianserin (e.g., Bolvidon) and mirtazapine (e.g., Remeron) are about as effective as SSRIs, but they too have side effects, such as drowsiness, increased appetite, and weight gain.

As serotonin, norepinephrine and dopamine are broken down within neurons through the enzyme monoamine oxidase (MAO), inhibiting this enzyme ought to increase these neurotransmitters and diminish depressive mood. The first monoamine oxide inhibitors (MAOIs) had modest antidepressant effects, but a new generation of these agents, which include moclobemide (Manerix), seems to be more potent.

Among the antidepressants mentioned above that inhibit the reuptake of both dopamine and norepinephrine, an agent such as bupropion is as effective as SSRIs, but isn't accompanied by sexually related side effects or weight gain. But, because it has been associated with increased blood pressure and seizure in vulnerable individuals, it is not prescribed for patients withdrawing from alcohol or benzodiazepines, anorexia nervosa, bulimia, or in individuals with brain tumors. Under the name Zyban, bupropion has also been used to diminish smoking, social phobia, anxiety comorbid with depression, as well as hyposexuality, obesity and adult attention deficit disorder. Interestingly, among its other actions, this agent reduced inflammatory cytokines, and it has been suggested that it might be useful in auto-inflammatory conditions such as Crohn's disease and psoriasis, both of which are exacerbated by stressors.

Erythropoietin (EPO): not just for cyclists

One way of increasing a person's oxygen-carrying capacity is to take some of their blood and store it while the body naturally replenishes the supply of blood. Then, on the day before an endurance event, such as a bicycle race, their own blood is transfused back into them, thereby increasing their red blood cells to carry oxygen. An alternative method of achieving this end is to self-administer erythropoietin (EPO). You've likely heard of this method, even if it doesn't initially sound all that familiar. EPO is the stuff that that has become (in)famous because of its involvement in blood doping among professional cyclists. This is a growth factor that stimulates the production of red blood cells and protects them from death, thus enhancing performance in endurance sports.

In addition, EPO has beneficial actions in response to traumatic brain injury and stroke, especially when it or one of its analogues is administered during a brief window following stroke. There has also been evidence based on animal studies that EPO can have antidepressant effects, and EPO has produced brain activity changes in humans reminiscent of those associated with antidepressant treatments. It also appears that EPO can promote anti-inflammatory and antioxidant effects, and provoke an increase in the synthesis and levels of BDNF, and might thus be useful as an adjunctive treatment to ameliorate depressive disorders.

It has frequently been suggested that exercise might be a way of diminishing stress, probably because it acts as a way to distract oneself from ongoing stressors. However, it might also have positive effects by increasing EPO, which acts against the stress, as well as limiting activation of certain parts of the hippocampus so that anxiety and depression will be diminished. As useful as exercise could potentially be to ameliorate illness, those who are severely depressed tend to be lethargic and just want to sit and veg, or even never get out of pajamas. So, it's doubtful that they can readily be coaxed to engage in an exercise regimen. While it isn't meant as a long-term alternative to exercise, EPO could potentially enhance the effects of standard antidepressants (Hayley and Litteljohn, 2013).

Ketamine

Big Pharma had for some time lost its zest for developing new compounds to treat depression, but the quest wasn't entirely abandoned and some companies turned to treatments with targets that differed from the earlier medications. We've only touched upon glutamate in relation to stress and depression, but it has considerable potential in this regard. The focus on glutamate in relation to stress processes and depression increased as a result of the finding that drugs that block glutamate receptors, notably N-methyl-D-aspartate (NMDA) receptors, can have rapid antidepressant actions. It was, in fact, suggested that the positive effects of SSRI, SNRI, and electroconvulsive shock treatments might be due to their actions on these receptors.

Some remedies come about through diligent experimental analyses, but as we've seen, they frequently occurred serendipitously, which is what happened in relation to another compound that has important implications for the treatment of depression. Ketamine is frequently used as a general anesthetic and analgesic in veterinary practice, but when it was used in clinical settings to treat chronic pain it also seemed to diminish the symptoms of depression that often accompany this condition. Of particular significance was that the reduced depression was apparent very soon after treatment, rather than the 2–3 weeks necessary for standard antidepressants to have their positive effects.

Several clinical studies of ketamine's efficacy as an antidepressant followed this discovery and the results have been consistent and fairly remarkable. In otherwise treatment-resistant patients, ketamine reduced the symptoms of depression within a few hours of the drug being administered. This was not a permanent fix, as the effects lasted for less than a week, after which poor mood returned. Subsequent studies confirmed that ketamine readily reduced suicidal ideation, and when administered on several occasions the drug's effects were somewhat longer lasting. Ketamine was effective about 50–60 percent of the time, but this was very impressive as these studies were conducted in patients who had been nonresponsive to other treatments.

In recent years several drug companies have continued to evaluate NMDA antagonists in the treatment of depression and have developed new compounds related to glutamate. These have had promising effects, diminishing symptoms of depression within 24 hours among otherwise treatment-resistant patients, and the positive effects lasted about a week, and with continued testing it will be known whether the drug can be taken repeatedly. One of these agents, lanicemine, acts like an antidepressant, but without some of ketamine's side effects. Likewise, one of the metabolites of ketamine, hydroxynorketamine, seems to be effective in animal models, and is not only more potent than ketamine itself, but could potentially be taken by mouth as opposed to intravenous injection as in the case of ketamine. There are several drugs already on the market that affect glutamate processes, and these too are being assessed for their antidepressant potential. Riluzole (Rilutek), which is used to treat amyotrophic lateral sclerosis (ALS), and memantine (Axura), which might have some effects on Alzheimer's symptoms, might also have antidepressant effects, although it is still a bit early to be sure.

Why would antagonizing glutamate receptors have positive effects at all? Duman and Aghajanian (2012) suggested that ketamine increases BDNF, which through its actions on the growth, proliferation and survival of cells, might be responsible for the positive effects obtained. It also seems that ketamine diminished the predominance of the default mode network that accompanies depression, and it is possible that the drug diminishes the inflexible ruminative features connected with depression. In a sense, ketamine might facilitate the individual's ability to break out of the negative cognitive rut that is characteristic of depressive disorders.

Deep brain stimulation

Parkinson's disease occurs as a result of the loss of dopamine neurons in a brain region known as the substantia nigra, and hence the standard treatment for this disorder was to use drugs that increased dopamine in the brain. However, the treatment could only go so far in attenuating the symptoms of the disorder. Moreover, as the treatment also affected dopamine in brain regions that were functioning normally, it could instigate the appearance of new behaviors linked to reward processes, such as a penchant for gambling. As an alternative to drug treatments, stimulation of particular neurons, a procedure referred to as deep brain stimulation or DBS, was developed to attenuate Parkinson's symptoms.

Transcranial magnetic stimulation (TMS)

Psychiatry, to some extent, was a victim of some of the early treatments of mental disorders, most notably lobotomy, in which aspects of the frontal lobes of the brain were removed or transected. Filmgoers likely remember *One Flew Over the Cuckoo's Nest*, adapted from Ken Kesey's book of the same name, or *Suddenly, Last Summer*, a somewhat older film adapted from a one-act play written by Tennessee Williams, both of which mock psychiatric practices.

Electroconvulsive therapy (ECT) is used for severe depression when other treatment methods have failed or when suicide risk is high. This treatment induces a brain seizure, and for reasons that still aren't fully understood, it quiets the depression that is otherwise present, and does so more quickly than medications. In the early days it was a gruesome treatment with many unwanted effects, some of them pretty terrible, but with improved technologies and understanding, more safeguards have been instituted. Still, in *One Flew Over the Cuckoo's Nest*, which changed the public face of psychiatry, evil Nurse Ratched, who lives in infamy for that one remarkable role, commented that ECT "might be said to do the work of the sleeping pill, the electric chair and the torture rack. It's a clever little procedure, simple, quick, nearly painless it happens so fast, but no one ever wants another one. Ever."

As the poor reputation of ECT continued, but with the realization that it reduced depressive symptoms, interest began to focus on the possibility that magnetic stimulation of the brain could also have positive effects, and the treatment could be administered safely. Transcranial magnetic stimulation (TMS) using electromagnetic induction causes the creation of weak electric currents that can influence brain neural activity. The effects of repeated TMS (rTMS) aren't as great as that of ECT, but are nonetheless relatively effective even when other treatments have failed. It isn't known how TMS comes to produce its positive actions, especially as the magnetic signals only spread to a depth of about 2 centimeters into the brain. There are new methods being developed that allow for deeper brain structures to be stimulated so that a greater number of patients could be helped. Although TMS is best known for its effects on depression, it has found its way into the treatment of anxiety disorders, neurodegenerative diseases, pain syndromes, and auditory hallucinations associated with schizophrenia, and there is reason to believe that it may be useful in the treatment of eating disorders. TMS isn't widely used yet, but it has a good track-record and might find a place in conventional treatment, provided that a movie isn't made about it.

This procedure was also used to treat essential tremor, an illness that is characterized by tremor that is most apparent when individuals make purposeful motions like holding a tea cup. As well, DBS was approved for use in treating dystonia, a neurological disorder wherein sustained muscle contractions cause twisting and repetitive movements, as well as abnormal posture, and it has also been used to treat chronic pain. The procedure has been remarkably successful, and has been conducted on more than 100,000 occasions.

The success achieved spurred the use of this approach to diminish depression in patients for whom no other treatment seemed to work. Mayberg, Lozano and their colleagues (2005) stimulated the subgenual cingulate cortex (also referred to as BA25 or area 25), which, as we've discussed, is involved in appraisal processes, and which is reciprocally linked to other sites deemed important in depression. This area is a gateway through which several brain regions are interconnected, and it was reasoned that when problems exist, introducing a pacemaker into this region might facilitate this communication, or block the noise within the circuit that otherwise prevents proper functioning. This treatment elicited marked and lasting reductions of depression in patients who had been treatment resistant. When long-term stimulation could be provided through a battery pack implanted just beneath the collar bone, symptom relief was achieved for more than two years in more than half the patients, and some continued to experience relief after more than six or seven years. Most patients reported diminished feelings of depression immediately the implanted electrodes were turned on, and Dr Mayberg described patients as feeling lighter and more connected, and their mental churning or pain was alleviated. Significantly, patients not only came to the realization that the mental pain they had been experiencing was gone, but they also worked on what they ought to do to avoid recurrence of the illness. DBS fixes them for the moment, but patients need some form of therapy, such as CBT, to reach a full and lasting recovery. This procedure is being explored further in an effort to establish whether it can be used to diminish OCD, Tourette's syndrome, bipolar disorder, addictions, and anorexia.

Anti-inflammatory agents

If the inflammatory immune system is involved in the provocation or maintenance of depression as suggested, then drugs that act as anti-inflammatories ought to have a positive effect in diminishing signs of depression. As anti-inflammatory agents are ordinarily used in the treatment of several disorders, researchers and clinicians have been able to evaluate mood changes without placing patients at further risk. As expected, depressive symptoms were reduced among individuals being treated for rheumatoid arthritis or psoriasis using the TNF-α antagonist etanercept. Of course, these antidepressant-like effects might have occurred because of the diminution of physical symptoms and pain rather than being a genuine antidepressant effect. Still, the findings are interesting and are encouraging for further analyses of inflammatory processes.

Several studies in animals have provided compelling data supporting the usefulness of nonsteroidal anti-inflammatory agents (NSAIDs), such as ibuprofen, in diminishing depressive-like behaviors. In humans, these agents likewise augmented the positive effects provided by standard antidepressant medication. However, it's a good bet that their effectiveness may be tied to whether or not a particular instance of depression is accompanied by inflammatory disturbances. Anti-inflammatory drugs are not meant for the treatment of all cases of depression, nor are they being recommended as treatments for depression on their own. Instead, the possibility exists that they could be effective adjunctive treatments to enhance the effects of standard drugs among individuals expressing high levels of inflammatory markers.

Treating anxiety disorders

There's no shortage of antianxiety medications available, and agents such as diazepam (Valium), alprazolam (Xanax), chlordiazepoxide (Librium), and lorazepam (Ativan) have represented a major source of revenue for some drug companies. These agents fall within a class known as benzodiazepines that have their effects, in part, by influencing GABA receptor activity. These agents diminish anxiety quickly and have few side effects, and thus are also used as sedatives, hypnotics (inducing sleep), anticonvulsants, and muscle relaxants, as well as serving as a premedication for medical or dental procedures. The downside is that tolerance, physical dependence and withdrawal symptoms may develop, and thus they aren't recommended for long-term use. That said, pregabalin (Lyrica), a compound that affects GABA receptors but is distinct from benzodiazepines, is effective as an anxiolytic, tolerated well, and has fewer cognitive and psychomotor effects than benzodiazepines.

One of the most common alternatives to benzodiazepines in treating chronic anxiety has been SSRIs, although it may take several weeks to see positive effects, just as there is a delay in the alleviation of depression. Although SSRI treatment and CBT were both effective in attenuating generalized anxiety disorder in 50-60 percent of cases, the therapeutic gains from CBT were maintained after treatment discontinuation, which was less likely to be the case following medication. Both high doses of SSRIs and CBT were also moderately successful in the treatment of OCD, and were useful in panic disorder, more so when the CBT treatment focused on the fear of panic occurring in public situations, the perceived consequences of panic, and methods of coping with panic.

Treating PTSD

Despite the array of strategies that have been used in treating PTSD, it has proven to be a hard nut to crack. Many treatment strategies have been tried, and most have fallen by the wayside. Limited improvements were realized using family or interpersonal therapy, trauma management therapy, stress management/relaxation therapy, supportive therapy/ nondirective counseling, psychodynamic therapies, hypnotherapy, imagery/rehearsal training and virtual reality treatments, acceptance and commitment therapy, and a variety of pharmacological approaches. Yet, because of its seriousness, and the fact that so many soldiers have been returning home with PTSD symptoms, the search for better treatment strategies has been redoubled.

Individual CBT has been used with some success in treating PTSD, and this was even evident when the threat of further trauma persisted. Once more, however, CBT isn't for everybody, as some individuals simply don't have much faith in the procedures or don't comply with all the steps necessary. There may, however, be biological markers regarding who might gain most from CBT. Individuals who carried the short 5-HTT allele, which we discussed in relation to depressive disorders, were least likely to gain from CBT, although it's uncertain whether it predicted the usefulness of other treatments.

As stressors affect HPA functioning, and PTSD is accompanied by altered cortisol variations, efforts were made to treat PTSD by targeting cortisol activity. It generally appeared that cortisol manipulations didn't have much of an effect once PTSD was well entrenched, but if administered within six hours of the trauma, high-dose cortisol treatment limited the subsequent emergence of PTSD. Aside from pointing to HPA functioning as a culprit in the provocation of PTSD, these findings point to a "window of opportunity" during which the persistent adverse effects of trauma can be diminished. It was similarly observed that norepinephrine antagonists, such as the α_1 and β norepinephrine receptor antagonists

Eye movement desensitization and reprocessing (EMDR)

I'm pretty open to "alternative" therapies for psychological disorders, but when I first heard about one particular treatment for PTSD, that of eye movement desensitization and reprocessing (EMDR), even I thought it was a bit flaky. Yet, there is evidence supporting its effectiveness, and I've heard testimonials about it. In this procedure, patients are required to focus on an image of the traumatic event they experienced, and while they are doing this, the therapist has them engage in various eye movements, such as following a finger moving across their visual field. After several such sessions, some patients report a moderate reduction of their symptoms, and some even report marked relief. It isn't certain why this therapy has any positive effects, but it seems to be more than just a placebo effect. It is thought that during the session the memory of the trauma will be associated with nonthreatening stimuli, such as stimulation of visual or auditory senses, so that eventually the traumatic memory and the emotions that ordinarily accompany it will be separated from one another. Admittedly, this sounds strange and has been met by a bit of resistance by some therapists, but as we'll see, there may be scientifically sound reasons concerning its usefulness. What puzzles me most is how this therapy first came about, or what would have inspired a therapist to think of doing this.

prazosin and propranolol, respectively, could attenuate symptoms of PTSD. Interestingly, α_1 adrenergic antagonists reduced trauma-related nightmares and insomnia, whereas the β blocker, propranolol, was more useful in alleviating the emotional content of traumatic memories, and thus a combination therapy might be most effective. As in the case of cortisol treatments, timing is everything and the behavioral and physiological aspects of PTSD were most readily diminished if the β-adrenergic antagonist propranolol was administered soon after the trauma.

Why timing is so important for the effectiveness of treatments may have to do with the way memory processes operate. As described earlier, when new information is acquired, neurons within brain regions, such as the hippocampus, are involved in maintaining that memory for the short term, after which it goes through a consolidation phase when synaptic connections are strengthened, eventually being maintained in a long-term way. Once memories have been consolidated they are hardy and difficult to alter, but when they are still in short-term stores or during the process of being consolidated, they can easily be disrupted or modified. This can be achieved by cognitive manipulations, introduction of alternative emotional responses, or by pharmacological intercessions that modify norepinephrine activity. Unfortunately, the golden hours during which these manipulations are effective are just that – a few hours – and there may not be the opportunity to administer treatments during this time.

As it happens, memory has several interesting aspects that researchers and clinicians can use to their advantage in treating PTSD. Juries seem to believe that eye-witness testimony is highly reliable, but lawyers for both the defense and the prosecution know full well that it's not. Memories are malleable, and they can be altered not only when they are in short-term storage, but also when they are retrieved from long-term storage. When a memory is active, meaning that the neurons are actively engaged in retrieving the memory, a therapist can alter this memory simply by providing individuals with new ideas

"Critical" and "debriefing" are great buzzwords

In an effort to thwart the development of PTSD, a support team might appear to "debrief" traumatized individuals, using a procedure often referred to as "critical incident stress debriefing." This procedure is widely used, usually delivered anywhere from a few hours to a few days after the trauma. Even though there has been only modest support for its usefulness, and it is even discouraged by some experts in the field, it continues to be used, possibly because it sounds right. Better to do something, even if it's pointless, than to sit on your hands. In view of the findings pointing to the usefulness of disengaging trauma memories from the emotional responses associated with them, these trauma teams might be better off using an approach in which the debriefing is accompanied by procedures that facilitate the dissociation of memories and emotions. It was at one time accepted that even if unwanted memories were suppressed, they might find their way into the unconscious and thus affect later behavior. This view has been challenged, and it has even been suggested that the suppression of intrusive memories might cause the memory trace to be disturbed, thereby limiting psychological disturbances.

or stimuli that can be incorporated into the existing narrative. In the same way, when a traumatic memory is recalled it will elicit particular emotional responses and during this time the memory of the event and the emotional responses it elicits can be dissociated from one another. Thus, when patients are asked to recall a trauma memory, making it vulnerable to manipulation, the administration of drug treatments that affect memory and diminish anxiety can result in emotional responses being divorced from the memory of the event. The individual won't have forgotten the event, but it might no longer elicit the intense emotional responses that it previously did. These memories, having now been separated from the emotional turmoil otherwise elicited, can be reconsolidated in this new form, so that when they are subsequently recalled, the negative emotions no longer emerge. Such manipulations have disrupted fear memories in rodents, and there seems to be some promise regarding the efficacy of administering propranolol in modifying fear-related memories in humans. It is conceivable that eye movement desensitization and reprocessing, described earlier, might also have its positive effects by dissociating memories from the usual emotional responses elicited, thereby limiting the expression of PTSD.

An alternative to norepinephrine acting agents in the treatment of PTSD has involved drugs that influence the transmitter, glutamate, which may affect learning and memory processes through its effects on NMDA receptors. It will be recalled that PTSD may reflect a disturbance of the normal forgetting of traumatic events, and D-cycloserine (Seromycin), which stimulates NMDA receptors and thereby facilitates fear extinction, has diminished PTSD symptoms in some patients, especially if the drug was used in combination with CBT or exposure therapy.

The search for effective treatments of PTSD is continuously evolving. Given that neuropeptide Y might promote resilience, nasal spray containing neuropeptide Y has been considered as a way of diminishing PTSD symptoms, and the endocannabinoid anandamide was also reported to diminish symptoms of PTSD through its fear-reducing features. As well, stimulating neuropsin, a substance present in the amygdala, seemed to hold some promise as a mediator of trauma symptoms. The use of novel combination therapies, such as antidepressant drugs paired with the GABA acting agent pregablin, which was initially used in reducing seizures, has also been effective in treating PTSD, and it appears that MDMA (more commonly known as the street drug ecstasy) combined with fairly extensive psychotherapy or exposure therapy has yielded some positive effects among those with chronic PTSD. How these treatments will evolve in their capacity to alleviate PTSD is a matter of empirical research. But there seems to be optimism that effective treatments might become available sooner than later.

Herbal (naturopathic) treatments

There are divergent attitudes toward natural products. On the one side are the folks who think that this stuff is a load of malarkey and shouldn't be used for any serious illness. On the other are those who think that natural medicines are the way to go as anything natural must be good for us. There have been many medicines that have come from naturally occurring substances, such as penicillin for fighting infection, aloe vera for the treatment of burns, tamoxifen for breast cancer treatment, opium to reduce pain, digitalis as a heart stimulant, and aspirin as an anti-inflammatory and pain suppressant. Moreover, in recent years the hallucinogenic agent psilocybin, originally obtained from "magic" mushrooms, which inhibits negative emotions has been or is being assessed in the treatment of OCD, cluster headaches, depression and anxiety, as well as to bring new life perspectives to those with terminal cancer.

The spread of herbal medicines in the last few decades has been remarkable. Positive effects of ginseng have been reported, sometimes ascribed to anti-inflammatory actions; black tea has been alleged to diminish diabetes; green tea extract has been used in an effort to keep chronic lymphatic leukemia from progressing, as well as to diminish the severity of atherosclerosis in men; Chinese wolfberries were said to diminish diabetes-related vision problems; essential plant oils were touted as having antibiotic-like properties; and it seems omega-3 from fish oils diminishes inflammation, acts against diabetes, and alleviates stress-related heart problems, as does the plant hormone abscisic acid. That's hardly the end of it as the intestinal side effects of chemotherapy were diminished by an ancient Chinese medicine that comprised skullcap, licorice and the fruit of the buckthorn tree; consumption of nuts has been linked to diminished risk of dying of cancer or heart disease; and the polyphenols that come from red wine and green tea have also been purported to slow down the course of prostate cancer, as well as the course of Alzheimer's disease.

The clash of cultures

Like particular foods, yoga has also been associated with a variety of positive feelings and diminished pain among those with fibromyalgia and rheumatoid arthritis, and it may have multiple other benefits through its actions on inflammatory processes. I mentioned this to an acquaintance who had become a health food junkie (and who seemed to have had his frontal cortex hijacked) after he spent two weeks at a "health spa," but who didn't much care for yoga. He responded that that "those yoga people, despite all their faults, often limit their diets to vegetables, fruit and nuts. But, then they try to give the credit for their good health to yoga when it's really the right food doing the job. Those yoga types will do anything to promote their cause."

These are only a few of the dozens and dozens of examples regarding the positive effects of natural products. So why are there detractors of natural products, and why are there so many of them? I suppose the problem comes from the fact that many compounds have not been rigorously tested and haven't yet met the test of replicability in independent labs. Even trusted old favorites, such as Echinacea for colds, have been questioned, and recent detailed analyses concluded that depending on what part of the plant is used, Echinacea may have some positive effects, but these are generally small. The fact is that not everything that comes from the ground or grows on trees is beneficial to your health. For instance, coumarin, ephedra, and calamus oil are natural products that have been banned. Sugars and salt are natural, too, but that doesn't mean that the more you eat of them the better off you are. The simple fact is that the glut of natural products that have been claimed to increase health aren't actually marketed as drugs and thus don't have to go through the same rigorous, expensive and time-consuming processes necessary to put drugs on the market.

All sorts of "remedies" are found on the shelves of health food stores and supermarkets even though they have little or no genuine value. Indeed, in countries such as England more than 90 percent of over-the-counter herbals don't offer information concerning their safe use, even though they might have negative effects in some individuals.

Separating the wheat from the chaff

Homeopathy is a form of alternative medicine that subscribes to the principle that a substance that causes illness symptoms in otherwise healthy people can be used to cure people who are sick. To achieve cures, a given substance is selected based on the individual's symptoms, personality features, and psychological condition. This substance is then diluted, diluted again, and again, repeatedly, until there are no or hardly any of the original molecules remaining, and this is then consumed by the patient. This procedure was first developed back in 1796 by Samuel Hahnemann based on his premise that "like cures like." As wacky as it sounds, and it is wacky, there's an odd element that sounds right. We do fight illness using elements of an illness. This is, after all, what the immune system is doing when it uses the memory of previous viruses to fend off new viral challenges.

Homeopathy has become increasingly complex as it has attempted to gain credibility. Evaluation of patients has become more extensive, repertories (manuals) that link symptoms to treatments have become more extensive, and new medicines have been created for homeopathic use. One can even get an academic degree after three years of intensive study at a homeopathic college or institute. However, before running off to become a practitioner or supplicant, consider that it's been known for some time that homeopathy is based on pseudoscientific notions and that it has no healing powers whatever. There have been reviews and analyses performed year after year, assessing a wide variety of different physical illnesses. Repeatedly, the results have been the same. The treatments are no better than a placebo, and virtually every medical association in Western countries has come to the same conclusion. With so much information it's astonishing that homeopathic colleges continue to flourish and virtually every medium-sized town or larger city has multiple homeopathic centers.

For instance, ginko and garlic can increase risk of bleeding, and Asian ginseng is not appropriate for those with diabetes, and there have been indications that acai berries, some herbal teas, cumin and turmeric may have negative actions on the effectiveness of chemotherapy. As well, many herbals have effects that can produce problems among individuals taking heart medications. Likewise, the fad for colon cleansing may be seeing its end (another bad pun) as it too may have several fairly negative consequences.

There are certain natural products that have stirred up more controversy than others, such as whether Echinacea really can help you beat a cold, and whether St John's Wort can be effective as an antidepressant. In the latter instance, several reports indicated that it was better than a placebo and had fewer side effects than SSRIs. Curiously, these effects were most notable in Germany where it has been used for some time and had built up a very positive reputation, and hence the expectancy of relief with this treatment was substantial – a sort of culture-dependent placebo effect. Later studies, however, revealed that St John's Wort was ineffective in the treatment of chronic low-grade depression, and a study conducted through the National Center for Complementary and Alternative Medicine in the US indicated that the effectiveness of this substance in ameliorating depressive illness was on a par with that of a placebo.

There's little question that poor nutrition will render individuals susceptible to all sorts of illnesses, and this can also leave people less able to deal with stressors. There's hardly a food group that isn't important for us in one fashion or another, but either because of realities or fads, certain foods have been getting particular attention. The omega fatty acids, which comprise unsaturated fats and thus are better for your health than those that come from animal or dairy fat, have been especially highlighted. Omega-3 fatty acids obtained from a variety of foods, such as fish oils, are important for building cell membranes and for cell health and they act against excessive inflammatory responses. At one time there were indications that polyunsaturated fatty acids (PUFAs) had a protective role in depressive illness and in diminishing distress, but subsequent research seemed not to support this conclusion. In fact, many illnesses have been linked to PUFAs, including those that involve immunological disturbances or are related to neuronal degeneration. There has been the view that the benefits of omega-3 are obtained primarily when omega-6, another fatty

First the news that there is no Santa, and now this! Say it ain't so, Joe

One of the safe bets when it came to daily supplements seemed to be that taking certain vitamins, including multivitamins, was good for us. As kids, our daily routine was for caring parents to shovel vitamin tablets at us. Who could resist eating a cute pastel-colored Barney or Wilma? We're told that was all a crock and we've been wasting our money. Not only do vitamins not improve our health and resilience, but some, such as beta-carotene, selenium, and vitamin E could be harmful when present in high doses, even promoting cancer. I suppose that supplements might be useful if a person has a problem that disturbs the natural amounts of particular substances, possibly because of poor eating habits, lack of sunlight or a deficiency in a particular biological system. But, otherwise, there seem not to be any benefits.

It just doesn't figure

Why is it that despite the lack of data, many people prefer alternative medicines, such as Traditional Chinese Medicine (TCM) over standard Western medical treatments? It seems this preference is particularly notable when the cause of an illness is uncertain, as the holistic aspects of TCM are better able to align with uncertainty than Western medicine. Oddly, as well, without any evidence, some people are under the impression that TCM gets at the root of illnesses rather than masking symptoms.

A recent analysis of more than 1,600 earlier studies that included TCM revealed that of 190 compounds assessed, those that were manufactured were 10 to 100 times more powerful than the equivalent natural products. The judicious combination of the natural products could potentially get them to equal the effectiveness of a man-made remedy, but this would entail considerable research and still the likelihood of achieving this would be low.

acid, is present, although if omega-6 is too high relative to omega-3 it can have negative health consequences, including effects on heart disease. So, once again, it's difficult to get an accurate reading of whether and when certain PUFAs have positive effects.

Increasingly I've been finding it more difficult to figure out what foods I should be eating and which I should be ignoring. You might similarly have found that that it's hard to distinguish hype from reality, and like me, you probably get most of your information from lousy sources, including what you hear from your friends, who also obtained their information from lousy sources. So, I decided to read up on foods that could have potential positive effects on psychological health and reduce the influence of stressors. My initial foray comprised an internet search that left me stunned by the amount of information available, especially in relation to which foods would affect neurotransmitters and hormones, and which illnesses they could prevent or cure. Some of this information didn't seem to be backed up by any scientific literature, and the dogmatic presentation of the information was sometimes a turn-off. However, some of the conclusions were based on seemingly scientific research, although I confess that this line of research isn't my expertise. Still, "integrative medicine," which comprises a combination of evidence-based medicine and alternative approaches, seems a fair bet. If a standard medication doesn't diminish symptoms, then why not go for an alternative or combination treatment, but bear in mind that this suggestion is predicated on the assumption that a standard medication was tried first.

At this point I've still been going by two basic rules: first, if it looks and tastes fantastic, then you better not have too much of it; and second, even if eating certain foods won't make you healthier, smarter or happier, poor nutrition will have some serious negative effects. An addendum to these rules might be that since expectancies have powerful effects on our well-being, for those people who feel better shopping at natural food stores and believe that it makes them healthier, then all the best to them. Over the years I've met many people who are into health foods, and those who are new converts tend to be very ardent about it and feel compelled to tell me that the foods I eat are poison. I can feel them bristle even as I begin to reply with "Yes, but ..." So, now I say nothing, as I dig into my poisonous fries and hamburger, but think yummy, yummy, poison.

Before you go...

Stressful events could come to promote pathological conditions through disturbances of a single or a combination of neurobiological processes. In some instances, the development of pathology could stem from a series of biological changes that culminate in a particular essential neurochemical disturbance. If an illness occurs owing to a dysfunction of one step in a series of sequential steps, then the effectiveness of the treatment might depend on altering the right step of this process. For example, let's take the scenario in which a stressor leads to an excessive inflammatory response, causing CRH changes, which then promotes altered serotonin, culminating in illness. We can treat the illness by modifying serotonin, but the underlying problem, the disturbance of inflammatory processes would persist, and hence when the medication is stopped, the illness likely would reemerge. Thus, it is necessary to identify where in the sequence a disturbance occurs for each person, and then treat them accordingly.

As complicated as this might sound, the complexity is actually still greater. Not only might there be several steps along a chemical pathway, but there may be several pathways that all end up affecting a particular neurochemical process. Essentially, we could get from A to D through any of several paths, just as we can get from Paris to Los Angeles through different airplane routes. If multiple routes exist in the processes leading to depression, then a treatment ought to be most effective in alleviating the illness if it maps onto the specific path that is disturbed. As well, illness might not be determined by any single substrate, but might develop because of multiple neurochemical processes, and consequently single treatment strategies might be less than fully effective in eliminating symptoms. In the absence of markers to direct us toward the root (or route) of the illness, an effective treatment might not be reliably obtained.

Even if we could identify and treat the neuronal process that leads to illness, we need to keep in mind that the initial problem arose because of inappropriate cognitive functioning, such as disturbed appraisals or inadequate coping, and thus it would obviously be advantageous to apply treatment strategies that focus on specific aspects of the cognitive/behavioral processes. Drug treatment might make a situation more manageable so that the individual is better positioned to reconsider the ways they appraise and cope with challenges, and how to deal with future stressors. Thus, a combination of drug treatment and cognitive behavioral therapy might be particularly efficacious. It can't be said often enough, however, that the choice of treatment ought to be dictated by characteristics of individuals reflected by genetic factors, certain markers in blood or cerebrospinal fluid (CSF), specific brain disturbances, the individual symptoms presented, psychosocial factors, and how individuals appraise and cope with stressors, as well as the nature of the stressors that led to pathology. "One size fits all" is fine for socks, but not for the treatment to restore mental health.

22

Epilogue

It's OK to go now...

In this short book we've traveled through varies aspects of the stress process, the relationship between stress and both psychological and physical illnesses, and what can be done to preclude or ameliorate stressor-induced illnesses. To be sure, in many respects the treatment of each topic was fairly superficial, particularly in relation to stress-elicited neurobiological changes, and we only scratched the surface of treatment strategies. This shouldn't be in the least surprising considering that multiple books and literally thousands of research reports have been published for each of the illnesses we covered and the many treatment approaches. Nonetheless, this book should have helped you gain some insight into what stressors, stress and distress involve, and it should have provided you with several bits of advice that I hope will help you deal with stressors, or get you to think about seeking help when you can't deal with events on your own.

My sincere hope is that neither you nor those who are close to you are experiencing any significant problems and that you have been reading this book out of interest. However, if you're already in a situation that has caused you distress, but you're too proud to seek help, then that's just not your best option. Sometimes we're lucky and bad things just simply go away, but more often they don't, and the longer problems persist, the more likely it is that they'll be increasingly difficult to resolve and their impact on your well-being will be more profound. You'd probably seek help if you believed that you had a heart problem, experienced suspicious stomach symptoms, repeatedly woke up with frontal headaches, or noticed signs of diabetes, and thus it's hard for your close ones to really understand or accept why you feel too proud to seek help for mental issues. This said, there's a high likelihood that you're not seeking help because of the stigma associated with mental health problems. If other people engage in discrimination and stigmatization, then they have a serious problem that you might advise them on some day, but today you have to take care of yourself, and so go seek help before things get worse.

Others have said the following before me, but it's worth repeating again and again and again, until pride and stigma, the two devils of mental health, are diminished. Mental health problems, more often than not, come about because of unfortunate

Stress and Your Health: From Vulnerability to Resilience, First Edition. Hymie Anisman.
© 2015 John Wiley & Sons, Ltd. Published 2015 by John Wiley & Sons, Ltd.

experiences endured, often without our having any say in the situation. These stressful experiences may tax our behavioral and neurobiological coping resources, rendering us more vulnerable to illness. Ultimately, psychological problems reflect "a flaw in brain circuitry and not a flaw in character."

References

Abizaid, A. (2009). Ghrelin and dopamine: new insights on the peripheral regulation of appetite. *Journal of Neuroendocrinology*, 21, 787–793.

Aknin, L. B., Sandstrom, G. M., Dunn, E. W., and Norton, M. I. (2011). Investing in others: prosocial spending for (pro)social change. In R. Biswan-Diener (ed.), *Positive Psychology as Social Change*. New York: Springer, pp. 219–234.

Babiak, P. and Hare, R. D. (2006). *Snakes in Suits: When Psychopaths Go to Work*. New York: HarperCollins.

Beck, A. T. (1970). Cognitive therapy: nature and relation to behavior therapy. *Behavior Therapy*, 1, 184–200.

Beck, A. T., Rush, A. J., Shaw, B. F., and Emery, G. (1979). *Cognitive Therapy for Depression*. New York: Guilford.

Best, D., Lubman, D. I., Savic, M., Wilson, A., Dingle, G., Haslam, S. A., Haslam, C., and Jetten, J. (2014). Social and transitional identity: exploring social networks and their significance in a therapeutic community setting. *Therapeutic Communities: The International Journal of Therapeutic Communities*, 35, 10–20.

Blier, P., Ward, H. E., Tremblay, P., Laberge, L., Hébert, C., and Bergeron, R. (2010). Combination of antidepressant medications from treatment initiation for major depressive disorder: a double-blind randomized study. *American Journal of Psychiatry*, 167, 281–288.

Bombay, A., Matheson, K., and Anisman, H. (2014). The intergenerational effects of Indian Residential Schools: implications for the concept of historical trauma. *Transcultural Psychiatry*, 51, 320–338.

Branscombe, N. R., Slugoski, B., and Kappen, D. M. (2004). Collective guilt: what it is and what it is not. In N. R. Branscombe and B. Doosje, B. (eds), *Collective Guilt: International Perspectives*. Cambridge: Cambridge University Press, pp. 16–34.

Brave Heart, M. Y. (2003). The historical trauma response among natives and its relationship with substance abuse: a Lakota illustration. *Journal of Psychoactive Drugs*, 35, 7–13.

Cardoso, C., Orlando, M. A., Brown, C. A., and Ellenbogen, M. A. (2014). Oxytocin and enhancement of the positive valence of social affiliation memories: an autobiographical memory study. *Social Neuroscience*, 9 (2), 186–195.

Dallman, M. F. (2010). Stress-induced obesity and the emotional nervous system. *Trends in Endocrinology and Metabolism*, 21, 159–165.

Disner, S. G., Beevers, C. G., Haigh, E. A., and Beck, A. T. (2011). Neural mechanisms of the cognitive model of depression. *Nature Reviews Neuroscience*, 12, 467–477.

Duman, R. S. and Aghajanian, G. K. (2012). Synaptic dysfunction in depression: potential therapeutic targets. *Science*, 338, 68–72.

Duman, R. S. and Monteggia, L. M. (2006). A neurotrophic model for stress-related mood disorders. *Biological Psychiatry*, 59, 1116–1127.

Fredrickson, B. L. (2004). The broaden-and-build theory of positive emotions. *Philosophical Transanctions of the Royal Society B*, 359, 1367–1377.

Haslam, S. A. and Reicher, S. D. (2005). The psychology of tyranny. *Scientific American Mind*, 16 (3), 44–51.

Haslam, S. A., Reicher, S. D., and Platow, M. J. (2011) *The New Psychology of Leadership: Identity, Influence and Power.* New York: Psychology Press.

Haslam, S. A., O'Brien, A., Jetten, J., Vormedal, K., and Penna, S. (2005). Taking the strain: social identity, social support, and the experience of stress. *British Journal of Social Psychology*, 44, 355–370.

Hayley, S. and Litteljohn, D. (2013). Neuroplasticity and the next wave of antidepressant strategies. *Frontiers in Cellular Neuroscience*, 20, 218.

Hebb, D. O. (1955). Drives and the C.N.S. (conceptual nervous system). *Psychological Review*, 62, 243–254.

Heim, C. and Nemeroff, C. B. (2001). The role of childhood trauma in the neurobiology of mood and anxiety disorders: preclinical and clinical studies. *Biological Psychiatry*, 49, 1023–1039

Hirsch, M. (2001). Surviving images: Holocaust photographs and the work of postmemory. *Yale Journal of Criticism*, 14, 5–37.

Hoffman, E. (2004). *After Such Knowledge: Memory, History, and the Legacy of the Holocaust.* New York: Public Affairs.

Jetten, J., Haslam, C., and Haslam, S. A. (2012). *The Social Cure: Identity, Health and Well-Being.* New York: Psychology Press.

Jetten, J., Haslam, C., Haslam, S. A., Dingle, G., and Jones, J. M. (2014). How groups affect our health and well-being: the path from theory to policy. *Social Issues and Policy Review*, 8, 103–130.

Kabat-Zinn, J. (1990). *Full Catastrophe Living: Using the Wisdom of Your Body and Mind to Face Stress, Pain, and Illness.* New York: Delacourt.

Kahneman, D. (2011). *Thinking, Fast and Slow.* New York: Farrar, Straus, & Giroux.

Kahneman, D. and Tversky, A. (1974). Judgment under uncertainty: heuristics and biases. *Science*, 185, 1124–1131.

Koob, G. F. and Le Moal, M. (2008). Addiction and the brain antireward system. *Annual Review of Psychology*, 59, 29–53.

Kreisel. T., Frank, M. G., Licht, T., Reshef, R., Ben-Menachem-Zidon, O., Baratta, M. V., Maier, S. F., and Yirmiya, R. (2014). Dynamic microglial alterations underlie stress-induced depressive-like behavior and suppressed neurogenesis. *Molecular Psychiatry*, 19, 699–709.

Kushner, H. S. (1978). *When Bad Things Happen to Good People.* New York: Anchor.

Lazarus, R. S. and Folkman, S. (1984). *Stress, Appraisal, and Coping.* New York: Springer.

Lupien, S. (2012). *Well Stressed: Manage Stress before It Turns Toxic.* Mississauga, ON: John Wiley & Sons.

Maier, S. F. and Seligman, M. E. (1976). Learned helplessness: theory and evidence. *Journal of Experimental Psychology: General*, 105, 3–46.

Marmot, M. G., Rose, G., Shipley, M., and Hamilton, P. J. (1978). Employment grade and coronary heart disease in British civil servants. *Journal of Epidemiology and Community Health*, 32, 244–249.

Matheson, K. and Anisman, H. (2003). Systems of coping associated with dysphoria, anxiety and depressive illness: a multivariate profile perspective. *Stress*, 6, 223–234.

Matheson, K. and Anisman, H. (2012). Biological and psychosocial responses to discrimination. In J. Jetten, C. Haslam, and S. A. Haslam (eds), *The Social Cure.* New York: Psychology Press, pp. 133–154.

Mayberg, H. S., Lozano, A. M., Voon, V., McNeely, H. E., Seminowicz, D., Hamani, C., and Kennedy, S. H. (2005). Deep brain stimulation for depression. *Neuron*, 45, 651–660.

McEwen, B. S. (2007). Physiology and neurobiology of stress and adaptation: central role of the brain. *Physiological Reviews*, 87, 873–904.

McEwen, B. S. and Wingfield, J. C. (2003). The concept of allostasis in biology and biomedicine. *Hormones and Behavior*, 43, 2–15.

Merali, Z., McIntosh, J., Kent, P., Michaud, D., and Anisman, H. (1998). Aversive and appetitive events evoke the release of corticotropin-releasing hormone and bombesin-like peptides at the central nucleus of the amygdala. *Journal of Neuroscience*, 18, 4758–4766.

Mukherjee, S. (2010). *The Emperor of All Maladies: A Biography of Cancer*. New York: Scribner.

Mychasiuk, R., Schmold, N., Ilnytskyy, S., Kovalchuk, O., Kolb, B., and Gibb, R. (2011). Prenatal bystander stress alters brain, behavior, and the epigenome of developing rat offspring. *Developmental Neuroscience*, 33, 159–169.

Nei, M. (2013). *Mutation-Driven Evolution*. Oxford: Oxford University Press.

Northoff, G. (2014). *Unlocking the Brain*. New York: Oxford University Press.

Reicher,S., Haslam, S. A., and Rath, R. (2008). Making a virtue of evil: a five-step social identity model of the development of collective hate. *Social and Personality Psychology Compass*, 2, 1313–1344.

Roth, T. L., Lubin, F. D., Funk, A. J., and Sweatt, J. D. (2009). Lasting epigenetic influence of early-life adversity on the BDNF gene. *Biological Psychiatry*, 65, 760–769.

Sapolsky, R. M., Romero, L. M., and Munck, A. U. (2000). How do glucocorticoids influence stress responses? Integrating permissive, suppressive, stimulatory, and preparative actions. *Endocrine Reviews*, 21, 55–89.

Segal, Z. V., Williams, J. M. G., and Teasdale, J. (2002). *Mindfulness-Based Cognitive Therapy for Depression: A New Approach to Preventing Relapse*. New York: Guilford Press.

Shonkoff, J. P., Boyce, W. T., and McEwen, B. S. (2009). Neuroscience, molecular biology, and the childhood roots of health disparities: building a new framework for health promotion and disease prevention. *Journal of the American Medical Association*, 301, 2252–2259.

Sklar, L. S. and Anisman, H. (1979). Stress and coping factors influence tumor growth. *Science*, 205, 513–515.

Sklar, L. S. and Anisman, H. (1981). Stress and cancer. *Psychological Bulletin*, 89, 369–406.

Stewart, J. (2000). Pathways to relapse: the neurobiology of drug- and stress-induced relapse to drug-taking. *Journal of Psychiatry and Neuroscience*, 25, 125–136.

Szyf, M. (2009). Epigenetics, DNA methylation, and chromatin modifying drugs. *Annual Review of Pharmacology and Toxicology*, 49, 243–263.

Taha, S., Matheson, K., Cronin, T., and Anisman, H. (2014). Intolerance of uncertainty, appraisals, coping, and anxiety: the case of the 2009 H1N1 pandemic. *British Journal of Health Psychology*, 19 (3), 592–605.

Taylor, S. E., Klein, L. C., Lewis, B. P., Gruenewald, T. L., Gurung, R. A., and Updegraff, J. A. (2000). Biobehavioral responses to stress in females: tend-and-befriend, not fight-or-flight. *Psychological Review*, 107, 411–429.

Ury, W. (1993). *Getting Past No*. New York: Bantam.

Volkow, N. D., Wang, G. J., Fowler, J. S., Tomasi, D., Telang, F., and Baler, R. (2010). Addiction: decreased reward sensitivity and increased expectation sensitivity conspire to overwhelm the brain's control circuit. *Bioessays*, 32, 748–755.

Walker, C. D. (2010). Maternal touch and feed as critical regulators of behavioral and stress responses in the offspring. *Developmental Psychobiology*, 52, 638–650.

Index

Note: Page numbers in *italics* refer to Figures; those in **bold** to Tables.

Stress and Your Health: From Vulnerability to Resilience, First Edition. Hymie Anisman.
© 2015 John Wiley & Sons, Ltd. Published 2015 by John Wiley & Sons, Ltd.

type 1, 122
type 2 *see* type 2 diabetes
discrimination, 267
drug remedies, stress and stress-related
    disorders
  biomarkers, 250
  effects of drugs, 250
  herbal *see* herbal (naturopathic) treatments
    for stress
  homeopathy, 263
  "inclusion criteria," 249
  PET analysis, 250
  pharmacotherapy, depression treatment,
    246–7
  placebo and nocebo responses, 247–8
  protocols, 250
  selecting the right treatment and related
    caveats, 249–50
  selective serotonin reuptake inhibitors
    (SSRIs), 246
  treating anxiety disorders *see* anxiety
    disorders
  treating depression *see* depression
  treating PTSD *see* posttraumatic stress
    disorder (PTSD)
  yoga, 262
dysthymia, 152

early life stress
  abuse, 101, 102
  childhood cancer, 104
  "indiscriminate friendliness," 104
  poverty, 103
  psychological and physical
    disturbances, 103
  stressor experiences, 101
eating and energy regulation, associated
    hormones
  CRH, 60
  eating as self-medication, 61
  ghrelin, 60
  leptin, 60
  neuropeptide Y (NPY), 60
  stress and eating responses, 61
electroconvulsive therapy (ECT), 163
emotion-focused coping, 36–8
empathy, 48
epigenetic effects, trauma *see* trauma,
    intergenerational effects
epinephrine (adrenalin), 54
erythropoietin (EPO)
  oxygen carrying capacity, increase in, 255
  traumatic brain injury and stroke, 255
estrogen and testosterone
  alpha female and male tendencies, 65

anabolic steroids, 66
"bad-boy" behavioral style, 65
cognitive coping methods, females, 64
estrus cycle, mood alterations, 64
external sources, 66
finasteride, 67
high/low levels, impact, 64, 67
performance enhancing drugs, 66
sex-related behavioral differences, 64–5, 66
stressor-provoked neurochemical
  responses, 64
exposure therapy
  classical conditioning, 233–4
  extinction, 234
  forced exposure, 234
  prolonged exposure therapy, 234
  systematic desensitization, 234
  "the law of effect," 233
eye movement desensitization and
  reprocessing (EMDR), 260

fast and slow thinking
  decision making, 22–3
  guideposts and anchors, 25–7
  heuristic view, 23
  "processing fluency," 24
fibroblast growth factor (FGF-2), 80–82, 98,
    164, 193
finding meaning, 38–9
Five Facet Mindfulness Questionnaire
  (FFMQ), 239
forgiveness and trust
  apologies, 46, 47
  barriers, 47
  empathy, 48
  family conflicts, 48
  half truths, 46
  negative rumination, 46
functional magnetic resonance imaging
  (fMRI), 154

gamma-aminobutyric acid (GABA)
  depression, 163–4
  dysfunctional GABA activity, 79
  posttraumatic stress disorder (PTSD), 187
  stress-related disturbances, 79
generalized anxiety disorder (GAD)
  neurotransmitters, 173
  symptoms, 172–3
genetics
  behavioral phenotype, 16
  chromosomes, 16
  environmental conditions, 14
  "epigenetic" changes, 14
  gene mutations, 15

Index 277

International Statistical Classification of Diseases and Related Health Problems (ICD-10), 150
interpersonal psychotherapy (IPT)
  method, 237
  period of 12-16 weeks, 237

job-related distress in workplace
  absenteeism and presenteeism
    health deterioration, 212
    reason and effects, 213
  attention management, 217
  bullying *see* bullying in workplace
  burnout, 212
  financial strain, 217
  immune, endocrine and neurotransmitter functioning, disruption, 217
  job strain, 112–13
  managerial tips, 218–19
  POSEC method, 218
  social identity, 215
  social support in the workplace, 215–16
  status and job strain, 212
  stressors, 212
  time management and juggling, 217–18
  trust in the workplace, 216
  unemployment, 216–17

life span
  early life, 101–4
  older age, 106–7
  prenatal experiences *see* prenatal stress
  transitional periods, 104–5
loneliness
  chronic, 40
  multiple group memberships, 42
  "transitional" periods, 42
loss and grief
  bereavement, 208
  child, loss of, 208
  "complicated grief," 209
  coping methods, 209
  loss-orientation, 209
  restoration-orientation, 209
  social support, 209

meditation
  effects, 237
  meditation-centered practices and CBT, 238
  positive physiological changes, 237
  short-term positive effects, 238
  sleep, effects, 238
melancholic depression, 152
metabolic syndrome, 123
Middle East respiratory syndrome (MERS), 131

The Million Women Study, UK, 142
Mindful Attention Awareness Scale (MAAS), 239
mindfulness
  Acceptance and Commitment Therapy (ACT), 240
  appraising stressors, 239
  coping methods, 239
  default mode network (DMN), 240–241
  Five Facet Mindfulness Questionnaire (FFMQ), 239
  meditation-centered practices and CBT, 238
  Mindful Attention Awareness Scale (MAAS), 239
  mindfulness-based cognitive therapy (MBCT), 239
  mindfulness-based stress reduction (MBSR), 239
  task-positive network (TPN), 240
  TPN-DMN balance, 240–241
mixed emotions, 31
monoamine oxidase (MAO), 255
multiple sclerosis (MS), 18, 79, 134, 135, 236

Narcotics Anonymous, 197
National Institute of Mental Health (NIMH), 150
negative social interactions, 91
neurobiological explanation, depressive disorders, 158–9
neurodermatitis, 129
neuronal and glial processes
  astrocytes and microglia, 71–2
  axon, 70
  hormones, 70–71
  lock-and-key arrangement, 70
  reuptake, 70
  synapse, 70
neuropeptide Y (NPY), 188
neuroplasticity, 81
neurotransmitter process
  acetylcholine (ACh), 72–5
  cannabinoids, 79–80
  corticotropin releasing hormone (CRH), 76–8
  gamma-aminobutyric acid (GABA), 79
  glutamate, 78–9
  neuronal and glial processes, 70–72
  serotonin, norepinephrine and dopamine, 75–6
neurotrophic factors
  growth factors, 80–81
  neurogenesis, 81
  neurotrophins, 80

Printed and bound by CPI Group (UK) Ltd, Croydon, CR0 4YY

09/06/2025

14685969-0001